American Batsford Chess Library

Chess Wizardry:

The New ABC of Chess Problems

John Rice

An ICE Book
International Chess Enterprises, Seattle

International Chess Enterprises, Inc.
2005 Fifth Avenue, Suite 402
Seattle, Washington 98121-2850

P.O. Box 19457
Seattle, Washington 98109-1457

First published 1996

Typeset by John Nunn
and printed in Great Britain by
Redwood Books, Trowbridge, Wilts
for the publishers,
B. T. Batsford Ltd, 4 Fitzhardinge Street, London W1H 0AH

British Library Cataloging-in-Publication Data.
A catalog record for this book is
available from the British Library.

First published in the United States in 1996 by
International Chess Enterprises, Inc.
Originally published in Great Britain in 1996 by
B. T. Batsford.

ISBN 1-879479-33-8 (An ICE Book: pbk.)

First American edition – 1996

Printed in the United Kingdom
All first editions are printed on acid-free paper

A BATSFORD CHESS BOOK
Editorial Panel: Mark Dvoretsky, Jon Speelman
General Adviser: Raymond Keene OBE
Specialist Adviser: Dr John Nunn
Commissioning Editor: Graham Burgess

Contents

Preface

Figurine algebraic notation is used in this book. The squares on the diagram are each given a letter and a number, the letters a-h running from left to right and the numbers 1-8 from bottom to top. So the bottom left-hand square is a1 and the top right-hand square h8. In every position White moves up from the bottom of the board.

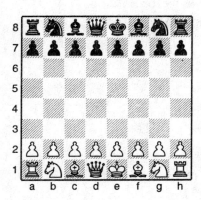

Moves are written as follows:

1 ♖e3	: White rook plays to square e3.
1 ♖e3+	: White rook plays to e3 and gives check.
1 ♖be3	: White rook on the b-file plays to e3; clarification of the file of departure would be used if the other white rook were on the e-file or on f3, g3 or h3 and could also play to e3.
1 ♖5e3	: White rook on the fifth rank plays to e3 (i.e. not white rook on e1 or e2).
1...♖e3	: Black rook plays to e3.
1 ♖xe3	: White rook captures a black unit on e3.
1 e3	: White pawn plays from e2 to e3.
1 dxe3	: White pawn on d2 captures a black unit on e3.
1 e8♕	: White pawn on e7 promotes to queen on e8.
1 dxe8♕	: White pawn on d7 promotes to queen by capturing on e8.
1 0-0	: White castles with ♖h1.
1 0-0-0	: White castles with ♖a1.

1 ♖~   : White rook plays a random move, i.e. the rook leaves the square it is on and plays to no square in particular.

1 ♖~e   : White rook plays a random move on the e-file.

1 ♖~3   : White rook plays a random move on the third rank.

1 ♖e~   : White rook on the e-file plays a random move.

1 ♖3~   : White rook on the third rank plays a random move.

The symbol > is used in to indicate a threat. When there is no threat, (-) follows White's first move.

The symbol ➜ refers the reader to an entry contained in the alphabetical listing in Section II.

The symbols ! and ? are used in a way that differs somewhat from that in literature about competitive chess playing. The question mark, ?, denotes a move that fails to meet the stipulation of the problem, e.g. fails to force mate in two when there is a solution possible. Also ?? is used to indicate that an intended, vital move is illegal. The exclamation mark, !, is used to signify or emphasise a move that does solve the problem, or a move by Black that prevents White from achieving his aim.

Throughout the book, a shorthand notation for referring to specific pieces is used: the figurine for the piece in question, followed immediately by the square it is on. Thus 'the ♖e3' refers to a rook on the square e3. The context will always make it clear whether such references are to pieces or to chess moves.

No special symbol is used to indicate that a move delivers mate.

When a year is given, it is sometimes followed by I or II (e.g. 1988/I). This signifies the first or second half of the year.

Technical terms appear either in bold type (e.g. **Grimshaw**), indicating that there is an entry under that word in Section II, or else in italics (e.g. *variation*), in which case the term, if not self-explanatory, is defined in Section I or at the appropriate point in the text. The reader will find that in Section II the solution to each problem is given alongside the diagram, in addition to any references in the text. This arrangement was welcomed as a feature of *An ABC of Chess Problems* (Faber & Faber, 1970), of which the present work is a thoroughly revised and updated edition, with over 250 new problems.

The author would like to express his thanks to all who have helped with the preparation of this book. Those who gave particularly valuable assistance for the first edition included Barry Barnes, the late Anthony Dickins, Michael Lipton, Robin Matthews and Chris Reeves. Useful suggestions for this new publication have been made by Sir Jeremy Morse, M.Parthasarathy, Mark

Ridley, Ivor Sanders and Ian Shanahan, and thanks are due in particular, for their very helpful critical comments and suggestions, to Barry Barnes, Colin Russ, Colin Sydenham and Kjell Widlert. One further acknowledgement is appropriate, to the computer program *Kalulu*, developed by Steve Dyson. The very clear and comprehensive solution-display makes it an easy matter to test problems for soundness.

Section I

What are Chess Problems?

Every regular player of the game of chess will have realised at one time or another what an extraordinary game it is: what possibilities, real or potential, what subtlety, and above all what infinite variety! Studying and analysing a chess position, whether from actual play or specially composed, will help you to a familiarity with the pieces and what they can do, singly or in combination. Some of the potential possibilities offered by the chessmen can be turned into realities by the problem-composer. The composer is master of both the white and the black pieces; his powers extend beyond those of the over-the-board player. How often have you, battling against your opponent, wished that just one more square next to his king were guarded by one of your men, or blocked by one of his, so that you could bring off a brilliant mate in three? The problemist can put the pieces just where he wants them, so that the strategy of your brilliant mate in three, expressed in a problem, can become actual instead of merely theoretical. In arranging the pieces to suit his purpose, the composer aims to show some worthwhile idea, in as elegant and economical a form as possible – in other words, he hopes to create something of beauty, to be appreciated and enjoyed by his audience, the solvers.

1

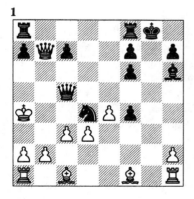

POSITION FROM ACTUAL PLAY

Keres-Bronstein, Zurich 1965
Black to play
(Throughout this section, a commentary on each position will be found in the text.)

Diagram no. 1 is not a problem but a position taken from over-the-board play. Settings of this type are frequently found in chess magazines and some newspapers, and the reader is invited to discover a line of play which will lead to a decisive advantage for one side or the other, or maybe to a clear draw. 'Decisive advantage' implies considerable material superiority, or at least sufficient for a win to be achieved at some later stage in the game. In no. 1 one of White's replies to Black's first move leads to mate on Black's seventh move, while another leads to a gain of material for Black. White's plight, admittedly, looks pretty desperate: his king is being hunted, he has a couple of undeveloped minor pieces, his rooks are not doing much good at present, and his queen is apparently chasing stray pawns. But players, especially grandmasters, have been known to get themselves out of worse jams than this. However, it is Black's move, and 1...♕b6, with the very obvious threat of 2...♕xb7, is good enough to finish the game off in a few more moves. White must choose between exchanging queens and withdrawing his own queen to d5. The latter move allows Black to win material with an eventual knight-fork: 2...♕a6+ 3 ♕a5 ♕c6+ 4 ♔a3 ♘c2+ 5 ♔b3 ♘xa1+ (if 3 ♔b4, 3...♖fb8+ 4 ♔c5 ♘e6+). 2 ♕xb6 seems to be White's best bet, but the consequences turn out to be even more disastrous than those of 2 ♕d5. Black recaptures with the ♙a7: 2...axb6+ 3 ♔b4, and now there follows a sacrifice which is designed to create what a problemist would term a **square-vacation**: 3...♖a4+! 4 ♔xa4 ♖a8+ 5 ♔b4. At this point the position is the same as it was after 3 ♔b4, with the important difference that f8 is not now occupied by a black unit. This square has been vacated, and Black can accordingly proceed 5...♗f8+, forcing 6 ♔c4, and now comes 6...b5+ 7 ♔d5/♔xd4 ♖d8#! In bringing about this mate, Black gets rid of three of his own men and forces the white king to one of the squares he has in mind right from the start of the manoeuvre, d4 or d5. The sacrifice followed by square-vacation is basic to the scheme.

It must be emphasised that no. 1 is not a chess problem, even though it may have one or two features to be found occasionally in problems. A problem is always a composed position, and very often it does not look as if it might have occurred in a game. It should, however, be a legal position; this is one of the problemist's conventions. In a *direct-mate* problem you are always told in how many moves the win must be achieved, and the win is invariably a clear-cut affair, i.e. it is always a mate. White, playing up the board, must play and force mate within the stipulated number of moves, whatever Black may reply. There are therefore three clear reasons why no. 1 is not a chess problem: (1) it is not a composed position; (2) mate is forced in only one line; variations lead to gain of material which will doubtless prove decisive in the end, though perhaps not straightaway; and (3) it is not a forced mate for White in a stipulated number of moves.

2

ENDGAME STUDY

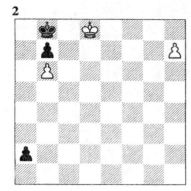

D.Joseph
British Chess Magazine 1922
White to play and win

Nor is no. 2 strictly a chess problem, though it is much nearer to be being one than no. 1 is. It is a composed position, and so not a contest between two players, but between composer and solver. In fact, as is the case with most chess problems as well, the composer had a two-fold aim in producing this position. Quite apart from presenting the solver with a challenge, the composer sought to achieve something artistic, a manoeuvre with the chess pieces with a claim to be regarded as beautiful. The stipulation 'White to play and win' means that this position is of a type known as an *endgame study*. These may be draws or wins, usually for White, and very often look as if they could have occurred in over-the-board play. Mate is rarely forced in such a position, the outcome being normally decided by material factors.

In no. 1 we saw how Black manipulated the white forces, especially the king, in forcing the win. In no. 2 White must manipulate the black forces. The first move for each side is obvious: 1 h8♕ a1♕. For White it is now a question of forcing the black queen to a square from which she will be unable to defend against a threat of mate along the top rank. 2 ♕e8? will not do, because Black replies with 2...♕g7!. 2 ♕f8? is also no good, since Black can play 2...♕a3!, followed by 3...♕d6+ if White continues 3 ♕e8?. Only 2 ♕g8! will work, to which Black's best reply is 2...♕a2 (if then 3 ♕xa2? stalemate!). Now the black queen can no longer reach g7, which means that White can proceed with 3 ♕e8!, forcing 3...♕a4. Play continues 4 ♕e5+ ♔a8 5 ♕h8!, and Black is now powerless to prevent 6 ♔e7+ other than by sacrificing his queen, which White can now capture without the risk of stalemate.

We have so far studied two positions, of which the first was not a problem at all, and the second resembled a problem only to a certain extent. But no. 3 is in every way a problem, and a fine one at that. It is a direct-mate in four moves, which means that White, to play, must inflict mate on his fourth

3

FOUR-MOVE DIRECT MATE

W.Speckmann
1st prize, *Die Schwalbe* 1960
White to play and mate in four

move at the latest, against any black defence. It is a *threat-problem*: White's first move threatens a mate which Black must parry if he is to attempt survival. A problem where White plays a first move which simply compels Black to make some mistake that will weaken his position (i.e. puts him in *zugzwang*) is known as a *block-problem* or *block*. White's first move is called the **key** of the problem, and unless the composer specifies to the contrary, a problem must have only one key. If a different white first move will also lead to forced mate within the stipulated number of moves, this move is known as a *cook*, and the problem is said to be *unsound* because *cooked*.

Our four-move direct-mate no. 3 has a strategic feature in common with the composed ending no. 2: White manipulates one of the black pieces to his own advantage. The black bishop is forced to move to a certain square (g4) so that it will prevent another black line-piece (queen, rook and bishop are line-pieces) from exerting its influence westwards to c4. In solving this problem, you should notice that every white move must either check or threaten immediate mate, because Black, if given time, can get a rook to his second rank and delay the mate with nuisance checks.

In fact White's key is 1 ♕e6, which threatens immediate mate by 2 ♕c8. Black has two possible *defences*, i.e. moves which prevent the threat from working. We'll look first at 1...b4; if now 2 ♕c8+, the black king escapes to b5. While the black pawn is on b5, that square is blocked; the square-vacation 1...b4 *unblocks* it. This move is clearly advantageous to Black, as it gives his king a **flight** (a square to which a king can move). But it carries a disadvantage, which White exploits: the line of squares from e2 to a6 has been opened, and White can therefore play 2 ♕xe2+. **Line-opening** is a very common way in which Black can weaken his own position. Black's two possible replies to 2 ♕xe2+ are 2...♖c4 and 2...c4, after both of which White plays 3 ♕a2+, followed by 4 ♕a5 mate after the king has moved to his flight b5.

Why could White not play 1 ♕a2+ (or 1 ♕a3+) straight away? Because Black can reply 1...♖a4, and there is now no mate in another three moves. The white move ♕a2+ is not sensible until after 1...b4 has *interfered* with the black rook's guard of a4, and prevented the ♖f4 from playing to that square. Black **interference**, which occurs when the influence of a black line-piece is obstructed by the move of another black unit, is a second common black self-weakening move.

After 1 ♕e6 b4, why won't 2 ♕a2+ do? Because after 2...♔b5, 3 ♕a5+ is not mate, as the black king can escape to his new flight c4. Therefore Black must first be induced to block that square with his rook (2 ♕xe2+ ♖c4) or with his pawn (2 ♕xe2+ c4). When a black king-flight, either actual or potential, is blocked by a black unit in the course of the solution of a problem, we speak of a **self-block**, a third very common self-weakening move.

So far we've examined only one of Black's possible defences to White's threat. If White were to play 1 ♕g8? right at the outset, to threaten 2 ♕c8 or 2 ♕a8 mate, then 1...b4! would be an adequate defence, as Black has three pieces, his bishop and two rooks, to prevent White from exploiting the line-opening. So White must get all of these pieces out of the way somehow. As we have seen, 1 ♕e6 threatens 2 ♕c8 mate. Black's second defence is 1...♗g4, which gets the bishop where White wants it. Now, once White can compel ...b4, there will be only one black piece guarding c4, the square on which White wants to mate after the b♙b5 has moved. To get rid of that one remaining piece, White continues 2 ♕a2+, and Black's forced reply is 2...♖a4. Now 3 ♕g8 can be played: it threatens 4 ♕a8#, and Black's attempt to defeat this threat by 3...♗c8 fails because of 4 ♕xc8#. His only other defence is 3...b4, which is now an interference with the ♖a4, and 4 ♕c4# results. The point of all White's manoeuvres is now clear: the bishop must be forced to move to g4 (*decoyed* to interfere with the ♖h4), and then the ♖f4 must be decoyed to a4 so that 3...b4 becomes a fatal interference. Play through the solution to this problem once again to savour the strategy to the full. Because the composer has placed the pieces precisely where he wants them, he has been able to express a chess idea in a perfect form, and at the same time he has presented us with a challenge, a problem to solve using our powers of analysis and our experience of the chess pieces.

You may well have realised by now that nos. 2 and 3 differ from the game position no. 1 in one important respect not so far touched on. In the composed positions, both the study and the problem, there is no unit on the board which does not play some part, however small, in the solution. (The term 'solution' is used here, and throughout the book, to refer not just to the key but to the entire play, both virtual and actual, of the problem. What is meant by *virtual play* will become clear in due course.) In no. 1, however, several of the pieces and pawns on the board do not participate at all in the play as far as we examined it. The four-mover no. 3 contains only three white pieces, but each plays a vital rôle, even though the king and bishop are not in fact called upon to move. Their function is to prevent the black king from moving too far, and they fulfil this by guarding, between them, four squares in the king's *field* (i.e. the squares around him). The bishop guards (or 'controls' or 'holds') a7 and a5, and the king b6 and b7. As we have seen, the black king is allowed to move only as far as b5 in the course of the problem's solution; the white forces and his own men conspire against him to prevent him from going any further. The three black line-pieces and the ♙b5 are, of course, integral to the composer's idea. Only the presence of the other pawns remains to be accounted for. Those on f6 and h5 clearly prevent the black rooks from inflicting disastrous checks on the white king – disastrous because they would prevent White from mating on his fourth move as stipulated. The pawns on c6 and c5 prevent 2...♖c4 from being a check, and each has a further function: the one on c6 stops a defence against the threat 4 ♕a8# by 3...♗f3 in the second variation we looked at, while the ♙c5 prevents a cook by 1 ♕a2+ ♖a4 2 ♕e6 (threatening 3 ♕c8) b4 3 ♕xe2+ (no mate after 3...c4!). Every unit on the board, therefore, is essential in one way or another, sometimes in more than one way. It should always be one of the composer's principal aims to express his idea with as little force as possible; in other words, with the greatest possible **economy**.

4

**TWO-MOVE DIRECT MATE:
BLACK KNIGHT-WHEEL**

G.Heathcote
1st prize, *Hampstead and Highgate Express* 1905
White to play and mate in two

The next two problems carry the stipulation 'White to play and mate in two' (this is normally shortened to 'Mate in two'). No. 4 is an old and famous composition. In comparison with nos. 2 and 3, the board is crowded, but the composer's idea demands a good deal of force. Everyone familiar with the chess pieces knows that a knight standing in the middle of the board has a maximum of eight possible moves. In this problem every move by the ♞d4 defeats White's threat, and all eight defences lead to new mates. This is known, for brevity's sake, as a black **Knight-wheel**, and the problem is a **task**, because the composer has managed to achieve, in this case, a maximum possible number of new mates introduced by moves of one black knight.

We'll examine the method by which the knight in question defeats the threat by each of his moves, and how the moves all permit White to play a different mating move. White's key is 1 ♖cc7, and the threat is 2 ♞c3. The square d4 is not only blocked by the black knight but also guarded by the ♗b2. This means, however, that White cannot mate by 2 ♞c3 after this black knight has moved, for the black king would then have a flight, d4. The knight-defences are therefore examples of square-vacation, a device we have already met in connection with the game position no. 1. The knight defeats the threat by departure from d4; it allows new mates by reason of its arrival on each of eight squares.

The moves 1...♞c6 and 1...♞e6 are self-blocks: each allows a white piece holding the square on which the knight arrives to abandon its guard: 1...♞c6 permits the ♖c7 to mate on d7, while 1...♞e6 leads to a mate on the same square by the other rook. The defences 1...♞b5 and 1...♞f5 are interferences, for in each case the arrival of the knight cuts a black line of guard: 1...♞b5 2 ♖c5; and 1...♞f5 2 ♖e5. Three other defences by the black knight are also interferences: 1...♞f3, which cuts the black queen's guard of e4 and so permits 2 ♛e4; 1...♞e2, leading to 2 ♛xh5 because the guard-line from the ♗d1 has been cut (interestingly, 1...♞f3 cuts this same guard-line d1-h5 but does not allow 2 ♛xh5 because the knight can interpose from f3 on the check-line by 2...♞e5 or 2...♞g5); and 1...♞c2, which interferes with the same bishop on the other side and leads to 2 b4. This last move is a **battery**-mate: the ♗a2 and △b3 constitute a ♗+△ battery, which opens as the pawn moves. It is a *direct battery* because the rear piece is aimed directly at the black king.

Two of the defences by the knight introduce self-blocks, and five are interferences; what about the eighth? 1...♞xb3 is a *self-pin*: by capturing the pawn, the knight pins itself on b3, and so allows White to mate by 2 ♛d3 because the knight cannot return to d4. A mate which is permitted because a black unit is pinned and which is invalid if that unit is not pinned, is referred to as a *pin-mate*. This fine problem contains a splendid mixture of strategy – self-blocks, interferences, a pin-mate, a battery-mate – and at no time is the defending knight captured by White. With twenty-one men on the board, can this problem be described as economical? Well, the white queen, two rooks, ♗a2 and ♞a4 all give mates and also guard squares in the black king's field, and the ♗b2 and the ♞b7 likewise do important guard-duty. It is normally agreed that the white king must be on the board, even if he plays no direct part in the proceedings. Here he is used to prevent a cook. If the composer had placed him on, e.g., a8, White could mate in two by 1 ♕g8+ ♘e6 2 ♕xe6, and the problem would be unsound. So the white king stands on g8, and must be shielded from checks on the g-file, hence the ♙g7, which also stops the cook 1 ♕f7+. Economy of white force is much more important than economy of black force, and so a composer would much prefer to use a black pawn rather than a white pawn. But a black pawn on g7 would be able to play to g5 after 1 ♖cc7 ♘e2! 2 ♕xh5?, and consequently the problem would again be unsound, this time by reason of *no solution*.

The function of most of the black units the composer has used in this problem is clear. But what of the ♗g1 and the pawns? The ♙h2 prevents the black queen from guarding h5, while that on e3 prevents the ♗g1 from playing to d4 after 1...♘xb3, and to c5 after 1...♘b5, and also stops Black from defending with 1...♕f3, after which there would be no mate by 2 ♘c3. The ♙a7 prevents the ♘a4 from mating on b6, and the ♙a6 stops both 1...a6 and 1...♖a6. Neither of these moves would defeat the threat, and White would thus be allowed a choice of mating moves. Such a choice of mates is called a **dual** (or sometimes triple or quadruple if the choice is between three, or four, mates). A dual is serious if, for example, it occurs in one of the composer's intended main variations. It used to be thought that almost any dual was serious if it could be avoided easily, and certainly Heathcote, in 1905, would have been dissatisfied with his problem if he had not taken steps to avoid the duals after 1...a6 and 1...♖a6. He even added the ♗g1 to prevent the relatively harmless dual (2 ♘c3 or 2 ♕e4) after moves by the black queen along the rank. Nowadays composers would omit this bishop, and most would leave off the ♙a6 as well. This would not be regarded as slipshod construction; it is simply that attitudes towards duals have softened, while attitudes towards economy of force have become more rigorous.

It has been mentioned already that the composer of a problem will generally want to demonstrate a particular idea. The idea underlying a problem is commonly referred to as the *theme*, a term which virtually defies definition. The theme may cover the possibilities inherent in the position before the key is played; it may involve the key itself; it may be simply the play which follows the key; or it may be any combination of these. The theme of the problem may be displayed in the strategy (e.g. interferences, self-blocks, pin-mates, etc.), or by the pattern of the play – the relationship between different elements within the solution, or between different *variations*. In the problemist's vocabulary, the term 'variation' refers to black defences plus white continuations. The theme of no. 4 is the complete black knight-wheel, with its eight distinct variations. The key of this problem is not *thematic*, because it is not related to the theme.

5

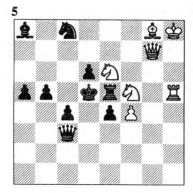

CROSS-CHECKS + SELF-PINS
AND BATTERY MATES

C.Mansfield
Version, *Magasinet* 1933
Mate in two

The key of no. 5, however, is certainly thematic, because it directly introduces the problem's theme. The diagram position contains three batteries, two white and one black. There is the direct battery consisting of the ♗g8 and the ♘e6. On the fifth rank White has a *masked* battery, consisting of ♖h5+♘f5 and in addition one black unit, the ♖e5, the masking piece. Black also has a masked battery directed at the white king: ♕+♖, with the white queen as the masking unit. If the white queen were to move off the line c3-h8, she would *unmask* the battery and thereby allow Black a couple of discovered checks by moves of the rook.

Solvers with a knowledge of problem history would look instinctively for a move by the white queen as a possible key to this problem, for checks by Black were a favourite theme of Comins Mansfield, the composer. As in over-the-board play, White may have three ways of countering a black check: (1) by moving his king; (2) by capturing the checking piece; (3) by interposing one of his own men on the line of check. In the two-move problem White's replies to black checks must themselves give mate, of course. A reply of type (3) is known as a **cross-check**, and we see two examples in no. 5. The thematic key 1 ♕a7 threatens 2 ♕xa8. Black's two checks are 1...♖xf5+ and 1...♖xe6+, and these two moves, as well as discovering check, are self-pins. 1...♖xf5+ allows the direct ♗+♘ battery to open: 2 ♘ed4 – cross-check, because the black line of check is closed. This is also a pin-mate: Black cannot play 2...♖f7 to parry the mate because the rook has pinned itself on f5. 1...♖xe6+ not only gives check and pins the rook again, but also unmasks the ♖+♘ battery and so allows the cross-check pin-mate 2 ♘fd4. The black self-pin is exploited in each variation.

It is worth noticing that after 1...♖xf5+ White's knight is forced to play to d4 rather than to g7 to counter the check, because of the black king-flight c6, which must be guarded. (After 1...♖xe6+ the same applies to the mate by the

♘f5, but there is a second reason why 2 ♘g7? would not mate: Black could play 2...♛e5!.)

The theme of this problem is, therefore, not simply 'cross-checks', but 'cross-checks + self-pins, leading to battery-mates covering a flight'. But we have not yet examined all of Black's defences. There are four other variations, and because they are not part of the principal theme of the problem, they constitute what is known as **by-play**. This usually adds to the interest and attractiveness of a problem, and often arises naturally from the placing of the main pieces involved in the thematic play. Mansfield was a master of good by-play; let us see how he incorporated some into no. 5. The black king may play to his flight, and if he does so the white ♗+♘ battery becomes *indirect*, because it will now fire at a flight of the king rather than directly at him. The defence 1...♚c6 allows an opening of this now indirect battery by 2 ♘d8. If it were Black's turn to play in the diagram position, White would have no immediate mating reply to 1...♚c6. The flight is therefore *unprovided*, and White's key, while good in respect of the checks it allows, has the weakness that it *provides* for the strong black defence 1...♚c6. If a black defence has a mate provided for it in the diagram position, the mate is called a *set mate*, and the whole variation (black defence followed by white set mate) is termed *set play*.

Black has three more defences: 1...♗b7, which merely *unguards* b7 and so allows the simple capture 2 ♛xb7; 1...♗c6, a self-block on the flight, leading to 2 ♘c7; and all moves by the ♘c8 (1...♘xa7/♘b6/♘e7), which, like 1...♗b7, are unguards, since they permit 2 ♘e7. No other black moves defeat the threat. This by-play is an integral part of the problem; no force has been added to achieve it. 2 ♘e7 must be prevented from occurring as a mate in the initial position – hence the need for the ♘c8. And White must not be allowed to mate in one by 1 ♛b7, which accounts for the ♗a8. It may well have been a stroke of luck for the composer that 1...♗c6 automatically allowed 2 ♘c7, but he had to use the black queen instead of merely a ♗c3 so that 2 ♘e3 would not work just as well.

Some of the strategic devices we have encountered so far reappear in no. 6, in which White is to play and mate in three moves. The Russian composer of this work is one of the world's leading problemists. The key is 1 ♘a4, which carries the threat of 2 ♘xb6+ ♘xb6 3 ♖c5. Black has two defences that involve the closing of the white line of guard from d2 to d4. 1...♖d3 defeats the threat because, after 2 ♘xb6+ ♘xb6, 3 ♖c5? is not mate: Black has a flight, d4. However, this move interferes with the ♗f1, and White may play 2 ♗c4+. The only reply open to Black is 2...♚xd4, whereupon White may play 3 ♗c3 – a pin-mate, as the ♖d3 has become pinned through the king's move. There are three basically distinct ways in which a piece may become

6

INTERFERENCES + PIN-MATES

V.F.Rudenko
3rd prize, *Schach-Echo* 1960
Mate in three

pinned: (1) by its capturing an enemy piece on a battery-line, as in no. 5; (2) by a move of the king, as here; (3) by a move of a third piece, a method which will be exemplified in no. 9.

The strategy of the variation 1...罩d3 2 奧c4+ etc. is repeated when Black defends by 1...奧d3, which also closes the white queen's line of guard. White may now play 2 ᐒc3+, since the guard of the 罩h3 over c3 has been interfered with. Black's sole reply is again 2...當xd4, and White's third move, another pin-mate, is 3 罩c4, exploiting the pin of the 奧d3 resulting from the king-move. Notice the very close connection between the two variations we have so far looked at: in the first the 罩h3 interferes with the 奧f1, while in the second it is the bishop that interferes with the rook.

Many a composer would have been satisfied to have constructed a three-mover with just these two main variations. Not so Rudenko, however. He has *doubled* the theme by incorporating a second pair of variations which **echoes** the first pair. This composer's great success in composing **tourneys** (the name given to competitions for problem composing) is mainly due to his boldness in striving for a maximum effect and the ingenuity he displays in achieving it, as in this problem. Black can defeat White's threat by moving either his 罩h7 or his 奧d8 to e7, cutting the line of guard e8-e6. If 1...罩e7, White exploits first the interference with the bishop: 2 ᐒf6+ 當e6 – and then the pin of the rook: 3 奧xd7. And if 1...奧e7, then 2 罩xd7+ is played, followed, after 2...當e6, by 3 罩d6. Notice how the white 奧b5 and 罩c7 get actively involved in both pairs of variations in this fine problem, which also contains a pleasant by-play variation: 1...d6 2 奧c6+ 當c4 3 ᐒb2.

We'll now give pin-mates a rest for a time and turn our attention to an extremely popular and very common theme: **unpin** of White by Black. We have already seen several ways in which Black can create weaknesses in his own position, for example by self-block, by interference with one of his own men, by opening a white line, etc. A black defence may also unpin a pinned white unit, which is thus free to mate. The unpin may be effected in one of two ways: (1) by withdrawal, when the pinning piece moves off the pin-line; and (2) by interference, when another black unit plays on to the pin-line. Interference unpins are found in no. 7.

7

UNPIN OF WHITE BY BLACK + DUAL AVOIDANCE

C.Mansfield
Good Companions 1919
Mate in two

White plays 1 &h2, to threaten 2 &c7 mate. Black's main defences are 1...&g3, which cuts the white bishop's line to c7, and 1...&c3, which cuts the white rook's line of guard to c7. The mates are delivered by the white knight, which is unpinned by these two defences. As is usual in a Mansfield problem, there is interesting by-play: 1...d6 2 ⬛c6 (a simple unguard); 1...d5 2 ♛g6 (an interference with the black queen, which enables the white queen to move off the pin-line in order to mate); and 1...⬛a8 2 ⬛xb7 (another unguard).

Five variations altogether, consisting of two interference unpins, two unguards and an interference. Not much, you might think. But there is in fact a good deal more to this problem than that. We have not so far examined exactly which knight-mate White plays after which unpin, and why. If White had a choice of mates after the two bishop-defences, the problem would be worthless. It is the fact that White does not have such a choice that makes this problem really interesting. Each bishop-defence cuts a white line of guard. Thus 1...&g3 closes the line of the &h2. If White now played 2 ♘c4?, Black could play 2...♚c7!. So the knight must play to d5, precisely because the bishop has arrived on g3. And 1...&c3 closes the line of the ⬛c1, so that White must carefully not play 2 ♘d5? (2...♚c6!), and must instead choose 2 ♘c4. In other words, it looks as if White will have a choice of mates, a dual. But as the defending black piece arrives on a particular square, one of the apparent alternative mates is eliminated and only the other one remains. The device (it is not a theme) is known as **dual avoidance**. A clear understanding of the principle of dual avoidance is essential for a full comprehension of what many chess problems are all about.

8

DUAL AVOIDANCE + BLACK CORRECTION

T.Ebend
1st prize, *Parallèle 50* 1949
Mate in two

Here is another example of it. The key of no. 8, 1 ♘c1, threatens 2 cxb3. The main defences, those which exemplify the dual-avoidance scheme, are 1...♘d4 and 1...♘d5. The arrival of a black unit on the line d6-d3 seems to allow White a choice of mates by 2 ♘xd6 or 2 cxd3, for the black rooks' guard of each other is interfered with. But 1...♘d4 unpins the B♗e4, so that 2 cxd3? would be answered by 2...exd3!, and only 2 ♘xd6 will work. In similar fashion the move 1...♘d5 unpins the black queen to guard d6: 2 ♘xd6? is therefore ruled out and White must choose 2 cxd3. The mate which occurs in one variation is avoided in the other. White's choice depends on Black's arrival square, in both no. 7 and no. 8.

Just as there was more to no. 7 than unpins, interferences and unguards, so there is more to no. 8 than the dual-avoidance variations studied so far. It will be seen that any move by either black knight will defeat the threat. The departure of the knight from b3 allows White to mate by 2 ♕c5. The knight, in moving *at random*, commits the *general error* of unguarding c5. But by arriving on d4 the knight *corrects* the general error by cutting the white bishop's guard of c5. 1...♘d4 is therefore a **correction** move, which nevertheless creates a new weakness (interference with the ♖d3) and allows the new mate 2 ♘xd6, as we have already seen. The other black knight performs a correction as well. If 1...♘c~ (the symbol ~ is used to indicate that a piece moves at random, creating a general error), then White plays 2 ♕b5 mate. 1...♘d5 is the correction: the white queen cannot now reach b5. The term *Black Correction* was coined by a famous composer and problem editor, Brian Harley, in 1935. The simplest form of black correction occurs when a black piece tries to put right, by its arrival, the error committed by its departure, but there are many other possibilities.

Mention has already been made of set play: black moves with white mates already prepared for them in the diagram position. A problem in which every possible black move has a set mate is known as a *complete block*. One where most of Black's moves have set mates and the key merely provides mates for the rest of them without threatening anything is called an *incomplete block*. A complete block may be (1) a waiting-move problem, or *waiter*, when White's key is a neutral move which simply waits for Black to commit himself (incomplete blocks are also waiters); (2) a *block-threat*, in which the key surprisingly introduces a threat; or (3) a **mutate**, in which the key abandons one or more of the set mates and replaces them with new ones. New mates replacing set mates are called *changed mates*, or *changes*.

9

MUTATE: HALF-PIN

K.A.K.Larsen
1st prize, Good Companions Complete
Blocks Tourney, April 1921
Mate in two

No. 9 is a mutate. Black has only three set defences: 1...♗xb7, and the moves of the pawns on d7 and e7. These pawn-moves are of particular interest, for if one of the pawns moves, the other remains pinned by the ♖f7. This arrangement (two black units on a line between the black king and a white line-piece) is termed a **half-pin**. The half-pin is of interest only if White exploits the pin when mating. The set play of no. 9 shows two pin-mates: 1...e6 2 ♕c6 (2...dxc6?? impossible); and 1...d6+ 2 cxd6 (2...exd6??). White has no neutral move, which would simply transfer to Black the obligation to move, though there are several near-misses, notably 1 ♔e4?, refuted by a pinning defence 1...♗xb7!. The key 1 ♘d8 still leaves Black in zugzwang, but changes the set replies to the pawn-moves and adds a variation: 1...♔xd8 2 ♕xd7 (an *added mate*). Now 1...e6 allows 2 ♘xe6, and 1...d6+ leads to 2 ♕xd6. The pin is again exploited each time, so that the half-pin can be said to be *complete*, both before and after the key. This is a *two-phase* problem; the set play is the first phase, and the play following the key (sometimes called the *actual play*, but more accurately termed the *post-key play*) is the second phase.

10

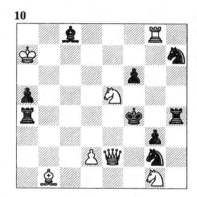

MATE TRANSFERENCE: SELF-BLOCKS + WHITE INTERFERENCE

O.Strerath
1st prize, *Problemisten* 1950
Mate in two

No. 10 is also a two-phase problem, but whereas in no. 9 the black defences remain the same in the two phases, here the black defences change and White's mates remain the same. This kind of changed play is known as **mate transference**, because the mates are transferred from one group of defences to another. Black's defences, in both phases of no. 10, are self-blocks, but of a type we have not previously seen. If in the diagram position Black were to play 1...♘g5, White could exploit the fact that the knight has blocked g5 and play 2 ♘g6, a **white interference** mate, so called because White has been permitted to cut his own rook's guard of g5. There is a second white interference in the set play: 1...f5 2 ♘d3 – the black pawn blocks f5 so that White, in mating, may close the line of guard of his ♗b1 to that square. A white-interference mate may be permitted in two ways: (1) by self-block, as in this example; or (2) by line-opening: Black's defence may open one white line of guard so that White is able to close another. The post-key play of no. 10 shows the same two mates, but this time after different black moves. The key 1 ♕b5 is a square-vacation threatening 2 ♘e2, and Black's thematic defences are 1...♗g4 and 1...♖e4. The former blocks g4, a square which is still doubly guarded by White even after the key (it had a triple guard before), and now White replies with 2 ♘g6. The key turns out to be an **ambush** of the white queen behind the ♘e5, and now the line of guard is opened to hold g5, the square on which the set self-block took place. Black's second defence 1...♖e4 leads to 2 ♘d3, because of the block of e4. Once again the queen's ambush is used, this time to hold f5, again the square of the set self-block.

Black's set defences do not defeat the threat, nor do they lead to a repetition of the set mates. And Black's post-key defences have no mates set for them. Accuracy, of both defences and mates, is an extremely important feature of mate-transference problems.

11

TRIES

M.Niemeijer
Tijdschrift van de Nederlandsche Schaakbond 1919
Mate in two

No. 11 is also a complete block; if it were Black's turn to play, White would be able to mate whatever he did. This means that a waiting-move will solve the problem, so let's set about finding one. The white king does not seem to be doing anything useful; surely one of his moves would be good enough? We'll try 1 ♔a2, which seems to maintain the block position. Not quite, however, since Black can play 1...♖h2!, and now the set mate 2 ♗g3 will not work, because the bishop is pinned. 1 ♔a2? is therefore a **try**, a move which very nearly solves the problem but fails to a single black defence. The try is *refuted* by the one move 1...♖h2!. It is usual to place a question mark (?) after a white try, and an exclamation mark (!) after a black refutation.

The fact that we have found a try by the white king suggests that there may be others. What about 1 ♔c3? This too is only a try, for Black can play 1...♖xc6!, and the mate set for this move, 2 ♕f5, is prevented, again by pin. There is a third try, 1 ♔a3?, which is refuted by a third pinning defence, 1...♗f8!, for 2 ♕g5 is now impossible. The key is the only king-move which does not allow the pin of another white unit: 1 ♔a4!. (The exclamation mark is used here to distinguish this move from the tries.) The subsequent play is not of much interest; it consists, in fact, of five simple unguard variations. The whole point of the problem lies in the tries, which are closely related to one another by the fact that they are all refuted by pinning moves. They therefore share a *common error*, that of permitting Black a single pinning refutation.

12

ZAGORUIKO: PROMOTIONS

O.Stocchi
Version, 2nd prize, *L'Italia Scacchistica*
1958
Mate in two

A try of a very different kind is found in no. 12. The play of this problem revolves round the move of the ♟e2 to e1 and its choice of promotion piece. In a two-move problem the choice normally lies between queen and knight, since the queen's powers include those of both rook and bishop. (For this reason a white mating-move choice between queen and rook or between queen and bishop is not regarded as constituting a **dual**.) In a three-mover or longer problem, however, the theme may demand a white promotion to rook or bishop, e.g. if stalemate is to be avoided (this occurs very occasionally in two-movers as well), or even a similar promotion by Black, e.g. to attempt to force stalemate. Nos. 9 and 10 are two-phase problems; no. 12, on the other hand, has three phases. The set play is 1...e1♕ 2 ♖d4; and 1...e1♘ 2 ♗e3. In addition to the key, White has another plausible-looking first move, a try which very nearly solves but fails to a single black defence. And this try, 1 ♘e3?, looks so plausible because it introduces two new mates to follow the promotions on e1: 1...e1♕ 2 ♕c2; and 1...e1♘ 2 ♘f1. The original set mates are not playable because the knight that makes the try abandons its guard of c3 (so that 2 ♖d4? is no longer mate after 1...e1♕), and of e3, the square on which it arrives (2 ♗e3? therefore being impossible after 1...e1♘). Play introduced by a try is known as *virtual play*. A further virtual mate in no. 12 is 2 ♘e4, which follows 1...♗a3 after the try. 1...♗a3 is, in fact, a random move by the bishop: 2 ♘e4 can be played because the bishop has opened the white queen's line of guard to e1. The correction 1...♗b2! prevents 2 ♘e4 by pinning the ♘c3, and is the move which refutes the try, for Black's only other available move, 1...♔e1, is met by 2 ♕xc1.

The correct white first move is 1 ♘f2!, which puts Black in a zugzwang position. This is a *flight-giving* key, because the black king is granted a second flight, e3. A key which deprives Black of a flight is called a *flight-taking* key, while one which allows one flight but takes another is a *give-and-take* key. Some of the conventions covering keys, especially with regard to their strength, are discussed in Section II (→ **Keys**). After 1 ♘f2! Black's two promotions lead to a further pair of white mates: 1...e1♕ 2 ♕d3; and 1...e1♘ 2 ♘fe4. The latter mate also follows 1...♗a3 and 1...♗b2 (the bishop cannot correct its general error this time), while 1...♔e1 leads once again to 2 ♕xc1 and 1...♔e3 is met by 2 ♕d3. The theme of this problem is the changed replies to the two promotion-moves. These replies are, in fact, doubly changed, since there are three pairs of mates altogether, one pair in the set play, one pair in the virtual play (after the try), and the third pair in the post-key play. Thus one pair appears in each of the three phases of the problem. Problems of this type, in which at least two black defences are followed by different mates in at least three phases of play, fit into the framework known as **Zagoruiko**, named after a Russian composer who made a number of fine examples of it. No. 12 is one of the most economical and beautiful settings; rarely has so much rich and interesting play been achieved with so few pieces. The thematic defences are self-blocks, and in each phase there is dual avoidance, for White would have a choice of two mates if the pawn could remain on e1 unpromoted, but is forced to choose one or the other according to Black's choice of queen or knight.

A two-phase problem may have either set play or virtual play in addition to the post-key play. A three-phase problem may consist of set, virtual and post-key play (like no. 12), or may have two virtual-play phases, each introduced by a white try. Problems with more than four phases are rare, though you will find an extraordinary setting under **Tasks** (no. 267). The term 'Zagoruiko' applies only when at least two of White's mates are changed in at least three phases; it does not cover changes of Black's defences (mate transference). Examples of three-phase mate transference are, in any case, much rarer than those of three-phase change.

* * * * *

You will have heard of the Sicilian Defence and know that it refers to an opening based on 1 e4 by White followed by 1...c5 by Black. The jargon of problems is no more confusing and no harder to pick up than that of over-the-board play. Many of the terms are self-explanatory, e.g. self-block, interference. A theme with a name that is not self-explanatory has usually been called after a composer who has paid particular attention to it, and in some cases produced the pioneer example, or alternatively after a town or country associated in some way with a composer or group of composers. The name may have been bestowed on the theme originally in honour of a composer, but the reason for its retention is normally that it is much quicker and easier to use than a descriptive phrase would be. As you tackle more problems and start to read problem-sections of chess magazines (where they exist), or even problem-magazines themselves (see the Bibliography at the end of the book), you will inevitably meet more technical terms than the few mentioned in this first section. That is where Section II of this book can help you. All the most important problem themes and mechanisms are explained and illustrated, and so are a good many other things associated with chess problems of all types. The entries are arranged alphabetically, so that you can turn immediately to any new theme you may encounter and familiarise yourself with it by studying the examples quoted. A section of further problems for solving will be found towards the end of the book. It is not recommended that the beginner should read straight through Section II from A to Z. You should perhaps start by looking at the essays on some of the terms introduced in Section I, such as **flight, interference, self-block**. Note, however, that some of the elementary terms defined in this first section are not included in the alphabetical survey.

Section II

Themes and Terms

Added Play → Mutate

Albino

A white pawn standing on the second rank, anywhere from b2 to g2, may have up to four moves available (two forward, two captures). A problem showing the four possible moves of a single white pawn at some stage during the solution illustrates an Albino. In a two-mover these four moves are most commonly found as mates, which means that the pawn in question must be part of a battery, either diagonal (♗+♙) or orthogonal (♖+♙). No. 13, a **mutate**, has a diagonal battery, with the queen as rear piece.

ALBINO (+ ROYAL BATTERY)

13

H.D'O.Bernard
2nd prize ex aequo, Good Companions,
May 1917
Mate in two

Set 1...	♗b~	2 ♘b3
	♗xd2	2 ♖xd2
Key 1 ♕a1 zugzwang		
	♗xa5	2 b4
	♗xd2	2 b3
	♗a3	2 bxa3
	♗c3	2 bxc3
	♘c~	2 ♔e7
	♗h7	2 ♔f7
	♖xg6+	2 ♔xg6
	♖h4	2 ♔g5
	♘xf5	2 ♔xf5
	♗xe6	2 ♔xe6

In the diagram position the battery is not yet set up: random moves of the ♗b4 lead to 2 ♘b3, while the correction 1...♗xd2 is answered by 2 ♖xd2. The key replaces these two mates by four, all from the ♕+♙ battery. Notice how the self-pin 1...♗xd2, by attempting to gain a flight at c4, forces 2 b3. This is really two problems in one, for in addition to the play just outlined there are also six mates from the **Royal Battery** in the north-east corner of the board. All of these mates, however, occur in both set and post-key pay. The composer has achieved a double **task**: an Albino combined with the maximum possible number of mates from a ♗+♔ battery.

ALBINO + PICKANINNY

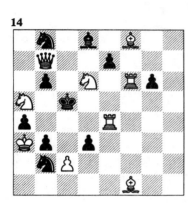

14

A.C.Reeves
Probleemblad 1965
Mate in two
Try 1 cxb3? (>2 b4)
       ...   exd6!
Try 1 c3?   (>2 ♖e5)
       ...   exf6!
Try 1 c4?   (>2 ♕d5)
       ...   e6!
Try 1 cxd3? (>2 d4)
       ...   e5!
Key 1 ♖b4! (>2 ♘e4)
       ...   exd6 2 ♗xd6
                   ♘c4 2 ♖xc4
                   ♘c6 2 ♕xc6

A second way of presenting an Albino in two-move form is to make each pawn-move a try. This is found in no. 14, where the composer has brilliantly arranged that each of the four white pawn-tries is defeated by each of the four possible moves of a black pawn, standing, like the white pawn, on its starting square. 1 cxb3? threatens 2 b4 but fails to 1...exd6!, which obtains a flight for Black on b5. 1 c3? looks rather more promising, since it threatens 2 ♖e5 (which will cover b5 after 1...exd6). But 1...exf6! directly guards e5 (notice that 1...exd6 does not, as the pawn is pinned). 1 c4? threatens 2 ♕d5, but Black guards d5 with 1...e6!. Finally 1 cxd3? (>2 d4) fails to 1...e5!. So White must give up trying to do things with this pawn, and must instead play 1 ♖b4! (>2 ♘e4). Black has three defences leading to new mates, but these are of minor importance by comparison with the intricate try-play. Like the previous problem, this is a double task (Albino tries answered by the four moves of a single black pawn), but unlike the previous problem, no. 14 features a close connection between the two tasks. The four possible moves of a black pawn appearing at some stage in the problem's solution are known as a **Pickaninny**.

15

ALBINO (+ PIN-MODELS)

G.Heathcote
The Observer 1927
Mate in three

Key 1 f3 (>2 ♕e5/♕e7/cxb7+)
... ♗xf3 2 ♕e7+ ♔d4 3 dxe3
... ♕d6 3 d4
♕c2 2 ♕e5+ ♔xc4 3 d3
♘c3 2 cxb7+ ♔d4 3 dxc3

In the three-mover or longer problem the moves of the Albino may, of course, be found as continuations or mates, with (or more elegantly without) a battery. In no. 15 the four moves occur as mates on White's third move, after self-pinning play by Black in each variation. This attractive problem also illustrates **model mates**, of a type known as *pin-models*.

Allumwandlung → Promotion

Ambush

A white line-piece **A** is placed behind a piece **B** of either colour, so that when **B** moves, **A**'s line is opened. This arrangement, known as an Ambush, is illustrated by the key of no. 16.

The white queen ambushes herself behind the ♘d3 so as to threaten 2 ♘b4. The queen's line of guard to the flight b3 is opened as soon as the knight leaves d3. Notice that 1 ♘b4+? cannot be played straightaway, as this move interferes with the queen's guard of b3 while she is still on b7. The key not only gives the flight and sacrifices the queen to two enemy units, but also allows Black a check: 1...♕xf3+. This is answered by 2 ♖e4, a battery-mate permitted by the fact that the black queen has abandoned her guard up the g-file of the ♗+♖ battery. The white rook, in mating, can **shut off** the black queen and black rook simultaneously. A similar shut-off occurs after 1...♖xf3: 2 ♖g4. A double-checkmate from the battery follows 1...b1♕, while if the black king takes his flight the ambushed queen becomes the rear piece of a new direct battery and White mates with 2 ♘c1. While the

16

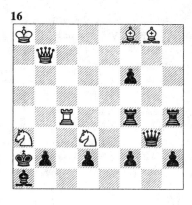

AMBUSH

J.A.Schiffmann
1st prize, *Bristol Times and Mercury*
1927
Mate in two

Key 1 ♕f3 (>2 ♘b4)
... ♕xf3+ 2 ♖e4
   ♖xf3 2 ♖g4
   b1♕ 2 ♖c2
   ♔b3 2 ♘c1

black king remains on a2, the white queen and ♘d2 form an *indirect battery*. An ambush key setting up a direct battery is found in no. 13 (**Albino**).

Andernach Chess

This is a form of **fairy chess**. On making a capture, units other than kings change colour. This novel idea was first introduced in 1993 by the German composer, editor and publisher Bernd Ellinghoven at the annual meeting of fairy chess enthusiasts held each year since 1975 in the small town of Andernach, on the Rhine. No. 17 was awarded a share of the first prize in the tourney for Andernach chess problems organised that year.

17

ANDERNACH CHESS (HELPMATE)

K.Widlert
1st prize ex aequo, Andernach 1993
Helpmate in two:
(a) diagram; (b) ♙g7→f7

(a) 1 ♗xd3=w♗ ♖h4 2 ♖xh4=w♖ ♗c4
(b) 1 ♖xd3=w♖ ♗d6 2 ♗xd6=w♗ ♖g3

[NB: Black's moves are given first in helpmates.]

It is a **helpmate** in two: Black, playing first, co-operates with White to enable White to give mate. In the diagram position White needs another piece, so Black provides one by capturing the ♘d3 with the ♝e4, allowing White 2...♝c4 as the mating move. But the ♖c4 is in the way: White cannot simply play a capture on this square, because then his new bishop will become black once again! Wherever the ♖c4 plays to on Black's second move, it will guard c4 and so prevent the mate. White's first move is thus determined: 1...♖h4. This enables the black rook to disappear by playing 2 ♖xh4=w♖, and the mate on c4 is now playable. Position (b) is arrived at by a shift of the ♘g7 to f7. Now the mate will be with a new white rook up the g-file. Once again there is a black unit in the way, the ♝g3. So the first moves create the white rook and enable the ♝g3 to disappear: 1 ♖xd3=w♖ ♝d6. Now 2 ♝xd6=w♝ allows the mate 2...♖g3. Do not overlook the fine orthogonal/diagonal **correspondence** in this problem.

Annihilation → Clearance

Anti-Bristol

The Anti-Bristol is an **interference** in which like-moving black pieces interfere along the same line (contrast **Holzhausen** and **Wurzburg-Plachutta** interferences, in which the thematic pieces are not on the same line). Mutual anti-Bristol interference occurs when piece **A** interferes with piece **B** in one variation, and **B** with **A** in another. No. 18 presents three pairs of mutual anti-Bristols, i.e. six anti-Bristol interferences altogether.

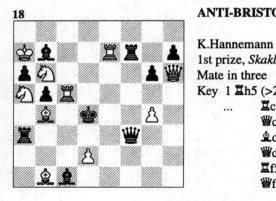

18

ANTI-BRISTOL

K.Hannemann
1st prize, *Skakbladet* 1919
Mate in three
Key 1 ♖h5 (>2 ♝c5)

...	♖c3	2 ♘b3+
	♕c3	2 ♕e3+
	♝d5	2 ♘c6+
	♕d5	2 ♖e4+
	♖f5	2 ♕g7+
	♕f5	2 ♕f4+

The key 1 ♖h5 threatens the *short mate* 2 ♝c5 (a short threat is common with this theme). 1...♖c3 allows 2 ♘b3+, White exploiting the black rook's interference with the black queen's guard of b3. The rook is now **overloaded,** being unable to retain its guard over both b3 and c5. In the analogous variation 1...♕c3 2 ♕e3+, it is the black queen which becomes overloaded, White exploiting her interference with the ♖a3. The second pair of variations involves the black queen and the ♗b7 (1...♗d5 2 ♘c6+; and 1...♕d5 2 ♖e4+), while the queen again and the ♖f7 feature in the third pair (1...♖f5 2 ♕g7+; and 1...♕f5 2 ♕f4+). The theme is called *anti-Bristol* as it is the weakening manoeuvre which is the opposite (or **antiform**) of the strengthening manoeuvre of the *Bristol* (➔ **Clearance**). In the anti-Bristol the pieces get in each other's way by moving towards each other, whereas in the Bristol the pieces get out of each other's way by moving away from each other.

Anticipation

If you compose a problem which someone else has made before, your problem is *anticipated*, and the other composer's work is an *anticipation*. Deciding whether a problem is completely new (or *original*) is nearly always a difficult and sometimes an embarrassing business. A problem is *completely anticipated* if the theme, the play and the positions of the principal pieces in the two settings are identical, or so nearly identical as to make no material difference. If, however, the two problems resemble one another in some but not all respects, the newer one is said to be *partially anticipated* by the older. A composer who knows that his problem is partially anticipated but feels that his version adds something really worthwhile to the previous setting will publish his problem as 'by X, after Y' if the difference is considerable, or as 'by Y: version by X' if the difference is only slight. A version of someone else's problem should ideally appear in the same publication as the first setting. Such versions are not normally eligible to compete in composing **tourneys**.

It is sometimes a difficult matter to determine the exact date of a problem. Contributions to a *formal tourney* are usually given the date of the deadline for receipt of entries for that tourney if they appear in the award, while for reprint purposes the date of the award is generally given. All other problems are dated from the day or month when they first appear in print.

There are one or two conventions concerning anticipations. In the first place, a composer should not submit for publication a problem which he knows to be completely anticipated. If he does so, he is guilty of plagiarism, the problemist's most serious crime. If he suspects that his work may be anticipated, he should submit it to the editor of a well-established problem section in a magazine, or of a magazine catering entirely for problemists. If the editor, too, is in doubt about anticipation, he will know where to seek advice before deciding whether to publish.

Secondly, a problem which has been awarded some distinction in a composing tourney will lose that distinction and be removed from the award if a complete anticipation is found within a few months of the publication of the award. In the event of a partial anticipation, it will be the judge's responsibility to decide whether the problem should keep its place, be downgraded, or even come out of the award altogether.

Thirdly, a point which, regrettably, is not universally observed: no problemist should offer his services as the judge of a tourney without a sound knowledge of the history and development of the type of problem for which the tourney is being organised. It is, after all, only fair to the contestants that the judge should have such knowledge.

On the whole question of anticipation, little advice can be offered to the beginner other than this: if you think your problem is worthwhile, show it to an expert. You will at least be advised as to whether it stands a chance of being original and whether it is worth publishing. If it isn't, don't despair – try again!

Anti-critical Play → Critical Play

Antiform

FORM : ANTIFORM (UNBLOCK AND SELF-BLOCK)

19

N.G.G.van Dijk
1st prize, *Chess Life* 1956
Mate in two

Set 1...   ♖4xb5 2 ♖3d4
             ♖6xb5 2 ♖c3
             ♘xb5   2 ♕e6
Key 1 ♕f1 (>2 ♖c3)
    ...   ♖4xb5 2 ♕f4
             ♖6xb5 2 ♕c1
             ♘xb5   2 ♕f7
             ♖b3   2 ♖3d4

Look at the set defence 1...♖4xb5 in no. 19: this is a **self-block**, allowing 2 ♖3d4. Why does it not also allow 2 ♖c3? Because 1...♖4xb5, as well as blocking b5, *unblocks* b4, which White must take care to guard when mating. Unblock (also known as **square-vacation**) is the opposite of self-block. Self-block and unblock therefore stand in the relation FORM : ANTIFORM of the same basic tactic. The two other set defences in this problem are self-blocks but not unblocks: 1...♖6xb5 2 ♖c3; and 1...♘xb5 2 ♕e6. The key 1 ♕f1 (>2 ♖c3) changes the replies to these three self-blocks, and also permits a second unblock/self-block variation: 1...♖b3 2 ♖3d4 (a transferred mate, since this is the move which followed 1...♖4xb5 in the set play).

20

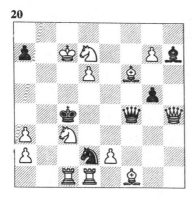

GOETHART AND ANTI-GOETHART

E.I.Umnov
1st prize, *64* 1929
Mate in two

Key 1 ♔c6 (>2 ♘e4)
      ...   ♘~   2 ♘e5
             ♘f3   2 e4
             ♘e4   2 ♖d4

The unity of a problem is increased if a Form : Antiform relationship can be seen in the play. This is the case with no. 20. The key 1 ♔c6 threatens 2 ♘e4, a move which unpins the black queen. If the black knight departs from d2, the threat fails because the now unpinned queen can capture the ♖c1. A random move of the knight allows 2 ♘e5. It is the correction 1...♘f3 that produces the interesting strategy. 2 ♘e4? still fails on account of 2...♕xc1!. But because the black knight has closed the line f4-f1, White can play 2 e4 – an unpin of the black queen made possible by the fact that the reply 2...♕xf1 has been prevented. An unpin of this type is known as a **Goethart unpin**. Black's defensive play with his knight may therefore be termed *Anti-Goethart*, since White is prevented from executing a Goethart unpin by 2 ♘e4.

Babson Task

This **task** involves the four promotions of a black pawn (to queen, rook, bishop and knight) answered by matching white promotions. The idea dates from the early years of the 20th century, when an American composer, Joseph Ney Babson, published a **selfmate** in three which achieved the task (1914), albeit with the white promotions shared between three pawns. In 1926 H.W.Bettmann won $25 and first prize in the 'Babson Task Tourney' for a selfmate setting in which both the black and white promotions are made by single pawns. It was long thought that the task might be impossible to achieve in direct-mate form, and it was not until 1983 that the first wholly correct examples appeared. No. 21 is the best of them.

BABSON TASK

21

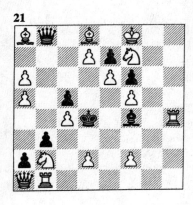

L.V.Yarosh
1st prize, *Shakhmaty v SSSR* 1983
Mate in four

Key 1 a7   (>2 axb8♕/♖/♗/♘)
    ...   axb1♕ 2 axb8♕ ♕xb2
3 ♕xb3 ♕xa1 4 ♖xf4
       axb1♖ 2 axb8♖ ♖xb2
3 ♖xb3 ♔xc4 4 ♕a4
       axb1♗ 2 axb8♗ ♗e4
3 ♗xf4 (>4 ♗e3/♗e5)
       axb1♘ 2 axb8♘ ♘xd2
3 ♕c1 ♘e4 4 ♘c6

The excellent waiting key 1 a7 threatens the four promotions by capture on b8. When Black replies by capturing on b1, White must proceed with care. 1...axb1♕ forces 2 axb8♕, because only a white queen will cope with both 2...♕xb2 (3 ♕xb3) and 2...♕e4 (3 ♖xf4). 1...axb1♖ is followed by 2 axb8♖, so that after 2...♖xb2, 3 ♖xb3 is not stalemate (3...♔xc4 4 ♕a4). Likewise stalemate is avoided after 1...axb1♗ by means of 2 axb8♗ ♗e4 3 ♗xf4. Finally 1...axb1♘ leads to 2 axb8♘ ♘xd2 3 ♕c1, with mate on c3 or e3, unless Black plays 3...♘e4, when the newly promoted knight mates on c6 (a **white interference** mate). The composer has successfully provided for all first moves by the black queen if Black does not play the promotions, though inevitably some of this **by-play** leads to alternative continuations – quite irrelevant when set against the outstanding task achievement.

Banny → Reversal themes

Battery

The W♗e6 and the W♖f5 in no. 22 constitute a battery: if the rook moves away, the bishop's line of attack on the black king is opened. In the diagram position the battery is controlled by the ♗a2, and the control of this bishop

22

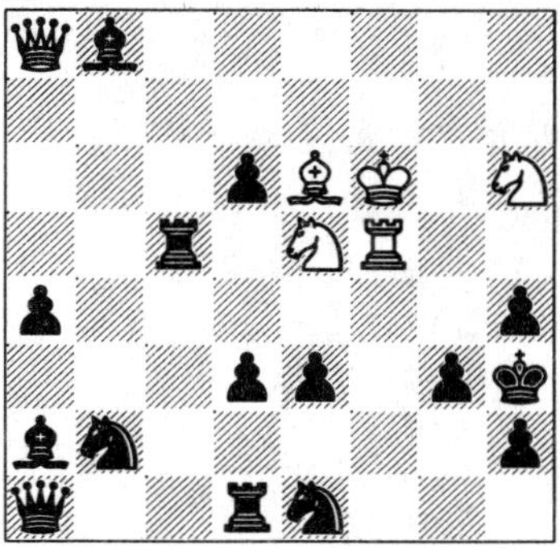

BATTERY MATES

L.I.Loshinsky
2nd prize, Olympic Tourney 1964
Mate in two
Key 1 ♘g6 (>2 ♘f4)

... ♘c4+	2 ♖e5
♘g2	2 ♖d5
g2	2 ♖f3
d5	2 ♖f2
♖c4	2 ♖f4
h1♕	2 ♕xh1
♖xf5+	2 ♗xf5

cannot be *shut off* by 2 ♖d5 until after the key, 1 ♘g6. Even then White cannot play 2 ♖d5 until Black has blocked g2 with 1...♘g2, for this is a **white interference** mate: the rook is allowed to interfere with the white queen's guard of g2. The key threatens 2 ♘f4, and Black, in addition to the variation just examined, has four more defences allowing mate by the battery: the **cross-check** 1...♘c4+ 2 ♖e5 (in this variation the black ♕+♘ battery opens); a second self-block with white interference, 1...g2 2 ♖f3; a black interference, 1...d5, which forces 2 ♖f2, as White must regain control of g2; and another black interference with shut-off, 1...♖c4 2 ♖f4. Two further variations round off this attractive work, which is notable chiefly for the extraordinary economy of the white force.

A battery is found in a large number of problems where it is a strategic device rather than the main theme. Many such examples will be found throughout this book. Like no. 22, however, the next four problems show batteries as the central idea. No. 23 has two of them, and each gives a total of four mates. Each battery is controlled by two black pieces, and when one moves away to defend against the threat, White is able to shut off or capture the other one. In addition there are four double-checkmate variations, three of them white interference mates permitted by black self-blocks.

The batteries in these two problems are all *direct*, since the rear piece is aimed straight at the black king. If the rear piece is aimed instead at a black flight-square, potential or actual, we speak of an *indirect* battery. No. 24 has batteries of both kinds. The indirect battery, consisting, after the key, of ♖e7+♘e4, is aimed at e3, the flight granted by the key, 1 ♘e4. The threat 2 ♘xc2 is an opening of the direct battery that is already in position in the diagram (i.e. ♕d7+♘d4). A second direct battery is set up by the key, consisting of the ♖a3+♗b3. This battery opens when the black king moves to

23

BATTERY MATES

E.Rukhlis
1st prize, *Shakhmaty v SSSR* 1945
Mate in two
Key 1 ♕b6 (>2 ♕xd6)

...	♘c7	2 ♘b7
	♖d8	2 ♘xa6
	♗e4	2 ♘ce6
	♗c4	2 ♘b3
	♖xb6	2 ♘h5
	♕f3	2 ♘e8
	♘e3	2 ♘ge6
	♕xf5	2 ♘xf5
	d5	2 ♕f6

24

DIRECT AND INDIRECT BATTERIES

V.Chepizhny
1st prize, *The Problemist* 1982/I
Mate in two
Key 1 ♘e4 (>2 ♘xc2)

...	♚e3+	2 ♗c4
	♖xe4	2 ♗e6
	cxd4	2 ♗d5
	♘xf7	2 ♗xf7
	♖xf5	2 ♘xf5
	♗c4	2 ♗xc2
	♘b8	2 ♘xc5
	♗f2	2 ♘xf2

his flight-square, discovering check from the ♗b5 (so Black, too, has a battery): 1...♚e3+ 2 ♗c4. The ♖+♗ battery opens to give four further mates: 1...♗c4 2 ♗xc2; 1...cxd4 2 ♗d5; 1...♖xe4 2 ♗e6; and 1...♘xf7 2 ♗xf7. The indirect battery formed by the key opens twice: 1...♘b8 2 ♘xc5 – here the ♖e7 guards e3, as in the diagram; and 1...♗f2 2 ♘xf2. Because of the need to place a guard on e3, the mating possibilities of the ♕+♘ battery are limited to the threat plus one more opening: 1...♖xf5 2 ♘xf5.

Interest can be added to the activity of a white battery by the introduction of changed play. In no. 25 there are three set openings of the ♗+♖ battery,

25

CHANGED BATTERY MATES

R.E.Burger
1st prize, *U.S. Problem Bulletin* 1984
Mate in two

Set	1...	♜d7	2 ♖g7
		♝e6	2 ♖g8
		♝xg5	2 ♖f6
		♞e4	2 fxe4

Key 1 ♞e6 (>2 ♛f7)			
	...	♜d7	2 ♖f6
		♝xe6	2 ♖xg4
		♝g5	2 ♖h6
		♞e4	2 fxg4
		♞d5	2 ♞d4

the rook arriving on g7, g8 and f6. The scope of the battery is restricted by the need for the rook to retain control of g5 after 1...♜d7 and 1...♝e6; it cannot leave the g-file until g5 is blocked: 1...♝xg5 2 ♖f6. The key switches the rook's necessary control from g5 to e6, thereby changing the three mates: 1...♜d7 2 ♖f6; 1...♝xe6 2 ♖xg4; and 1...♝g5 2 ♖h6. A further (albeit non-thematic) change occurs after 1...♞e4.

26

BATTERY PLAY + CROSS-CHECKS

H.-P.Rehm
1st prize, *Neue Zürcher Zeitung* 1986
Mate in three

Key 1 ♛e2	(>2 ♖e3+ ♚d4 3 ♛d3)
... ♞f4,♞e3+	2 ♖b7+ ♚c5 3 ♛e3
♞xe7,♞b6+	2 ♖f3+ ♚d4 3 ♛d3
♞c3+	2 ♖dd5+ ♞xe2 3 ♖xb3
♞b4+	2 ♖bd5+ ♞xa6 3 ♖xb3

Battery-play in the three-mover is illustrated by no. 26. There is already a battery set in the diagram position: ♝a6+♖b5. The key sets up a second: 1 ♛e2, with the threat of 2 ♖e3+ ♚d4 3 ♛d3. By opening the line a8-h1, the key allows Black's ♝+♞ battery to get to work with checks. There are six possible arrival squares for the knight, and four distinct variations ensue.

1...♘f4+ and 1...♘e3+ allow 2 ♖b7+ ♚c5 3 ♕(x)e3, while 1...♘xe7+ and 1...♘b6+ lead to 2 ♖f3+ ♚d4 3 ♕d3. Notice that this continuation is not threatened, because the ♖d3 must place a prospective guard on e5 in the threat. Moves of the black knight open the line b5-e5, so that this is no longer necessary after the checks. The two remaining moves of the ♘d5 are **corrections** with **self-block**: 1...♘c3+ allows 2 ♖dd5+ ♘xe2 3 ♖xb3; and after 1...♘b4+ play continues 2 ♖bd5+ ♘xa6 3 ♖xb3. These last two variations illustrate the theme known as **Umnov I**: White plays to a square just vacated by a black piece.

A battery is *masked* if there is another piece standing on the battery-line. White does not always have to wait until a black masking piece has moved in order to mate with a masked battery: a pin-mate may arise with the piece still there. In no. 27, however, the battery opens four times as the black rook leaves e5.

27

MASKED BATTERY (PIN-MATES)

V.F.Rudenko
1st prize, *Problemnoter* 1961
Mate in three

Key 1 ♗d5 (>2 ♘c2+ ♘xc2 3 ♘f3)
... ♖xd5 2 ♖g8+ ♖e5 3 ♖d8
    ♖xe4 2 ♖h7+ ♖e5 3 ♖h4
    ♖xe6 2 ♖xf7+ ♖e5 3 ♘e6
    ♖xf5 2 ♖xg6+ ♖e5 3 ♘f5

Pin-mates result when this rook is forced back to the battery-line to parry White's second-move checks. In each variation White exploits the fact that the black rook has captured a white piece, by occupying the square or line of the capture. The key 1 ♗d5 threatens 2 ♘c2+ ♘xc2 3 ♘f3; and Black defends by obtaining a flight for his king on e5. 1...♖xd5 leads to 2 ♖g8+ ♖e5 3 ♖d8 – the white rook cannot mate from this direction until his black opponent has cleared the white bishop out of the way. An analogous variation is 1...♖xe4 2 ♖h7+ ♖e5 3 ♖h4. With its two other moves the black rook removes white pawns to enable knights to mate: 1...♖xe6 2 ♖xf7+ ♖e5 3 ♘e6; and 1...♖xf5 2 ♖xg6+ ♖e5 3 ♘f5. The four variations display a *rook's cross* for Black and White.

Further problems with batteries as the principal idea will be found under **Half-battery**.

Block

A problem in which White's key makes no threat but merely puts (or keeps) Black in a zugzwang position is termed a *block*. When the key creates the block (i.e. by providing mates for black defences which have no set mates), we speak of an *incomplete block*. If Black's moves all have set mates in the initial position, the block is complete. A complete block may be a *waiter*, in which case a simple waiting-move will solve. Or it may be a *mutate*, with a key that changes one or more of the set mates. Mutates are also known as *White-to-play* problems. Alternatively, but much more rarely, it may be a *block-threat*, in which the key sets up a threat and very likely abandons some of the set mates.

INCOMPLETE BLOCK
(WAITING KEY)

A.F.Mackenzie

28

1st prize, *Mirror of American Sports* 1886

Mate in two

Key 1 ♘g7 zugzwang

...	♖c~3	2 ♖c8
	♖c~c	2 ♕xd3
	♖c4	2 ♖d6
	♗b8	2 ♖xc3
	♖d~	2 ♖d6
	♔e4	2 ♖e6
	♗g2	2 ♕xg2
	♗f3	2 ♕xf3
	♗e4	2 ♕xf7
	♘~	2 ♕f5
	♘d6	2 ♖c5
	♘e5	2 ♘f6
	♘h6	2 ♕xh1

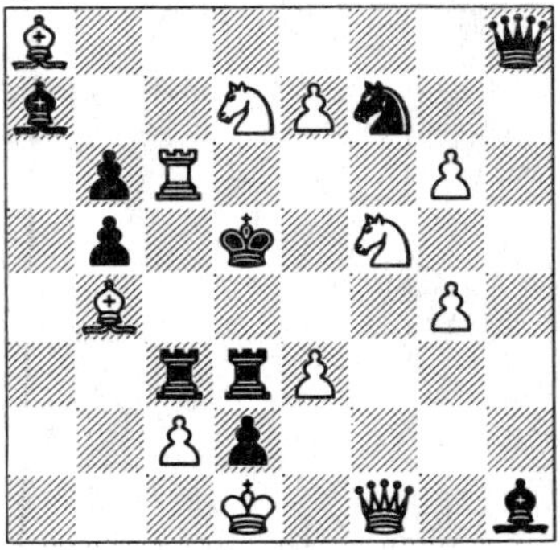

No. 28 is an incomplete block. Some, but not all, of Black's defences have set mates; the key 1 ♘g7 does no more than complete the block, introducing mates to answer those defences that lack replies in the initial position.

No. 29, on the other hand, is a complete block: every black defence has a set mate, and the solver has only to find a move that will hold the position. As

29

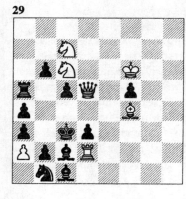

COMPLETE BLOCK: WAITING TRIES AND KEY

N.G.G.van Dijk
1st prize, *Banska Bystrica* Tourney 1964
Mate in two

Try	1 ♔e7?	♖a7!	(2 ♘b5?)
Try	1 ♔e6?	♗b3!	(2 ♕xd3?)
Try	1 ♔xf5?	c4!	(2 ♕d4?)
Try	1 ♔g5?	♗xd2!	(2 ♗e5?)
Key	1 ♔g6!	zugzwang	

readers who have studied no. 11 in Section I will soon realise, it is important not to play a move which will allow Black to pin a crucial white unit. There are four tries by the white king: 1 ♔e7?, 1 ♔e6?, 1 ♔xf5? and 1 ♔g5?. Only 1 ♔g6! does not allow a fatal pin.

The **Mutate**, a special kind of complete block with changed mates, is illustrated by no. 193.

The block-threat, though never very common, was once a fairly popular type of problem, on account of the element of surprise of the key and subsequent play. No. 30 is typical of its period.

BLOCK-THREAT

30

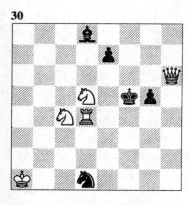

W.B.Rice
Good Companions 1915
Mate in two

Set	1...	g4	2 ♖f4
		e6	2 ♕h7
		e5	2 ♘d6
		♗~	2 ♘xe7
		♘~	2 ♘de3
Key	1 ♘f4 (>2 ♕e6)		
	...	g4	2 ♕g6
		gxf4	2 ♖xf4
		♔g4	2 ♕h3

The composer was born in Philadelphia in 1895, and is no relation of the author of this book. The set play has three self-blocks and two unguard variations, but the key 1 ♘f4 destroys all these lines by giving a flight-square on g4 and threatening 2 ♕e6. One of the pre-key mates returns after the key, but following a different defence (this is known as **mate transference**).

The problem was first published by the *Good Companions* in one of their Folders. The Good Companion Chess Problem Club was an international society of problemists which was founded by James Magee, with the support of Alain White, in America in 1913. Its famous Folders of original work contain some of the finest problems ever composed.

Bohemian School

31

MODEL MATES, BOHEMIAN STYLE

M.Havel
Version, 2nd prize, *Szachy* 1956
Mate in three

Key 1 ♔f8 (>2 ♕xd3+ cxd3 3 ♖e5)
  ...   ♔e3 2 ♖xd3+ cxd3 3 ♕e1
  f2   2 ♕e2+ ♔xd5 3 ♘e7

The composers of the Bohemian School were and are the principal exponents of **model-mate** problems. Mobility of force, especially white, and economy and beauty of mate are their ideals, strategy and difficulty being of only subsidiary interest. No. 31 is a clear example of the style by the greatest of all Bohemian composers. The key 1 ♔f8 threatens the sacrifice 2 ♕xd3+, which leads to the model mate 3 ♖e5 after 2...cxd3. In the two variations the black king is mated on different squares, and the white pieces perform completely different mating- and guard-duty – a typical feature of the best Bohemian work: 1...♔e3 2 ♖xd3+ cxd3 3 ♕e1 – the queen mates and the knights guard squares; and 1...f2 2 ♕e2+ ♔xd5 3 ♘e7, one of the knights giving the mate and the queen guarding three squares in the black king's new field.

Brede Cross-check

A three- or more-move device in which White parries a check by playing on to the check-line a piece which Black then unpins, allowing it to mate. See no. 66, under **Cross-check**.

Brede Square-vacation

The departure from a square of the white queen (according to Weenink in *The Chess Problem*) or of any white unit (Harley in *Mate in Three Moves*), so that a knight can occupy that square to give mate. See no. 265, under **Square-vacation**.

By-play

Variations not directly connected with or a part of the problem's principal theme are usually termed by-play. There is more about this under the heading **Economy**.

Bristol → Clearance

Castling

Castling is permitted in a chess problem, provided king and rook are on their home squares, unless it can be proved that either piece must have moved in the hypothetical game leading to the diagram position. Such a proof involves the application of **retrograde analysis**, and a problem where this forms the principal idea may be found under this heading.

32

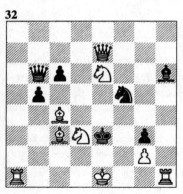

CASTLING IN TRY AND KEY

M.Lipton
4th place, GB v Israel 1960-1
Mate in two
Try 1 0-0? (>2 ♖ae1/♖fe1)
    ...   ♚e4+ 2 ♘ec5
           ♚e2+ 2 ♘d4
           bxc4!
Key 1 0-0-0! (>2 ♖de1/♖he1)
    ...   ♚e4+ 2 ♘g5
           ♚e2+ 2 ♘ef4

No. 32 is a witty two-mover in which White's selection of key-move involves a choice between long and short castling. After the try 1 0-0? (>2 ♖ae1/♖fe1), Black defends by opening the ♕+♚ battery to give check: 1...♚e4+, and 1...♚e2+. White replies with the **cross-checks** 2 ♘ec5 and 2

②d4 respectively. The try is refuted by 1...bxc4!, so White must instead play 1 0-0-0!, with similar threats. The same two black defences now open a check-line from the bishop, and again cross-checks ensue: 1...♔e4+ 2 ②g5; and 1...♔e2+ 2 ②ef4.

33

CASTLING PREVENTION

A.Kraemer and W.Massmann
Die Welt 1955
Mate in five
Try 1 ♕h6? 0-0-0!
Key 1 h6! ♗c6 2 ♕e1+ ♔d8 3 ♕e8+ ♔xe8 4 h7 (>5 h8♕)
       ... ♗c4 2 ♕a3 ♖c8 3 ♕a8 ♖xa8 4 h7 (>5 h8♕)
              ... ♔f8 3 ♕e7+ ♔g8 4 ♕xf6

In the five-mover no. 33, Black cannot castle in the initial position for the obvious reason that the white queen guards c8. The point of the problem lies in the ways in which White continues to prevent Black from castling. The try 1 ♕h6? (>2 ♕h8) is refuted by 1...0-0-0!. The key is 1 h6!, and now Black's two best defences are 1...♗c6 and 1...♗c4, which allow the defence 2...0-0-0 after 2 h7?. In one variation White prevents castling by forcing the king to move, while in the other it is the rook that has to move. In each case the white queen is sacrificed before mate can be given. 1...♗c6 2 ♕e1+ ♔d8 3 ♕e8+ ♔xe8 4 h7 – and mate by 5 h8♕ cannot now be avoided, as 4...0-0-0? is no longer legal. 1...♗c4 leads to 2 ♕a3 (>3 ♕xa8) ♖c8 3 ♕a8! ♖xa8 4 h7 – and once again castling is out. In the different variations the black king and black rook return to their original squares, thus making it seem that castling might again be possible. The problem also shows an idea known as **Umnov I**: in each line the white queen occupies a square just vacated by a black piece.

Checks by Black

Checks inflicted by Black at some stage in the course of a problem's solution always contain an element of surprise, and this is very likely the reason for their great popularity with both composers and solvers. There are many examples throughout this book of black checks parried by White in all sorts of ways, the most interesting way being by **cross-check**, under which heading several fine examples will be found.

34

BLACK CHECKS (ZAGORUIKO)

C.Goldschmeding
Problem 1957
Mate in two
(version suggested by C.Mansfield)

Set 1...   ♖b7+ 2 cxb7
             ♖xc6+ 2 ♕xc6

Try 1 ♕a1?   (>2 ♘~)
    ...   ♖b7+ 2 ♘xb7
             ♖xc6+ 2 ♘xc6
             ♖xb5!

Key 1 ♕f1!   (>2 ♖xb6)
    ...   ♖b7+ 2 ♖xb7
             ♖xc6+ 2 ♖xc6

No. 34 shows checks answered by capture of the checking piece, but with changed play in three phases. Checks by the rook on b7 and c6 are answered in the set play by 2 cxb7 and 2 ♕xc6. White tries 1 ♕a1?, threatening a mate by the new ♕+♘ battery, and the same checks are now answered by 2 ♘xb7 and 2 ♘xc6. However, the try fails to 1...♖xb5!, which means that White must instead play 1 ♕f1!, threatening 2 ♖xb6. Now 1...♖b7+ allows 2 ♖xb7, while, because the queen now guards b5, 2 ♖xc6 can be played in reply to 1...♖xc6+. The changes are not particularly subtle, but the economy of the setting is remarkable.

BLACK CHECKS

35

C.S.Kipping
Manchester City News 1911
Mate in three

Try 1 ♔b5? ♖g8! (2 ♘d4+? ♔a7!
3 ♘b5?)

Key 1 ♔a5! e1♕+ 2 ♔b6 ♕b1+ 3 ♘cb4
          ...   ♕a5+ 3 ♘xa5
                    ♕e3+ 3 ♘e4
                    ♕e5 3 ♘xe5
                    ♕e7 3 ♘xe7
                    ♕e6 3 ♘c7
        ...   ♖g8 2 ♘d4+ ♔a7 3 ♘b5
             ♔b7 2 ♘e7+ ♔a7 3 ♘c8

No. 35 is one of the most famous problems ever composed. The key invites Black to promote his pawn to a queen and give check at the same time! Furthermore, the reply to the check is another quiet king-move, apparently inviting checks from several directions: 1 ♔a5! e1♕+ 2 ♔b6!. But Black's checks are now all answered by a shut-off mate from the ♗+♘ battery, e.g. 2...♕b1+ 3 ♘cb4; 2...♕e3+ 3 ♘d4, etc. Black's alternative first-move defences lead to immediate openings of the battery: 1...♖g8 2 ♘d4+ ♔a7 3 ♘b5; and 1...♔b7 2 ♘e7+ ♔a7 3 ♘c8. It is because the knight needs b5 in order to mate there in the first of these two variations that White cannot start 1 ♔b5? (1...♖g8! 2 ♘d4+ ♔a7! – no mate).

Chinese pieces

The four Chinese pieces are **fairy chess** units. They are represented as figurines by pieces given a quarter-turn to the right and on diagrams by highlighted squares. Their moves are as follows:

Pao: moves like a rook but captures an enemy unit by hopping along rook-lines over another unit of either colour. Check is therefore given over another unit.

Vao: moves like a bishop but captures an enemy unit by hopping along bishop-lines over another unit of either colour. As with the Pao, check is given over another unit.

Leo: combines the powers of Pao and Vao.

Mao: moves and captures like a knight, but it jumps in two steps from its starting square via the orthogonally adjacent square, which must therefore be unoccupied. So a Mao a1 can move to b3 only if a2 is clear: the first step of its move is orthogonal, the second diagonal.

In the diagram position of no. 36, the black Pao b8 could move to any square on the top rank or to b7 or b6, or it could capture on b4. The Vao h6 has three moves available, to f8, g7 and g5, and it also helps to guard d2 (over the unit on f4). The Mao f4 guards d3 via e4, but d3 is not also guarded by the Mao c1, because c2 is occupied.

The solver will soon see that the Mao c1 is pinned by the Pao g1, and that moves by the ♘e1 would give check, simultaneously unpinning the Mao (a curious effect that is, of course, quite impossible with orthodox force). The set checks with unpins are: 1...♘xf3+ 2 ♗a2; and 1...♘xd3+ 2 ♗e2. Why can the mating moves not be played the other way round? With the black knight on f3, 2 ♗e2? is not mate, because of 2...♘d2!, closing the Mao's check-line. Similarly, if the black knight is on d3, 2 ♗a2? fails to 2...♘b2!.

36

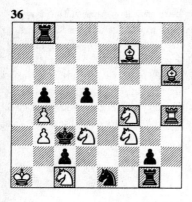

CHINESE PIECES

J.M.Rice
Die Schwalbe 1964
Mate in two
Paos h4, b8, g1; Vaos f7,h6; Maos c1,f4

Set	1...	♞xf3+	2 ♙a2
		♞xd3+	2 ♙e2
Key	1 ♜h3(>2 ♙xd5)		
	...	♞xf3+	2 ♙e2
		♞xd3+	2 ♙a2
		♜xb4	2 ♞dxe1
		d4	2 ♞fxe1

The point of the problem lies in the **reciprocal change** of the two mating moves, achieved by means of a simple key-move 1 ♜h3. In the initial position this Pao helps to guard d4 and b4, so that after the captures on f3 and d3 by the black knight White does not have to provide an extra guard on these squares. By placing an additional guard on d3, the key threatens 2 ♙xd5. Now the black knight's captures on f3 and d3 are self-pins! Consequently the white ♙c1, in mating, can provide the guard needed on d4 (after 1...♞xf3+ by 2 ♙e2) and b4 (after 1...♞xd3+ by 2 ♙a2), and the black knight cannot defend by interposing on the Mao's check-line. There are two further defences based on the Mao's unique move: 1...d4 defeats the threat by occupying the square orthogonally adjacent to d5. On d4, however, the pawn creates a self-block, allowing the battery-opening 2 ♞fxe1. 1...♜xb4 blocks b4 and defeats by threatening to interpose on d4. Now, of course, 2 ♞dxe1 is mate.

Circe

Circe is a form of **fairy chess** in which a unit, when captured, is reborn on its original square in the game array. In the case of rooks and knights, the colour of the square on which the capture is made determines the rebirth square (e.g. a white rook captured on a2 is reborn on h1; a white knight captured on the same square reappears on b1). Pawns are reborn on the second rank of the file on which the capture is made. The rebirth of the unit occurs instantaneously. If the appropriate rebirth square is already occupied, the captured unit disappears completely, as in a normal capture. Castling is permissible with a reborn rook.

37

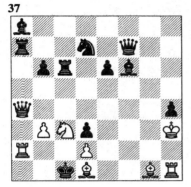

CIRCE
N.A.Macleod
1st prize, *British Chess Magazine* 1980-2
Mate in two: Circe

Key 1 ♗g4 (>2 ♕a3)
...   ♗xc3   2 ♗f2
        ♖xc3   2 ♗xb6[♙b7]
        e5   2 ♗c5
        ♘c5   2 ♗d4

The key of no. 37, 1 ♗g4, threatens 2 ♕a3 by unblocking d1, so that 2...♖xa3[♕d1]?? would be an illegal move, the black king being in check from the queen. It is useful to consider why moves of the ♗g1 are not threats. In the diagram position the W♘c3 is under attack, so that an attempt to mate by e.g. 2 ♗h2? would be refuted by 2...♖xc3[♘g1]! or 2...♗xc3[♘g1]!. Black defeats the threat of 2 ♕a3 by capturing this knight, which disappears because g1 is occupied. 1...♗xc3 threatens to interpose on b2, but allows 2 ♗f2 – the ♖+♗ battery can now open, but the black queen must be shut off. 1...♖xc3 defeats the threat more subtly, for now 2 ♕a3? would be answered by 2...♖xb3[♙b2]!. But 2 ♗xb6[♙b7] is playable, and no other opening of the battery will work, as the ♗a8 must be shut off by means of the Circe capture on b6. Two further defences threaten a capture of the ♙b3: 1...e5 and 1...♘c5. Each of these moves is an **interference** with one of the two black line-pieces attacking the ♘c3, so that, in mating with the ♖+♗ battery, White can shut the other off: 1...e5 2 ♗c5; and 1...♘c5 2 ♗d4.

Various curious effects can be achieved that are peculiar to the Circe rules of play. Since a piece may be immune from capture because it would give check from its rebirth square (like the white queen after the key in no. 37), mating pieces may guard themselves, from their rebirth square. No. 38, a **helpmate**, illustrates this property in both of its solutions, which consist entirely of captures and Circe rebirths. 1 ♗xg3 replaces the white bishop on c1 for an eventual mate on g5, but before this can work, the line h8-e8 must be blocked because of the check that would arise from the reborn black rook. Hence White's first move 1...♖xd5[♘g8]. Now Black must clear the line c1-g5 and capture the white rook so that it is reborn on h1, from where it pins the ♖h5: 2 ♕xd5[♖h1]. Now 2...♗xg5[♖h8] is mate, the bishop guarding itself from c1. The second solution shows analogous play, forming an attractive orthogonal/diagonal **correspondence**: 1 ♕xd3[♖h1] ♗xe5[♘b8] (the

38

CIRCE: HELPMATE

K.Gandew
2nd prize, *Schach-Echo* 1974
Helpmate in two: 2 solutions – Circe

1 ♗xg3[♗c1] ♖xd5[♘g8]
2 ♕xd5[♖h1] ♗xg5[♖h8]

1 ♕xd3[♖h1] ♗xe5[♘b8]
2 ♗xe5[♗c1] ♖xh5[♖a8]

check to be avoided is now from a8); 2 ♗xe5[♗c1] – pinning the ♖g5 –
2...♖xh5[♖a8] mate (self-guard of the rook from h1).

Circe was invented by P.Monréal and J.-P.Boyer, and was first introduced
in 1968. It has proved to be one of the most fertile of fairy forms, and many
variants have developed.

Clearance

CLEARANCE KEY

39

H.Grasemann
1st prize, *Horizont* Tourney 1947
Mate in three

Key 1 ♕g8 (>2 ♗f7+ ♔b1 3 ♗xg6)
            ...   ♗f5   2 ♗e6+
                       ♗e4   2 ♗d5+
                       ♗d3   2 ♗c4+
                       ♗c2   2 ♗b1+
Try 1 ♕f7?   ♗h7!
Try 1 ♕d3?   ♗c3!
Try 1 ♕b4?   ♗c2!
Try 1 ♕a3?   ♗f8!

The key of no. 39 is the very surprising move 1 ♕g8!. This threatens 2
♗f7+ ♔b1 3 ♗xg6. The white queen clears the line a2-g8 for the bishop, but
stays on that line, going past the square (f7) which the bishop is to occupy.
Clearance of this type is known as *Bristol-clearance*. The try 1 ♕f7? makes

it quite clear why the queen must play as far as g8: Black can reply 1...♗h7!, and the black bishop cannot now be captured. Other tries by the queen to squares off the line a2-g8 are refuted by moves of one or the other black bishop: 1 ♕d3? ♗c3!; 1 ♕b4? ♗c2!; 1 ♕a3? ♗f8!.

40

CLEARANCE

A.Hüfner
1st hon. mention, *Schach* 1956
Mate in three

Key 1 ♖fe2 zugzwang
.... ♗xe2 2 ♘h4 ♗~ 3 ♕b2
.... ♗xg2 2 ♖a2 ♗~ 3 ♕b2

Two further types of clearance are to be found in no. 40. The white queen could mate on b2 if the ♘g2 and the ♖f2 were removed, and it will be White's task to shift these pieces. In this he is aided by Black, who is placed in zugzwang by the key, 1 ♖fe2. This move is a particular type of clearance known as *annihilation*: the rook cannot clear the line completely, and so plays to a square on which it can be captured by Black. (It also incidentally prevents other moves by the black bishop.) The capturing piece subsequently moves away, and in so doing opens the line to allow White to mate. After 1...♗xe2, White continues 2 ♘h4 – not a clearance, but a *line-vacation*, since the knight leaves the line in question altogether. The bishop must then move, and White follows with 3 ♕b2. In the other variation 1...♗xg2, the white rook carries out a Bristol-clearance (2 ♖a2) like the one in no. 39, so that White can mate by 3 ♕b2 after 2...♗~. The two moves by the white rook, 1 ♖fe2 and subsequently 2 ♖a2, form a clearance in stages (known in German as *Stufenbahnung*, but without an established name in English problem terminology).

Further examples of clearance are found under **Doubling**, **Turton** and **Zepler-Doubling**.

Cook

A cook is a solution not intended by the problem's composer. Cooked problems are not eligible to compete in tourneys, although it is usually permissible for a composer to submit a corrected version of a cooked problem before the closing date for receipt of tourney-entries. In today's world of powerful home-computers and strong solving programs, all problems except those with very long solutions can and should be thoroughly tested before being submitted for publication. A solver seeing C+ beside a diagram will know that the problem has been subjected to computer testing.

Correction

(a) Black

Correction is not a theme in itself, though problems exist in which it is the principal feature. Rather it is a mechanism whereby moves, either black or white, are related to one another. Where black moves are concerned, the mechanism works in the two-mover as follows. Defence 'a' makes an error which allows a white mate. A second defence 'b' makes the same or an equivalent error but has in addition a *correcting* effect which rules out White's mate. However, a new error is now caused which permits a different mating move. Defence 'a' is described as *primary*, and defence 'b' as *secondary*.

The mechanism is seen at its clearest when defences 'a' and 'b' are made by the same unit.

BLACK CORRECTION

41

T.Tikkanen
1st prize, BABY Tourney 1960
Mate in two
Key 1 ♕f8 zugzwang

...	♘c~	2 ♖xe5
	♘xe4	2 ♘c7
	♖~	2 ♕d6
	♖xe6	2 ♕c5
	♘e~	2 ♕a8
	♘c6	2 ♘xc3
	♔xe4	2 ♘xc3
	♔xe6	2 ♕f7
	♔c6	2 ♕c5

In no. 41 Black is in zugzwang after 1 ♕f8. If the ♘c3 moves *at random* (i.e. to no square in particular), it makes the *general error* of opening the line c2-c6, so that one of Black's three flights (c6) is guarded, and a second guard is put on c4. This enables White to mate by 2 ♖xe5, the other two flights (e4 and e6) now being held by the mating piece. The mate following a general error is termed the *secondary threat*. The *correction* move (secondary defence) is the capture of the mating piece: 1...♘xe4. The new error is **self-block** of e4, so that mate is now possible by 2 ♘c7.

The two other black pieces in this problem also illustrate the correction mechanism when they move. A random move by the ♘e5 opens e4-e6 and at the same time unguards c6, allowing mate by 2 ♕a8. The correction is clearly 1...♘c6, which again is a self-block of a flight, permitting 2 ♘xc3. When the ♖g6 moves at random, h7-e4 is opened and 2 ♕d6 will mate, while 1...♖xe6, guarding the mating square, once again blocks a flight, and 2 ♕c5 follows. The variations of this fine problem are completed by three king-flights, one of which (1...♚xe6) leads to a pin-mate (2 ♕f7).

BLACK CORRECTION: ZAGORUIKO

42

B.Zappas
1st prize, *Schach* 1959
Mate in two

Set	1...	♘~	2 ♕xa3
		♘c5	2 ♕c7
Try	1 ♘b4?	(>2 ♖d3)	
	...	♘~	2 c5
		♘c5	2 ♘b5
		♖f6!	
Key	1 ♘c7!	(>2 ♖d3)	
	...	♘~	2 ♖xe6
		♘c5	2 ♘cb5

Random and correction moves of a single piece are found in three phases in no. 42. In the set play, 1...♘~ unguards the line a3-d6 and allows 2 ♕xa3, while the self-block correction 1...♘c5 leads to 2 ♕c7. Any move by the ♘d5 eliminates both these mates by removing White's second guard of c7. If White tries 1 ♘b4? (threat 2 ♖d3), Black defends by pinning the white rook. 1...♘~ allows 2 c5, and the secondary defence is again a self-block, which White this time exploits with a self-interference mate: 2 ♘b5. Black may also defend against the primary threat with any move by his rook, but a random move unguards e5 and so permits 2 ♕e5. However, the rook may correct by shutting off the white bishop's guard of this square: 1...♜f6!. This is the move that refutes the try, and because it is a correction it fits in most harmoniously with the theme of the problem. The key 1 ♘c7! carries the same primary threat as the try, but the secondary threat and the mate following the secondary defence are again changed: 1...♘~ 2 ♜xe6; 1...♘c5 2 ♘cb5. A further change between virtual and post-key play may also be noted: after 1 ♘b4? Black may defend with 1...♛xg7, which leads to 2 ♘c8. After the key this defence permits 2 ♘e8.

CHANGED BLACK CORRECTION (TERTIARY)

43

M.Parthasarathy
1st prize, *The Problemist* 1989/I
Mate in two

Try 1 ♛b6?		(>2 ♘xd6)
...	♘~	2 ♛xe6
	♘f7	2 ♜xf4
	♘f5	2 ♘c3
	♘xb5!	
Key 1 c3!		(>2 ♘xd6)
...	♘~	2 ♛e5
	♘f7	2 ♛xf4
	♘f5	2 ♘c5

No. 43 introduces us to an aspect of correction not encountered in the previous two problems. The try 1 ♛b6? threatens 2 ♘xd6, which will naturally be defeated by any move of the ♘d6. The secondary threat, which follows the knight's random move, is 2 ♛xe6. There are two corrections that cut the line f8-f4: 1...♘f7 and 1...♘f5. It seems that 2 ♜xf4 will be the mate whichever defence Black plays. However, only 1...♘f7 allows this mate. This is because 1...♘f5, while committing the same error as 1...♘f7, prevents 2 ♜xf4 by unpinning the ♘g6. The new error committed by this defence is self-block of the flight, allowing 2 ♘c3. Because 1...♘f5 is 'secondary' to the secondary defence 1...♘f7, it is termed a *tertiary* defence. A third correction by the knight refutes the try. After the key 1 c3, with the same threat, the secondary threat following 1...♘~ is 2 ♛e5, and again the knight corrects by playing to the f-file. The secondary defence 1...♘f7 allows 2 ♛xf4, and the tertiary defence 1...♘f5, again blocking the flight, leads to 2 ♘c5.

Once one has absorbed the notion of tertiary play, it is reasonable to wonder whether further degrees of correction are possible. In no. 44 the general error and the corrections are made by different units.

44

BLACK CORRECTION (QUATERNARY)

C.Goldschmeding
1st hon. mention, *Probleemblad* 1943
Mate in two

Key 1 ♕f8 (2 ♘e7)
...   ♗d5   2 ♕c8
      ♘cd5 2 ♖xc4 (2 ♕c8?)
      ♘bd5 2 ♘b8 (2 ♕c8? ♖xc4?)
      d5 2 ♕c5 (2 ♕c8? ♖xc4? ♘b8?)

The threat 2 ♘e7, introduced by the square-vacation key 1 ♕f8, is defeated by the line-opening defence 1...♗d5, which, however, blocks the flight d5 and allows 2 ♕c8. This secondary threat is, in turn, defeated by 1...♘cd5, which makes the same error as 1...♗d5 (self-block on the flight-square) but corrects it by preventing the secondary threat from working (2 ♕c8? ♘c7!). But the new error is an interference with the ♗e6, so that 2 ♖xc4 is playable. The further defence 1...♘bd5 not only prevents the primary threat (2 ♘e7) and the secondary threat (2 ♕c8), but also prevents 2 ♖xc4 by opening a line of guard from a4. At the same time it commits the new error of opening a line of guard to c5, thus permitting 2 ♘b8. This is, therefore, a tertiary defence. But that is not all, for 1...d5 commits all the errors of the defences we have so far examined, namely block of d5, interference with ♗e6, and line-opening to c5, and at the same time it carries the same correction-effects, viz. prevention of 2 ♕c8 (by square-vacation and line-opening) and prevention of 2 ♖xc4 (by direct guard), plus one more: prevention of 2 ♘b8 (by line-opening). Finally, of course, there is a further error: 2 ♕c5 will mate because of the opening of the white queen's line. If 1...♘cd5 is tertiary, then 1...d5 must be termed *quaternary*. This highly complex problem can be said to illustrate *arrival correction*, the term used when Black's series of defences bring different pieces to the same square or line. In the previous example, arrival correction is seen in the knight's secondary and tertiary defences on the f-file.

While preparing the mate-in-three section of the Faber book *Chess Problems: Introduction to an Art* in 1961, Robin Matthews discovered that there were few really satisfactory examples of quaternary correction in three moves at the time, and so set about composing one. Because a knight can arrive on a maximum of two squares on a straight line, it is necessary to use a bent line, in three-move form, if the same knight is to correct its random arrival error twice over, the second correction being itself a correction of the first.

45

BLACK CORRECTION (QUATERNARY)

R.C.O.Matthews
1st prize, *The Observer* 1964
Mate in three

Key 1 &c6   (>2 &e3+ dxe3 3 d4/&f3)
    ...   &f~   2 &xe7+ &e6 3 &xe6
          &g6   2 c3 (>3 cxd4)
          &e6   2 &xb2 (>3 &c4)
          &d5   2 &b5 (>3 &xd4)

The key of no. 45, 1 &c6, threatens 2 &e3+ dxe3 3 d4. Obviously a random move by the &f4 defeats the threat by square-vacation, and such a random move (e.g. 1...&h3) enables White to continue 2 &xe7+ &e6 3 &xe6. Three knight-moves prevent this: 1...&g6, 1...&e6 and 1...&d5, and all three interfere with the &h6 by ensuring that the defence 2...&d6 does not defeat a threat of mate on d4. After 1...&g6 White continues 2 c3, the secondary threat which itself carries the third-move threat 3 cxd4. 1...&e6 and 1...&d5 correct against 2 c3 by either guarding d4 or threatening to capture on c3. However, both these knight-moves interfere with the &e8! This is because the move 2...&xf7 is no longer a defence against a threat of mate on c4 if e6 or d5 is blocked. 1...&e6 allows 2 &xb2, followed by 3 &c4. But this will not do after 1...&d5, because Black can defend with 2...&e3 or 2...&b6. However, 1...&d5 is a self-block, for it permits White to continue with 2 &b5, and now the defence 2...&xc6 (which would previously have obtained a flight for Black on d5) cannot prevent the threatened mate 3 &xd4.

A summary of these variations with the appropriate terminology might be helpful. White's key carries the primary threat 2 &e3+. Black's &f4 moves at random and commits the general error of unguarding e6, so that the secondary threat 2 &xe7+ can be played. The secondary defence 1...&g6 corrects, but interferes with the &h6 to allow 2 c3 (the tertiary threat). 1...&e6 commits the same error as the secondary defence, but corrects it by guarding d4:

this is therefore the tertiary defence. The error inherent in this defence is that of preventing 2...♗xf7 as an adequate defence against 3 ♘c4 mate after 2 ♔xb2. The quaternary defence 1...♘d5 commits the same errors as both the secondary defence and the tertiary defence, but corrects both by threatening 2...♘xc3 if White were to continue 2 c3?, or 2...♘e3/♘b6 after 2 ♔xb2?. The quaternary defence carries the final error of self-block of d5, so that 2 ♘b5 may be played without the fear of 2...♗xc6 to prevent 3 ♗xd4.

46

BLACK CORRECTION

A.Casa
3rd prize, *L'Echiquier de Paris* 1953
Mate in two
Key 1 ♕d7 (>2 ♕f5)
  ... ♘ce7 2 ♕xe7
     ♘d4 2 ♘xg5 (2 ♕e7?)
     ♘d~ 2 ♕d3 (2 ♕e7? ♘xg5?)
     ♘e3 2 ♘d2 (2 ♕e7? ♘xg5? ♕d3?)
     ♘f4 2 ♖e3 (2 ♕e7? ♘xg5? ♕d3? ♘d2?)
     ♘db4 2 ♕d4 (2 ♕e7? ♘xg5? ♕d3?)

This survey of correction by Black ends with a controversial two-mover, no. 46. The key, 1 ♕d7, carries the threat 2 ♕f5. The ♘c6 can guard f5 by playing to either e7 or d4, pinning its colleague on d5 as it moves. 1...♘ce7 is the primary defence, allowing 2 ♕xe7. 1...♘d4 corrects because 2...♘e6 would defeat 2 ♕e7?, but, with d4 blocked, White can play 2 ♘xg5. Moves of the ♘d5 bring in the same errors as we have already seen, namely unguard of e7 (the ♘c6 is now pinned) and removal of the need for the white knight to guard d4 (this time by line-opening rather than self-block, an 'equivalent' error). But both 2 ♕e7? and 2 ♘xg5? are eliminated by the opening of a line of guard from a5. 1...♘d~ is therefore the tertiary defence, with the new reply 2 ♕d3. This d-knight has correction moves available: 1...♘e3 is a quaternary defence, because it commits every previous error and prevents every previous mate, but, by interfering with the ♗g5, enables White to play 2 ♘d2. Finally we have a *quinary* defence: all four previous errors are committed and all four previous mates prevented by 1...♘f4, which rules out 2 ♘d2 by cutting the line h2-e5. 2 ♖e3 can now be played, because the interference with the ♗g5 has taken place one square further up the line. There is a further correction by the d-knight, 1...♘b4, only quaternary, however, as it is of the same degree as 1...♘e3, i.e. it commits three errors and thereby rules out three mates.

Here is a summary of what happens in the post-key play of this complex problem:

1...♘ce7: error: unguards e7, allowing 2 ♕xe7.

1...♘d4: error: unguards e7;
correction: threatens to interpose on e6;
error: blocks d4, allowing 2 ♘xg5.

1...♘d~: error: unguards e7;
correction: unblocks d5 and opens rook's line from a5-e5;
error: opens queen's line of guard to d4;
correction: opens rook's line from a5-g5;
error: allows queen through to mate on d3.

1...♘e3: error: unguards e7;
correction: unblocks d5 and opens rook's line from a5-e5;
error: opens queen's line of guard to d4;
correction: opens rook's line from a5-g5;
error: opens queen's line to d3;
correction: closes line from a3 through d3 to f3;
error: closes bishop's line from g5 to d2, allowing 2 ♘d2.

1...♘f4: all the errors and corrections listed for 1...♘e3, plus:
correction: closes white bishop's line of guard h2-e5;
error: closes bishop's line from g5 to e3, allowing 2 ♖e3.

What has given rise to controversy here is firstly the question of 'equivalent errors' (self-block and line-opening are not strictly the same thing), and secondly the notion that correction can be split between two black units, though of course in Goldschmeding's example of arrival correction there are four black units involved. It is certainly true that in Casa's problem there are two reasons why 2 ♕e7 could never be played after a move of the ♘d5: not only is the black rook's line from a5 opened, but also 1...♘d~ is a square-vacation that gives Black a potential flight on d5. Some critics also feel that the additional correction 1...♘b4 obscures the pattern. Be that as it may, many composers have found this problem inspirational.

(b) White

The principle of correction can be applied to white pieces as well as to black. White Correction is a try-play theme when presented in two-move form, and is illustrated by nos. 47-50. In no. 47 a random move by either white knight threatens mate by a move of the other knight, and Black has only his rook and pawn with which to parry any such threat.

47

**WHITE CORRECTION
(HALF-BATTERY)**

B.P.Barnes
Commended, *British Chess Magazine*
1961
Mate in two
Try 1 ♘b~? ♖c7!
Try 1 ♘c4? b3! (2 ♕a4?)
Try 1 ♘c~? ♖xd5!
Key 1 ♘b5! (>2 ♘b~)
    ... ♖xd5 2 ♕a7
     b3 2 ♕a4

If the ♘b2 moves at random, 1...b3 leads to 2 ♕a4, but 1...♖c7! refutes, as the ♕+♘ battery cannot now open to give mate. So White corrects with 1 ♘c4!?, which cuts out 1...♖c7? as an adequate defence. But 1...b3! now refutes, since the queen can no longer play to a4. A random move by the ♘c3 again threatens a battery-opening; 1...b3 leads, as before, to 2 ♕a4, but 1...♖xd5! refutes. The correction 1 ♘b5! (an anticipatory closure of the line d5-a5) is the key: this is the only safe move that either knight can make. 1...♖xd5 is now answered by 2 ♕a7, but the post-key play is not of great importance, for the point of the problem lies in the tries.

WHITE CORRECTION

48

H.Ahues
2nd prize, *Schach-Echo* 1960
Mate in two
Set 1... ♗xd5 2 ♘d2
Try 1 ♗d~? (>2 ♖d4)
    ... ♗xd5!
Try 1 ♗e5? ♗xd5 2 ♕xf4
    ... ♗a7! (2 ♖e5?)
Try 1 ♗f6? ♗xd5 2 ♗xf5
    ... ♖d8! (2 ♘f6?)
Key 1 ♗g7! ♗xd5 2 ♘g5
    ... ♔xd5 2 ♕f3
     ♗a7 2 ♖e5
     ♖d8 2 ♘f6

The same is true of no. 48, but here the composer has incorporated some changed play after each try. The move which refutes the random move of the ♗d4, instead of being ruled out as a defence, as happens in no. 47, is here followed by a new mate which differs according to the arrival square of the bishop. Furthermore, this defence has a set mate, which is abandoned as soon as the bishop moves. Set: 1...♗xd5 2 ♘d2. Try 1 ♗d~? (>2 ♖d4) ♗xd5!. Correct the general error of moving this bishop with 1 ♗e5!?, so that 1...♗xd5 is followed by 2 ♕xf4. But now 1...♗a7! refutes, since 2 ♖e5? cannot be played. So correct again with 1 ♗f6!?. Now 1...♗xd5 leads to 2 ♗xf5, but there is nothing after 1...♖d8! (2 ♘f6? is impossible). The key is the further correction 1 ♗g7!!, which introduces yet another mate after 1...♗xd5: 2 ♘g5. 2 ♖e5 and 2 ♘f6 follow 1...♗a7 and 1...♖d8 respectively, while 1...♔xd5 permits 2 ♕f3. White correction is here presented with great clarity and unity: the correction tries both fail because the bishop occupies a square required by another white unit, and these tries and the key are united not only by the fact that they are corrections of a random move, but also because each closes a black line in order to effect the thematic changes.

WHITE CORRECTION: TERTIARY PLAY

49

A.C.Reeves
2nd hon. mention, *British Chess Magazine* 1965
Mate in two

Try	1 ♗e5?	(>2 ♖d4)
...	♗f2	2 ♘d2
	♘c2!	
Try	1 ♘ce5?	(>2 ♖d4)
...	♘c2	2 ♗xd3
	♗f2!	
Key	1 ♘ge5!	(>2 ♖d4)
...	♗f2	2 ♕g4
	♘c2	2 ♕xf3
	c5	2 ♗a7

Readers who have studied the examples of Black Correction showing tertiary play will doubtless wonder whether such effects are obtainable with White Correction. No. 49 shows one way in which this may be achieved. 1 ♗e5? represents a random arrival on e5, and threatens mate by the unpinned ♖d6. 1...♘c2! refutes. 1 ♘ce5? improves on this by arranging a mate to follow 1...♘c2, namely 2 ♗xd3. But Black can now play 1...♗f2!, since White has committed a secondary error by giving up the mate 2 ♘d2. The key, 1 ♘ge5!, like the try 1 ♘ce5?, corrects the primary error committed by 1 ♗e5? – failure to cope with 1...♘c2 (2 ♕xf3 can now be played). While maintaining the secondary error made by 1 ♘ce5? – abandonment of the mate 2 ♘d2 after 1...♗f2 – 1 ♘ge5! is a *tertiary correction*, opening the line h3-f3 and so permitting 2 ♕g4 after 1...♗f2. It is the retention of the secondary error in the key-move which makes this problem an example of tertiary play, and a comparison of the nature of the key with that of no. 48 will clarify the point. In Ahues' example the key succeeds merely because it does not commit a secondary error.

WHITE CORRECTION:
QUATERNARY PLAY

50

C.G.S.Narayanan
Version, *The Problemist* 1989
Mate in two
Try 1 ♘d~? (>2 ♖c5/♖xb4)
...   ♘xf2   2 ♕h5
         e3   2 ♕f3
         ♕xc4!
Try 1 ♘f5? e3   2 ♕f3
...   ♕xc4   2 ♘fe7
         ♘xf2!
Try 1 ♘f3? ♘xf2   2 ♘xf4
...   ♕xc4   2 ♘ge7
         e3!
Key 1 ♘e2! ♘xf2   2 ♘exf4
         e3   2 ♕xd3
         ♕xc4   2 ♘c3

No. 50 shows how White Correction can be taken one degree further. 1 ♘d~? (e.g. 1 ♘c2?), threatening 2 ♖c5 and 2 ♖xb4, does nothing to disturb the set mates following the defences 1...♘xf2 and 1...e3 (2 ♕h5 and 2 ♕f3 respectively), but fails to provide a mate in reply to 1...♕xc4!. 1 ♘f5!?, with the same threats, corrects by providing such a mate (2 ♘fe7), but commits the error of preventing 2 ♕h5 after 1...♘xf2!. The further correction 1 ♘f3!!? again provides for 1...♕xc4 (2 ♘ge7) and now provides also for 1...♘xf2 with the new mate 2 ♘xf4. But there is a new error, namely occupation of the square f3, so that Black can defend with 1...e3! (2 ♕f3? is no longer playable). If 1 ♘f5!? is secondary, then 1 ♘f3!!? is tertiary, and that makes the key, 1 ♘e2!!!, quaternary. The knight has again occupied the line d1-f3-h5, but, although mates are not available on f3 or h5, there are new mates to compensate: 1...♘xf2 2 ♘exf4, and 1...e3 2 ♕xd3. There is also yet another new mate to follow 1...♕xc4: 2 ♘c3. With each step, to f5, f3 and e2 successively, the knight makes the same errors as before, but, by its arrival, eliminates the effect of each one in sequence. Readers might find it helpful to use the following summary in conjunction with a study of the full solution:

1 ♘d~?	error: no provision for 1...♕xc4;
1 ♘f5!?	correction: provides for 1...♕xc4 (2 ♘fe7);
	error: eliminates 2 ♕h5 as mate after 1...♘xf2;
1 ♘f3!!?	correction: provides for 1...♕xc4 (2 ♘ge7);
	error: eliminates 2 ♕h5 as mate after 1...♘xf2;
	correction: provides for 1...♘xf2 (2 ♘gxf4);
	error: eliminates 2 ♕f3 as mate after 1...e3;
1 ♘e2!!!	correction: provides for 1...♕xc4 (2 ♘c3);
	error: eliminates 2 ♕h5 as mate after 1...♘xf2;
	correction: provides for 1...♘xf2 (2 ♘exf4);
	error: eliminates 2 ♕f3 as mate after 1...e3;
	correction: provides for 1...e3 (2 ♕xd3).

Purist critics would perhaps claim that there should be a mate set in reply to 1...♕xc4, so that 1 ♘d~? would commit the error of abandoning this set mate. In the field of white correction, however, this theoretical shortcoming is commonly ignored. Narayanan's excellent problem, whose only small defect is the double threat, regrettably won no award, because it appeared in an incorrect form in *The Problemist* at a time when unsound problems could not be considered by the judge. On this occasion the judge was Colin Sydenham, who has made an in-depth study of two-move correction ideas and who has mentioned his disappointment that he was unable to honour the problem appropriately.

White Correction may be found in the second-move continuations of a three-mover. Really convincing examples, like no. 51, are rare, however. The key 1 ♕g7 sets up a block position. Note that it does not threaten 2 ♘e~+?, even though 2...♔c5 is met by 3 ♕g1, because of 2...♗e4!. The ♘e4 cannot afford to move until the black bishop has done so. 1...♗b1, unguarding a4, allows the continuation 2 ♘c3+ ♔c5 3 ♘xa4 – not 2 ♘e~+?, because 2...♗e4! is still playable (2 ♘c3+ ♗e4 3 ♕xc7). 1...♗d1 removes the bishop from its potential guard of the line h6-d6, which means that White may play 2 ♘f6+, followed by 3 ♘d7 after 2...♔xd6 or 2...♔c5, and 3 ♕xc7 after 2...♗f3. (2 ♘e~+? fails to 2...♗f3!) The black bishop can avoid the error of unguarding a4 and at the same time correct the error of relinquishing control

51

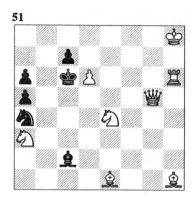

WHITE CORRECTION + BLACK CORRECTION

J.Scheel
1st prize, U.S. Chess Federation
Tourney 1946-8
Mate in three
Key 1 ♕g7 zugzwang

... ♗b1	2 ♘c3+ ♔c5	3 ♘xa4
♗d1	2 ♘f6+ ♔c5/♔xd6	3 ♘d7
♗b3	2 ♘c5+ ♔xc5	3 ♕g1
♗xe4	2 ♗xe4+ ♔c5	3 ♕g1
♔d5	2 ♖h5+	
♘~	2 ♕xc7+	

of the line h6-d6, by playing 1...♗b3. Now 2 ♘e~+ will work, because 2...♗d5 is followed by 3 ♕xc7. But the white knight cannot simply depart from e4: it must arrive somewhere. 2 ♘g5+, 2 ♘g3+ and 2 ♘f2+ cannot be played, because 3 ♕g1 must remain possible as a reply to 2...♔c5. 2 ♘f6+? fails to 2...♔xd6! (3 ♘d7? ♗e6!), and 2 ♘d2+? and 2 ♘c3+? will not work, on account of 2...♔c5 (3 ♕g1? ♗b4!). So it turns out that the only 'random' move available to the knight is 2 ♘c5+!. This beautiful combination of white and black correction-play is enriched by the fact that the three thematic variations, and also the line 1...♗xe4 2 ♗xe4+ ♔c5 3 ♕g1, end in **model mates**.

Correspondence

Many simple themes show some degree of correspondence, either formal or strategic. The complete **half-pin** is a good illustration of correspondence between black defences, as is the **Grimshaw**, while the arrangement known as the **half-battery** yields correspondence between white moves. Correspondence between white play and black play is, however, less frequently found. It is well exemplified by no. 52, by Colin Sydenham, whose researches into correspondence in the 1970s and 1980s led to articles in *The Problemist* and also to the production of a number of very interesting problems.

Here there is a set cutting-point between the lines of a black rook and a black bishop on b5, with resulting potential for mates on c4 and c5 after 1...♖b5 and 1...♗b5. However, in the diagram position no mates are available on these squares. The W♘d4 stands initially on the cutting-point of two white lines, those of the ♖e4 and the ♗e3. The key 1 ♘b5 switches the knight from the white cutting-point to the black one and, by guarding the set

52

CORRESPONDENCE

C.P.Sydenham
1st prize, *British Chess Magazine* 1979
Mate in two

Set 1...   ♔c3   2 ♗d2
Key 1 ♘b5 (>2 ♕c5/♕xc4)
      ...   ♖xb5   2 ♖xc4
                ♗xb5   2 ♗c5
                ♔xb5   2 ♕b6

flight c3, it threatens 2 ♕c5 as well as 2 ♕xc4. These mates are separately forced by 1...d6 and 1...d5. Readers familiar with the **Novotny** might well expect that the captures of the key-piece would separate the threats as well, but this is not the case: 1...♖xb5 does not allow 2 ♕xc4 because the queen must hold the square a5, which the black rook has vacated. But 2 ♖xc4 is now playable. 1...♗xb5 rules out 2 ♕c5 because c3 is no longer guarded. 2 ♗c5 works as the mate because the bishop, in moving from e3, opens a line from h3 to allow the rook to hold c3. So the effect of the key is to threaten Novotny-style mates which are eliminated by the captures on b5, and at the same time to bring into play two white line-pieces, equivalent to the black pieces which make those captures. The rook-capture leads to a rook-mate, and the bishop-capture to a bishop-mate. Another interesting line-effect occurs when the black king captures on b5. Two further black lines are opened to guard c5 and c4, so that the white queen cannot mate on either of these squares after 1...♔xb5 and must instead play 2 ♕b6. Incidentally, the set flight has a set mate which makes good use of the white pieces on e3 and h3: 1...♔c3 2 ♗d2.

In no. 53 White has three tries with his knight, which are refuted by equivalent moves of the black ♘g7: 1 ♘a4? ♘e8!; 1 ♘d1? ♘h5!; 1 ♘xc4? ♘xe6!. In each case the white move eliminates a set mate, thus enabling the black knight to exploit the error. The composer skilfully ensured that this formal correspondence is not the only interesting feature of the problem, for the key introduces a further defence leading to a queen-mate on a5.

The excellent key of no. 54, 1 ♕b7, threatens 2 ♘g3 (>3 ♕e4) ♘d5 3 ♘c6. Black's three best defences by the ♘e3 are answered by moves of the ♘e4 in precisely the same direction: 1...♘f1 2 ♘f2; 1...♘f5 2 ♘f6; and 1...♘c4 2 ♘c5. Each time 3 ♕e4 is threatened, and the white knight chooses its square in order to cater for further defences by the black knight. Readers

53

CORRESPONDENCE: TRIES

C.Mansfield
2nd prize, *The Observer* 1961
Mate in two

Try	1 ♘a4?	(>2 ♕d4)
	... ♘e8!	(2 ♕xa8?)
Try	1 ♘d1?	(>2 ♕d4)
	... ♘h5!	(2 ♕h1?)
Try	1 ♘xc4?	(>2 ♕d4)
	... ♘xe6!	(2 ♗c6?)
Key	1 ♖xc4!	(>2 ♖d4)
	... ♘e8	2 ♕xa8
	♘h5	2 ♕h1
	♘xe6	2 ♗c6
	bxc4	2 ♕a5
	d1♕	2 ♕xd1

CORRESPONDENCE

54

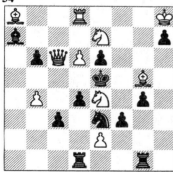

S.Brehmer
1st prize, *Schach* 1969
Mate in three

Key 1 ♕b7 (>2 ♘g3 {>3 ♕e4} ♘d5 3 ♘c6)

... ♘f1	2 ♘f2 (>3 ♕e4) ♘d2 3 ♘d3
	... ♘g3 3 ♘xg4
♘f5	2 ♘f6 (>3 ♕e4) ♘g3 3 ♘xg4
	... ♘xd6 3 ♘d7
♘c4	2 ♘c5 (>3 ♕e4) ♘d2 3 ♘d3
	... ♘xd6 3 ♘d7
♘d5	2 ♘c6+ ♔f5 3 ♕xh7

might like to compare this correspondence effect with that found in Goldsch-meding's no. 276 (→ **Tries**).

The six-mover no. 55 is a superb example of precise correspondence between white and black moves. The try 1 ♘e7? (>2 ♘xd5#) is met by 1...♘e3!, the two knights both playing on to the e-file. The second try 1 ♗d6? (>2 ♘e7 ♘e3 3 ♗xc5#) fails to 1...♗d4!, with the bishops both playing on to the d-file. (There is more matching play in this try: 1 ♗d6? ♗d4! 2 ♘e7? ♘e3 3 ♗f4? ♗f6! 4 ♗xe3 ♗xe7!.) The key 1 ♗h6!, threatening 2 ♘e7

55

CORRESPONDENCE

H.-P.Rehm
1st place, 3rd WCCT 1986-8
Mate in six

Try 1 ♘e7? (>2 ♘xd5) ♘e3!
(2 ♗h6? ♗xh4 3 ♗xe3 ♗xe7!)
Try 1 ♗d6? (>2 ♘e7 ♘e3 ♗xc5) ♗d4!
(2 ♘e7? ♗e3 3 ♗f4 ♗f6 4 ♗xe3 ♗xe7!)
Key 1 ♗h6! (>2 ♘e7 ♘e3 3 ♗xe3 ... 4 ♘xd5)

    ... ♗xh4 2 ♗f8 ♗f2 3 ♗d6 ♗d4
4 ♘e7 ♘e3 5 h4 (6 ♗xc5/♘xd5)
                         3 ... ♘d2
4 ♘e7 ♘b3 5 cxb3 ... 6 ♘xd5

♘e3 3 ♗xe3 ... 4 ♘xd5#, introduces a wonderful sequence of corresponding moves: 1...♗xh4 2 ♗f8 ♗f2 3 ♗d6 ♗d4 4 ♘e7 ♘e3 5 h4! (zugzwang – the point of the manoeuvre was to gain a tempo for White) ♗~/♘~ 6 ♗xc5/♘xd5#.

56

CORRESPONDENCE (DIAGONAL/ORTHOGONAL)

M.Tribowski
5th prize, *Schach* 1987
Mate in two

Try 1 ♖h1?   (>2 ♖xg1)
   ...   ♖g3!
Try 1 ♗e8?   (>2 ♗xd7)
   ...   ♗f5!
Key 1 ♖f3!   (>2 ♗h5)
   ...   ♖h1   2 ♖g3
            ♗e8   2 ♗f5
            ♘xf3 2 ♕e4

    Correspondence of a different kind is seen in no. 56. White tries 1 ♖h1? (>2 ♖xg1), but 1...♖g3! defeats, the two rooks moving the same number of squares in opposite directions. This play is echoed by a similar manoeuvre by the bishops at the top of the board: 1 ♗e8? (>2 ♗xd7) ♗f5!. After the key 1

♖f3! (>2 ♗h5) we find more matching play: 1...♖h1 2 ♖g3, and 1...♗e8 2 ♗f5. What we have here, therefore, is correspondence between orthogonal and diagonal effects, as well as between white and black moves. As with most correspondence schemes, this makes for great unity. It is perhaps unfair to point out that the composer was obliged to add an otherwise useless W♗b7 to get his scheme to work: 1 ♗e8? must fail only to 1...♗f5!, not to 1...♗c8 as well!

57

CORRESPONDENCE (DIAGONAL/ORTHOGONAL): HELPMATE

C.J.Feather
Moultings 5 1991
Helpmate in two: 2 solutions

1 ♕xg8 ♖f3 2 ♔e6 ♖e2
1 ♕xf8 ♗c4 2 ♔f6 ♗c3

Orthogonal/diagonal correspondence is a feature of many **helpmates**. No. 57 is a fine example by a master of the genre: first the black queen captures a white unit and opens a line for another white unit, which then plays to a square where it shuts off a black line-piece in anticipation of the mate. After a move by the black king to a square which White would now control if the black queen had not made a capture on the first move, White gives a long-range mate, on the d-file in one solution, and on the diagonal c3-f6 in the other. When he is in the mood for composing, Chris Feather is so prolific that he prefers to publish most of his work (and it is of very high quality) in home-produced booklets which he sends out to friends. These booklets bear names associated with his own, hence *Moultings* and *Hatchings*. An anthology of his problems is also available, entitled *Pluckings* (F.Chlubna, Vienna 1995).

Critical Play

A critical move is one in which a piece passes over a square (known as the *critical square*) with the result that any other piece moving subsequently to that square will produce an interference. The key of no. 58, 1 ♕c1, threatens a **Novotny** interference on f5: 2 ♗f5. If now 2...♗xf5, 3 ♕f4, and if 2...♖xf5,

58

CRITICAL PLAY

R.C.O.Matthews
2nd prize ex aequo, *Die Schwalbe*
1954/II
Mate in three

Key 1 ♕c1 (>2 ♗f5 ♗xf5 3 ♕f4
                  ♖xf5 3 ♖e6
                  d3 3 ♕c3)

   ...   ♖f1   2 ♘d2 (>3 ♘xc4)
             ...   ♗f5 3 ♘f7
                 ♖f5 3 ♖e6
        ♗c8   2 ♘d6 (>3 ♘xc4)
             ...   ♗f5 3 ♕f4
                 ♖f5 3 ♘g4
        ♗d7   2 d6+ ♚e6 3 ♕xc4
        ♘xg5 2 ♕xg5+
        ♖f3   2 exf3

3 ♖e6. Black can foil White's plans by playing his ♖f8 and ♗h3 over the critical square so that the interference is avoided. 1...♖f1 and 1...♗c8 are termed *anti-critical* moves with respect to the square f5, because they prevent the intended interference from working. However, they turn out to be critical at the same time. Let us examine exactly what happens when 1...♖f1 is played. 2 ♗f5? will not work as a continuation because, with the black rook to the south of f5, there is a guard on f4, where the white queen would like to mate. But now White can play 2 ♘d2 (>3 ♘xc4). Black defends by playing bishop or rook to f5 to cut the white bishop's line of guard to e4. And because the rook is no longer on f8, 2...♗f5 is an interference, allowing 3 ♘f7. 2...♖f5 allows 3 ♖e6 once again. Closely related play follows Black's second anti-critical/critical move, 1...♗c8. White plays 2 ♘d6 (>3 ♘xc4), and again there are interferences on the critical square: if 2...♖f5, 3 ♘g4 is mate, while if 2...♗f5, 3 ♕f4 reappears. It is instructive to work out how the composer has differentiated White's continuations after the two black anti-critical defences: in each case the white knight plays to a square where it shuts off a white unit whose mate (on f4 for the queen and on e6 for the rook) is no longer required.

Critical play may be conveniently classified as in the following table:

Critical move made by	Advantage gained by	Subsequent occupation of critical square by
A Black	(i) White	(a) Black
		(b) White
	(ii) Black	(a) Black
		(b) White
B White	(i) White	(a) Black
		(b) White
	(ii) Black	(a) Black
		(b) White

No. 58 illustrates type A(i)(a).

Type A(i)(b) is the very common arrangement of shut-off by White after Black has played across a critical square. No. 59 is a justly famous example, in which anti-critical play is also featured, in each of Black's thematic defences.

59

CRITICAL AND ANTI-CRITICAL PLAY

M.Barulin, G.Golubev, A.P.Guliaev, L.Loshinsky, E.Umnov and V.I.Schiff
64 1932
(In memoriam L.Isaev)
Mate in two
Key 1 ♖b5 (>2 ♘e4)

...	♛d5	2 ♗g4
	♛a8	2 ♘b7
	♖e5	2 ♘xf4
	♖xe7	2 ♘e6

The key 1 ♖b5 threatens 2 ♘e4, which simultaneously shuts off the black queen and e-rook from the line b5-h5. Black defends by playing these two pieces on to or beyond that line, so that 2 ♘e4 becomes ineffective as a shut-off. Such defences are anti-critical with respect to e4. 1...♛d5 allows 2 ♗g4. 1...♛a8, however, prevents this mate by pinning the ♗c8. But in playing to a8 the black queen crosses not only e4 but also a second critical square, b7.

White is thus able to play 2 ♘b7, again shutting off the black queen, but this time on the other side of the fifth rank. Note that the ♖e2 is pinned as soon as the queen leaves the line d1-h5. An analogous pair of defences is made by this rook, the queen becoming thematically pinned. 1...♖e5, crossing e4 anti-critically, leads to 2 ♘xf4. 1...♖xe7, however, removes the second guard from h4 so that 2 ♘xf4? no longer mates. But, like 1...♕a8, this defence crosses a second critical square, this time e6, so that 2 ♘e6 becomes play-able.

60

CRITICAL PLAY

J.Kohtz and C.Kockelkorn
Schachaufgaben 1875
Mate in five

Tries 1 ♗b2? 1 ♗c3? 1 ♗d4? ♗h1!
(>2...g2!)
Key 1 ♗e5 ♗h1 2 ♗xg3 (>3 ♗d6 ... 4
♗f8 ... 5 ♗g7)

A black critical move to Black's advantage, whether the subsequent inter-ference is carried out by Black or White, cannot be shown in a problem of fewer than four moves. No. 60, a miniature five-mover, gives an indication why this is so. It is clear that White must eventually mate on g7 with the bishop. Black's only hope of preventing this lies in the creation of stalemate, which might be done by means of the critical move 1...♗h1, followed by the interference 2...g2, *incarcerating* the bishop. If by this time White is about to play 3 ♗f8 (e.g. 1 ♗b2?, 2 ♗a3?), stalemate ensues. White must therefore select his key with care, so as to forestall Black's stalemate plans. 1 ♗e5! must be played, so that 2 ♗xg3 removes the offending pawn after 1...♗h1. Black's threatened manoeuvre illustrates critical-play category A(ii)(a).

A critical move made by White to his own advantage, with a white piece subsequently occupying the critical square (a three- or more-move tactic), is the main feature of the **Indian** and **Turton** themes, under which headings ex-amples will be found.

Nos. 61 and 62 show critical play by white pieces as tries, with Black gaining the advantage from the crossing of the critical square.

In no. 61 the try 1 ♖g2? (>2 ♕h4) fails to 1...♖xf4! because 2 ♘g4? cannot be played: the knight cannot afford to cut the rook's guard of g5.

61

CRITICAL TRIES

E.Visserman
3rd prize, *Schach* 1959
Mate in two
Try 1 ♖g2?   (>2 ♕xh4)
    ...   ♖xf4! (2 ♘g4?)
Try 1 ♖xd5?   (>2 ♕xh4)
    ...   ♗xf4! (2 ♗e5?)
(Try 1 ♖g4?   (>♕xh4)
    ...   ♖h5! (2 ♘g4?))
(Try 1 ♖e5?   (>2 ♕xh4)
    ...   ♗b6! (2 ♗e5?))
Key 1 ♖h5! (>2 ♕xh4)
    ...   ♖xf4 2 ♘g4
             ♗xf4 2 ♗e5
             (♘xg6 2 ♖f5)
             (♘f7 2 ♖e6)

Similarly 1 ♖xd5? is refuted by 1...♗xf4!, because 2 ♗e5? would again close the rook's line of guard to g5. Two further tries show square-block rather than critical play: 1 ♖g4? fails to 1...♖h5!, since 2 ♘g4? is not now playable; and 1...♖e5? rules out 2 ♗e5? after the refutation 1...♗b6!. With 1 ♖h5! White plays his rook to a square where it neither crosses nor blocks a square needed for mating. The critical tries illustrate category B(ii)(a).

62

CRITICAL TRIES

H.Ahues and A.Volkmann
1st prize, SV Dortmund-Hombruch-
Barop 1951
Mate in two
Try 1 ♗a2?   ♘b3!
Try 1 ♗a8?   ♘b7!
Try 1 ♗g8?   ♘e6!
Try 1 ♗h1?   ♘e4!
(Try 1 ♗c6?   ♖d8!)
Key 1 ♗c4!   (>2 ♖d5)
    ...   ♘c~   2 ♘d3
             ♖d8   2 ♘c6
             ♘f6   2 ♗d6

Critical tries where Black plays the subsequent interference move (type B(ii)(b)) are less subtle than those found in no. 61, but lend themselves to economical presentation, as is shown in no. 62.

To vacate d5 in order to threaten 2 ♖d5, the bishop tries playing to a2, a8, g8 and h1, but whichever direction it chooses, its guard of d5 can be shut off by the ♘c5, so that the white-interference mate 2 ♘d3 becomes unplayable. The bishop must therefore remain inside the range of the black knight (i.e. must avoid crossing a critical square). 1 ♗c6? fails to 1...♖d8 (2 ♘c6?), so only 1 ♗c4! will do. As with many problems showing common-error tries, the main interest of the work lies in the try-play; what happens after the key is of less interest. Incidentally, a chess problem containing no pawns, like this one, is often dubbed an *aristocrat*.

Pericritical play, in which a piece moves round, rather than across, a critical square, is illustrated by no. 213, and is also found in no. 82 (**Doubling**) and no. 245 (**Roman**).

Cross-check

It has long been one of the problem composer's favourite devices to allow Black, invariably the underdog in the direct-mate problem, a chance to carry out one last attack on the white king before his own king finally succumbs. One of White's three possible ways of parrying a black check is by placing a piece on the check-line. In the two-mover any such move must also be a mating move, either by direct checkmate or with the use of a battery. Such a reply to a black check is known as a cross-check.

CROSS-CHECKS

63

C.Mansfield
2nd prize, *La Settimana enigmistica*
1935
Mate in two

Key 1 ♔f5 (>2 ♗xc5)

...	♗d4+	2 ♗e5
	♗e3+	2 ♘c5
	♗xd6+	2 ♘b5
	♖f1+	2 ♘f2
	♖d1	2 ♘d2
	♘d7	2 ♕d5
	♘c7	2 ♕xc7

The great master of the cross-check was undoubtedly Comins Mansfield. The key of no. 63, 1 ♔f5, is entirely thematic in that it exposes the white king to the checking defences which form the main variations of the problem. The ♝c5 produces three of these variations. The threat is 2 ♝xc5, and this same move follows checks by the bishop if it moves to b4 or a3. But if Black plays 1...♝d4+, 2 ♝c5? fails to 2...♝f6!. So the shut-off 2 ♝e5 must be played – a double shut-off, because not only the check-line but also the bishop's line from d4 to f6 must be closed. 1...♝e3+ allows no mate from the ♖+♝ battery on the sixth rank (2 ♝f4? does not parry the check). But this defence interferes with the ♖e1, so that White can now play 2 ♘c5. Supposing Black plays 1...♝xd6+, a move which allows neither the ♖+♝ battery nor the ♝+♘ battery to function? This is a *self-pin*: the black bishop cannot return to c5, and so the previously *masked* battery consisting of ♖+♘ can open with the mate 2 ♘b5. A further check introduced by the key is 1...♖f1+, which White can meet with the cross-check 2 ♘f2. Three by-play variations complete a typical Mansfield cross-check masterpiece.

64

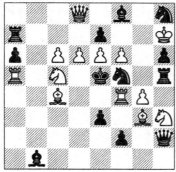

CROSS-CHECKS

G.F.Anderson
1st prize, *The Observer* 1961
Mate in two
Key 1 ♕b6   (>2 ♘e4)

...	exf6+	2 ♘b7
	exd6+	2 ♘d7
	♘f~+	2 ♘e4
	♘d4+	2 ♖f5
	♘xd6+	2 ♘d3
	♔xf6	2 ♕b2
	♔xd6	2 ♖d4

The composer of no. 64 succeeded, after years of effort, in obtaining five cross-checks, though with the slight drawback that one of them (after random moves by the ♘f5) is the threat. That threat is 2 ♘e4, introduced by the key 1 ♕b6, which gives a second flight on d6 to add to the existing one on f6. It is the presence of these flights that makes the mechanism work. The ♟e7 blocks one of them with each of its moves, and the ♘c5, opening the ♖+♘ battery, can play to the seventh rank to parry the check, guarding the non-blocked flight by arrival: 1...exf6+ 2 ♘b7; and 1...exd6+ 2 ♘d7. As noted, random moves by the ♘f5 allow the threat, but there are two **corrections**:

1...♘d4+, allowing 2 ♖f5 (self-block on d4); and 1...♘xd6+ 2 ♘d3 (self-block on d6). In both of these variations the f-rook guards the flight f6. There are two new mates after the black king moves to his flights: 1...♚xf6 2 ♕b2, and 1...♚xd6 2 ♖d4. The fact that 1...♚xf6 has no mate set in the diagram position is a small blemish in an otherwise excellent piece of construction.

An example of changed play after cross-checks is no. 32 (→ **Castling**).

65

CHANGED CROSS-CHECKS

Y.G.Vladimirov
1st place, USSR Championship 1960
Mate in three

Set	1...	♕b4+ 2 ♘d6+ ♚g5 3 ♗f4
		♕h4+ 2 ♘g5+ ♚xg5 3 ♗f4
Key	1 ♕a8 (>2 c8♕+)	
	...	♕b4+ 2 ♖d6+ ♚e4 3 ♘g5
		♕h4+ 2 ♗f6+ ♚e4 3 ♘d6
	(...	♕xe5+ 2 ♖xe5+ ♗xe5 3 c8♕)

Cross-checks are, of course, frequently found in three-movers and longer problems, and may occur at any stage in the course of the solution. In no. 65 Black's set checks with the queen on b4 and h4 are answered by cross-checks from the ♘f7, followed by mate on the third move by the bishop, exploiting Black's first-move unpins. After the key 1 ♕a8 (>2 c8♕+ ♚e4 3 ♖d4) the unpins are exploited straightaway: 1...♕b4+ 2 ♗d6+; and 1...♕h4+ 2 ♗f6+. In each case Black's only possible second move is 1...♚e4, and now White's original second-move continuations reappear as third-move mates: 3 ♘g5 and 3 ♘d6.

A special kind of three- and more-move cross-check, known as the *Brede cross-check*, is featured in no. 66, where it is combined with pin-mates. The key 1 ♚b8 (three threats, 2 ♕e5+, 2 ♘xe7+ and 2 ♘d4+) unpins the ♘c6 but exposes the white king to checks from two directions. 1...♗g3+ is answered by 2 ♘e5+. The white knight is now pinned, and is unpinned again by Black's second-move reply to the check from the rook, 2...♖d6. Now the knight is free to mate, and can exploit the fact that the ♗f3 was pinned by Black's first move: 3 ♘xg4. In the parallel variation 1...♖b1+, the knight becomes pinned on the b-file: 2 ♘b4+. Now the ♗f3 is again left pinned as Black parries White's second-move check with 2...♗b6. This move once again unpins the white knight to allow the pin-mate 3 ♘d5. Brede cross-check consists in its simplest form of a white cross-check with a subsequent

66

BREDE CROSS-CHECKS

G.J.Bouma
1st prize, *De Waarheid* 1965
Mate in three

Key 1 ♔b8 (>2 ♕e5+/♘xe7+/♘d4+)
    ...   ♗g3+ 2 ♘e5+ ♖d6 3 ♘xg4
             ♖b1+ 2 ♘b4+ ♗b6 3 ♘d5

unpin by Black of the piece which has parried Black's original check; this piece then mates. In the present example the theme is shown in two variations, with the embellishments of a highly thematic key permitting the checks and unpinning the piece which is to parry them, and a black half-pin line which gives rise to eventual pin-mates. The only weakness of the problem is the triple threat.

Cyclic Play

Before attempting to understand the intricacies of Cyclic Play, the reader is advised to study the problems under **Reciprocal Play**. Whereas reciprocal play requires two related elements, cyclic play needs at least three. The nature of the cycle depends on the theme into which it is incorporated. Some of the commonest types of cyclic play are discussed here.

    Cycles limited to the post-key play of a two-mover are found in the first three examples.

    No. 67 illustrates an **interference** cycle, in which the important pieces are the black rooks and bishops. For clarity these units are referred to here as W (the ♖e1), X (♗d4), Y (♖d3) and Z (♗c6). The key 1 ♘g8 threatens 2 g6, and each of the four thematic pieces can defend against the threat. If Black plays 1...♖e5, White replies 2 ♘f6 – W has interfered with X. 1...♗e3 leads to 2 g4; here X interferes with Y. After 1...♖f3, the mate is 2 ♔g2, which exploits the interference of Y with Z. Finally Z defends, and in so doing interferes with W: 1...♗e4 2 ♗e8. The cycle is complete: each piece defends once and is interfered with once. It will be observed that the interferences all take place on different squares. A four-piece interference cycle in a two-mover with all the interferences on the same square has been achieved, but at the cost of a checking key.

67

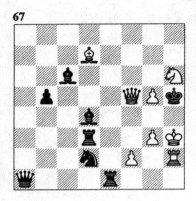

INTERFERENCE CYCLE

G.F.H.Packer
2nd hon. mention, *British Chess Magazine* 1944
Mate in two

Key 1 ♘g8	(>2 g6)
... ♖e5	2 ♘f6
♗e3	2 g4
♖f3	2 ♔g2
♗e4	2 ♗e8

Dual avoidance is basically a reciprocal idea: the move avoided in one variation usually appears as the mate in the other, and vice versa. No. 68 shows how a familiar dual-avoidance theme (**Mari**) can be extended to show cyclic avoidance.

68

CYCLIC DUAL AVOIDANCE

S.Brehmer
1st prize ex aequo, *Die Schwalbe* 91st Theme Tourney, 1949
Mate in two

Key 1 ♖d3 (>2 ♖e3)
... ♖xc3 2 ♘f2 (A) not 2 ♘d6? (B)
♗xd3 2 ♘d6 (B) not 2 ♗d5? (C)
♘xd2 2 ♗d5 (C) not 2 ♘f2? (A)

In each of three variations, only one white move will mate, while a second must be avoided. The possibility of playing the third does not arise at all. The threat carried by the key, 1 ♖d3, is 2 ♖e3, and Black's three thematic defences are 1...♖xc3, 1...♗xd3 and 1...♘xd2. Each of these moves opens a white line, which White must avoid closing again with his mating move. 1...♖xc3 opens b8-f4, but only 2 ♘f2 (mate A) can be played, because 2 ♘d6? (mate B) would re-close this line. After 1...♗xd3, which opens a5-f5, only mate B will do, as mate C (2 ♗d5?) would close the line again. Finally 1...♘xd2, opening f1-f5, permits only mate C, since mate A would interfere with the white queen on the newly-opened line.

Black correction and cyclicity are by no means incompatible concepts, as is amply demonstrated by no. 69. Each of four black units has one random move and one correction move.

CYCLIC BLACK CORRECTION

69

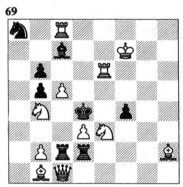

J.Retter
1st prize, *BABY* Theme Tourney 1962
Mate in two

Key 1 ♖e5		zugzwang
...	♗~	2 ♖e4 (A)
	♗xe5	2 ♘f5 (B)
	f~	2 ♘f5 (B)
	fxe3	2 ♖d5 (C)
	♖d~	2 ♖d5 (C)
	♖xd3	2 ♘c6 (D)
	♖c~	2 ♘c6 (D)
	♖xc5	2 ♖e4 (A)

The white mate which follows the correction move of piece W reappears after the random move of piece X; piece X's correction move then leads to the same mate as the random move of piece Y, and so on until the cycle is complete. The key 1 ♖e5 puts Black in zugzwang. Black's four thematic units are his bishop, the ♙f4, and the two rooks. If the bishop moves at random, 2 ♖e4 (mate A) results. The correction 1...♗xe5 blocks e5 and allows 2 ♘f5 (B). This mate also follows 1...f3, the random move of the pawn. (It is quite legitimate to regard this single move as a random move, since the error which it commits, viz. opening of the line h2-e5, would still be there if the pawn were entirely removed from the board.) The pawn corrects by capturing the ♘e3, thereby blocking e3 and introducing mate C, 2 ♖d5. 1...♖d~, by opening c1-e3, permits C again, but 1...♖xd3 corrects. However, this is a further self-block, and White can accordingly proceed with mate D, 2 ♘c6. 1...♖c~ allows this same mate by opening b1-d3, but this rook corrects by playing to c5. This is the defence which completes the cycle, since, by blocking c5, it re-introduces A, 2 ♖e4 – and we are back where we started.

Cyclic effects are commonly found spread over various phases of the problem's solution. *Cyclic refutation* is the name given to an arrangement in which Black has three thematic defences and White's three tries fail to each in turn. The key, of course, provides mates for all the defences. This arrangement is perhaps not strictly cyclic, but it is convenient to illustrate it here. There are lots of dull examples where White's mates remain the same all the time. The scheme becomes interesting, however, when changed play is introduced. No. 70 is a very simple example with some changed mates.

CYCLIC REFUTATION

M.Locker
2nd prize, *Stella Polaris* 1966
Mate in two

70

Try	1 ♕h2?		
	...	♚c5	2 ♕c7
		♚d3	2 ♕e2
		d3!	
Try	1 ♗c6?		
	...	♚d3	2 ♗b5
		d3	2 ♕d5
		♚c5!	
Try	1 ♗a8?		
	...	d3	2 ♕d5
		♚c5	2 ♕c6
		♚d3!	
Key	1 ♗b7!	zugzwang	
	...	♚c5	2 ♕c6
		♚d3	2 ♗a6
		d3	2 ♕d5

Black's three thematic defences are 1...♚c5 (X), 1...♚d3 (Y) and 1...d3 (Z). The try 1 ♕h2? provides for X and Y with 2 ♕c7 and 2 ♕e2 respectively, but fails to Z. 1 ♗c6? deals with Y and Z: 1...♚d3 2 ♗b5; and 1...d3 2 ♕d5; but it is defeated by X. 1 ♗a8? is good enough to cope with Z and X (2 ♕d5 and 2 ♕c6), but Y remains unprovided. The key 1 ♗b7! sets up mates for all three defences: 1...♚c5 2 ♕c6; 1...♚d3 2 ♗a6; and 1...d3 2 ♕d5. Six different white mates appear in the course of the solution of this famous miniature.

It will be readily seen that the maximum number of white mates demanded by the cyclic refutation scheme, if all mates are changed, must be nine (two after each try, and three after the key). Like many ideals in the chess problem world, this maximum is hard to obtain, but it is shown in spectacular fashion by no. 71. The tries and key are all made by the same piece. If the ♘d5 were removed from the board completely, the threat of 2 ♖e4 would be refuted by all three of the thematic defences: 1...exf5 (X), 1...♚xe5 (Y)

71

CYCLIC REFUTATION

M.Parthasarathy
1st prize ex aequo, *British Chess Magazine* 1966
Mate in two

Try	1 ♘dxe3?	exf5	2 ♘xf5
		♚xe5	2 ♖xe6
		♗xe5!	
Try	1 ♘xb4?	♚xe5	2 ♕c3
		♗xe5	2 c3
		exf5!	
Try	1 ♘c3?	♗xe5	2 ♘e2
		exf5	2 ♖d5
		♚xe5!	
Key	1 ♘c7!	(>2 ♖e4)	
	...	exf5	2 ♖xd6
		♚xe5	2 ♖f8
		♗xe5	2 ♘xe6

and 1...♗xe5 (Z). 1 ♘dxe3? introduces mates for X and Y: 1...exf5 2 ♘xf5; and 1...♚xe5 2 ♖xe6. But 1...♗xe5! refutes. 1 ♘xb4? deals with Y and Z (2 ♕c3 and 2 c3), but fails to X. The third try 1 ♘c3? brings in mates to answer defences Z and X, but Y remains unprovided. Now comes the delight of the problem, the key 1 ♘c7! and the play it introduces: 1...exf5 2 ♖xd6; 1...♚xe5 2 ♖f8; and 1...♗xe5 2 ♘xe6. The new battery-mate after 1...♚xe5 is especially impressive.

An idea related to cyclic refutation is *cyclic mating permutation*. This scheme requires basically three phases rather than four, and the same mates recur in cyclic pattern after different black defences. There are two fundamentally different ways of showing cyclic mating permutation. In no. 72 there are three black line-pieces each guarding a pair of mating squares. With his tries and key White shuts off each of these pieces in turn, so that the defences by the other two lead to two of the thematic mates. Each try is refuted by the piece that has been shut off, which means that in the post-key play there must be a new mate to follow the defence by the black piece which the key shuts off. A random move by the ♖c5 threatens mate by 2 ♗c5, but would fail to the three defences 1...♗f2, 1...♖xd4 and 1...♖xa5. The try 1 ♖c8? brings in the following play: 1...♗f2 2 d8♕ (mate A); 1...♖xd4 2 dxe8♘ (B). Each time White, having shut off one black guard unit, must mate on the square from which Black removes the second guard in defending

72

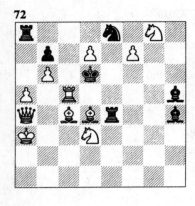

CYCLIC MATING PERMUTATION

B.P.Barnes
4th prize, *Die Schwalbe* 1960
Mate in two

Try 1 ♖c8?		(>2 ♗c5)
...	♗f2	2 d8♕ (x-A)
	♖xd4	2 dxe8♘ (y-B)
	♖xa5!	(z!)
Try 1 ♖g5?		(>2 ♗c5)
...	♖xd4	2 f8♕ (y-C)
	♖xa5	2 d8♕ (z-A)
	♗f2!	(x!)
Key 1 ♖e5!		(>2 ♗c5)
...	♖xa5	2 dxe8♘ (z-B)
	♗f2	2 f8♕ (x-C)
	♖xd4	2 ♖e6 (y-D)

against the threat. This try fails to the defence by the piece shut off, namely 1...♖xa5!. 1 ♖g5? leads to 1...♖xd4 2 f8♕ (C), and 1...♖xa5 2 d8♕ (A), but fails to 1...♗f2!. The choice of mating square follows the same pattern as before. The key 1 ♖e5! re-introduces mates B and C: 1...♖xa5 2 dxe8♘ (B); and 1...♗f2 2 f8♕ (C). Finally 1...♖xd4, which looks as if it ought to defeat, is followed by the new mate 2 ♖e6. Mates A, B and C each appear twice in the course of the solution, after different defences in the three phases.

The second way of setting cyclic mating permutation is exemplified by no. 73. Here the white ♖+♘ battery on the a-file is controlled by three black pieces, the queen and the two rooks. White's initial move shuts off the first of these, a second moves away or is interfered with to defend against the threat, and finally the third is shut off by the mating move. 1 ♘d8? (>2 ♕b3) ♖d5 2 ♘c5 (A); 1...♕xf7 2 ♘c7 (B); but 1...♗g8!. Black closes the line White has just closed, so that no mate is now possible. 1 ♘ec7? ♕xf7 2 ♘b8 (C); 1...♗g8 2 ♘c5 (A); but 1...♖d5!. The next phase is usually the last in this sort of problem, but here the composer has introduced a fourth phase which in fact repeats the thematic mates of the third. The reason for this fourth phase becomes plain in due course. The third try is 1 ♘ec5?, and the ensuing play: 1...♗g8 2 ♘c7 (B); 1...♖d5 2 ♘b8 (C); but 1...♕xf7!. Once again the try fails to a defence by the piece which has just been shut off. The key 1 ♘d4! shuts off the same piece, and so the thematic play which follows is the same as that following 1 ♘ec5?. But now 1...♕xf7, which refuted the try, is answered by the new mate 2 ♘xc2. Mate A, which does not appear in the

73

CYCLIC MATING PERMUTATION

C.Goldschmeding
1st prize, *Probleemblad* 1960
Mate in two

Try	1 ♘d8?	(>2 ♕b3)	
	... ♖d5	2 ♘c5	(x-A)
	♕xf7	2 ♘c7	(y-B)
	♗g8!		(z!)
Try	1 ♘ec7?	(>2 ♕b3)	
	... ♕xf7	2 ♘b8	(y-C)
	♗g8	2 ♘c5	(z-A)
	♖d5!		(x!)
Try	1 ♘ec5?	(>2 ♕b3)	
	... ♗g8	2 ♘c7	(z-B)
	♖d5	2 ♘b8	(x-C)
	♕xf7!		(y!)
Key	1 ♘d4!	(>2 ♕b3)	
	... ♕xf7	2 ♘xc2	
	♔a4	2 ♘c5	

post-key play after any of the thematic defences, does in fact come in again after the black king's move to the flight which the key grants: 1...♔a4 2 ♘c5.

Yet another type of cyclic effect is found in the next two problems. Black has three set-play or virtual-play defences X, Y and Z, which allow respectively mates A, B and C. After the key the same defences and mates recur, but in a different pattern: X, Y and Z now lead respectively to B, C and A. This arrangement, known as a *cyclic shift*, is often referred to as the *Lačný theme*, after the distinguished Slovak composer who made one of the first examples of it.

The thematic defences of no. 74 are 1...♔a5 (X), 1...♘a~ (Y) and 1...♘b~ (Z). After the try 1 ♗d2? the mates are 2 ♖xa6 (A), 2 ♕xc5 (B) and 2 ♖b7 (C). The try is refuted by 1...♘c3!. The key 1 ♖a1! shifts the mates in the following manner: 1...♔a5 (X) is now followed by mate B, 2 ♕xc5 (the ♘a4 is pinned, but the ♘b4 is not); 1...♘a~ (Y) now leads to mate C, 2 ♖b7 (a5 is now guarded by the ♖a1, and there is no second guard on c5); while 1...♘b~ (Z) now allows mate A, 2 ♖xa6 (the white rook must guard a5 in mating, and can release its control of c7).

No. 75 extends the pattern to include a fourth defence and mate. W, X, Y and Z are therefore followed by A, B, C and D in the virtual play, and by B, C, D and A after the key. There are very few examples of this difficult scheme

74

CYCLIC SHIFT

V.F.Rudenko
1st prize, *Chervony girnik* 1975
Mate in two
Try 1 ♗d2?

	♔a5	2 ♖xa6	(x-A)
	♘a~	2 ♕xc5	(y-B)
	♘b~	2 ♖b7	(z-C)
	♘c3!		

Key 1 ♖a1!   zugzwang

	♔a5	2 ♕xc5	(x-B)
	♘a~	2 ♖b7	(y-C)
	♘b~	2 ♖xa6	(z-A)

CYCLIC SHIFT

75

M.Krizovensky
1st prize, *Šachové umění 1982*
Mate in two
Try 1 ♕a8?

	♔e6	2 ♗g4	(w-A)
	♘d~	2 ♘d4	(x-B)
	♔e4	2 ♖xf4	(y-C)
	♘g4	2 ♗d3	(z-D)
	♘d7!		

Key 1 ♘e5!   zugzwang

	♔e6	2 ♘d4	(w-B)
	♘d~	2 ♖xf4	(x-C)
	♔e4	2 ♗d3	(y-D)
	♘g4	2 ♗xg4	(z-A)

to be found. 1 ♕a8?, waiting for Black to respond, introduces the following play: 1...♔e6 (W) 2 ♗g4 (A); 1...♘d~ (X) 2 ♘d4 (B); 1...♔e4 (Y) 2 ♖xf4 (C); and 1...♘g4 (Z) 2 ♗d3 (D). Other moves by the ♘f6 allow 2 ♕xd5, except 1...♘d7!, which refutes. By subtly switching the lines of guard and crucially occupying e5, the key 1 ♘e5! (-) effects the desired shift of mates: W, X, Y and Z now lead respectively to B, C, D and A.

No. 76 is a three-move version of this very complex scheme. Both the try 1 ♗xg6? and the key 1 ♗xe6! threaten 2 h8♘ followed by 3 ♘f7. After the try the variation play works like this: 1...♕xg3 (W) leads to 2 ♘g4+ (A) ♔d5

76

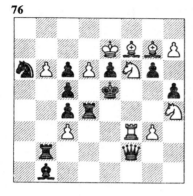

**CYCLIC SHIFT
(+ SIERS BATTERY)**

J.Retter
1st place, Israel v Sweden 1986
Mate in three

Try 1 ♗xg6?	(>2 h8♘ ... 3 ♘f7)
... ♛xg3	2 ♘g4+ ♚d5 3 ♘e3
♜xd6	2 ♘xh5+ ♚d5 3 ♘f4
♘c7	2 ♘e8+ ♚d5 3 ♘xc7
♜xb6	2 ♘d7+ ♚d5 3 ♘xb6
♜g4!	

Key 1 ♗xe6!	(>2 h8♘ ... 3 ♘f7)
... ♛xg3	2 ♘xh5+ ♚e4 3 ♘xg3
♜xd6	2 ♘e8+ ♚e4 3 ♘xd6
♘c7	2 ♘d7+ ♚e4 3 ♘xc5
♜xb6	2 ♘g4+ ♚e4 3 ♘xf2

3 ♘e3; 1...♜xd6 (X) to 2 ♘xh5+ (B) ♚d5 3 ♘f4; 1...♘c7 (Y) to 2 ♘e8+ (C) ♚d5 3 ♘xc7; and 1...♜xb6 (Z) to 2 ♘d7+ (D) ♚d5 3 ♘xb6. The try fails, however, to 1...♜g4!. Because the key sets up a slightly different pattern of guards from the try, the post-key play finds defences W, X, Y and Z leading to mates B, C, D and A respectively. The white ♗+♘ battery in this problem is known as a *Siers battery*, and the knight, opening the battery on move 2 and then mating from a new direction on move 3, is referred to as a *Rössel* (see under **Knight-tour**).

Related to the cyclic shift is an arrangement which is called *cyclic change* or *cyclic Zagoruiko*. Black has two defences, X and Y, which are followed by mates A and B in the first phase, by B and C in the second, and finally by C and A after the key. The first-ever example of this scheme, despite its double-checking try and key, won first prize in a theme tourney in 1961. At the time it was thought that checking tries and key would be necessary to achieve this cyclic pattern at all, but soon after this tourney several more orthodox settings appeared, mainly by Russian composers, such as no. 77.

Black's defences are 1...♘xe5 (X) and 1...♘xd4 (Y). These are followed by 2 ♘c7 (A) and 2 ♗xb7 (B) – pin-mates in each case – after the try 1 ♛xd3? (refuted by 1...♜a3!). 1 ♛f5?, with the same threat of 2 ♛f3, introduces mates B and C: 1...♘xe5 2 ♗xb7 (B); and 1...♘xd4 2 ♘b6 (C); but this fails to 1...g4!. The key 1 ♗f8! (>2 ♛h1), by providing an additional guard for d6 and c5, completes the cyclic pattern: 1...♘xe5 2 ♘b6 (C); and 1...♘xd4 (A). Note that mate B cannot appear in the post-key play because

77

CYCLIC CHANGE

E.Livshits
1st hon. mention, *Shakhmaty v SSSR*
1962
Mate in two

Try	1 ♕xd3?		(>2 ♕f3)
	...	♘xe5	2 ♘c7 (x-A)
		♘xd4	2 ♗xb7 (y-B)
		♖a3!	
Try	1 ♕f5?		(>2 ♕f3)
	...	♘xe5	2 ♗xb7 (x-B)
		♘xd4	2 ♘b6 (y-C)
		g4!	
Key	1 ♗f8!		(>2 ♕h1)
	...	♘xe5	2 ♘b6 (x-C)
		♘xd4	2 ♘c7 (y-A)

the black knight cannot pin itself. This splendid problem is only slightly marred by the fact that the key-piece is not wholly in play in the diagram.

A great deal of attention has been paid to cyclic play in the three-mover. As in the two-mover, the cyclicity may take several forms, but post-key cycles still predominate and are often concerned with the relationship between White's second and third moves. Before examining two examples of this type of cycle, here first is a kind of interference-cycle impossible to achieve in the two-mover. In the three-mover one can create an interference with a knight, or with a pawn away from its starting square, by making it impossible for the knight or pawn to move to the square where the interference takes place, in order to defend. Such an interference is usually termed **obstruction**. No. 78 illustrates *cyclic obstruction*: in the first variation black unit X obstructs unit Y; in the second Y obstructs Z; and finally Z obstructs X.

The key 1 c5 threatens 2 ♘g7+ ♖xg7 3 ♖e8. The obstructions take place on c5: 1...♗xc5 obstructs the ♘a4 and prevents it from defending by 2...♘xc5 after White's continuation 2 bxc8♕ (>3 ♕xd7). 1...♘xc5 obstructs the rook, so that White can play 2 bxa8♘ without fear that his threat of 3 ♘xc7 will be defeated by 2...♖xc5. Finally 1...♖xc5 obstructs the bishop: 2 bxc8♘ (>3 ♘f8) can now be played, since 2...♗xc5? is now impossible. Considerable unity and interest is achieved in this example of the theme by the fact that each of White's continuations is a promotion of the △b7. The composer of this problem, Dr Karl Fabel, was a very versatile problemist, perhaps best known for his work in the field of retrograde analysis.

78

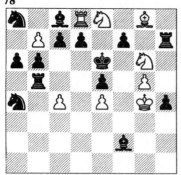

CYCLIC OBSTRUCTION

K.Fabel
1st prize, *Deutsche Schachzeitung* 1965
Mate in three

Key 1 c5   (>2 ♘g7+ ♖xg7 3 ♖e8)
    ...   ♗xc5 2 bxc8♕ (>3 ♕xd7)
            ♘xc5 2 bxa8♘ (>3 ♘xc7)
            ♖xc5 2 bxc8♘ (>3 ♘f8)

One of the most popular three-move cyclic themes is *cyclic overload*. A black unit becomes overloaded if it is expected to guard too many squares at once: White, with his second move, draws the unit away from its guard of a square or line on which White plans to mate on his third move. (See also **Overloads, Anti-Bristol** and **Wurzburg-Plachutta**.)

79

CYCLIC OVERLOAD

M.Keller
1st prize, *Schweizerische Arbeiterschachzeitung* 1966
Mate in three

Key 1 ♕a3 (>2 ♘c5+ ♗xc5 3 ♕d3)
    ... ♗xa3 2 ♗xc6+ ♕xc6 3 ♘g5   (A-B)
        ♖xa8 2 ♘g5+ ♕xg5 3 exf3   (B-C)
        ♖xh3 2 exf3+ ♕xf3 3 ♗xc6 (C-A)

In no. 79 the black queen, despite having support from behind in the shape of two rooks and a bishop, cannot maintain her control over all three of the squares c6, g5 and f3. The key 1 ♕a3 threatens 2 ♘c5+, with 3 ♕d3 as the mate following 2...♗xc5. In each variation one of the black support pieces leaves its post, thus weakening the defences and allowing White to exploit the black queen's overload. 1...♗xa3 leads to 2 ♗xc6+ (move A) ♕xc6 3 ♘g5 (move B). 1...♖xa8 pins the white queen but permits the continuation 2 ♘g5+ (B) ♕xg5 3 exf3 (C). 1...♖xh3 defends by eliminating one of the guards over f4, and is followed by 2 exf3+ (C) ♕xf3 3 ♗xc6 (A). White's continuations are determined not only by Black's removal of his double control over the mating squares, but also by the fact that each of Black's first moves is the capture of a crucial white unit. The composer of this problem, now a Grandmaster of Composition and one of the world's leading problemists, was still in his teens when this work appeared.

80

CYCLIC OVERLOAD (DOUBLED)

R.C.O.Matthews
1st prize, *British Chess Magazine* 1968
Mate in three
Key 1 ♕a4 (>2 ♕xc4)

... ♗a5 2 ♕c2+ d3 3 ♖xe3   (A-B)
♘e5 2 ♖xe3+ dxe3 3 ♘c3 (B-C)
♖xh6 2 ♘c3+ dxc3 3 ♕c2 (C-A)
♖xc6 2 ♖xe3+ dxe3 3 ♕c2 (B-A)
♘c5 2 ♘c3+ dxc3 3 ♖xe3 (C-B)
♕xh6 2 ♕c2+ d3 3 ♘c3   (A-C)

Cyclic overloads are featured once more in no. 80, but this time there are two complete and distinct cycles. The same three white moves are used throughout, but every possible pairing and sequence of these moves is seen in the six variations. The two cycles run AB-BC-CA, and BA-CB-AC. The moves of the second cycle thus represent a total reversal of those of the first cycle. The key is 1 ♕a4, with the threat of 2 ♕xc4 (>3 ♕d3/♖xe3/♘c3). The thematic defences of the first cycle are 1...♗a5 (X), 1...♘e5 (Y) and 1...♖xh6 (Z). X allows 2 ♕c2+ (A) d3 3 ♖xe3 (B). Y leads to 2 ♖xe3+ (B) dxe3 3 ♘c3 (C). Z gives 2 ♘c3+ (C) dxc3 3 ♕c2 (A). The overloaded unit is the ♙d4, and this is the case in the second cycle as well: 1...♖xc6 2 ♖xe3+ (B) dxe3 3 ♕c2 (A); 1...♘c5 2 ♘c3+ (C) dxc3 3 ♖xe3 (B); 1...♕xh6 2 ♕c2+ (A) d3 3 ♘c3 (C). It is interesting to work out how these continuations are motivated, and why the cyclic pattern of this highly ingenious problem arises.

Cylinder Boards

The Cylinder board belongs to the realm of **fairy chess**. There are three types:

1) the vertical cylinder, on which the h- and a-files are joined together, so that the board is like a tin-can without top and bottom;

2) the horizontal cylinder, on which the first and eighth ranks are joined together (the tin-can is now on its side);

3) the anchor-ring, which combine the properties of the vertical and horizontal cylinders (imagine that the can is bent so that the open ends are sealed together).

A bishop on b1 on an empty vertical cylinder will have access to c2, d3, e4, etc., and also to a2, h3, g4, f5, e6, d7 and c8. On a horizontal cylinder this same bishop would be able to move north-west to a2, north-east to c2, d3, etc., and also south-west to a8 and south-east to c8, d7, e6, f5, g4 and h3. On an anchor-ring a bishop on b1 would be able to reach all the squares mentioned for the bishop on a vertical cylinder, plus those for the bishop on a horizontal cylinder. Moves on all kinds of cylinder are not limitless: they must come to a definite stop. Pawn-promotion on a horizontal cylinder or anchor-ring is permissible only if specifically stated.

CYLINDER BOARDS

81

C.R.Flood
A Guide to Fairy Chess 1967
Series-helpmate in three
(a) Normal board
(b) Vertical cylinder
(c) Horizontal cylinder
(d) Anchor-ring
Black pawns promote on first rank of diagram

(a) 1 h1♕ 2 ♕xd5 3 ♕b5 b3
(b) 1 h1♖ 2 ♖h5 3 ♖b5 b3
(c) 1 h1♗ 2 ♗g2 3 ♗b5 b3
(d) 1 h1♘ 2 ♘a7 3 ♘b5 b3

No. 81 is a fairly simple *series-helpmate* (see under **Series-movers**) with four solutions which differ according to the type of board. (Black plays three consecutive moves to reach a position where White can mate in one.) On a normal board Black plays 1 h1♕ 2 ♕xd5 3 ♕b5 and now White mates with 3...b3. If the board is a vertical cylinder, this will not work, since 1 h1♕? would be check (h1 to a2), and under the rules of the series-helpmate Black may not inflict check until the last move of the series. The solution is therefore 1 h1♖ 2 ♖h5 3 ♖b5 (via a5) b3. Clearly this solution, exploiting the properties of the vertical cylinder for the third move, will not work on a horizontal cylinder. Nor will the normal-board solution, since the queen on b5 would guard White's mating square b3 (via b8 and b1). The only 'horizontal' solution is 1 h1♗ 2 ♗g2 3 ♗b5 (via f1 and e8) b3. Promotions to queen, rook or bishop all fail on the anchor-ring board, however: 1 h1♕? and 1 h1♗? are both check, while 1 h1♖? fails because the mating-square is guarded after 3 ♖b5?. Black must therefore play 1 h1♘ 2 ♘a7 3 ♘b5 b3, thereby completing a neat *Allumwandlung* (see **Promotion**). Working out the solution of an anchor-ring problem is made easier if one bears in mind that the squares h1 and a8 are diagonally adjacent to one another, as are a1 and h8.

Dombrovskis → Reversal themes

Doubling

Doubling involves getting two white pieces on to the same line in such a way that the rear piece (seen from the point of view of the black king) supports the front piece (e.g. guards it) in the mate. Basically this is a three- and more-move manoeuvre, for doubling is really interesting only if White's key is a move by either the eventual front piece or rear piece along the doubling line (or one parallel to it) to enable the pieces to get into their correct positions. A single example will suffice here to show how doubling-schemes work in three-move form; further examples are found under **Turton** and **Zepler-doubling**.

82

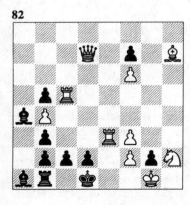

DOUBLING

Z.Maslar
1st prize ex aequo, *Problem* 1962-3
Mate in three

Key 1 ♖e8		zugzwang
...	c1♘	2 ♕e7
	c1♕/♖	2 ♖ce5
	c1♗	2 ♗e4
	♔c1	2 ♖d8

In no. 82 the key 1 ♖e8 prepares the way for four different subsequent manoeuvres by White, dependent on Black's reply. If 1...c1♘, then 2 ♕e7 puts Black in zugzwang, for 3 ♕e2 can be played after the knight has moved. If

1...c1♛ or 1...c1♜, White plays 2 ♜ce5, and then 3 ♜e1. 1...♚c1 forces 2 ♜d8, which threatens 3 ♛xd2, and if 2...d1♛+, 3 ♛xd1. Finally 1...c1♝ allows a continuation unrelated to the doubling found in the other variations: 2 ♝e4. This has to be played to avoid stalemate. Black then moves his king to e1 or e2, and White mates with 3 ♝c2. A white **critical** move – here 1 ♜d8 – followed by white interference to avoid stalemate – here 2 ♝e4 – is known as an **Indian**. In addition to the Indian, this problem contains two **Turtons** and a **pericritical** Turton.

Dresden

The Dresden is a three- or more-move theme consisting of the following. In the diagram position, if White made a certain threat, a black piece X would have an adequate defence. White therefore plays in such a way that Black is obliged to replace this defence by another, by piece Y, which will, however, let in a new weakness. The idea is clearly illustrated by no. 83.

Black's defence substitution may be carried out by any piece: the one that makes the original defence (termed the *Palitsch-Dresden*), the one giving the new defence (the *Brunner-Dresden*), or a third unit (this has no special name). In no. 83 Black's adequate defence by piece X is prevented and an inadequate defence by piece Y introduced through the move of another unit.

83

DRESDEN

E.Zepler
4th prize, *Dresdener Anzeiger* 1927
Mate in three

Try 1 ♛g2? (>2 ♛g8) ♜g4!
Try 1 ♛a2? (>2 ♜xa7) ♜a4!
Key 1 ♛f2! (>2 ♛g1 ... 3 ♛g8)
...   f4 2 ♛g2 ♜g5 3 ♛xc6
       b4 2 ♛a2 ♜a5 3 ♛g8

In fact, the Dresden idea is doubled here. If White were to try 1 ♛g2? (>2 ♛g8), Black would have the reply 1...♜g4!. Similarly, 1 ♛a2? (>2 ♜xa7) fails to 1...♜a4!. White therefore first plays 1 ♛f2! (>2 ♛g1), and of course 1...♜g4 is answered by 2 ♛/♜xa7. Black's thematic defences are 1...f4 and 1...b4, which allow the ♜d5 to defend against White's third-move threat 3 ♛g8 with 2...♜g5 and 2...♜b5 respectively. However, 1...f4 cuts out the defence 2...♖g4, so that White may continue 2 ♕g2. Black's new defence against the threat of 3 ♕g8 is 2...♖g5, but this move, unlike 2...♖g4, contains a weakness: the line g2-c6 is now open, and White can thus play 3 ♕xc6. Much the same thing happens on the other side of the board. 1...b4 prevents 2...♖a4, which means that 2 ♕a2 is now playable. The substitute defence 2...♖a5 contains a line-opening weakness analogous to that found in the first variation, for White can now mate with 3 ♕g8.

Most composers on the European continent insist on the presence of thematic tries to underline the logic of the Dresden idea, as is the case with the **Roman**, a closely related theme. However, the same arrangement of substitute defences by different pieces can be shown – and understood – without the tries.

84

DRESDEN

L.I.Loshinsky
2nd prize, Galitsky Memorial Tourney
1963-4
Mate in three

Key 1 ♘g7   (>2 ♘f5)
...   ♖c3 2 gxf3 ♖c4 3 ♕d7
             ♘c3 2 ♗b6 ♘e4 ♕e6
             ♗c3 2 ♗xb5 ♗d4 3 ♕xf3

The tries in no. 84 ought to be the three thematic white second moves, but in fact none of these can introduce a threat until after the key has been made. What is needed is an alternative way of considering the logic of the solution. After 1 ♘g7, why will 2 gxf3 not work as a threat? Because of 2...♘c3!, which prevents 3 ♕e4. Why will 2 ♗b6 not do? Because 2...♗c3! stops 3 ♕d4. Finally, what is wrong with 2 ♗xb5? The answer is that 3 ♕c4 is no use after 2...♖c3!. White's real threat is 2 ♘f5 (>3 ♘xe7). The three black moves just examined are in fact defences against this threat, each allowing one of the continuations mentioned. 1...♖c3 prevents Black from playing 2...♘c3, which means that 2 gxf3 can now be played. The substitute defence is 2...♖c4, a self-block allowing 3 ♕d7. 1...♘c3 rules out 2...♗c3 as a defence, so 2 ♗b6 is now playable. Again the substitute defence is a self-block: 2...♘e4, permitting 3 ♕e6. Finally 1...♗c3 obstructs the rook and prevents 2...♖c3. So White can continue 2 ♗xb5, and once more self-block is the weakness of the substitute defence: 2...♗d4 3 ♕xf3. This fine problem incidentally illustrates *cyclic obstruction*, and may thus be compared with no. 78. (However, no. 78 is not a Dresden: the black units simply get in each other's way, without introducing substitute defences.)

Dual

A white choice of mating move in a two-mover, or of continuation in a three- or more-mover, is termed a dual, the word covering triples, quadruples and other multiple choices. A dual is held to be serious if it follows a thematic black move, or an otherwise interesting or intelligent one, or one that defeats White's threat. This is particularly the case if the continuations or mates are not separately forced by other black moves. Some problemists regard duals arising in a block position as more serious than those which occur in a threat-problem. Duals arising when Black makes an unintelligent move (e.g. one that fails to defeat the threat) are of little importance, and there must be few composers who would bother to add extra force to prevent them.

Duals were formerly divided into two types, *major* and *minor*. A 'major dual' occurred when at least one of the choice of continuations or mates was not otherwise forced by Black, while the term 'minor dual' was applied to a choice of otherwise forced continuations or mates. This distinction, observed nowadays by only a very few composers, has been superseded by the division into 'serious' and 'harmless' outlined above.

Dual Avoidance

A black move may create a certain weakness and thereby seem to allow White a choice between two possible mates (or continuations in a three- or more-mover). However, this same black move may have an additional effect, advantageous to Black, which prevents one of the two mates or continuations, forcing White to pick his move with care.

Consider the black defence 1...♘xc6 in no. 85. (The key is 1 ♗g3, and the threat 2 ♕h5.) By blocking c6, Black appears to allow White to mate either by 2 ♔c3 (a **white-interference** mate) or by 2 ♖cd2. But because c6 has been blocked by a knight, 2 ♖cd2 is excluded on account of 2...♘d4!. Therefore only 2 ♔c3 will work, and the dual mate has been avoided.

This ingenious problem in fact has six dual-avoidance variations, paired in such a way that the white mate avoided in one variation is the one which must be played in another. We have seen that 1...♘xc6 forces 2 ♔c3, eliminating 2 ♖cd2. A further self-block on c6, 1...♕xc6, prevents 2 ♔c3? and allows only 2 ♖cd2. There are pairs of self-blocks on d6 and e6 as well: if a rook were to block d6, White could choose between 2 ♖e5 and 2 f4. 1...♘xd6

85

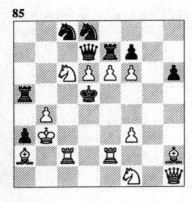

**DUAL AVOIDANCE
(SELF-BLOCKS)**

M.Myllyniemi
Die Schwalbe 1955
Mate in two

Key 1 ♗g3	(>2 ♕h5)
... ♘xc6	2 ♔c3 (not 2 ♖cd2?)
♕xc6	2 ♖cd2 (not 2 ♔c3?)
♘xd6	2 ♖e5 (not 2 f4?)
♕xd6	2 f4 (not 2 ♖e5?)
♘xe6	2 ♘e3 (not 2 ♖ed2?)
♕xe6	2 ♖ed2 (not 2 ♘e3?)

forces 2 ♖e5 (if 2 f4?, 2...♘e4!), while 1...♕xd6 allows only 2 f4 (2 ♖e5? ♕xe5!). A pawn blocking e6 would enable White to play either 2 ♘e3 or 2 ♖ed2. But 1...♘xe6 cuts out 2 ♖ed2? (2...♘d4!), while 1...♕xe6 eliminates 2 ♘e3? (2...♕xe3!).

86

DUAL AVOIDANCE

G.Latzel
1st prize, *Chess* 1948
Mate in two

Key 1 ♗c6	(>2 ♘f3)
... ♘d5	2 ♖c4 (not 2 ♕g7?)
d5	2 ♕g7 (not 2 ♖c4?)
♗d5	2 ♘xf5 (not 2 ♕g7?)
♖d5	2 ♘b3 (not 2 ♖c4?)

No. 86 presents a rather more complex dual-avoidance scheme. The key, 1 ♗c6, threatens 2 ♘f3, and Black can defend by playing any one of four units to d5, to cut White's control of e4. If a unit with no powers at all arrived on d5, White could choose between 2 ♕g7 (exploiting the interference with the ♖b5) and 2 ♖c4 (exploiting the interference with the ♗e6). 1...♘d5 allows only 2 ♖c4 (2 ♕g7? ♘f6!), while 2 ♕g7 follows 1...d5 (2 ♖c4? dxc4!). This pair of dual-avoidance variations is not unlike those of the previous example, except that here White exploits interference rather than self-block. Black's two other defences are also a pair, but of a different type, for here the dual avoided in one variation does not appear as the mate in the other. 1...♗d5 seems to allow 2 ♕g7 again, but in fact the bishop has opened the line of guard of the ♖d8 to e5. So 2 ♕g7? would fail to 2...♖e5!, and White must instead exploit the new error, unguard of f5 combined with interference, mating by 2 ♘xf5. After 1...♖d5 it looks as if 2 ♖c4? ought to be possible, but the rook has opened the queen's line of guard to c4. So White can only play 2 ♘b3, again exploiting the unguard plus interference.

Occasionally one comes across a problem in which dual mates that are avoided never occur at all, in any variation. Such dual avoidance is described as *total*, whereas the type examined so far, with avoided mates appearing in other variations, is known as *partial* dual avoidance.

87

TOTAL DUAL AVOIDANCE

J.Buchwald
Version, 3rd prize, *Christian Science Monitor* 1946
Mate in two

Key 1 ♖b4	(>2 c5)
... ♗xa3	2 ♕xc3 (2 ♗xc3?)
♘c6	2 ♕d5 (2 ♖d5?)
♘xe5	2 ♗e3 (2 ♕e3?)

Total dual avoidance is seen in no. 87. 1 ♖b4 threatens 2 c5. Each of the defences 1...♗xa3, 1...♘c6 and 1...♘xe5 appears to allow two mates, by unguarding a mating square. But in each case one of the two mates is prevented because the defending piece opens a black line to pin one of White's potential mating units. After 1...♗xa3 White could reply 2 ♗xc3 or 2 ♕xc3, were it not for the fact that the bishop is now pinned. Similarly 1...♘c6 permits only 2 ♕d5, 2 ♖d5? being impossible on account of the pin, and after 1...♘xe5 White has only 2 ♗e3 and not also 2 ♕e3?. The avoided mates are never allowed to occur.

In each of these problems the dual avoidance arises through some positive action on Black's part: his moves contain not only a weakness but also a compensating element to restrict White's choice of mate to a single move. Such strategy is usually referred to as *active dual avoidance*, to distinguish it from the *passive* variety, exemplified by no. 88.

Here Black's defence has no positive effect whatever, but White must nonetheless choose his mate with care so as not to annul the error of the black

88

PASSIVE DUAL AVOIDANCE

C.Mansfield
1st prize, Schiffmann Memorial
Tourney 1931
Mate in two

Key 1 ♘d5   (>2 ♘c3)
    ...   ♕xe5   2 ♘f4 (2 ♘e7?)
                 ♕xg4   2 ♘ge7 (2 ♘gf4?)
                 ♕xg6   2 ♗e6

move. 1 ♘d5 threatens 2 ♘c3, and Black defends by self-pinning his queen on e5 and g4. In mating, White must regain control of the new flight d5, and this can be done only by means of 2 ♘ge7 and 2 ♘gf4. If Black plays 1...♕xe5, 2 ♘e7? fails because it has the effect of unpinning the black queen who has just obligingly pinned herself. Therefore only 2 ♘f4 will work. In the analogous variation, 1...♕xg4 allows only 2 ♘ge7, since after 2 ♘gf4? the black queen is again mobile. Black himself does nothing to affect White's choice of mate, beyond self-pinning the queen to enable the mates to function at all. His rôle is negative, and the dual avoidance is therefore passive. A further queen self-pin, 1...♕xg6, is followed by 2 ♗e6: no dual avoidance here. More examples of dual avoidance will be found under **Herpai**, **Java**, **Mari** and **Stocchi**.

Duel

In no. 89 the white bishop battles for supremacy over the black rook. Four tries by the bishop up the long diagonal fail because White has no tempo-move available. White might, for instance, try 1 ♗d4? (>2 ♕d1+ ♔a2 3 ♕c2+ ♔a3 4 ♗c5+ ♖b4 5 ♕b1 ♔a4 6 ♕xb4). But Black replies by occupying b4 with the rook on his first move, so that 4 ♗c5? for White would bring about stalemate. The same happens if the bishop plays to e5, f6 or g7: the rook occupies b6, b7 and b8 respectively. The key is therefore 1 ♗h8!, which waits until Black has decided where to put his rook. Once the rook has committed itself, the bishop knows where to go: 1...♖b8 2 ♗g7!, and the rook must now unguard f8, to which the bishop can play on move 5: 2...♖~b 3 ♕d1+ ♔a2 4 ♕c2+ ♔a3 5 ♗g8+ ♖b4 6 ♕b1 ♔a4 7 ♕xb4. The other variations work in the same way: 1...♖b7 2 ♗f6!; 1...♖b6 2 ♗e5!; 1...♖b5 2 ♗d4!. So the duel originates in the try-play, where the rook chooses its move

89

DUEL

F.Davidenko
Special prize, *Shakhmaty v SSSR* 1987
Mate in seven
Try 1 ♗d4? ♖b5!
Try 1 ♗e5? ♖b6!
Try 1 ♗f6? ♖b7!
Try 1 ♗g7? ♖b8!
Key 1 ♗h8! (zugzwang) ♖b8 2 ♗g7
♖~b 3 ♕d1+ ♔a2 4 ♕c2+ ♔a3 5 ♗f8+
♖b4 6 ♕b1 ♔a4 7 ♕xb4
     ...   ♖b7   2 ♗f6 (5 ♗e7+)
           ♖b6   2 ♗e5 (5 ♗d6+)
           ♖b5   2 ♗d4 (5 ♗c5+)

according to where the bishop may be, and is carried over into the post-key play, where, thanks to the waiting key, the rôles are reversed: now the bishop can make the choice in accordance with the rook's arrival square. Duels are a not uncommon feature of longer problems, as well as being frequently encountered in endgame studies, but it is rare to find a problem where the duel is seen in both pre-key and post-key play, and a miniature at that. Incidentally, this problem also illustrates the *Vladimirov* theme (→ **Reversal themes**): White's try A is refuted by defence a; after the key, 1...a allows 2 A. Here we have three further tries in addition, each with the same effect.

Echo

90

CHAMELEON ECHO

Y.G.Vladimirov
Sovietsky Sport 1985
Mate in four

Key 1 ♖a2 zugzwang
  ... ♔c3 2 ♔f4 ♔d4 3 ♗b4 ♔xd3 4 ♖d2
     ♔xd3 2 ♗g7 ♔e4 3 ♗c4 ♔e3 4 ♖e2
     ♔e3 2 ♗b4 ♔d4 3 ♔f4 ♔xd3 4 ♖d2
     ♔e5 2 ♖a4 ♔f6 3 ♖f4+ ♔e5 4 d4

The excellent flight-giving key of no. 90, 1 ♖a2, sets up a block position, waiting for Black to commit himself. 1...♚c3 allows the continuation 2 ♔f4, and if now 2...♚d4, White hems in the black king with 3 ♗b4, followed (after 3...♚xd3) by 4 ♖d2#. We should study this mating position carefully: the squares c3 and d2 are held by the ♗b4, while the white king guards e3 and e4. The mating piece, the rook, holds d4, and the other bishop controls c4. Now let us see what happens if Black answers 1 ♖a2 with 1...♚xd3. White's second move is 2 ♗g7, and if now 2...♚e4, 3 ♗c4 ♚e3 4 ♖e2#. (In both lines of play, Black's second and third moves can be interchanged without affecting White's continuations.) Compare this second position with the one we have already examined: the ♗c4 guards the squares d3 and e2, the white king holds f3 and f4, the mating unit controls e4, and d4 is held by the other bishop. In other words, the second position reproduces, or *echoes*, the first position one file to the right. An echo where the black king is on a square of a different colour, as here, is known as a *chameleon echo*. This fine, clear-cut problem is completed by two further full-length lines of play, one of which ends in a pretty mate by the pawn: 1...♚e5 2 ♖a4 3 ♔f6 3 ♖f4+ ♚e5 4 d4.

Economy

'In der Beschränkung zeigt sich erst der Meister' (Goethe, *Natur und Kunst*).

The famous German poet was certainly not referring to economy in the chess problem when he wrote: 'The Master only reveals himself in restraint.' However, the principle applies. The finest chess problems, by the greatest masters of the art, are usually those where the idea or theme is shown with the greatest economy.

Different composers will have different views on what exactly is the most important feature of economy. The composers of the **Bohemian School**, for example, held that economy of mating forces should be the main aim. The result is that their problems have relatively few white units, and the mates are **models** or near-models. The New-German School, on the other hand, under the influence of J.Kohtz (1843-1918), considered that *purity of aim* (German *Zweckreinheit*) was all-important: there should be no extraneous elements to confuse the logic of the problem's play. This principle is discussed more fully under **Logical problem**.

Closely allied to purity of aim is what might be termed *economy of motivation*. This is a principle that has greater importance in some fields of chess problems than in others. Many composers of strategic three- and more-movers place emphasis on why certain white and/or black moves are played in preference to others. It is all-important that the reasons which the composer has planned really determine the thematic moves, so that they are not fixed by other factors. There are two books in which this concept is treated in some detail. One is an anthology of the work of Professor R.C.O.Matthews, entitled *Mostly Three-Movers* (Editions feenschach-phénix, 1995). The distinguished British expert Robin Matthews sets great store by economy of motivation, though he does not use this term himself, and the book reveals how he has applied the principle in his problems. The second book is all about **helpmates**: *Black to Play (Schwarz am Zug)*, by C.J.Feather, in English and German, published by F.Chlubna (Vienna) in 1994. The reason why, in the solution of a helpmate, a certain move works and another move does not interests the author much more than the strategy the move displays (e.g. interference, unpin, etc.). Chris Feather is likewise an expert in his field, and the book makes fascinating reading.

Other principles of economy in the chess problem concern time, space, play and force. A problem should not take three moves to say what can just as well be expressed in two. The Grimshaw, for example, is a two-move theme. It is possible to extend it to three moves by introducing some element which will delay the mate for a move, but this will not make it into a genuine three-move theme. Interference between unlike-moving pieces is common enough in three-movers, but interference between like-moving pieces (e.g. **Holzhausen, Wurzburg-Plachutta, Anti-Bristol**) is thematically more interesting and often more successful, because such interference lies outside the scope of the two-mover. A *built-up two-mover* is what it says it is: a three-mover showing a two-move theme with some uninteresting mate-delaying feature.

Economy of space is not easy to define, but it has to do with the way the chessboard is used. A problem position should ideally be as open as possible: ugly clusters of pieces, especially strings of pieces along a single rank, file or diagonal, should be avoided, for an attractive, open setting will appeal to the solver much more readily than a cramped one. Only when a composer is aiming at some special effect will he produce settings like no. 151 (→ **Key**).

Problems whose construction does not conform with the principle of economy of play are for the most part inferior works, and as such find no place in this book. The **by-play** of a problem should arise naturally from the composer's setting: no extra pieces should be added to achieve it, although it might be admissible to replace, say, a black pawn by a black knight, or even a white pawn by a white knight, if an extra variation of some interest can thereby be gained. Unity of play is normally regarded as preferable to quantity of variations in the direct-mate problem; therefore **fringe** variations, bearing no thematic relationship to the rest of the play and only arising through the addition of force, should be avoided.

This brings us naturally to economy of force, for it is obvious that one of the fundamental conventions is that no force should be added to a position merely to create fringe variations. Every piece on the board must have at least one function, and if it can have more than one, so much the better. A white unit used to give mate in one variation should, where possible, guard a black king-flight in another. A black unit added to prevent a **dual** might also serve to shield the white king from check, or to stop a crucial pin of a white piece. In general, economy of white force is more important than that of black force. So a serious dual, or a **cook**, will be stopped by a black pawn rather than by a white one (if the choice arises), one piece will be used instead of two, and so on. If the white queen has to be used where a rook would do just as well (e.g. if there are two rooks on the board already and a third is needed to pin a black piece), the composer will try to arrange for the queen's diagonal power to be used in some way, for example in giving mate in the by-play (but better to use the white queen as a rook only than to add lots of force just to give her something else to do). In a helpmate the composer should strive to ensure that all the white units on the board (other than king and pawns) play some part in each mate.

The process known as 'dressing the board' (i.e. adding pieces to the position solely to increase the difficulty of the problem – 'camouflage pieces') was very popular among the earliest composers, but is not considered appropriate nowadays. Every unit on the board must have some part to play in the composer's idea or theme, and preferably more than just a tiny part. In problems with two or more phases (those with set or virtual play or both), it is desirable that all the force should be used in some way in the play that follows the key. This is not always possible, however, and solvers and critics should be prepared to accept without prejudice positions in which this ideal is not achieved. A problem such as the astonishing nine-phase task no. 270 amply demonstrates the need for a broad-minded attitude to the question of force which plays no part in the key and post-key variations. Such force in no way 'dresses the board': it is an integral part of the problem, and if properly used, commits no offence against the principle of economy of force.

Excelsior

Excelsior is the name given (by Sam Loyd) to a pawn, white or black, standing on its game-array square in the diagram, which marches down the board and promotes in the course of the problem's solution.

Such a pawn is on e2 in no. 91. Where it stands, it blocks the line e4–e1, so allowing Black a refutation to the try 1 ♖e4? (1...♞e1!). The opening moves clear this line: 1 e4 ♞b4/♞d4/♞e3/♞e1 2 e5+ ♞c2. Now 3 ♖e4 is playable,

91

EXCELSIOR

O.Yefrosinin and A.P.Grin
1st prize, *Mat-Pat* 1987
Mate in ten
Try 1 ♖e4? ♘e1!
Key 1 e4! ♘~ 2 e5+ ♘c2 3 ♖e4 ♘xa3
4 ♖a4+ ♘c2 5 ♖a6 bxa6 6 e6 a5
7 e7 a4 8 e8♖ a3 9 ♖e4 ♘~
10 ♖ex♘
(3 ♖a6? bxa6 4 e6 a5 5 e7 a4 6 e8♖
stalemate!)

and Black's best reply is 3...♘xa3 (other knight-moves lead to immediate mate). White must now ensure that Black has moves available after the knight has been pinned on c2 again: 4 ♖a4+ ♘c2 5 ♖a6!. There are now four moves for the black a-pawn, just enough to allow the e-pawn to promote on move 8. However, there is a further surprise for the solver: promotion to queen will lead to stalemate, so only 8 e8♖! will work. Mate then follows in two more moves: 8...a3 9 ♖e4 ♘~ 10 ♖ex♘. Replacement of a sacrificed piece by promotion to a piece of the same type is known as the *Phoenix* theme. Notice that if White were to play his rook to a6 too early (e.g. on move 3), stalemate would ensue even with a rook-promotion, for the ♙a3 would leave the black a-pawn blocked one move too soon.

Fairy Chess

Nearly all the problems in this book are direct-mates: White, moving first, forces mate in a stipulated number of moves. Such problems, using only the six standard units and a normal board, are *orthodox*. Any problem which does not conform with the conventions of orthodox chess is an illustration of Fairy Chess, a vast and potentially limitless offshoot of the normal game. Here are some of the ways in which a fairy chess problem may differ from an orthodox one:

1) The problem may be a **selfmate**, or a **helpmate**, rather than a direct mate. Nowadays, these forms are also regarded as 'orthodox'. Other possible modifications to the conventional direct-mate stipulation include stalemate, **reflex-mate**, and **series-movers**.

2) The problem may contain new pieces, unknown in orthodox chess and with movements different from those of the standard units (e.g. **Grasshopper, Nightrider, Chinese pieces**).

3) The properties of the board may be altered: it may be reduced or increased in size, or converted into, e.g., a **cylinder** or **grid-board**.

4) The rules of play may be changed. The reader is referred to the entries under **Andernach chess**, **Circe**, **Madrasi** and **Maximummer** for a treatment of just four of the huge number of possibilities.

5) The solver may be required to determine from the diagram position whether castling, or an *en passant* capture, is possible or not, or what the last move was or whether the position is legal or illegal; or it may be necessary to determine all the moves of the hypothetical game leading to the diagram position (see **Proof games**). Solving of this sort requires **retrograde analysis**. Sometimes the solution of an otherwise orthodox problem may also involve such analysis.

6) The problem may be a *construction task*, a tour de force of constructional ingenuity, in which the composer aims at a record number of, e.g., possible captures, checks, mates, stalemates, stalemate-releases, etc.

Fairy chess was popularised in Britain by Thomas Rayner Dawson (1889-1951), one of the most brilliant creative minds of the chess problem world. He was for many years editor of the problem section of the *British Chess Magazine*, and also of the *Fairy Chess Review*, and many of Dawson's inventions first appeared in one of these two periodicals. He was also President of the British Chess Problem Society from 1931 to 1943. His handbook of fairy chess, *Caissa's Wild Roses* (1935), gives a full survey of the extent of the genre as known at the time.

Fleck Theme

White's key may carry more than one threat. Usually double-threats, triple-threats, etc., are regarded as blemishes, but there are certain problem ideas that depend for their effect on multiple threats. The Fleck theme is one of these. The idea is that each one of at least three white threats shall be forced separately, and singly, by Black. No. 92 is an illustration, in which no fewer than seven threats are uniquely forced, in turn, by all the moves available to Black.

If only some of Black's moves force a single threat, we speak of a *partial Fleck*; this one, however, is *total*, because only one threat will work whatever Black plays, and each of them appears at some point. If Black were to forgo his right to move, all seven threats would be playable, for they are *primary threats*. So the problem illustrates the *primary Fleck* theme.

No. 93 is an example of the *secondary Fleck* theme. (A full analysis of the concept of secondary play may be found under **Correction**.) A white mate permitted by the random move of a black unit – a move away from a square,

92

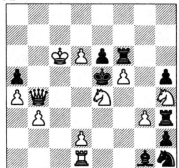

PRIMARY FLECK (SEVENFOLD THREAT SEPARATION)

P.Overkamp
2nd prize, Dutch Jubilee Tourney 1951-2
Mate in two

Key 1 ♘f2
  (>2 ♕e4/♕f4/♘d3/♖e1/♕c5/♕c3/d4)
...	♖xg3	2 ♕e4
	♘xf2	2 ♕f4
	♘xg3	2 ♘d3
	exf5	2 ♖e1
	♖xh4	2 ♕c5
	♖f~	2 ♕c3
	axb4	2 d4

SECONDARY FLECK

93

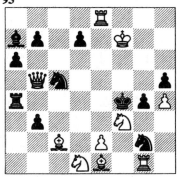

O.Stocchi
1st prize, *Christian Science Monitor*
1953
Mate in two
Key 1 ♘h2   (>2 ♖f1)
...	♘g~	2 ♗d2/♗g3/e3
	♘xh4	2 ♗d2
	♘e3	2 ♗g3
	♘xe1	2 e3
	♘c~	2 ♕f5/♕e5/♕g5
	♘e6	2 ♕f5
	♘e4	2 ♕e5
	♘d3	2 ♕g5

without any specific arrival effect – is known as a *secondary threat*. The secondary Fleck theme involves the accurate separation of three or more secondary threats by the moves of a single black piece. After the key, 1 ♘h2, of no. 93 the black ♘g2, moving at random, would allow White to mate by 2 ♗d2, 2 ♗g3 and e3. However, the knight must in fact arrive somewhere; it cannot merely hang in the air. These three white mates are forced in turn according to the knight's arrival square: 1...♘xh4 2 ♗d2 only; 1...♘e3 2 ♗g3 only; and 1...♘xe1 2 e3 only.

A similar arrangement is found after the three moves of the other black knight. 1...♘c~ seems to permit 2 ♕e5, 2 ♕f5 and 2 ♕g5. The knight's arrivals on e4, e6 and d3 force each of these replies in turn. The composer has had to use black pawns to 'plug' a6, b7 and d7 to prevent the knight from arriving on these squares. Without these plugs, the secondary Fleck introduced by the knight would be only partial.

94

PROGRESSIVE SEPARATION

J.Hartong
1st prize, *Il Due Mosse* Theme Tourney
1953
Mate in two
Key 1 ♕c7 (>2 ♕xd7)
   ... ♘b8   2 ♕e5/♕f7/♕h7/♕c5/♕a5
       ♘c5   2 ♕e5/♕f7/♕h7/♕c5
       ♘b6   2 ♕e5/♕f7/♕h7
      ♘xf8   2 ♕e5/♕f7
       ♘e5   2 ♕xe5
       ♘f6   2 ♘g7

No. 94 shows a curious type of secondary threat-separation scheme known as *progressive separation*. The key 1 ♕c7 threatens 2 ♕xd7. A random move by the ♘d7 (1...♘b8) allows five secondary threats to operate: 2 ♕e5, 2 ♕f7, 2 ♕h7, 2 ♕c5 and 2 ♕a5. After 1...♘c5 the first four of these will work, but the fifth, 2 ♕a5, is prevented. 1...♘b6 prevents both 2 ♕a5 and 2 ♕c5, but permits the other three. Only two mates, 2 ♕e5 and 2 ♕f7, follow the defence 1...♘xf6, while 1...♘e5 allows only 2 ♕e5. The number of mates available to White is progressively reduced, and once a mate has been eliminated from the sequence it never reappears. The final black knight-move, 1...♘f6, prevents all the secondary threats and allows 2 ♘g7.

An equally strange form of secondary threat-separation is seen in no. 95. White's threat of 2 ♕xd4, introduced by the key 1 ♗g1, is defeated by any move of the ♘d4. 1...♘b5 allows three secondary threats: 2 ♘b4 (A), 2 ♘f4 (B) and 2 ♕g2 (C). Six of the knight's other moves allow all possible combinations of these threats: A+B (after 1...♘f3), A+C (1...♘e6) and B+C (1...♘c6); A only (1...♘e2), B only (1...♘c2) and C only (1...♘f5). Such an arrangement is called *combinative separation*. As in the example of progressive separation above (no. 94), there is one knight-move that introduces a new mate, thereby completing the black knight-wheel: 1...♘xb3 2 ♕x⊃3.

95

COMBINATIVE SEPARATION

N.A.Macleod
Hon. mention, *American Chess Bulletin*
1954
Mate in two
Key 1 ♗g1   (>2 ♕xd4)
...   ♘b5 2 ♘b4/♘f4/♕g2 (ABC)
      ♘f3 2 ♘b4/♘f4   (AB)
      ♘e6 2 ♘b4/♕g2   (AC)
      ♘c6 2 ♘f4/♕g2   (BC)
      ♘e2 2 ♘b4   (A)
      ♘c2 2 ♘f4   (B)
      ♘f5 2 ♕g2   (C)
      ♘xb3 2 ♕xb3

Flight

A flight, or flight-square, is a square to which the black king has access. The more mobile the black king, the harder is White's task, for in mating it may be necessary to arrange an attack on two or more squares (the square where the king stands, and also his flight or flights) rather than merely one. After the king has moved to his flight, White's mate will need to cover both the king's original square and his new square.

Solvers usually enjoy problems featuring flights, as the play and mates are often made the more interesting by their very existence. Many problems in this book show flights as an incidental feature, combined with other, often unrelated, strategy. In nos. 96 and 97, however, the flights are thematised.

In the diagram position of no. 96, mates are set for all of the black king's moves: 1...♔d6 2 d8♕; 1...♔f6 2 f8♕; 1...♔d8 2 ♕g5; and 1...♔f8 2 ♕c5. When the king has access, as here, to his four diagonal flights, we speak of *star-flights*. *Plus-flights* is the term used if the king can move to all four orthogonal flights. The harmless-looking key of this problem, 1 ♕e4 (-), has the radical effect of changing the reply to each of Black's four king-moves: 1...♔d6 2 f8♕; 1...♔f6 2 d8♕; 1...♔d8 2 ♕h4; 1...♔f8 2 ♕b4. The changes following the king's moves to d8 and f8 are of a type known as *concurrent*: the queen merely mates on a different square but on the same line in relation to the black king. Such changes are held to be slightly inferior to a more complete alteration of the mating position. But this small drawback is more than counter-balanced in this problem by the character of the other two

96

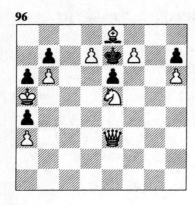

STAR-FLIGHTS (RECIPROCAL CHANGE)

J.Kiss
1st prize, Hungarian Problemists'
Theme Tourney 1942
Mate in two

Set	1...	♚d6	2 d8♕
		♚f6	2 f8♕
		♚d8	2 ♕g5
		♚f8	2 ♕c5
Key	1 ♕e4 zugzwang		
	...	♚d6	2 f8♕
		♚f6	2 d8♕
		♚d8	2 ♕h4
		♚f8	2 ♕b4

changes, which is of great interest. The mate which follows 1...♚d6 in the set play appears after 1...♚f6 in the post-key play, while the one set for 1...♚f6 recurs after 1...♚d6 following the key. Such an interchange of mating moves between two variations is known as *reciprocal change*, a thematic device to which composers have paid a great deal of attention. More examples will be found under **Reciprocal play**.

In the diagram position of no. 97 the black king has no flights at all. White's two tries and the key give him two in each case, in different pairings. The try 1 ♕a5? (>2 ♕xd5) gives flights on e6 and d4: 1...♚xe6 2 ♖e7; and 1...♚d4 2 ♕c3. However, 1...♕xg3! (set with the mate 2 ♗xg3) refutes this try. 1 ♘c5? (>2 ♘d7) gives d4 again and also f6 this time: 1...♚d4 2 ♘c2; 1...♚xf6 2 h8♕; and 1...♕xg3 2 ♘d3. But this try fails to 1...♕xe3!. The key 1 ♘d6! (>2 ♘g4) allows the black king to escape to f6 and e6: 1...♚xf6 2 ♘xd5; 1...♚xe6 2 ♘f7. The two queen-defences yield new mates: 1.. ♕xg3 2 ♘xd5; and 1...♕xe3 2 ♖xe3. This finely conceived problem, with its cycle of black king-flights, was unlucky not to be placed much higher in the third International Composing Match 1986-8 (W.C.C.T. = World Chess Compositions Tournament).

The expert composer will often incorporate a flight into his matrix, if the basic idea allows it. This is not in order to make things difficult for himself, but because the presence of a flight can add piquancy to the thematic play and provide an additional element of interest for the solver. It can also be of value in that most awkward of the composer's tasks: getting the problem sound!

97

FLIGHTS

M.Mladenović
8th place, 3rd W.C.C.T. 1986-8
Mate in two

Set	1...	♛xg3	2 ♗xg3
Try	1 ♛a5?		(>2 ♛xd5)
	...	♚xe6	2 ♖e7
		♚d4	2 ♛c3
		♛xg3!	
Try	1 ♘c5?		(>2 ♘d7)
	...	♚d4	2 ♘c2
		♚xf6	2 h8♛
		♛xg3	2 ♘d3
		♛xe3!	
Key	1 ♘d6!		(>2 ♘g4)
	...	♚xf6	2 ♘xd5
		♚xe6	2 ♘f7
		♛xg3	2 ♘xd5
		♛xe3	2 ♖xe3

Focal Effects

A black line-piece guarding potential mating squares in at least two different directions is said to *focus* those squares, which themselves are the *foci*, or focal points. Focal effects in the two-mover are at their most interesting when White apparently has a number of different ways of taking advantage of the fact that the black line-piece in question cannot retain its guard on more than one focal point at a time (as in no. 98), or else when White tries to disrupt Black's focal control of two squares (as in no. 99).

In no. 98 White has three tries which each introduce a pair of mates to follow the moves of the ♗g5 to north-west or south-west. 1 ♘h5? fails to 1...♗e7!, because 2 ♘f4? would allow 2...♚xe5!. Similarly 1 ♘f5? fails to 1...♗f4! (2 ♘e7? ♚xe5!). Nor is 1 ♘g4? any use, because of 1...♗xc1!, acquiring a flight (c6) over which White cannot regain control. The key, 1 ♘g6!, introduces a fourth pair of mates in reply to the bishop's moves. In the four phases the actual foci (White's mating squares) are four different pairs of squares. Two by-play variations involving mates by the white queen complete the play of this fine work.

98

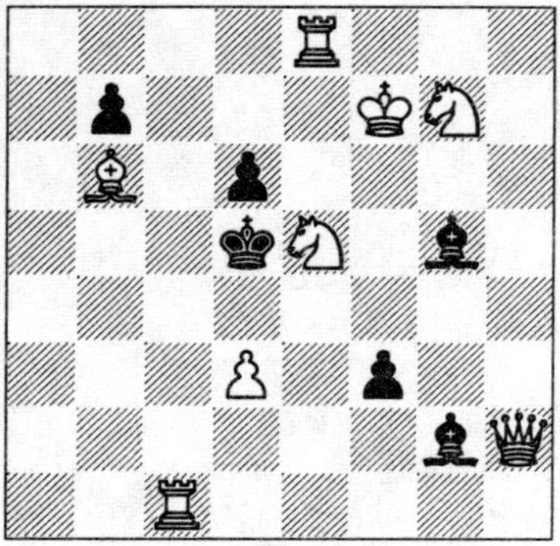

FOCAL EFFECTS (ZAGORUIKO)

N.A.Macleod
American Chess Bulletin 1961
Mate in two
Try 1 ♘h5?

...	♗d2	2 ♘f6
	♗d8	2 ♘f4
	♗e7!	

Try 1 ♘f5?

...	♗d2	2 ♘e7
	♗d8	2 ♘e3
	♗f4!	

Try 1 ♘g4?

...	♗d2	2 ♘f6
	♗d8	2 ♘e3
	♗xc1!	

Key 1 ♘g6!   zugzwang

...	♗d2	2 ♘e7
	♗d8	2 ♘f4
	(f2	2 ♕xg2)
	(♗h1	2 ♕a2)

The point of no. 99 (see diagram on page 105) lies in the tries, which aim to interrupt one of the two focal guards of the black line-pieces, queen and rook. 1 ♗c3? threatens 2 ♗b3, but Black refutes by pinning the white bishop with 1...♖f1!. 1 ♗d6?, cutting the queen's guard of c5, threatens 2 ♘c5, but fails to 1...cxd6!. 1 ♗f6? threatens an analogous mate on the other side of the black king, 2 ♘g5, but is refuted by 1...♕xf6!. The key cuts the guard-line of the black rook to f5: 1 ♗f4! (>2 ♕f5). In each phase Black can defend against the threat in other ways, but in so doing abandons one of his crucial focal guards, thereby letting in a white mate. International Master of Composition Barry Barnes is one of Britain's most successful two-move composers, as well as being a dedicated worker in the cause of chess problems. His problems combine originality with an enviable constructional finesse.

As things stand in the diagram position of no. 100 (see diagram on page 106), the W♘f6 focuses the two potential squares d7 and g4, but these are currently guarded by the B♖d4, supported by the black queen. The paradoxical key, 1 ♘b6, giving two further flights, seems to cut the ♖a6 and ♗a7 out of the play (compare the key of no. 212, under **Paradox**). But the key has the positive effect of strengthening White's attack on the square d7 and introducing another potential mating square, c4, one which the black queen does not hold. The black rook, focusing squares in three directions, will now find itself seriously **overloaded**, as the threat 2 ♘fd7+ ♖xd7 3 ♘c4 proves.

99

FOCAL EFFECTS: SHUT-OFFS

B.P.Barnes
Die Schwalbe 1964
Mate in two

Try	1 ♗c3?	(>2 ♗b3)
	...	♖xc3	2 ♕f5
		♕c5	2 ♘xc5
		♕g5	2 ♘xg5
		♖f1!	

Try	1 ♗d6?	(>2 ♘c5)
	...	♕xd6	2 ♘g5
		♖f5	2 ♕xf5
		♖b3+	2 ♗xb3
		exd6!	

Try	1 ♗f6?	(>2 ♘g5)
	...	♕c5	2 ♘xc5
		♖f5	2 ♕xf5
		♖b3+	2 ♗xb3
		♕xf6!	

Key	1 ♗f4!	(>2 ♕f5)
	...	♖xf4	2 ♗b3
		♕c5	2 ♘xc5
		♕g5	2 ♘xg5
		f6	2 ♕xe7

Black's alternative second move in this threat line, 2...♔d6, leads to 3 ♘bd5, which reintroduces the shut-off pieces on the a-file. The defence 1...♖d6 releases control of c4: 2 ♘c4+ ♔f4 3 ♘fd5, a mate from the originally indirect battery on the f-file. (2...♔xe8 allows 3 ♖e8.) The third move of this variation is played as second move after 1...♔f4: 2 ♘fd5+ ♔e5 3 ♘bd7. 1...♕d3 weakens the guard on g4: 2 ♘bd7+ ♖xd7 (2...♔f4 3 ♘fd5) 3 ♘g4. 1...♕g4+ has the same effect, but of course 2 ♘g4 is forced, with 3 ♘bd5 to follow 2...♔d6 (and 3 ♘d7 to follow 2...♖xg4). If the king takes another flight, 1...♔d6, White plays 2 ♘bd5+, forcing the king back to e5, when 3 ♘fd7 is mate. The focal position of the black rook has been most skilfully used by the composer to bring about a six-point cycle of continuations and mates, as shown by the letters A-F beside the solution. The black defence 1...♔xe6 leads to several continuations, an insignificant point when viewed in the context of the play as a whole.

100

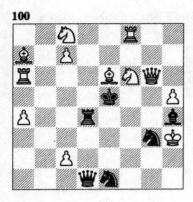

FOCAL EFFECTS + CYCLIC PLAY

J.M.Loustau
Die Schwalbe 1987
Mate in three

Key 1 ♘b6 (>2 ♘fd7+ ♖xd7 3 ♘c4	A-B
... ♚d6 3 ♘bd5	
...♖d6 2 ♘c4+ ♚f4 3 ♘fd5	B-C
... ♚xe6 3 ♖e8	
♚f4 2 ♘fd5+ ♚e5 3 ♘bd7	C-D
♕d3 2 ♘bd7+ ♖xd7 3 ♘g4	D-E
... ♚f4 3 ♘fd5	
♕g4+ 2 ♘xg4+ ♚d6 3 ♘bd5	E-F
... ♖xg4 3 ♘d7	
♚d6 2 ♘bd5+ ♚e5 3 ♘fd7	F-A
♖b4 2 ♘bd7+	
♕e2 2 ♘bd7+	

Four-Hands-Round

101

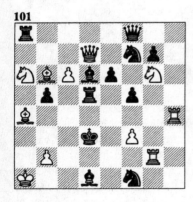

FOUR-HANDS-ROUND

N.G.G.van Dijk
Frederikborg Amts Avis 1957
Mate in two

Set 1...	♗e5	2 ♗xb5
	♖e5	2 ♘b4
Key 1 ♕xe6		(>2 ♕xd5)
...	♗c5	2 ♗xb5
	♖c5	2 ♘b4
	♗e5	2 ♕xf5
	♖e5	2 ♘f4

The reader should become familiar with the term **Grimshaw** (mutual interference between rook and bishop, or between pawn and bishop) in order to understand the arrangement known as Four-Hands-Round. This thematic idea consists of Grimshaw interferences on two squares, in which only one black rook and one black bishop take part. In other words, there are four variations, two in which the bishop interferes with the rook, and two where the rook interferes with the bishop. No. 101 shows the idea in the post-key play.

The Grimshaw interferences occur on c5 and e5. In this example the composer has ingeniously incorporated changed play of a rather unusual character. The black rook and bishop are **half-pinned** in the diagram position, and their set moves to e5 are followed by mates exploiting this half-pin. The key destroys these pin-mates, but the set mates now recur in answer to the moves of the bishop and rook to c5, rather than to e5 as previously. (Comparison may be made with the problems to be found under **Rukhlis**.)

102

FOUR-HANDS-ROUND

Tjoa Giok Hing
1st hon. mention, *Probleemblad* 1965
Mate in three

Key 1 ♕a7   (>2 ♖e1+ ♔d5 3 ♕a2)
    ...   ♗f6   2 ♗g6+ ♔xf4 3 ♗xd6
           ♖f6   2 ♖d4+ ♔f5 3 ♕xd7
           ♗d4   2 ♘d2+ ♔e3 3 ♕a3
           ♖d4   2 ♘c3+ ♔e3 3 ♖d3

No. 102 is a fine three-move rendering of Four-Hands-Round. The excellent withdrawal key 1 ♕a7 threatens 2 ♖e1+ ♔d5 3 ♕a2. Black defends by trying to obtain flights for his king, but each time he cuts a white line of guard, a black one is cut as well. White exploits the interferences in his second-move continuations, allowing the king a flight in each case. White's final move is then a pin-mate. 1...♗f6 allows 2 ♗g6+ ♔xf4 3 ♗xd6, while 1...♖f6 leads to 2 ♖d4+ ♔f5 3 ♕xd7. The Grimshaw interferences on d4 bring in the following play: 1...♗d4 2 ♘d2+ ♔e3 3 ♕a3; and 1...♖d4 2 ♘c3+ ♔e3 3 ♖d3.

Fringe Variation

A variation which is not part of a problem's principal theme and which is brought about by the addition of extra force is termed a fringe. Such variations are normally held to be an offence against the principles of **economy**.

Gamage Unpin

The key of no. 103, 1 ♖b4, threatens 2 ♖c3. If Black defends by playing 1...♗c5, White can mate by 2 ♕b5. This mating move is a Gamage unpin:

103

GAMAGE UNPINS

H.E.Funk
Good Companions 1923
(version by H.Knuppert)
Mate in two

Key 1 ♖b4 (>2 ♖c3)
...	♗c5	2 ♕b5
	♖e5	2 ♕h3
	♖c5	2 ♘xc5
	♗e5	2 ♗b5

the black bishop has interfered with the newly-pinned ♖d5, preventing it from capturing on b5. 1...♖e5 is a further Gamage unpin: 2 ♕h3 can be played, because 2...♗g3? has been ruled out by the black interference. The **half-pinned** position of Black's thematic pieces is an unusual feature; normally the piece which is unpinned by the mating move is completely pinned in the initial position.

Goethart Unpin

104

GOETHART UNPINS

C.Mansfield
Evening News 1933
Mate in two
Set 1...   ♘f3   2 ♘f2
             ♘e6   2 ♘c3
Key 1 ♘b3 (>2 ♘d4)
...	♘f3	2 ♘ed2
	♘e6	2 ♘ec5
	axb3	2 ♘xg5
	♖c3+	2 ♖xc3

In the set play of no. 104 Black has two moves with his knight which lead to mates of a type known as Goethart unpins: 1...♘f3 2 ♘f2; and 1...♘e6 2 ♘c3. In each variation the moving-piece of the white ♗+♘ battery can unpin, by interference, a black unit which would have been able to interpose on the check-line if the black knight had not intercepted its route. The moves 1 ♘f2+? and 1 ♘c3+? will not mate in the diagram position because of

1...♗e4! and 1...♖g6! respectively. The key 1 ♘b3, by depriving Black of his flight d1 and giving him instead a flight b3 (a *give-and-take key*), alters the mates set for the black defences given above, which both defeat the threat of 2 ♘d4. 1...♘f3 now allows 2 ♘ed2, while 1...♘e6 leads to 2 ♘ec5. Like the mates of the set play, these are Goethart unpins. A third mate by the ♗+♘ battery, 2 ♘xg5, occurs after the self-block 1...axb3. The *unprovided flight* and *unprovided check* (1...♖c3+, lacking a set reply) are serious drawbacks, hardly balanced by the sacrificial key, yet the problem is noteworthy for its four Goethart unpins spread over two phases.

Grab

GRAB (DOUBLE KNIGHT-WHEEL)

C.S.Kipping
Version, *The Problemist* 1936
Mate in three

105

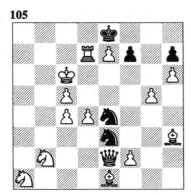

Key 1 f4   zugzwang

...		
♘d1	2 ♘xd1	
♘c2	2 ♘xc2	
♘xc4	2 ♘xc4	
♘d5	2 cxd5	
♘f5	2 ♗xf5	
♘g4	2 ♗xg4	
♘g2	2 ♗xg2	
♘f1	2 ♗xf1	
♘d2	2 ♗xd2	
♘c3	2 ♗xc3	
♘xc5	2 dxc5	
♘d6	2 cxd6	
♘f6	2 gxf6	
♘xg5	2 fxg5	
♘g3	2 ♗xg3	
♘f2	2 ♗xf2	
f6	2 ♕h5	

The key of no. 105, 1 f4, sets up a zugzwang position. White will eventually mate by means of 3 ♖d8, if both of Black's knights can be induced to leave the e-file to enable the white queen to guard e7. As it turns out, this is not a difficult business, for no matter which knight moves, and irrespective of where it arrives, it exposes itself to capture, so that the other knight is then forced to move (unless Black plays 2...f6/f5, which will allow 3 ♛h5). This problem therefore presents a doubling of the Grab theme: each of two black units is grabbed wherever it goes.

Grasshopper

The Grasshopper (🦗) is a **fairy-chess** piece. It moves along queen-lines, but must hop over another piece of either colour and land on the next square beyond. If that square is occupied by a unit of the same colour as the 🦗, the move is illegal; if by a unit of the opposite colour, the 🦗 captures it. The piece was invented by T.R.Dawson in 1912, and is one of the most popular of all fairy-chess units. The new possibilities which its move creates are considerable; some of them are seen in no. 106.

GRASSHOPPERS

106

T.R.Dawson
British Chess Magazine 1943
Mate in two
Key 1 ♘e3   zugzwang

...	🦗e6	2 ♘5g4
	🦗g6	2 ♗g4
	🦗e2	2 ♘3g4
	🦗g~	2 ♗e1
	🦗xf5	2 ♘xf5
	♘~	2 ♘f3
	h2	2 ♘g2
	g4	2 🦗f4

The white 🦗a4 has two moves available to it, to c6 and f4. If it moves to the latter square, the black king is in check. The black 🦗e4 is pinned in the diagram position, for if it were to move it would expose the black king to check from the 🦗a4. The key is 1 ♘e3 and, curious as it may seem, this unpins the 🦗e4! If Black now plays 1...🦗e6, White mates with 2 ♘5g4 – by moving away from e5, the white knight prevents the black grasshopper from returning to e4. The special property of the grasshopper makes it possible for a white unit to play to a square, rather than away from it, in order to achieve a sort of battery-mate (sometimes termed an *anti-battery* mate). Two other variations contain similar play: 1...🦗g6 2 ♗g4; and 1...🦗e2 2 ♘3g4. Each time White moves a unit to prevent the return of the grasshopper – a kind of shut-off in reverse. The non-return feature of the grasshopper occurs automatically (i.e. without any assistance from the opposite side) if the grasshopper crosses any empty squares before hopping, as in the variation 1...&d6 (or 1...&d3), allowing 2 &e1, since the grasshopper cannot return to g3. Two further variations feature grasshoppers: 1...&xf5 2 ♘xf5; and 1...g4 2 &f4.

The *Lion* is closely related to the Grasshopper. It too moves along queen-lines and hops over a unit of either colour, but it may land on any square beyond the hurdle, provided the intervening squares are unoccupied.

The *Locust* is another related fairy-chess unit. Again the move is along queen-lines, but the Locust can only move by capturing an enemy unit, and this it does by hopping over that unit to the next square beyond, capturing as it goes.

For fairy-chess units with capturing power similar to that of Grasshopper and Lion, see **Chinese pieces**.

Grid-Chess

The grid-board, a **fairy-chess** board, was invented by W.Stead in 1953. As can be seen from the accompanying diagram (no. 107), the board is divided not only into its usual 64 squares, but also into 16 larger squares consisting of four squares each.

107

GRID BOARD
M.Seidel
3rd commendation, *feenschach* 1991
Mate in two
Key 1 d4   (>2 ♖e5)

...	♖xd4	2 ♕c4
	♗xd4	2 ♘c3
	♕e6	2 ♖f5
	♖e6	2 ♘f6
	♗e6	2 ♕b7
	♘e6	2 ♕d7
	♘xe8	2 ♕b5

All moves by both sides must cross at least one line of the grid, so that movement within a large square is impossible. Here, for instance, c5 and d6 are guarded by the ♘e4, as normal, but not also by the queen, because she stands in the same large square as the black king. The king is not in check from the queen, nor can he capture her. Some curious effects are possible on a grid-board, as this problem demonstrates. The key 1 d4 threatens 2 ♖e5.

Captures of the key-unit are answered by mates within the same square, so that no further capture is possible: 1...♖xd4 2 ♕c4; and 1...♗xd4 2 ♘c3. Four black units can play to e6 to defeat the threat. 1...♕e6 allows 2 ♖f5 (the black queen interferes with the black bishop). 1...♖e6 leads to 2 ♘f6, the knight being immune from capture within the same square. The two other defences on e6 allow the white queen to step back over a grid-line to deliver mate: 1...♗e6 2 ♕b7; and 1...♘e6 2 ♕d7. Finally 1...♘xe8 leads to another step back by the queen: 2 ♕b5.

Grimshaw

No. 108 is one of the most famous two-movers ever composed. The position is a complete block: every black move has a set mate.

DOUBLE GRIMSHAW + PAWN GRIMSHAW

108

L.I.Loshinsky
Commended, *Tijdschrift v.d. Nederlandse Schaakbond* 1930
Mate in two

Key 1 ♗b3		zugzwang
...	♗b7	2 ♖e7
	♖b7	2 ♖c6
	♗g7	2 ♕xf7
	♖g7	2 ♕e5
	♗f6	2 ♕g4
	f6	2 ♕e4
	f5	2 ♕d6
	♗xd4	2 ♘xd4
	♖xc7	2 ♘xc7

The key is the waiting move 1 ♗b3, which holds the block position so that Black is bound to commit an error permitting a white mate. Six of Black's moves are interferences, and it is these that form the theme of this superb problem. 1...♗b7 allows 2 ♖e7, because of the interference with the ♖a7. This black rook may in turn play to b7, where it interferes with the bishop and permits mate by 2 ♖c6. A pair of interference variations, in which piece X interferes with piece Y and vice versa, is known as a Grimshaw. (The name derives from a 19th-century composer who made an early example of the theme.) The remarkable thing about this problem is that it contains three

Grimshaws altogether, i.e. three pairs of interferences. A pair similar in character to the variations already examined may be seen on the other side of the board: 1...♗g7 2 ♕xf7 (bishop interferes with rook); and 1...♖g7 2 ♕e5 (rook interferes with bishop). The third Grimshaw involves the ♗h8 and the △f7: 1...♗f6 2 ♕g4 (the bishop prevents 2...f5); and 1...f6 2 ♕e4 (2 ♗e5? being impossible). A Grimshaw of this kind is known as a Pawn-Grimshaw, to distinguish it from the more usual ♖+♗ variety. In the orthodox two-mover a pawn can be interfered with only when it stands on its starting square, so that its double jump is prevented. To complete this problem, there are three further variations, a self-block by 1...f5 (2 ♕d6) and two straight recapture-mates after 1...♖xc7 and 1...♗xd4. It is extremely doubtful whether three Grimshaws can ever again be combined in a single phase as neatly as in this example. Its reward was a mere commendation!

GRIMSHAW (ZAGORUIKO)

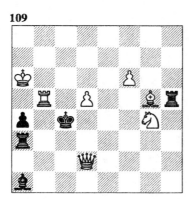

109

M.Manolescu
1st prize, Meredith section, *Revista de Sah* 1956
Mate in two

Set	1...	♗c3	2 ♘e3
		♖c3	2 ♘e5
Try	1 ♘f2?		(>2 ♕b4)
	...	♗c3	2 ♕d3
		♖c3	2 ♕f4
		♖b3!	
Key	1 ♗e3!		(>2 ♖b4)
	...	♗c3	2 ♕e2
		♖c3	2 ♕d4
		♖b3	2 ♖c5
		♖d3	2 ♕b4
		♖xe3	2 ♘xe3

No. 109 also has three Grimshaws, but spread over three phases: the black defences remain the same, but there are three different pairs of replies. The set mates following 1...♗c3 and 1...♖c3 are respectively 2 ♘e3 and 2 ♘e5. The try 1 ♘f2? (>2 ♕b4) automatically eliminates these mates, but introduces 2 ♕d3 and 2 ♕f4, thanks to the additional guard on d3. 1...♖b3! refutes. The key is 1 ♗e3!, with the new threat of 2 ♖b4. The set mates are ruled out because the bishop occupies one of the knight's mating squares and has opened the line of the black ♖h5 to guard the other. The try-play mates by the queen will not work either, because there is no second guard on d3. There is, however, a second guard on d4, which enables White to mate by 2 ♕e2 after 1...♗c3, and by 2 ♕d4 after 1...♖c3. The mechanism by which all these changes are brought about is extremely skilful. Furthermore, there is some good by-play to complete the problem. The move which refutes the try, 1...♖b3, leads after the key to 2 ♖c5, while the self-block 1...♖d3 re-introduces the threat of the try-play, 2 ♕b4. Finally the knight, which provides the set mates and makes the try, is given work to do after the key: 1...♖xe3 2 ♘xe3.

Grimshaw interferences have appealed to composers more than most other two-move themes. There are many examples throughout this book, especially under **Novotny**, a closely related theme.

CHANGED DOUBLE GRIMSHAW

C.G.S.Narayanan
1st prize, *The Problemist* 1975
Mate in two

110

Try 1 e5?		zugzwang
...	♗c7	2 ♕c8
	♖c7	2 ♕d8
	♗f7	2 ♖e7
	♖f7	2 e6
	♗e6!	
Key 1 ♕e5!		zugzwang
...	♗c7	2 ♗c8
	♖c7	2 ♖d8
	♗f7	2 ♕e7
	♖f7	2 ♕e6
	♗b6	2 ♘xb6
	♖c6	2 ♗xc6

No. 110 is one of quite a small number of examples of a difficult task: changed double Grimshaw. After the try 1 e5?, with no threat, there are replies to the Grimshaw defences on c7 and f7: 1...♗c7 2 ♕c8; 1...♖c7 2 ♕d8; 1...♗f7 2 ♖e7; and 1...♖f7 2 e6. But the try fails to provide for 1...♗e5!. The key 1 ♕e5! (-) changes the mates by switching the queen and altering the guards: 1...♗c7 2 ♗c8; 1...♖c7 2 ♖d8; 1...♗f7 2 ♕e7; and 1...♖f7 2 ♕e6. Now, of course, 1...♗e6 has an answer: 2 ♕xe6.

Half-Battery

A half-battery exists in its simplest form when two white units, X and Y, stand on a line between the black king and a white line-piece, such that if one of these units moves away a normal battery is formed. The half-battery theme, however, is an extension of this basic arrangement. Unit X moves to make a try, thereby perhaps introducing virtual play involving battery-openings by moves of unit Y. The key is made by Y, and the same, or different, black defences may lead to play in which X moves to open the battery. The try-play is not necessarily confined to a single white move, for the point of the problem may lie not only in the choice of which white unit to move, but also in that unit's destination.

111

HALF-BATTERY

G.Bakcsi
1st prize, FIDE Tourney 1962-3
Mate in two

Try 1 ♘xd5?	(>2 ♖d1)
... ♔d3	2 ♘f2
♔xd5	2 ♘c3
♗d6!	
Key 1 ♘xc5!	(>2 ♕b4)
... ♔c3	2 ♘xd5
♔xc5	2 ♘d3
♗xc5	2 ♕e5

In no. 111 the half-battery on the fourth rank yields different mates after the king-flights in virtual and post-key play. The try is made with the ♘f4: 1 ♘xd5? (>2 ♖d1). Black's defences against the threat are 1...♔d3 and 1...♔xd5. These are followed by 2 ♘f2 and 2 ♘c3 respectively, each mate being an opening of the newly-formed ♖+♘ battery. The try is refuted by 1...♗d6!, and so White, in order to threaten 2 ♕b4, plays 1 ♘xc5!. Black now has two new flights, c3 and c5. 1...♔c3 leads to 2 ♘xd5, while 2 ♘d3 follows 1...♔xc5. This time the battery consists of ♖+♘f4. This attractive setting illustrates **total change**: the theme remains the same throughout the problem's solution, but the thematic defences and mates are different in the two phases.

The amazing fertility of the half-battery can be judged from the large number of such problems which appear under other headings in this book.

Two further examples must suffice here, both showing a *direct* half-battery. *Indirect* half-batteries are not uncommon, nor are *masked* half-batteries, both direct and indirect.

HALF-BATTERY (RADICAL CHANGE)

112

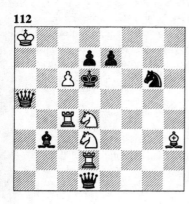

W. Issler
2nd prize, *Die Schwalbe* 1962
Mate in two

Try 1 ♘e5?		(>2 ♘f7)
...	e6	2 ♘f5
	♘xe5	2 ♘b5
	♗xc4	2 ♘xc4
	♛f1	2 ♘e2
	♛f3	2 ♘dxf3
	♘h8!	
Key 1 ♘e6!		(>2 ♛c5)
...	♛a1	2 ♘b2
	♛h5	2 ♘e5
	♛g1	2 ♘f2
	♛g4	2 ♘df4
	dxc6	2 ♛d8

No. 112, besides being a half-battery, illustrates **radical change**: not only do the thematic defences and mates change between the virtual and post-key play, but the variations also display different strategy in the two phases. 1 ♘e5? threatens 2 ♘f7, and four of Black's six defences lead to openings of the battery consisting of ♖+♘d4: 1...e6 2 ♘f5 (self-block + white interference); 1...♘xe5 2 ♘b5 (ditto); 1...♛f1 2 ♘e2 (unguard + shut-off); and 1...♛f3 2 ♘xf3 (unguard + capture). The fifth defence, 1...♗xc4, is answered by 2 ♘xc4, while the sixth, 1...♘h8!, refutes the try. The key is a move by the other knight, 1 ♘e6! (>2 ♛c5). The four thematic defences by the queen introduce shut-off mates from the new battery: 1...♛a1 2 ♘b2; 1...♛h5 2 ♘e5; 2...♛g1 2 ♘f2; 1...♛g4 2 ♘f4. The only weakness of this otherwise elegant problem is that the play following the try is strategically superior to that found after the key.

No. 113 is a three-move rendering in which the white half-battery works in combination with a black **half-pin**. The withdrawal key 1 ♛b1 threatens 2 ♛a1+, and 3 ♘bxc5 after 2...♔xd3. To defend, Black guards c5 with his

113

HALF-BATTERY (+ BLACK HALF-PIN)

W.Hebelt
1st place, International Team Match
1962-3
Mate in three
Key 1 ♕b1 (>2 ♕a1+ ♔xd3 3 ♘bxc5)
... ♕e7 2 ♘f2   ♖xf2 3 ♗f3
...   ♘xc4 3 ♗e6
♕xc7 2 ♗e2   ♖f1 3 ♘f2
...   ♘xc4 3 ♘ed6

queen, which in the initial position exercises a dual control over the half-battery on the fourth rank. 1...♕e7 allows White to continue 2 ♘f2 (>3 ♕a1). If Black replies 2...♖xf2, White can exploit two weaknesses simultaneously, namely the pin of the B♘e5 and the fact that the black rook has played across the **critical** square f3 and can therefore be shut off by 3 ♗f3. 2...♘xc4, on the other hand, leads to 3 ♗e6: the black rook is pinned and the white bishop, in mating, must re-close the line which Black has just opened, from the black queen (now on e7) to the battery-line on the fourth rank. In the second thematic variation, 1...♕xc7 leads to 2 ♗e2, with the same third-move threat of 3 ♕a1. 2...♖f1, again a critical move, allows 3 ♘f2, a shut-off which also exploits the pin of the ♘e5. 2...♘xc4 once again opens a line from the black queen which White must close in mating by 3 ♘ed6, the ♖f6 being now pinned. This excellent setting of the half-battery is ample proof of the theme's suitability for expression in three-move form.

Half-Pin

(a) Black

Two units are said to be half-pinned when one of them becomes completely pinned if the other moves. Such is the case with the black ♗d4 and ♘f4 in no. 114.

The key, 1 c3, threatens 2 ♕xd4, and Black has a total of five defences with his half-pinned units, after each of which White's mate would be ineffective but for the pin. 1...♗xc3 pins the knight, blocks c3 and so allows 2 d3. 1...♗c5 is a second self-block, and White again exploits the pin of the knight with 2 ♕d3. 1...♗e5, on the other hand, is an interference: 2 ♗xe6 is made possible not only by the pin of the knight but also because the ♖h5 is

114

HALF-PIN

C.Mansfield
1st prize, *El Ajedrez Argentino* 1921
Mate in two
Key 1 c3   (>2 ♕xd4)

...	
♗xc3	2 d3
♗c5	2 ♕d3
♗e5	2 ♗xe6
♘d5	2 ♕xc6
♘e2	2 ♘xe3
♗d5	2 ♕b4
♖d5	2 ♕b4

prevented from playing to d5 to interpose. Then there are two defences by the ♘f4 which allow White to exploit the pin of the bishop: 1...♘d5 2 ♕xc6; and 1...♘e2 2 ♘xe3. Both these defences are also interferences. It is most often the case with the half-pin, arguably the most fertile of all two-move themes, that the composer combines his half-pin with other strategy, such as self-blocks and interferences (as here), or **cross-checks** or **unpin** of White.

Successful doublings of the half-pin theme (i.e. with two distinct half-pin lines, and with each unit thematically pinned in at least one variation) are by no means uncommon, but there are few examples of the triple half-pin. No. 115 is particularly fine, with a key that changes one of the thematic mates.

115

TRIPLE HALF-PIN

B.Malmström
3rd prize, Good Companions 1923
Mate in two
Key 1 ♕c5 zugzwang

...	
♖xc5	2 d3
♘d3	2 ♘c3
♖xe2	2 ♕xc4
♘d4	2 ♘f2
♗g5	2 ♕f5
♕g5	2 ♕e3

1 ♕c5 creates a block position. The changed mate is that following 1...♗g5: before the key this is answered by 2 ♕xf3, while the post-key mate is 2 ♕f5. The other variation from this half-pin line is 1...♕g5 2 ♕e3. A

half-pin is not regarded as *complete* unless each half-pinned unit becomes thematically pinned in at least one variation. The two other half-pin lines in Malmström's problem are likewise complete.

116

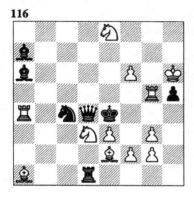

HALF-PIN: RECIPROCAL CHANGE

I.Grossman and A.Hirschenson
Probleemblad 1965
Mate in two

Set	1...	♞e5	2 ♖xe5
		♛xe3	2 ♞d6
Key	1 ♞f4 (>2 ♝f3)		
	...	♞e5	2 ♞d6
		♛xe3	2 ♖e5

Changed play centring on a half-pin arrangement is comparatively common, but no. 116 is a rather curious example. The set defences 1...♞e5 and 1...♛xe3 are met by 2 ♖xe5 and 2 ♞d6 respectively. The key 1 ♞f4 (>2 ♝f3) has the effect of reversing these two mates: 1...♞e5 2 ♞d6; and 1...♛xe3 2 ♖e5. This is known as **reciprocal change** and is quite unusual in half-pin problems.

HALF-PIN (ZAGORUIKO)

117

M.Parthasarathy
The Problemist 1966
(version by B.Zappas)
Mate in two

Set	1...	♞d4	2 ♛d6
		♛h7	2 ♛b2
Try	1 ♞xc5?	(>2 ♖e4)
	...	♞d4	2 ♞xd7
		♛h7	2 d4
	d5!	
Key	1 ♞d6!	(>2 ♖e4)
	...	♞d4	2 ♞f7
		♛h7	2 ♛xc5

Half-pin two-movers in three phases are rare, especially when the black defences remain exactly the same throughout the problem's solution. The set play of no. 117 has the variations 1...♘d4 2 ♕d6, and 1...♕h7 2 ♕b2. Both these mates are rendered impossible if the white knight leaves e4. The try 1 ♘xc5? (>2 ♖e4) introduces two new mates: 1...♘d4 2 ♘xd7, and 1...♕h7 2 d4. However, there is no mate to follow 1...d5!. The key 1 ♘d6!, with the same threat, brings in a third pair of mates: 1...♘d4 2 ♘f7, and 1...♕h7 2 ♕xc5. This fine problem is therefore a **Zagoruiko**.

Three examples follow of black half-pin in three-move form. In no. 118 the chief interest lies not so much in the strategy with which the half-pin is combined, as in the relationship between White's second and third moves.

118

HALF-PIN: CYCLIC EFFECTS

N.G.G.van Dijk
1st prize, *Stella Polaris* 1966
Mate in three

Key 1 ♕b2 (>2 ♗f6 ... 3 ♕d4/♕e5)

...	♖a1	2 ♖e3+ ♘xe3	3 ♘c5
	♖a3	2 ♘c5+ ♕xc5	3 ♖f4
	♖h8	2 ♖f4+ ♘xf4	3 ♘d6
	♖f8	2 ♘d6+ ♕xd6	3 ♖e3

The key 1 ♕b2 threatens 2 ♗f6 followed by 3 ♕d4 or 3 ♕e5. If Black defends with 1...♖a1 (threatening 2...♖xf1+), White proceeds with 2 ♖e3+ (A) ♘xe3 3 ♘c5 (B). 1...♖a3 allows 2 ♘c5+ (B) as the second move, forcing 2...♕xc5, and White then mates with 3 ♖f4 (C). 1...♖h8 leads to 2 ♖f4+ (C) ♘xf4 3 ♘d6 (D), while 1...♖f8 allows 2 ♘d6+ (D) ♕xd6 3 ♖e3 (A). A complete **cycle** of white second and third moves is combined with the half-pin.

The half-pin in no. 119 does not in fact exist until Black has made his first move. 1 ♗h3 threatens 2 ♘g4+, and the principal defences involve the capture of the ♙d5 by the ♗b7 and the ♙e6. After 1...♗xd5 White continues 2 ♖g4 (>3 ♕f4). Black's replies and White's mates are now such as might be found in a two-mover: 2...♘d4 3 ♖e4; and 2...♗e4 3 d4. 1...exd5 introduces a second situation reminiscent of the two-mover: 2 ♘e2 (>3 ♕f4) ♘d4 3 ♘c4; and 1...d4 3 ♕xd4. The half-pin is complete in each variation, so that there are in all four white mates exploiting the mechanism which Black himself is responsible for creating.

119

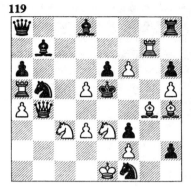

HALF-PIN

J.Montgomerie
Version, 1st prize, *British Chess Magazine* 1964
Mate in three

Key 1 ♗h3   (>2 ♘g4+ ♔f5 3 ♕e4)
  ...   ♗xd5 2 ♖g4   ♘d4 3 ♖e4
          ...   ♗e4 3 d4
          exd5 2 ♘e2   ♘d4 3 ♘c4
          ...   d4 3 ♕xd4
                      ♗xa5 3 ♖e7
          ♘xe3 2 ♕f4+
          ♘d4 2 ♕d6+
          ♘d6 2 d4+
          ♘xc3 2 ♕xc3+

A casual glance at no. 120 is unlikely to suggest the existence of a half-pin arrangement.

120

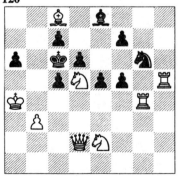

ANTICIPATORY HALF-PIN

J.J.Rietveld
2nd prize, *British Chess Magazine* 1963
Mate in three

Key 1 ♔a5   (>2 ♘b4+/♖c4)
  ...   fxg4 2 ♕c1 ♔xd5 3 ♕h1
          f4 2 ♕c3 ♔xd5 3 ♕f3
          e4 2 ♕c2 ♔xd5 3 ♕xe4

Yet there is one there all right, of a type known as *anticipatory* half-pin. 1 ♔a5 threatens 2 ♘b4+ cxb4 3 ♖c4, or 2 ♖c4 and 3 ♘b4. Black's main defences are with his pawns on e5 and f5, which move so as to prevent the ♖g4 from playing to c4. Whichever pawn moves, White can allow the king to escape to d5, whereupon the non-moving pawn becomes pinned and White can mate accordingly. 1...fxg4 allows 2 ♕c1 (>3 ♘b4), and if 2...♔xd5 then 3

♛h1. 1...f4 leads to 2 ♕c3 (>3 ♘b4), and now 2...♚xd5 is answered by 3 ♕f3. Finally 1...e4 permits 2 ♕c2, with 3 ♕xe4 to follow 2...♚xd5. In each variation of this elegant work the half-pin does not become effective until after the king-move. The play of the white queen to three different squares on the c-file gives the problem great unity. The double threat is unfortunate.

For another three-move extension of the half-pin theme, see under **Third-Pin**.

(b) White

The reader who has just studied nos. 114-120 will have no trouble recognising the black half-pin on the fifth rank in no. 121.

WHITE HALF-PIN + BLACK HALF-PIN

121

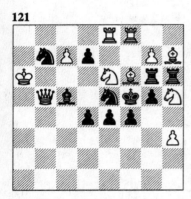

M.Lipton
3rd prize, *British Chess Magazine* 1966
Mate in two
Try 1 ♗d8+? ♘f7! (2 ♘xd4?)
Try 1 ♘xd4+? ♗xd4! (2 ♗d8?)
Try 1 ♘xf4? ♖xh5!
Try 1 ♘xg5? (>2 ♖xe5)

    ...   ♘c6   2 ♗d8
              d6!
Key 1 ♘d8! (>2 ♖xe5)
    ...   ♘e~   2 ♕xd7
          ♘c6   2 ♗xd4
          ♗e7   2 ♕xe5
          ♗d6   2 ♗e7
          d6   2 ♗xe5

However, this problem contains in addition a white half-pin: if either the ♗f6 or the ♘e6 were to move, the other would be left pinned. The nature of a white half-pin can be best appreciated if one examines plausible-looking check-tries (known as *cook-tries*) by these two units: 1 ♗d8+? fails to 1...♘f7!, because White cannot continue 2 ♘xd4?. Likewise 1 ♘xd4+? will not work because 2 ♗d8? is impossible after 1...♗xd4!. As well as these cook-tries, the solver should notice the try by the ♘e6 which leads to mate by the ♖+♗ battery on the f-file after unpins of the bishop: 1 ♘xg5? (>2 ♖xe5) ♘c6 2 ♗d8, but 1...d6! (2 ♗xe5? is ruled out because the bishop cannot relinquish its guard of g5). The key 1 ♘d8! (>2 ♖xe5) allows Black three defences which unpin the bishop: 1...♘c6 2 ♗xd4; 1...♗d6 2 ♗e7; and 1...d6 2 ♗xe5. In the first two of these variations the black half-pin is exploited, with **black correction**. The key also gives up two set half-pin lines: 1...♘f3 2 ♗xd4, and 1...♘f7 2 ♘xd4.

Hamburg

The Hamburg is a three- and more-move theme which can best be understood by reference to the very clear example of it, no. 122.

122

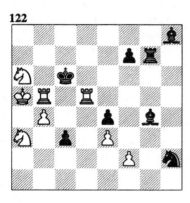

HAMBURG

S.Brehmer
2nd prize, German Ring Tourney 1948
Mate in three

Try 1 ♘c4?	♖g6!
Try 1 ♖d4?	♖g5!
Key 1 f4!	(>2 ♖b6+ ♔xd5 3 ♘c7)
... f6	2 ♘c4 ♖d7 3 ♖dc5
f5	2 ♖d4 ♖b7 3 ♖bc5

If White were to try 1 ♘c4?, with the double threat of 2 ♘e5 and 2 ♖d6, Black would have the adequate defence 1...♖g6! (opening a line to guard e5 and directly controlling d6). In addition, the try 1 ♖d4? (>2 ♖b6) is refuted by the pinning defence 1...♖g5!. White's object must therefore be to induce Black to eliminate these defences in turn, so that the moves shown as tries can be played instead as second-move continuations. This is done by means of 1 f4!, which threatens 2 ♖b6+ ♔xd5 3 ♘c7. Black's principal defences are made with the ♙f7, which opens the line of the ♖g7 to guard c7, the eventual mating-square. 1...f6 allows the continuation 2 ♘c4 (>2 ♖d6). Black has lost his previous adequate defence 2...♖g6, but this has been replaced by a new defence from the same piece, namely 2...♖d7. However, this is a self-block permitting 3 ♖dc5. The other move by the f-pawn, 1...f5, eliminates 2...♖g5 as a defence to 2 ♖d4. As in the try, the threat is 3 ♖b6, and Black's new defence, 2...♖b7, is a further self-block, leading this time to 3 ♖bc5. This attractive problem shows the Hamburg theme doubled. In its simplest form the theme involves the elimination by black unit Y of an adequate defence by unit X, and its replacement by a new defence by piece X which creates a new weakness. This theme is a close relation of the **Roman** and **Dresden** themes.

Hannelius → Reversal themes

Helpmate

Most of the problems in this book are direct-mates: the normal rules of the game of chess apply, in that White and Black are playing against one another, each trying to avoid being mated. In a helpmate, however, a spirit of co-operation exists: both sides play towards the common goal of the mate of the black king. It is normal for Black to play first, which means that in a helpmate in two, for example, each side has two moves. In the printed solution the black moves are given first, which is, of course, the reverse of the usual procedure.

Helpmates are sometimes fairly easy to solve, but occasionally one comes across a helpmate of extreme difficulty, such as no. 123. To test your powers as a solver, cover up the solution shown by the diagram and work out the succession of black move, white move, black move, white move which will end in mate of the black king. Remember, Black is trying just as hard as White to get to this mating position.

123

HELPMATE

F.E.Giegold
feenschach 1963
Helpmate in two

1 ♘b3 ♖xd7 2 ♚e6 ♘c5

Satisfactory helpmates in two or three moves with only a single line of play, as in no. 123, are a comparative rarity, though many fine single-line helpmates of greater length can be found, such as no. 124, a helpmate in eight.

124

HELPMATE

Z.Maslar
2nd prize, *Die Schwalbe* 1981
Helpmate in eight

1 ♔f3 ♘d3 2 ♗b3 ♔c3 3 ♔e4+ ♔d2
4 ♔d4 ♔e2 5 ♔c3 ♘b4 6 ♔b2 ♔d2
7 ♔a1 ♔c1 8 ♗a2 ♘c2

In this problem, the white king has to mark time by means of a **round-trip** followed by a **switchback** before moving to the square he will occupy in the mating position. A point worth noticing is the role of the black queen, which remains stationary throughout the solution.

In shorter helpmates it is usual to find at least two lines of play. Here is a brief survey of some of the methods by which such variety may be achieved.

1) The problem may have set play, which, in a two-move helpmate, will consist of white move, black move, white mate. In the actual play Black will have no waiting move at his disposal to preserve this set line, which must therefore be changed. No. 125 is a fine illustration, by a Grandmaster composer of outstanding ability.

125

HELPMATE: SET PLAY

P.A.Petkov
1st prize, *Schach-Echo* 1976
Helpmate in two (with set play)

Set 1...   ♗a5 2 bxa5+ ♘d6
     1 ♔a4 ♘a5 2 bxa5+ ♗d6

2) The position may be a **twin**. The twinning methods set out under the heading **Twin** apply to helpmates as well as to direct-mates. No. 126, by

126

HELPMATE: TWIN

J.M.Kricheli
1st hon. mention, *feenschach* 1971
Helpmate in two
(a) diagram; (b) ♗f2→e3

(a) 1 ♕f6 ♖h3 2 ♖d5 ♘c6
(b) 1 ♖g4 ♕xh7 2 ♗d5 ♘b5

one of the most talented of helpmate composers, has a second position and solution brought about by the simple shift of a single black unit. As in direct-mates, pieces are not added to a helpmate position which are not required in the solution or for purposes of soundness. Getting his helpmate sound is often the composer's chief worry, though the advent of personal computers and solving programs has helped a good deal.

127

HELPMATE: TWIN

H.-P.Rehm
1st prize, *Problem* 1960-1
Helpmate in two
(a) diagram; (b) remove ♖f3

(a) 1 ♕d5 exf3 2 ♔d4 ♘e6
(b) 1 ♘d5 ♘b7+ 2 ♔d4 e3

Twinning by the removal of a piece is seen in no. 127, in which each solution displays a black anticipatory **half-pin**, together with anticipatory self-pin, with resulting double pin-mate. Turning the whole board clockwise produces the twins of no. 128.

3) The position may have several solutions. In no. 129 Black must start by capturing a white unit, a seemingly paradoxical beginning which has become one of the helpmate composer's most popular devices. A thematic link between the solutions is regarded as essential. Here it is achieved not only by

128

HELPMATE: TWINS

V.Chepizhny
5th prize, Bohemian Centenary Tourney
1962
Helpmate in two
(a) diagram
(b) board quarter-turn clockwise
(c) board half-turn
(d) board quarter-turn anti-clockwise

(a) 1 c1♖ ♖xg5 2 ♖c3 ♗c2
(b) 1 b5 ♗c3+ 2 ♔c5 ♗a5
(c) 1 b3 ♖b4 2 f6 ♗f7
(d) 1 g2 ♗f4+ 2 ♔f2 ♗h2

129

HELPMATE: TWO SOLUTIONS

C.J.Feather
Moultings 2 1991
Helpmate in two: 2 solutions

1 ♕xf8 ♖f3+ 2 ♔g6 ♘xf8
1 ♖xh7 ♕b1+ 2 ♔f6 ♘xh7

the initial captures but also by the fact that the mate is given each time by the knight that has not been captured, on the square where the capture has been made. The composer of this problem, Chris Feather, is Britain's leading authority on helpmates. His book, *Black to play* (F.Chlubna, Vienna 1994), is an outstanding critical survey of the genre which can be enthusiastically recommended to all chess enthusiasts.

4) The *duplex* helpmate has two solutions, one normal (i.e. Black begins and is mated) and one with the colours reversed (i.e. White begins and is mated). No. 130 is by a composer who specialises in **ideal-mate** problems, and was first published as an original in his interesting book on the subject, *Ideal-mate Chess Problems* (1966). Note that in the second solution given White's moves appear first.

130

HELPMATE: DUPLEX

E.Albert
Ideal-Mate Chess Problems 1966
Helpmate in three: duplex

Black plays:
1 e5 ♔d3 2 ♔d5 ♖a6 3 ♗c5 e4
White plays:
1 ♔e5 ♔c6 2 ♖f4 ♔d7 3 e4 ♗b2

5) Variations are permitted, beginning either on White's first or on Black's second move. In practice this form is now seldom seen, composers preferring to work with multiple solutions, which give greater scope for analogous (and, indeed, contrasting) effects.

6) **Try-play** is accepted by some problemists as a legitimate helpmate device. The effect can be unconvincing, because the logic involved is at variance with the essential nature of the helpmate, viz. co-operation between the two sides, and making wrong moves is simply a failure to co-operate. But some examples have been produced which make out a good case for the acceptance of tries, such as no. 131, in which tries by the black knights fail because they open a black line which ultimately pins the piece White wants to use for mating.

131

HELPMATE: TRIES

N.A.Macleod
Commended, *British Chess Magazine* 1967
Helpmate in two

Try   1 ♘c5? ♔xd2 2 ♘b5
Try   1 ♘b5? ♔c2 2 ♘c5
Play   1 ♘xe6 ♖a8 2 ♔d7 ♘e5

Two off-shoots of the helpmate deserve a mention. One is the *helpstalemate*, which works just like a helpmate except that the eventual aim is a stalemate of the black king and forces. The other is the *series-helpmate* (see under **Series-movers**).

Herpai

The Herpai is a **dual avoidance** theme incorporating **black interference**. A black unit, in defending, moves to a square where it interferes simultaneously with two of its own pieces, thereby appearing to allow White a choice between two mates. However, some positive aspect of this black move, some *compensating effect*, will eliminate one of White's mates and so force him to select the other. Variations of this type are normally found in pairs, so that a second black move causing the same double interference will also carry some compensating element which will force White to choose the mate which has had to be avoided in the other variation. Reference to no. 132, in which the theme is combined with **unpin** of White, will clarify the nature of Herpai effects.

132

HERPAI

F.Fleck
1st prize, *Magyar Sakkvilàg* 1934
Mate in two

Key 1 h4 (>2 ♘g6)
  ... ♘ce5 2 ♘xe2 (2 ♘xe6?)
  ♘de5 2 ♘xe6 (2 ♘xe2?)

1 h4 threatens 2 ♘f6, and Black's principal defences are 1...♘ce5 and 1...♘de5. These two moves unpin the white ♘d4 and interfere with the black rooks' guard of each other, so that it seems that White will be able to play either 2 ♘xe2 or 2 ♘xe6, whichever black knight makes the defence. The compensating effect is that the black knights each open a line of guard from the black queen to one of the rooks. Consequently 2 ♘xe6? cannot be played after 1...♘ce5 because of 2...♕xe6!. Similarly 2 ♘xe2? is ruled out after 1...♘de5 because of 2...♕xe2!. White's choice is restricted not by the interferences themselves, but by the line-opening effects.

The Herpai effects of no. 133 are also achieved by means of black line-opening, but this example differs from the previous one in that the thematic

133

CHANGED HERPAI

E.Visserman
1st prize, *Limburgsch Dagblad* 1940
Mate in two

Set 1...   ♘ge6   2 ♘c6 (2 ♘g4?)
           ♘ce6   2 ♘g4 (2 ♘c6?)
Key 1 ♖f4 (>2 d4)
    ...   ♘ge6   2 ♗d6 (2 ♖f5?)
           ♘ce6   2 ♖f5 (2 ♗d6?)

mates are changed from set to post-key play, and so too are the black lines which are opened to create the dual-avoidance effects. In the set play 1...♘ge6 is answered by 2 ♘c6, which exploits the interference with the ♖g6, and not by 2 ♘g4?, exploiting the interference with the black queen, because the line of the ♖g6 has been opened to guard g4. In the analogous variation, 1...♘ce6, White must play 2 ♘g4 and not 2 ♘c6? because of the opening of the black queen's line to guard c6. (There is a further set interference variation, 1...♘b5 2 ♕e1, but this of course has nothing to do with the Herpai.) The key 1 ♖f4 (>2 d4), by granting the black king a new flight on f4, rules out the set mates, but introduces two new ones to follow the moves of the knights to e6. 1...♘ge6 leads to 2 ♗d6, not 2 ♖f5? because of the opening of the line h5-f5; and 1...♘ce6 allows 2 ♖f5, not 2 ♗d6? because b8-d6 has been opened. So in both set and post-key play the interferences on e6 appear to allow duals, but in each case one of the apparent mates must be avoided because of black line-opening. The composer has skilfully worked in a third change: 1...♘b5 now permits 2 ♘fd3 instead of 2 ♕e1.

Holst

In a 3-mover or longer problem White may have a try which fails to a black promotion defence. White must therefore induce the relevant pawn to promote to a different unit, so that his original plan can succeed.

If the ♙f2 in no. 134 were on f4, the problem would be a mate in 3. White would have the try 1 ♖c8? (threatening 2 ♖c3), failing to 1...e1♕!. The key would be 1 ♖d8! (>2 ♖d3), forcing the reply 1...e1♘ (1...e1♕ 2 ♖d3+ ♕c3 3 ♖xc3), and thus allowing the continuation 2 ♖c8, because the new black knight cannot prevent 3 ♖c3. This idea, which is named after a 19th-century Danish composer who was the first to use it, is closely related

134

HOLST

E.M.H.Guttmann
Miniatures Stratégiques 1935
Mate in four

Try 1 ♖c8? e1♕!
Try 1 ♖d8? e1♘! (2 ♖c8? f1♕+!)
Key 1 ♖g8 (>2 ♖g3)
...f1♘ 2 ♖d8 e1♘ 3 ♖c8 ... 4 ♖c3

to **obstruction**: promotion to knight denies Black the opportunity to promote to a queen.

The composer of this problem, which is in fact a 4-mover, has doubled the theme, for with the f-pawn on f2 1 ♖d8? also fails, to 1...e1♘!, because 2 ♖c8? would lead to 2...f1♕+!. So first White must induce a promotion to knight on f1 by playing 1 ♖g8! (>2 ♖g3). After 1...f1♘, 2 ♖d8 will now work, as 2...e1♘ is followed by 3 ♖c8 (>4 ♖c3). This is a fine **logical problem**: two successive *foreplans* are needed before the *mainplan* can succeed. A brilliant miniature.

Holzhausen

Holzhausen is the term used to denote interference between pieces of like motion (e.g. queen and rook, rook and rook, or queen and bishop). (Mutual interference between such pieces, where piece X interferes with piece Y in one variation, and vice versa in a second, is known as **Wurzburg-Plachutta**.)

No. 135 contains four Holzhausen interferences, all committed by the black queen. The key 1 ♕g5 sets up a threat of 2 ♘xg7+ ♔xd6 3 ♗e7. Black defends by means of **square-vacation**: the queen leaves c6 in order to obtain a flight for the king after 2...♔xd6. But the queen must retain her guard over c7, for otherwise White may play 2 ♘axc7. As she moves down the c-file, she interferes with four other black line-pieces in turn. If 1...♕c5, White can play 2 ♕xd5+, for Black cannot reply 2...♖xd5; the defence 2...♕xd5 has been substituted, and White now proceeds with 3 ♘axc7. Similarly 1...♕c4 leads to 2 ♕xg4+; 1...♕c3 allows 2 ♕e5+; and finally 1...♕c2 is followed by 2 ♕f5+. On each occasion the black queen is **overloaded**: she is required to take over the guard duty of another black piece and so can no longer perform

135

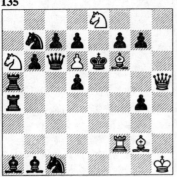

HOLZHAUSEN

A.P.Grin
Hon. mention, *British Chess Magazine*
1967
Mate in three

Key 1 ♕g5 (>2 ♘xg7+ ♔xd6 3 ♗e7)
... ♕c5 2 ♕xd5+
♕c4 2 ♕xg4+
♕c3 2 ♕e5+
♕c2 2 ♕f5+

her original task of guarding c7. The fact that the defences by the black queen are all answered by continuations from the white queen gives considerable unity to the problem. The composer, A.P.Grin, first came to prominence, under the name A.P.Guliaev, in the period around 1930 when Russian problemists were experimenting with white line-themes in the two-mover. At the time of writing (January 1996), Grin is still as active and enthusiastic as ever.

Ideal Mate

An ideal mate is a **model mate** in which all the force on the board, both black and white, is necessarily used, white king and pawns included. Such a mate represents the ultimate in terms of **economy** of force. No. 136 is a miniature five-mover in which both the set and the post-key lines terminate in an ideal mate.

136

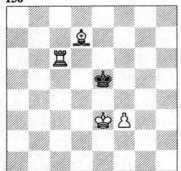

IDEAL MATE

W.Pauly
Deutsche Schachblätter 1924
Mate in five

Set 1...♔d5 2 ♗e8 ♔e5 3 ♗g6 ♔d5 4 ♗e4+ ♔e5 5 f4
Key 1 ♗c8 ♔d5 2 ♗b7 ♔e5 3 ♖g6 ♔f5 4 ♗e4+ ♔e5 5 f4

The mate is given by the white pawn; the white king guards the three squares to the south of the black king, and the rook holds the squares to the north, while the squares d5 and f5 are held by the bishop.

Illegal Position → Obtrusive Force

Incarceration → Paralysis

Indian

An Indian manoeuvre consists of a white **critical** move, followed by a self-interference on the critical square for the purpose of relieving stalemate, and finally a discovered mate. Such strategy, though with double checkmates, is found twice over in no. 137, once in the set play and again in the post-key play.

137

INDIAN

M.Niemeijer
La Liberté 1928
Mate in four

Set 1...b5 2 ♗c1 b4 3 ♖d2 ♔f4 4 ♖d4
Key 1 ♗xh6 b5 2 ♔g3 b4 3 ♖g5 ♔e3
4 ♖xe5

The set play runs: 1...b5 2 ♗c1 (the critical move, over d2) b4 3 ♖d2 (self-interference on the critical square) ♔f4 4 ♖d4. No waiting-move can hold this position, so White must substitute a different line: 1 ♗xh6 (critical move) b5 2 ♔g3 (to leave e3 eventually unguarded) b4 (stalemate threat) 3 ♖g5 (self-interference on the critical square) ♔e3 4 ♖xe5.

No. 138 is an amazing achievement, with two consecutive Indians in each of two lines. The key is 1 ♗h3, waiting. If 1...g6, play continues 2 ♗xb6 (critical move) d5 3 ♖d4 (self-interference) ♔xf2 4 ♖xd5+ ♔e1 5 ♗d4 (second self-interference) ♔xd2 6 ♗f2. If on the other hand Black opens with 1...d5, then 2 ♖xd5 g6 3 ♗d4 ♔xd2 4 ♗xb6+ ♔e1 5 ♖d4 ♔xf2 6 ♖dxd1. The order in which the Indian manoeuvres are played is reversed in the second line.

138

INDIANS

R.C.O.Matthews
1st prize, *Die Schwalbe* 1952
Mate in six

Key 1 ♗h3 g6 2 ♗xb6 d5 3 ♖d4 ♔xf2
4 ♖xd5+ ♔e1 5 ♗d4 ♔xd2 6 ♗f2
        ... d5 2 ♖xd5 g6 3 ♗d4 ♔xd2
4 ♗xb6+ ♔e1 5 ♖d4 ♔xf2 6 ♖dxd1

Interference

(a) Black

There are many problems in this book in which Black Interference is found
in one form or another. An interference occurs when one black piece closes
the line of another, and the idea becomes interesting, from the strategic point
of view, when White is able to exploit the interference, either immediately
(as in the two-mover) or at some later stage in the solution (which is possible
in three-movers and longer problems). Single-phase two-movers with the
emphasis on black interference are of particular interest when the interferences are related, as, for example, in the **Grimshaw**, and in nos. 139-142
given here.

139

INTERFERENCES: FIVE ON ONE SQUARE

L.I.Loshinsky
The Problemist 1930
Mate in two
Key 1 ♕f2   (>2 ♕xa7)
        ...   ♗d4   2 ♕xe2
            d4   2 ♗c4
            ♖d4   2 ♖h6
            ♘ed4   2 ♕a2
            ♘fd4   2 ♖a3

In no. 139 the interferences all occur on one square. The key 1 ♕f2 threatens 2 ♕xa7, and Black defends by playing any one of five units to d4 to prevent the white queen from reaching her destination. 1...♗d4 interferes with the ♖h4 and allows 2 ♕xe2. 1...d4 is a second interference with the rook, and also opens a white line (g8-c4) to permit 2 ♗c4. 1...♖d4, opening another white line (h3-h6), interferes with the bishop so that 2 ♖h6 can be played. The defences by the knights are both interferences with the rook combined with line-opening: 1...♘ed4 2 ♕a2, and 1...♘fd4 2 ♖a3. This is easily the most economical version yet composed of five interferences on one square. It seems unlikely that six such interferences can be achieved without some constructional defect such as a strong promotion-key.

INTERFERENCES: SIX ON ONE LINE

140

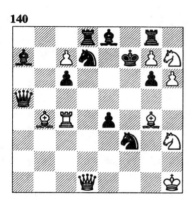

L.I.Loshinsky and G.Baev
1st prize, *Vetserniaia Moskva* 1933
Mate in two

Key 1 ♖xe4	(>2 ♖e7/♗e6)
... ♗c5	2 ♕b3
c5	2 ♕d5
♘c5	2 ♕xf3
♘de5	2 ♖f4
♘fe5	2 ♘3g5
g5	2 ♗h5
(♕e5	2 cxd8♘)

No such weakness is found in no. 140, where there are six interferences on a single line. The key, 1 ♖xe4, is poor, in that it brings the white rook into a prominent position and carries two threats, 2 ♖e7 and 2 ♗e6. The six interferences are all on the fifth rank, and in each case it is the line of the black queen that is closed. Three black units play to c5: 1...♗c5 2 ♕b3; 1...c5 2 ♕d5; and 1...♘c5 2 ♕xf3. The two knights play to e5: 1...♘de5 2 ♖f4; and 1...♘fe5 2 ♘3g5. The sixth interference variation is 1...g5 2 ♗h5.

The very entertaining no. 141 also displays interferences with the black queen, but here the five thematic defences each obstruct the queen in a different direction. The key 1 ♘d1 threatens 2 ♖xd2. 1...♘d5 interferes with the queen to the west, and White mates by 2 ♕xa6. 1...♘d4 interferes to the south-west, allowing 2 ♘xc3. The line to the south is closed by 1...♘e4,

141

INTERFERENCES: FIVE WITH BLACK QUEEN

G.P.Golubev
1st prize, *Die Schwalbe* 1931
Mate in two

Key 1 ♘d1	(>2 ♖xd2)
... ♘d5	2 ♕xa6
♘d4	2 ♘xc3
♘e4	2 ♕e3
♖f4	2 ♘xg3
♗g5	2 f4

leading to 2 ♕e3, while that to the south-east is closed by 1...♖f4, giving 2 ♘xg3. Finally 1...♗g5 interferes with the queen to the east and permits 2 f4.

A number of composers have concerned themselves with the task of incorporating as many interferences into a problem as possible. For a great many years the record stood at eight. In 1965 John Driver produced what was thought to be the first setting with nine. Subsequently Sir Jeremy Morse, who has made an exhaustive study of tasks of all kinds, publishing his findings in a series of articles in *The Problemist* and in a fine book entitled *Chess Problems: Tasks and Records* (Faber & Faber, 1995), discovered that a problem showing nine interferences, by H.J.Burgess (no relation to this book's editor), had in fact been published nearly twenty years before. It had remained unknown not because of its flight-taking key but because it had first appeared in the specialist publication *Braille Chess Magazine*. Since Driver's version appeared, there have been several more, mainly by H.W.Grant. No. 142 is perhaps his finest achievement.

The key, 1 ♗d4, is only moderate, but the nine interferences can be clearly seen, and there are four further variations to round off a remarkable problem, which includes two unpins and six mates by the **Royal battery** (♖+♔). Ten interferences have been achieved, but at the cost of a promotion-capture key.

Changed mates after black interferences are frequently found. One of the neatest three-phase settings is no. 143. The tries and key are all made by the ♘d4 and carry the threat 2 ♗d5. Black's thematic defences are 1...♘b4 (interfering on the line a5-e1) and 1...♘c7 (closing b8-g3). The try 1 ♘f3? introduces the mates 2 ♘3d2 and 2 ♖e5 after these defences, but fails to 1...♕a2!. After 1 ♘c2? the thematic mates are 2 ♘d2 and 2 ♘g3, but 1...d2! refutes. The key 1 ♘e2! introduces the third pair of mates after the interference defences: 2 ♘c3 and 2 ♘eg3.

142

NINE INTERFERENCES

H.W.Grant
1st prize, British Chess Federation
Tourney 1966-7
Mate in two

Key 1 ♗d4		zugzwang
...	♖b6	2 ♔d8
	♖c6	2 ♔xd7
	♗b5	2 ♗xd5
	♗c6	2 ♔xd6
	♘c3	2 ♘d2
	♘d2	2 exf4
	♖g7	2 ♔f8
	♗g7	2 ♕xg6
	♘g7	2 ♕xf4

INTERFERENCES (ZAGORUIKO)

143

H.L.Musante
Problem 1955
Mate in two

Try 1 ♘f3?		(>2 ♗d5)
...	♘b4	2 ♘3d2
	♘c7	2 ♖e5
	♕a2!	
Try 1 ♘c2?		(>2 ♗d5)
...	♘b4	2 ♘d2
	♘c7	2 ♘g3
	d2!	
Key 1 ♘e2!		(>2 ♗d5)
...	♘b4	2 ♘c3
	♘c7	2 ♘eg3
	(dxe2	2 ♗c2)

Any of the interferences obtainable in a two-mover can, of course, be shown in three-movers or longer problems. In a three-mover the interferences may perhaps not occur until Black's second move, or alternatively there may be some reason why mate cannot be given straightaway. Such strategy, however, being of essentially two-move character, is generally less interesting when expressed in three- or more-move form than the sort of interference which cannot normally be shown in a two-mover. Some remarks on interference between like-moving pieces will be found under **Anti-Bristol, Holzhausen** and **Wurzburg-Plachutta**.

144

ANTICIPATORY INTERFERENCE

L.I.Loshinsky
1st prize, *Probleemblad* 1965
Mate in three

Try 1 ♘d4? (>2 ♕d6+)
    ... ♘ce4 2 ♗e5+ ♕xe5 3 ♘e2
        ♘de4 2 ♘e2+ ♕xe2 3 ♗e5
        ♗a3!
Key 1 ♘b4! (>2 ♕d6+)
    ... ♘ce4 2 ♖f3+ ♕xf3 3 ♘d5
        ♘de4 2 ♘d5+ ♕xd5 3 ♖f3

A special type of interference is seen in no. 144, a fine three-mover with both virtual and post-key play. White has a try, 1 ♘d4?, carrying the threat 2 ♕d6+. Black defends by guarding d6 with each of his knights: 1...♘ce4 allows the continuation 2 ♗e5+, for after 2...♕xe5 White can mate by 3 ♘e2. The black knight, by moving to e4, closes the line e5-e2, although the black queen is not yet on this line. Similarly 1...♘de4 permits 2 ♘e2+, with 3 ♗e5 to follow after 2...♕xe2. Interferences of this sort, where the piece whose line of guard is closed is not yet in position, is known as *anticipatory interference*. This try of White's is refuted by 1...♗a3!. The key is 1 ♘b4!, with the same threat of 2 ♕d6+. Similar anticipatory interferences now take place, but with changed continuations and mates: 1...♘ce4 2 ♖f3+ ♕xf3 3 ♘d5; and 1...♘de4 2 ♘d5+ ♕xd5 3 ♖f3. In each phase White's second move in one variation is his third move in the other; careful study of the play will show why the moves cannot be played in the reverse order.

(b) White

White Interference occurs when a white unit, in playing to a particular square, cuts the line of a second white unit. In the two-mover a white-interference mate may be permitted by a black self-blocking defence, as in the two principal variations of no. 145, a famous example featuring withdrawal **unpin** of the white ♘b7.

145

WHITE INTERFERENCE: UNPINS

A.Ellerman
1st prize, Guidelli Memorial Tourney
1925
Mate in two
Key 1 ♖d7 (>2 ♕f4)

...	♕d4	2 ♘d6
	♕e5	2 ♘c5
	♕h8+	2 ♘d8
	♗f2	2 ♕xh1
	♗f3	2 ♕d3
	♖d4	2 ♖e7

The key 1 ♖d7 threatens 2 ♕f4. 1...♕d4 defeats the threat by closing the line d7-d3, but allows the white-interference mate 2 ♘d6 (the queen has blocked d4). In the companion variation, 1...♕e5, the mate 2 ♘c5 is permitted because the ♖a5 need no longer guard e5. The main play of this fine problem is completed by a third unpin of the knight with **cross-check**: 1...♕h8+ 2 ♘d8; and there are three further variations, two black interferences and a self-block. The rook that makes the key move must select his destination with care: 1 ♖d8? ♕f2! (2 ♘d8?); 1 ♖d6? ♕d4! (2 ♘d6?); 1 ♖d1? ♕d2!.

146

WHITE INTERFERENCE: BATTERY MATES

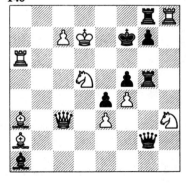

N.A.Macleod
1st prize, British Chess Federation
Tourney 1972-3
Mate in two
Key 1 ♕b2 (>2 ♘c3)

...	♖b8	2 ♘b4
	♖e8	2 ♘e7
	♖g6	2 ♘f6
	g6	2 ♘b6
	(♕xb2	2 ♘xg5
	♖d8+	2 cxd8♘)

A white interference mate may also be permitted by a black line-opening defence. Two such defences are seen in no. 146, along with two self-blocking defences. The excellent key 1 ♕b2 threatens 2 ♘c3, a line-closing defence which does White no harm as long as the queen is not required to guard f6 or g7. By playing to b8 or e8 to threaten to interpose on the mating line, the ♖g8 opens the line of guard of the ♖h8 to f8, and so allows the ♘d5 to play to b4 or e7 respectively. Each of these mates not only shuts off the black rook but also cuts the line of guard of the ♗a3 to f8, a closure made possible by the opening of the line from h8 to f8. The two self-blocking defences are 1...♖g6 (threatening to interpose on e6), answered by the shut-off 2 ♘f6 (the knight arrives on the same line as in the threat, b2-g7); and 1...g6, which prevents the threat by unblocking g7 (2 ♘c3? ♔g7!) but allows a further white interference mate, 2 ♘b6. The only slight weakness of this splendid problem is the passive role of the white queen, whose orthogonal power is not utilised and who has to be prevented from mating on f6 by the ♗a1.

For another form of white interference mate, see under **Goethart unpin**.

White mates which will not work because of white interference are found in a number of themes, e.g. the **dual-avoidance** theme known as **Java**. No. 147 shows one way in which white interferences can be used in try-play.

WHITE INTERFERENCE TRIES

147

Touw Hian Bwee
1st prize, *Schach-Echo* 1980-1
Mate in two
Try 1 ♖b6? (-) b3! (2 ♗a5?)
Try 1 ♗f6? (-) g2! (2 ♖f2?)
Try 1 ♖e7? (>2 ♕e2) ♖h2! (2 ♗xg5?)
Try 1 ♖f6? (>2 ♖d6) ♖h6! (2 ♗xg5?)
Try 1 ♗b6? (>2 ♗e3) c5! (2 ♖d6?)
Try 1 ♗e7? (>2 ♗xb4) ♘xa6! (2 ♖d7?)
Key 1 ♗a5! (>2 ♗xb4)
    ...   c5   2 ♖d6
        ♘xa6 2 ♖d7

This is a *block* position, so White tries to maintain the block with 1 ♖b6?. This, however, fails to 1...b3!, because 2 ♗a5 has been eliminated. Similarly after 1 ♗f6? Black can refute with 1...g2!, since 2 ♖f2 has been ruled out. So White tries to introduce a threat: 1 ♖e7? (>2 ♕e2) fails to 1...♖h2! (2 ♗xg5 cannot be played). 1 ♖f6? (>2 ♖d6) is refuted by 1...♖h6! for the same reason. 1 ♗b6? (>2 ♗e3) is answered by 1...c5! because White has lost the chance to play 2 ♖d6. And 1 ♗e7? (>2 ♗xb4) is met by 1...♘xa6!, since 2

罝d7 is no longer available. In a problem of this kind, the key and subsequent play are often not of great interest, for the whole point lies in the try-play. The highly talented composer of this work has at least ensured that the two white rooks get a look in after the key 1 ♗a5! (>2 ♗xb4), mating on the d-file in response to 1...c5 and 1...♘xa6.

WHITE INTERFERENCE: CRITICAL TRIES

148

M.Lipton
1st hon. mention, *Probleemblad* 1960
Mate in two
Try 1 ♗a7+? 罝bd5! (2 ♘c5?)
Try 1 ♗a1+? ♘cd5! (2 罝c3?)
Try 1 ♗g1+? ♘ed5! (2 罝e3?)
Try 1 ♗f6+? 罝gd5! (2 ♘e5?)
Key 1 ♗g7+!

...	罝bd5	2 ♘c5
	♘cd5	2 罝c3
	♘ed5	2 罝e3
	罝gd5	2 ♕xg3

In the very curious no. 148 White's **critical** tries fail because of resulting self-interference. The four tries and key all give check, and the black defences are consequently self-pins which lead to pin-mates. The ♗d4 is the crucial piece: wherever it moves, Black is in check, but the bishop must choose its arrival square with care. 1 ♗a7+? will not do, because, after 1...罝bd5!, 2 ♘c5? would give Black a flight on d4. 1 ♗a1+? fails to 1...♘cd5!, because 2 罝c3? would be a similar white interference allowing 2...♚d4!. 1 ♗g1+? is refuted by 1...♘ed5! (2 罝e3?), while 1 ♗f6+? is answered by 1...罝gd5! (2 ♘e5?). The solver may well wonder where this bishop can safely go. The answer is to g7, where it cuts the line of the black queen down the g-file, thereby allowing the mate 2 ♕xg3 after 1...罝gd5. Black's three other defences are followed by the pin-mates which could have been played after the tries had it not been for the ensuing white interference.

Java

The **dual avoidance** theme known as Java is so called because it was used as the basis for a number of problems by the Danish composer H.V.Tuxen when he was living in Java in the 1930s. The first published example of it, however, is thought to be by Mansfield, appearing as no. 7 in this book. The mechanism of the theme is as follows: a black defence appears to allow two white mates, each of which would close a white line of guard to a doubly-guarded square in the black king's field. But by closing one of the white guard-lines, this defence forces White to choose the mate which will not allow Black a flight through **white interference**. A second black defence, by means of a different line-closure, will force the selection of the mate which White had to avoid in the first variation.

149

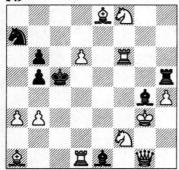

DOUBLE JAVA

O.Strerath
1st place, Hamburg v Würzburg 1948
Mate in two

Key 1 ♕g2	(>2 ♗d4)
... ♗d2	2 ♘d3 (2 ♘e4?)
♗c3	2 ♘e4 (2 ♘d3?)
♗f3	2 ♘e6 (2 ♘d7?)
♗xd1	2 ♘d7 (2 ♘e6?)

This is not as complex as it sounds. The key of no. 149 is 1 ♕g2, threatening 2 ♗d4. Black's defences, which unpin the ♘f2, are 1...♗d2 and 1...♗c3. The square d5 is guarded by the white queen and the ♖d1. If Black plays 1...♗d2, White must not reply 2 ♘e4?, because Black would then have a flight on d5. Therefore 2 ♘d3 is the only possible mate. 1...♗c3 closes the line a1-d4, so that 2 ♘d3?, closing d1-d4, would permit 2...♔d4!. So 2 ♘e4 must be played. This very ingenious problem has a further pair of Java-type variations, in which the ♗g4 abandons its control of the potential mating-squares e6 and d7. 1...♗f3 cuts the line g2-c6, thereby ruling out 2 ♘d7?, as 2...♔c6! would follow. And 1...♗xd1 destroys one white guard of d6, so that White must not close the other by playing 2 ♘e6?. This last variation suffers from the impurity that Black captures the guarding piece instead of cutting its line of guard.

Key

A great deal has been written and spoken about what constitutes a good key. Problemists seem to be generally agreed that a good key should in some way increase the strategic possibilities open to Black, e.g. by allowing flights, checks, etc. Yet a key can still be good without doing this, simply by being surprising, unexpected or paradoxical. After all, a problem is among other things a challenge for the solver, even if composers seldom allow this aspect to form more than a small part of their aims.

It is far easier to define a bad key than to say what constitutes a good one. A key is usually thought to be bad if any of the following things occur:

a)   a black piece (other than a pawn) is captured;

b)   the black king is deprived of a flight – especially one with no set mate – unless another flight is offered in exchange;

c)   a mobile black piece is pinned (except when such a key is part of the theme);

d)   an out-of-play white piece is moved to a prominent and powerful position;

e)   White adds to his strength by promoting a pawn to a queen (promotion to rook, bishop or knight is normally admissible, mainly because of the element of surprise);

f)   a strong unprovided black defence (e.g. check or capture of an important white unit) is prevented or provided for.

Several other possible features of a bad key could be listed here, but might in any problem be accompanied by compensating elements which would mitigate the badness. Many problemists would unhesitatingly add to the list any move which checks the black king. However, a checking key should be regarded as bad only if the play it introduces could have been shown without such a key.

Nos. 150 and 151 have keys of a sort which unfailingly appeal to the beginner. No. 150 has a *multi-sacrifice* key: the ♖f5 offers itself on e5 to no fewer than eight different black units. The mates which follow the captures are not of great strategic interest, though the budding composer would do well to notice how the white queen is used to give mate on four different squares. The point of the problem lies in the **task** achievement of an eightfold sacrifice key.

No. 151 is not the most attractive position in the book! There is some set play: 1...dxe6 2 ♕xe6; 1...e4 2 ♕d4; 1...♘xf8 2 hxg5; 1...dxc5 2 ♕xe5; and 1...♗xf7 2 ♖xf7. The solver should consider what Black's last move can have been in this very tightly locked position, and it will not take him long to realise that only the ♙g5 can have moved last, and indeed must have made its double jump from g7 (on g6 it would have been checking the white king). Since ♙g7-g5 can be proved to have been Black's last move, White is justified in capturing this pawn *en passant*: 1 fxg6 e.p. is therefore the key! This cluttered setting yields a surprising amount of variety. The first three set

150

SACRIFICIAL KEY

N.G.G.van Dijk
8th hon. mention, 3rd FIDE Tourney
1961
Mate in two
Key 1 ♖fe5 (>2 ♖d8)

...	♛xe5	2 c6
	dxe5	2 ♕xd5
	♖dxe5	2 ♕c6
	♖exe5	2 ♗b5
	♗xe5	2 ♕f5
	fxe5	2 ♕xg4
	♘4xe5	2 ♘xf6
	♘6xe5	2 ♘f8

151

EN PASSANT KEY

K.S.Animitsa
2nd prize, *Mat* 2nd Theme Tourney 1974
Mate in two

Set 1...	dxe6	2 ♕xe6
	e4	2 ♕d4
	♘xf8	2 hxg5
Key 1 fxg6 e.p.		zugzwang
...	dxe6	2 ♕f3
	e4	2 ♕f5
	♘xf8	2 g5
	♘g5	2 hxg5
	dxc5	2 ♕xe5
	♗xf7	2 ♖xf7

mates listed above are all changed: 1...dxe6 2 ♕f3; 1...e4 2 ♕f5; and
1...♘xf8 2 g5. The other two set mates are retained, and there is an *added*
mate: 1...♘g5 2 hxg5.

In what circumstances can a checking key be justified? Problems with
such keys most commonly feature king-flights or pin-mates. No. 152 is by
far the most economical rendering to date of *plus-flights*: the black king is
allowed access to all four of his orthogonal flights.

The checking key 1 ♘f7+ is of the *give-and-take* variety: two flights are
granted (c6 and e6), while the king is deprived of access to e5. In addition to

152

CHECKING KEY: PLUS FLIGHTS

N.G.G.van Dijk
American Chess Bulletin 1961
Mate in two

Key 1 ♘f7+

...	♚d7	2 c8♕
	♚e6	2 ♕f5
	♚xd5	2 ♕c4
	♚c6	2 ♕b5
	♚c5	2 ♕c4

the plus-flights, the king also has the diagonal flight c5. The key of this problem cannot reasonably be held to be bad, since Black's mobility is scarcely restricted by it. He is bound to move his king in any case, since it is the only piece he has. (However, a checking key does restrict the black king's freedom after he accepts a flight, since his original square is guarded by the key, unless the checking unit is captured.)

153

CHECKING TRIES AND KEY: STAR-FLIGHTS OF BOTH KINGS

M.Lipton
1st prize, Segal Memorial Tourney 1962
Mate in two

Try 1 ♔f2+?	♚f5!	(2 g4?)
Try 1 ♔f4+?	♚d7!	(2 c8♕?)
Try 1 ♔d4+?	♚f7!	(2 gxf8♕?)
Try 1 ♔d2+?	♚xd5!	(2 c4?)
Try 1 ♔d3+!		
...	♚xd5	2 ♗a3
	♚f5	2 g4
	♚d7	2 c8♕
	♚f7	2 gxf8♕

No. 153 presents the extraordinary task of *star-flight* tries by the white king answered by star-flight refutations by the black king. The tries fail because the units which are supposed to deliver the mates after the black king's moves are pinned by the white king's moves. 1 ♔f2+? fails to 1...♚f5!

because 2 g4? cannot be played. 1 ♘f4+ will not do because the ♗c7 is pinned and cannot mate by 2 c8♕ after 1...♔d7!. 1 ♘d4+? fails to 1...♔f7! because of the pin of the ♗g7 (2 gxf8♕?), while 1 ♘d2+ is refuted by 1...♔xd5! (2 c4?). Remarkable as it may seem, the key 1 ♘d3+ also pins the ♗c2, but provides a new mate to follow 1...♔xd5: 2 ♗a3. An amazing task, typical of this original and talented composer who, regrettably, has had little time for composition in recent years owing to a busy professional life as a Professor of Economics.

154

CHECKING TRIES AND KEY: WHITE SELF-OBSTRUCTION

W.Speckmann
2nd hon. mention, *Schach* 1957
Mate in two

Try 1 ♖c7+?	♔e8!	(2 ♕b8?)
Try 1 ♕c7+?	♔f8!	(2 ♖c8?)
Try 1 ♖e5+?	♔d8!	(2 ♕d6?)
Try 1 ♕e5+?	♔f8!	(2 ♖f5?)
Key 1 ♕e2+!		

Another unusual task is found in no. 154. The try 1 ♖c7+? fails to 1...♔e8!, because the white queen is prevented by the rook from playing to b8 to mate. Similarly 1 ♕c7+? is refuted by 1...♔f8!, since 2 ♖c8? cannot now be played. This pair of tries therefore illustrates *mutual interference* between the two white pieces. There is a further pair of such tries: 1 ♖e5+? ♔d8! (2 ♕d6?); and 1 ♕e5+? ♔f8! (2 ♖f5?). The key must avoid any obstruction: 1 ♕e2+!. The post-key play, in which the black king moves to five flights, is of secondary importance; what matters is the try-play. The distinguished composer of this problem, Dr Werner Speckmann, is an acknowledged expert in the field of **miniatures**: a very large number of his problems have seven pieces or fewer.

Knight-tour

A knight placed somewhere near the middle of the board may have access to a maximum of eight squares. When a white knight visits each of these eight squares in the course of the solution of a problem, we speak of a knight-tour. Naturally, if the tour is complete on the second move of a two-mover, it must be with the aid of a battery, as in no. 155.

155

WHITE KNIGHT-TOUR + SCHIFFMANN DEFENCES

K.A.K.Larsen
Special prize, Schiffmann Memorial
Tourney 1930
Mate in two

Key 1 ♗f3		(>2 ♘g5)
...	♛xe5	2 ♘f2
	♘xe5	2 ♘d6
	♘xc3	2 ♘xc3
	♘xd2	2 ♘xd2
	♘xc5	2 ♘xc5
	♘xf6	2 ♘xf6
	♖xg3	2 ♘xg3
	♖xe5	2 ♛g8

The key, 1 ♗f3, sets up the battery and threatens one of the eight knight-moves, 2 ♘g5. Five of the knight's potential arrival squares are initially occupied by white units, and if the knight were to play to either of the other two, he would allow Black a flight-square through **white interference**. In fact, 2 ♘f2 and 2 ♘d6 are the mates after Black's principal defences, 1...♛xe5 and 1...♘xe5. These moves are of the special type known as **Schiffmann defences**: the black pieces pin themselves to prevent the threat from working, since in each case 2 ♘g5? would be an unpin permitting a black second-move defence (2...♛e4! or 2...♘xf3!). 1...♛xe5 allows 2 ♘f2 because Black has opened the white queen's line of guard to c5, and White can therefore shut off the bishop's line of guard to that square. Similarly 1...♘xe5 opens the white queen's guard-line to e6, so that the line of the ♖a6 can be shut off by 2 ♘d6. (A further example of this white line-opening and line-closing strategy will be found under **Interference – White**.) Black has five further defences to the threat of 2 ♘g5, each involving the capture of a white unit on a square to which the ♘e4 has access. The tour is therefore complete, in the threat and seven variations. There is an eighth variation, a third Schiffmann defence: 1...♖xe5 2 ♛g8. J.A.Schiffmann, after whom this type of defence is named, died in 1929 at the early age of 26. Since Larsen's problem was entered for the tourney organised in memory of Schiffmann, it is reasonable to assume that the three Schiffmann defences were intended as the principal feature. Their combination with the complete knight-tour is a notable achievement.

156

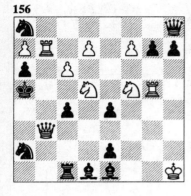

DOUBLE WHITE KNIGHT-TOUR

N.G.G.van Dijk
1st prize, *Die Schwalbe* 133rd Theme
Tourney 1961
Mate in two

Try 1 ♘g3?   (>2 ♘d~)

... ♛b8	2 ♘c7
♛e8	2 ♘e7
g6	2 ♘f6
♝xg3	2 ♘f4
♝d2	2 ♘e3
♝/♘c3	2 ♘xc3
♝/♘b4	2 ♘xb4
♘b6	2 ♘xb6
h6!	

Key 1 ♘c3!   (>2 ♘f~)

... ♛b8	2 ♘d6
♛e8	2 ♘e7
g6	2 ♘g7
h6	2 ♘xh6
♝h4	2 ♘xh4
♝g3	2 ♘xg3
♝d2	2 ♘e3
♝xc3	2 ♘d4
♘xc3	2 ♛b4
♘b6	2 ♛xb6

No. 156 won first prize in a theme tourney for **half-battery** problems organised in the German problem magazine *Die Schwalbe* and judged by Michael Lipton, one of the earliest exponents of the theme. Van Dijk's superb problem shows a double white knight-tour, one after the try and the second after the key. In each case the eight knight-mates are all threats, separated by various black moves. It is interesting to notice that the key is made by the knight nearer to the black king, which means that the knight further away makes the post-key tour. As a result, the defences 1...♘b4, 1...♘xc3 and 1...♘b6, each answered by one of the knight-moves in the virtual play, must lead to completely different mates after the key, as the ♘f5 cannot reach b4, c3 and b6 to capture the defending pieces. It is a tribute to this composer's extraordinary skill that he has succeeded in arranging two new mates by the queen after these defences: 1...♘b4/♘xc3 2 ♕(x)b4; and 1...♘b6 2 ♕xb6.

The white knight-tour in the three-mover is comparatively common, but the theme gains in interest when the knight, having discovered check on White's second move, then gives mate on the third move, after the black king has moved to a flight-square. This idea, known as the *Rössel* theme, was the subject of a book by Theodor Siers, *Rösselsprünge im Schachproblem* (1948). (The Rössel theme need not necessarily motivate a complete knight-tour. Indeed, the theme can be shown with a white bishop or white rook as the thematic piece, using what is often termed a *Siers battery*.) Again Nils van Dijk provides a good example, no. 157.

157

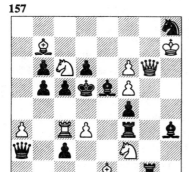

WHITE KNIGHT-TOUR (RÖSSEL)

N.G.G.van Dijk
Version, 1st prize, *The Problemist* 1965
Mate in three

Key 1 ♗d2   (>2 ♘a7+ ♔d4 3 ♘xb5)
...   ♕b3   2 ♘a5+   ♔d4   3 ♘xb3
      ♕c4   2 ♘b4+   ♔d4   3 ♘xc2
      ♗xf6 2 ♘d4+   ♔e5   3 ♘xf3
            ...   ♔xd4 3 ♕xf6
      ♗xc3 2 ♘e5+   ♔d4   3 ♘f3
            ...   ♔xe5 3 ♗xc3
      ♗xf5 2 ♘e7+   ♔d4   3 ♘xf5
      c4   2 ♘d8+   ♔~   3 ♘e6
      ♗d4   2 ♘b8+   ♔e5   3 ♘d7
      ♖b1   2 ♕g8+

The key is 1 ♗d2, with the threat 2 ♘a7+ ♔d4 3 ♘xb5. The nature of the Rössel theme can be clearly seen from this threat: the knight moves, giving check from the bishop; the black king moves to his newly-gained flight; and finally the knight gives mate. The seven main variations show exactly this pattern. Black defends by guarding b5 (the eventual mating-square of the threat), or else by obtaining a new flight for himself. 1...♗xf6, for instance, leads to 2 ♘d4+ ♔e5 3 ♘xf3. If 2...♔xd4, then 3 ♕xf6. 1...♕b3 allows 2 ♘a5+ ♔d4 3 ♘xb3. 1...c4 is a variation of particular strategic interest, for it allows 2 ♘d8+ ♔d4/♔c5 3 ♘e6. This mate would not be possible without the *anticipatory interference* created by Black's first move, which makes

158

WHITE KNIGHT-TOUR: TRIES

G.Latzel
5th hon. mention, *Die Schwalbe* 1956
Mate in two

Try	1 ♘xg3?	♚f4!
Try	1 ♘f2?	gxf2!
Try	1 ♘d2?	♚e6!
Try	1 ♘c3?	♚d4!
Try	1 ♘c5?	dxc5!
Try	1 ♘xd6?	g2!
Try	1 ♘f6?	d5!
Key	1 ♘g5!	

3...♛xe6? impossible. The knight-tour is completed by the four further black defences: 1...♛c4 2 ♘b4+; 1...♝xc3 2 ♘e5+; 1...♝xf5 2 ♘e7+; and 1...♝d4 2 ♘b8+.

No. 158, an amazing miniature, shows a complete white first-move knight-tour. The seven tries by the knight are all refuted in different ways, and the key is simply the only one of the knight's available moves which does not commit a fatal error of some kind, such as exposing the knight to capture or causing an interference with the mobility of the white rook. The wonderful economy of this setting makes it all the more remarkable that it gained only fifth honourable mention in the tourney in which it competed, though perhaps the flight-taking key (entirely excusable in this instance) had something to do with it.

Knight-wheel

Curiously enough, black knights do not tour: they wheel. One of the finest of all examples of the black knight-wheel is Heathcote's masterpiece discussed in Section I (no. 4). At the time of writing (January 1996), no composer has yet achieved a complete knight-wheel in which each knight-defence is an interference leading to a different mate, except by using promoted force. The present record of seven interferences by a black knight has been achieved several times; no. 159 is an example. (A problem by Alberto Mari shows eight knight-interferences, but two of them lead to the same mate.)

The key of Beers' problem, 1 ♘a5, threatens 2 ♖c4, and Black defends by opening a line of guard from the ♝g8. The only non-interference variation is 1...♘xc7 2 ♛xc7.

159

BLACK KNIGHT-WHEEL: SEVEN INTERFERENCES

W.A.Beers
Atlanta Journal 1934
Mate in two
Key 1 ♘a5 (>2 ♖c4)

	...		
	♘e7	2	♗d6
	♘f6	2	♕xf8
	♘f4	2	♕xg1
	♘e3	2	♕d4
	♘c3	2	♘xd3
	♘b4	2	♗b6
	♘b6	2	♘xb7
	♘xc7	2	♕xc7

Le Grand

First introduced in 1958 by the Dutch brothers Henk and Piet le Grand, after whom it was later named, this idea may be defined as follows: in two phases of play, the threat and the reply to a prominent black defence are interchanged. It is therefore a form of **reciprocal change** involving the threat as one of the elements.

No. 160 is a good example with rich by-play. The try 1 ♖g5? threatens 2 ♕f5 [A]. If Black plays 1...♖xa7, then 2 ♖g4 [B] follows. However, 1...♗xe4! refutes this try. The key 1 ♕h5! threatens mate B (2 ♖g4), and now 1...♖xa7 leads to mate A (2 ♕f5). There are, additionally, changed mates after defensive moves by each of the other black pieces.

The le Grand has turned out to be enormously fruitful: ingenious composers have combined it with many other ideas (e.g. the **reversal themes**) to produce problems of great complexity.

One such is no. 161, where it is seen in the play introduced by the two tries: 1 ♘b4?, threatening 2 ♕xc6 [A] and giving 1...♗xb2 2 ♕d6 [B], but refuted by 1...♘xe3!; and 1 ♘b5?, threatening 2 ♕d6 [B] and giving 1...♗xb2 2 ♕xc6 [A], refuted by 1...♘xd3!. The key 1 ♖b4! (>2 ♖c4) reintroduces mates A and B after the very defences that refute them in the try-play (the *Dombrovskis* theme – see **Reversal themes**): 1...♘xe3 2 ♕xc6 [A], and 1...♘xd3 2 ♕d6 [B].

A cyclic form of the le Grand is seen in no. 162 (see page 153). 1 ♖e7? threatens 2 ♕d5 [A], and after 1...e5 comes 2 ♖d4[B]. 1...♖a5! refutes. 1

160

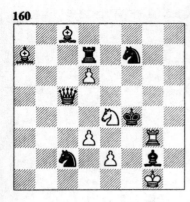

LE GRAND

F.Pachl
1st prize, *Schach-Echo* 1986
Mate in two
Try	1 ♖g5?	(>2 ♕f5)
	...	♖xa7	2 ♖g4
		♘h6	2 ♕e5
		♘e3	2 ♕xe3
		♘d4	2 ♕c1
		♗h3	2 ♕f2
		♘xg5	2 ♕xg5
		♗xe4!
Key	1 ♕h5!	(>2 ♖g4)
	...	♖xa7	2 ♕f5
		♘h6	2 ♕g5
		♘e3	2 ♗xe3
		♘d4	2 e3
		♗h3	2 ♖f3

LE GRAND + DOMBROVSKIS

161

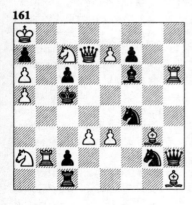

I.Kiss
Probleemblad 1985
Mate in two
Try	1 ♘b4?	(>2 ♕xc6)
	...	♗xb2	2 ♕d6
		♘xe3!
Try	1 ♘b5?	(>2 ♕d6)
	...	♗xb2	2 ♕xc6
		♘xd3!
Key	1 ♖b4!	(>2 ♖c4)
	...	♘xe3	2 ♕xc6
		♘xd3	2 ♕d6

♖f6? threatens 2 ♖d4 [B], and 1...e5 leads this time to 2 ♘d6 [C]. But this try fails to 1...c3!. The key, 1 ♗f4!, threatens 2 ♘d6 [C], and 2 ♕d5 [A] now re-appears after 1...e5. Notice how skilfully the composer has utilised the ♖a4 in the two refutations, and the white queen in mating on h1 after a defence by the black queen.

162

LE GRAND (CYCLIC)

M.Mladenović
1st prize, *Die Schwalbe* 1989
Mate in two

Try	1 ♖e7?		(>2 ♕d5)
	...	e5	2 ♖d4
		♖a5!	
Try	1 ♖f6?	(>2 ♖d4)	
	...	e5	2 ♘d6
		c3!	
Key	1 ♗f4!		(>2 ♘d6)
	...	e5	2 ♕d5
		♕d4	2 ♖xd4
		♕e5	2 ♕h1

163

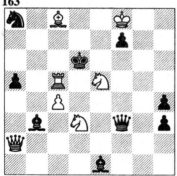

LE GRAND

M.Keller and D.Kutzborski
1st prize, *Deutsche Schachblätter* 1989
Mate in three

Key 1 ♕b2 (>2 ♕d4+ ♕d5 3 ♕xd5)
...♗c3 2 ♕h2 (>3 ♘xf7) ♕xd3 3 ♖c6
   ♗f2 2 ♕a3 (>3 ♖c6) ♕xd3 3 ♘xf7

Reciprocal change between threat and mate following a defence is a relatively common occurrence in three- and more-movers. The key of no. 163, 1 ♕b2, threatens 2 ♕d4+ ♕d5 3 ♕xd5. Black has two main defences: 1...♗c3, which leads to 2 ♕h2 (>3 ♘xf7 [A]); if 2...♕xd3, 3 ♖c6 [B]; and 1...♗f2, allowing 2 ♕a3 (>3 ♖c6 [B]); if 2...♕xd3, 3 ♘xf7 [A].

A less interesting variant of the le Grand, where Black's defence differs between the two phases, has been termed the *pseudo le Grand*.

The le Grand pattern may be summarised as follows: Try (>2 A); 1...a 2 B. Key (>2 B); 1...a 2 A. This is the pseudo le Grand: Try (>2 A); 1...a 2 B. Key (>2 B); 1...b 2 A. A and B are white moves; a and b represent black moves.

Line-opening

Line-opening can take a great many forms. Black may open a line (i.e. remove a unit from a rank, file or diagonal) for White to mate, either by allowing the mating piece to make use of the opened line, or, perhaps more interestingly, by enabling a white piece to guard a black king-flight so that another piece may relinquish its guard of that flight. Alternatively Black may open one of his own lines in defence of a threat. Or again a white try may fail because it makes the error of opening a black line. There are many possibilities, and the reader will find examples throughout the book.

The *open-gate* type of Black-for-White line-opening is a dull strategic idea, unless it is shown in combination with some other theme, or else, as in no. 164, the composer has aimed at a **task** rendering of it.

LINE-OPENING

164

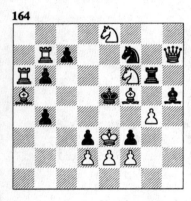

J.Fulpius
Die Schwalbe 1978
Mate in two
Key 1 &c8 zugzwang

	b3	2 &c3
	b5	2 ♖e6
	c6	2 ♖e7
	♘d6	2 ♕e7
	♘d8	2 ♕xc7
	♖xf6	2 ♕e4
	♖xg4	2 ♕f5
	&xg4	2 ♕h2
	dxe2	2 d4
	fxe2	2 f4

The key 1 &c8 completes the block, and there follow ten line-opening variations. Arrival effects allow the ♘f7 to introduce two differentiated mates (1...♘d6 2 ♕e7 and 1...♘d8 2 ♕xc7), and the rook's moves to f6 and g4 likewise force White to choose between two mating squares, e4 and f5. The two-move record for line-openings of this type is currently twelve, also achieved by Jaques Fulpius, but in a setting with a strong promotion key and an unprovided check.

Line-openings of a more subtle character are found in no. 165. The key, 1 ♖d6, granting a second flight d6, threatens 2 ♖e6. Black defends against this

165

LINE-OPENING +
DUAL AVOIDANCE

F.Fleck
L'Italia Scacchistica 1939
Mate in two
Key 1 ♖d6 (>2 ♖e6)

...	♘c~	2 ♕xf6	(2 ♘f7?)
	♘cxd6	2 ♘d7	(2 ♘xc6?)
	♘f~	2 ♘f7	(2 ♕xf6?)
	♘fxd6	2 ♘xc6	(2 ♘d7?)
	♔xe4	2 ♕e7	

threat by moving his knights to open lines of guard from the queen and the ♗a2. At the same time the knights open white lines of guard to the flight e4. Consequently, in mating, White simply has to take care of the flight d6. But there is more line-opening yet. If the ♘c4 moves at random, 2 ♕xf6 is mate. But the knight can correct by capturing the rook that guards f6: 1...♘cxd6. This apparently allows mate by either 2 ♘xc6 or 2 ♘d7, since the defence is a self-block. But the knight has also opened the line of the black rook from c2, so that 2 ♘xc6? would fail to 2...♖xc6!, and so only 2 ♘d7 will work. Random moves of the other black knight allow 2 ♘f7. Why not 2 ♕xf6? Because of the opening of the rook's line from f2 to guard f6. (And why could 2 ♘f7? not be played after the random move of the ♘c4? Because of the opening of the line a2-f7.) The correction move of the ♘f5, 1...♘fxd6, seems to allow White a choice once again, between 2 ♘d7 and 2 ♘xc6. But again because of the opened line h3-d7 only 2 ♘xc6 will mate. Black's opened lines are used, therefore, not only to defeat the threat, but also to force a unique choice of mate. (For problems with similar strategy, see **Dual avoidance**.) A fine addition to the complex line-play of this problem is the variation 1...♔xe4 2 ♕e7 – a double **pin-mate**.

Line-opening is naturally a very common feature of three-movers and longer problems. A brief note on some of the possibilities may be found under **Clearance**. Line-opening of a very simple kind is seen in no. 166.

The key 1 e3 puts Black in zugzwang, leaving him with a choice of four moves by his bishop. Wherever the bishop goes, White plays a quiet move to enable him to take advantage of the fact that the bishop is bound to open a line on its second move, e.g. 1...♗xc5 2 e6 ♗~ 3 ♕h5.

Jan Hartong, the composer of this work, was an outstanding all-round problemist who did much to encourage beginners and popularise chess problems.

166

LINE-OPENING

J.Hartong
4th prize, Kecskemet Chess Club 1927
Mate in three

Key	1 e3	zugzwang		
...	♗xc5	2 e6	♗~	3 ♕h5
	♗xe5	2 c6	♗~	3 ♕h5
	♗xc3	2 ♕c4	♗~	3 ♕c2
	♗xe3	2 ♕d3	♗~	3 ♕f3

Line themes

There are five lettered themes associated with white line effects in the post-key play of a direct-mate problem. These themes came to prominence as a result of intensive researches by Soviet composers in the 1920s and 1930s, though the basic features were already well known before this period.

Theme A: Black defeats a white threat involving the closure of a white line of guard by cutting another white line of guard.

167

THEME A

B.Harley
Hampshire Post 1914
Mate in two
Key 1 ♘g4 (>2 ♘d2)

...	♘e3	2 ♘f2
	♘f5	2 ♘g5
	e5	2 ♘f6
	♗e5	2 ♖xe5
	(♖c2	2 ♕d3)
	(♗c3	2 ♕xb1)

No. 167 is an early illustration by Harley. The key, 1 ♘g4, threatens mate by 2 ♘d2, closing the rook's line of guard to d4 and d5. Black defends by closing White's second guard-line to these squares: 1...♘e3, causing a **self-block**, allows the **white-interference** mate 2 ♘f2. 1...♘f5 produces a similar effect, allowing mate by 2 ♘g5. Two further defences, 1...e5 and 1...♗e5, also illustrate Theme A, but lead to less interesting mates, 2 ♘f6 and 2 ♖xe5 respectively. A couple of nice interference variations round the problem off.

An extension of Theme A involves the *Levman* defence: White's second line of guard is not opened until the threat is played. No. 168 is a fine illustration.

LEVMAN DEFENCES

168

F.Fleck
2nd prize, British Chess Federation
Tourney 1936-7
Mate in two

Key 1 ♗c3 (>2 ♘d7)

...	♘e4	2 ♖xf3
	♗e4	2 ♕xg5
	♕e4	2 ♘xe8
	♘e6	2 ♖f7
	♗e6	2 ♘ec4
	♖e6	2 g8♘

The ♖a7 guards e7, and this guard-line will be closed by the threat, 1 ♗c3, which in turn threatens 2 ♘d7. In the mate the ♖e3 will guard e7, so Black defends, in six variations, by interposing on the rook's line, after which 2 ♘d7? will fail to 2...♔e7!.

Theme B: In defending, Black opens a white line of guard to a square, thus enabling White, in mating, to close another line of guard to the same square.

Such defences are sometimes called *Somov*, after the composer of no. 169. The key 1 f4 threatens 2 ♖e5. 1...♖e6 opens the line h8-d4 to allow 2 c4 to mate. 1...♗d6 opens e8-e5, so that 2 ♘e3 is playable. Finally 1...d6 opens e8-c6, permitting mate by 2 ♖b5. These are all, of course, **white interference** mates. In a variant of Theme B, Black's defence is a self-block allowing a white-interference mate.

Theme C: Black cuts either one of two white lines of guard, thus forcing White, in mating, to open the correct one of two other lines of guard. The two variations thus display **dual avoidance**.

169

THEME B

E.N.Somov
3rd prize, *Shakhmaty* 1928/I
Mate in two

Key 1 f4   (>2 ♖e5)
...   ♖e6   2 c4
             ♗d6   2 ♘e3
             d6   2 ♖b5
             (♖e1   2 ♖d4)

THEME C

170

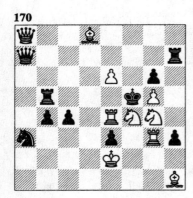

L.Aprò
Shakhmaty v SSSR 1934
(Version by K.Braithwaite,
The Problemist 1983)
Mate in two

Key 1 ♘g2   (>2 ♖f3)
...   ♕b7   2 ♘2xe3   (2 ♘4xe3?)
             ♕e7   2 ♘4xe3   (2 ♘2xe3?)
             ♖hb7   2 ♘h4   (2 ♘h6?)
             ♖e7   2 ♘h6   (2 ♘h4?)
             (♖d5   2 ♕xd5)
             (♖bb7 2 ♖e5)

No. 170, with two pairs of Theme C defences, is a fine example. After the key, 1 ♘g2 (>2 ♖f3), the black queen can defend by cutting two guard-lines, a8-e4 and d8-g5. Mate is given by a white knight on e3: 1...♕b7 2 ♘2xe3 (not 2 ♘4xe3?, because the line h1-e4 must be opened); and 1...♕e7 2 ♘4xe3, to open g3-g5 (and so not 2 ♘2xe3?). The ♖h7 can defend analogously, with mate given on the h-file: 1...♖hb7 2 ♘h4 (not 2 ♘h6?); and 1...♖e7 2 ♘h6 (not 2 ♘h4?).

In a variant of Theme C, Black's defences unblock potential flight-squares, which White must guard in mating by opening the appropriate line.

Theme D: Two squares in the black king's field are each guarded by two white line-pieces. In defending, Black cuts one of the guard-lines. White then cuts the second line with his mating move, opening a third guard-line in the process.

171

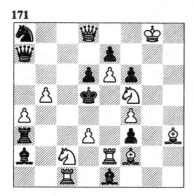

THEME D

M.M.Barulin
Greater Russian Tourney 1931
Mate in two
Key 1 ♕c8 (>2 ♕c6)

...	♕c7	2 ♘ce3	(2 ♘fe3?)
	♕d7	2 ♘fe3	(2 ♘ce3?)
	(♕b7	2 ♕xb7	
	♕b6	2 ♘xe7	
	♖c3	2 ♘b4	
	fxe2	2 ♗g2)	

In no. 171, the c5-square is guarded after the key, 1 ♕c8 (which threatens 2 ♕c6), by the white queen and the ♗f2. 1...♕c7 cuts the line c8-c5, and the mate 2 ♘ce3 cuts f2-c5 but opens a new line of guard from c1. Similarly, after 1...♕d7 (cutting c8-e6), 2 ♘fe3 mates by opening h3-e6 at the same time as e2-e6 is closed. In each case mate must not be given by the wrong knight on e3, which means that here, too, there is **dual avoidance**.

A variant of Theme D involves white guard-lines running respectively to two squares blocked by black units. When one of these units moves, White's mating move closes the relevant line of guard but opens another line of guard by way of compensation. Dual avoidance arises through the need to open the correct lines.

Theme E: Black opens a white line of guard so that White, in mating, can close another line to the same square (as in Theme B). Additionally, however, the mating move would allow the black king to escape to a different square if it did not simultaneously open another guard-line. In the variant of the theme, the black defence blocks a potential flight instead of opening a white guard-line.

Both forms of the theme are to be found in no. 172. 1 ♕d2 threatens 2 ♕h2. The defence 1...♖b2 opens a2-e6, allowing 2 ♘bc6, which opens a3-d6 as it closes b6-e6, so that 2...♔d6? cannot be played. After 1...dxc3, 2 ♘ec6 is mate, opening e8-e6 as it closes b6-e6 (2...♔e6? not available). The self-blocks 1...♘xe6 2 ♘bc6 and 1...♘d6 2 ♘ec6 show the variant form of the theme. Notice that there is no dual avoidance here.

172

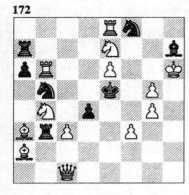

THEME E

M.M.Barulin
Il Problema 1932
Mate in two

Key 1 ♕d2 (>2 ♕h2)
...	♖b2	2 ♘bc6
	dxc3	2 ♘ec6
	♘xe6	2 ♘bc6
	♘d6	2 ♘ec6
	(♘g6	2 ♘d3)

The composer of these last two problems, Mark Barulin, was one of the leading Soviet composers of his time, and his name is often linked to these five white line-themes.

In 1978 the distinguished German composer Herbert Ahues published an article in a special issue of *Die Schwalbe*, outlining three further line-themes based on white try-play.

Theme F: A square in the black king's field is guarded by two white line-pieces. In each try White closes one of these lines, thus allowing Black to refute the try by closing the other.

The closure by Black will either give his king a flight or will prevent a white mate from working because it would give a flight. The former effect is seen in no. 173, which combines Theme F tries (which form a **Novotny** on d3) with Theme A defences (here **Grimshaw** interferences) after the key. 1 ♖d3? threatens both 2 ♘xc4 and 2 ♗f3, but because the white rook has closed the white bishop's line of guard to f5, Black can refute by closing the white queen's guard-line to that square: 1...e6!. Analogous play is seen after 1 ♗d3?, with the same threats. This move closes the line d1-d5, so that 1...♗d6! refutes by closing the line d7-d5. The key, 1 ♔g7!, threatens 2 ♗f4, a closure of the line h4-d4. Now we see Theme A at work: Black defends by occupying d3, thus closing b1-e4 and d1-d4. The try-play threats reappear as mates: 1...♖d3 2 ♘xc4; and 1...♗d3 2 ♘f3.

Theme G: In each try White closes a line of guard, with the result that a mating move will not work because it would close a second line of guard to the same square.

173

THEME F (+ THEME A)

H.Ahues
Schweizerische Schachzeitung 1992
Mate in two

Try	1 ♖d3?	(>2 ♘xc4/♘f3)
	... e6!	
Try	1 ♗d3?	(>2 ♘xc4/♘f3)
	... ♗d6!	
Key	1 ♔g7!	(>2 ♗f4)
	... ♖d3	2 ♘xc4
	♗d3	2 ♘f3
	♗c1	2 ♕c7
	♘e6+	2 ♕xe6

THEME G

174

H.Prins
2nd prize, *Die Schwalbe* 1984
Mate in two

Try	1 ♖b3?	(>2 ♕a8)
	... ♘e3!	(2 ♘d6?)
Try	1 ♗b3?	(>2 ♕a8)
	... ♘xf4!	(2 ♘f2?)
Key	1 ♕d7!	(>2 ♕c6)
	... ♘e3	2 ♘d6
	♘xf4	2 ♘f2
	(♖b6	2 ♕xd4)

No. 174 shows the effect with masked guard-lines (not an essential feature). 1 ♖b3? (>2 ♕a8) closes a2-d5, so that 2 ♘d6?, closing d8-d5, cannot be played after 1...♘e3!. Similarly 1 ♗b3? (>2 ♕a8), which closes a3-f3, fails to 1...♘xf4!, because 2 ♘f2?, closing f1-f3, is no longer mate. The key 1 ♕d7! (>2 ♕c6), making no line-closing error, allows the play to work smoothly: 1...♘e3 2 ♘d6; and 1...♘xf4 2 ♘f2.

Theme H: Three white lines of guard are aimed at the same square. In each try White closes one of them; Black's defence closes a second and refutes the try because the mating move would close the third.

175

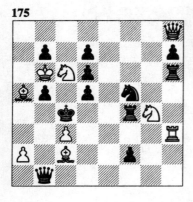

THEME H

S.Dittrich
Schach 1988
Mate in two

Try	1 ♘c~?	(>2 ♕c8)
	... d4!	
Try	1 ♘d4?	(>2 ♕c8)
	... ♕b4!	(2 ♗d3?)
Try	1 ♘b4?	(>2 ♕c8)
	... ♘d4!	(2 ♘e3?)
Key	1 ♘e7!	(>2 ♕c8)
	... ♕b4	2 ♗d3
	♘d4	2 ♘e3

The thematic square in no. 175 is c3, guarded by the ♗a5, the ♕h8 and the ♖h3. White's thematic mates, 2 ♗d3 and 2 ♘e3, would close the rook's line. A random try by the ♘c6 (threatening 2 ♕c8) fails to 1...d4!. There are two thematic **correction** tries: 1 ♘d4!?, closing h8-c3, and so refuted by 1...♕b4!, closing a5-c3 (2 ♗d3? will not work); and 1 ♘b4!?, which closes a5-c3 and thus allows Black to defend with 1...♘d4!, closing h8-c3 and ruling out 2 ♘e3?. The key 1 ♘e7! succeeds because it carries no line-closing effect. Notice the attractive **correspondence** between the thematic white tries and black refutations, with **reciprocal** effects. There is potential for a cyclic setting of the theme, but this has not yet been achieved.

Lion → Grasshopper

Locust → Grasshopper

Logical problem

The *Logical school*, sometimes called the *New German school*, derives from the early years of the 20th century. The term 'logical' is applied to problems displaying a strategic combination that requires a process of reasoning on the part of the solver. In the initial position from which will flow a three- or more-move 'logical combination' of the more usual type, White seems to have a sequence of moves leading to mate (his *mainplan* – German *Hauptplan*), but Black has a defence. Therefore White must first execute a

176

LOGICAL PROBLEM (ROMAN)

E.Pedersen
1st prize, *Skakbladet* 1942-3
Mate in three

Try 1 ♕b6? (>2 ♕b3)
    ... ♖b1!
Key 1 ♔a6! (2 ♕a2+ ♔b4 3 ♕a5)
    ... ♖h2 2 ♕b6   (>3 ♕b3)
                ...   ♖b2 3 ♕a5
          ♔b4 2 ♕b2+ ♔c5 3 ♕b6
          ♖a1 2 ♔a5   ♖~ 3 ♕a2

foreplan (German *Vorplan*) which deals with this defence in some way. It is implicit in the thinking of New German composers that White's sole purpose in carrying out his foreplan is to deal with the black defence. He must not at the same time improve his position in some other way. This cardinal principle is known as *purity of aim* (German *Zweckreinheit*).

No. 176 exemplifies the idea in miniature form. White would like to mate by playing 1 ♕b6, threatening 2 ♕b3. But Black has the defence 1...♖b1!. White must therefore play a different first move in order to threaten something else and thereby to force the rook to leave the bottom rank. 1 ♔a6! has this effect, for it threatens 2 ♕a2+ ♔b4 3 ♕a5. 1...♖a1 is easily countered: 2 ♔a5!, and the rook must move, after which 3 ♕a2 is playable. However, Black has the defence 1...♖h2. White has hereby achieved his objective: the rook cannot now reach b1, so he can continue with his main-plan: 2 ♕b6 (>3 ♕b3). The black rook's 'good' defence on b1 has been replaced by a 'bad' defence on b2, for 2...♖b2 is followed by 3 ♕a5, White exploiting the **self-block** by the rook on b2. This is a self-block **Roman**, and its logic may be compared with that of no. 247, by Møller, under that heading. There is one further line in Pedersen's attractive problem: 1...♔b4 2 ♕b2+ ♔c5 3 ♕b6 – a mate which is an **echo** of that with the queen on a5 and the black king on b4.

The celebrated German composer and writer Dr Werner Speckmann is the author of an exhaustive treatise on the New German school, entitled *Das logische Schachproblem* (Walter Rau Verlag, Düsseldorf, 1965; 2nd edition, extensively revised, 1980). One of his compositions appears as no. 3, on page 10 in Section I. It provides a further illustration of the logic underlying problems of the New German school. The mainplan 1 ♕g8? fails to 1...b4, so White must first carry out his foreplan with 1 ♕e6! (>2 ♕c8). If now 1...b4, then 2 ♛xe2+. So Black plays 1...♝g4, which simultaneously removes the bishop from its guard of c4 and shuts off one of the black rooks. Now White forces a critical move by the other black rook with 2 ♛a2+ ♜a4, and at last the main-plan works: 3 ♛g8 (>4 ♛c8/♛a8). Black's only resource is 3...b4, allowing 4 ♛c4.

FOUR FOREPLANS

177

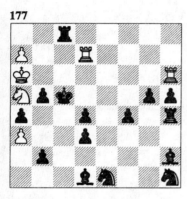

H.Lepuschütz
Deutsche Schachzeitung 1936
Mate in six

Try 1 ♖b6? (>2 ♖xb5) b1♛!
Try 1 ♖hd6? (>2 ♖d5) ♝b3 2 ♖b6
     1   ...   ♝f3!
Try 1 ♖e6? (>2 ♖e5) ♞f3 2 ♖ed6
     1   ...   f3!
Try 1 ♖f6? (>2 ♖f5)   ♞g3 2 ♖e6
     1   ...   ♝g4!
Key 1 ♖g6! (>2 ♖xg5)
    1...♝g4 2 ♖f6 ♞g3 3 ♖e6 ♞f3
    4 ♖ed6 ♝b3 5 ♖b6 ♖b8/♝c4
    6 ♖c6/♞b7

No. 177 shows a sequence of foreplans required to eliminate a series of black defences. The mainplan is to mate with the ♖h6 on b5, but the immediate 1 ♖b6? fails to 1...b1♛!. The try 1 ♖hd6? (>2 ♖d5) allows 2 ♖b6 (>3 ♖xb5) after 1...♝b3, because 2...b1♛? is now ineffective. But the ♝d1 can defend from the other direction with 1...♝f3!, so this move must be eliminated if White is to make progress. 1 ♖e6? (>2 ♖e5) provokes the defence 1...♞f3, which allows 2 ♖ed6 because the ♝d1 can no longer occupy f3. But 1...f3! refutes. Therefore this pawn-move must also be eliminated as a defence: 1 ♖f6? (>2 ♖f5) ♞g3 2 ♖e6! – and 2...f3? is useless. But Black has one last trick up his sleeve: 1...♝g4!. So the key is 1 ♖g6! (>2 ♖xg5), and now Black's defences allow White's tries to work in sequence as continuations: 1...♖g4 2 ♖f6 (>3 ♖f5) ♞g3 3 ♖e6 (>4 ♖e5) ♞f3 4 ♖ed6 (>5 ♖d5) ♝b3 5 ♖b6 (>6 ♖xb5). White has successfully manipulated all the black defenders so that there is nothing much left for Black to do: 5...♖b8/♖c6 6 ♖(x)c6, and 5...♝c4 6 ♞b7. A marvellous piece of work. A further example of this type of idea, with two foreplans in miniature form, is no. 134, under **Holst**.

There is a second, less familiar, type of logical problem. This is known in German as an *Auswahlkombination* (approximate English translation: *option-combination*). White appears to have two or more ways of forcing mate in the stipulated number of moves, but Black has a single defence which refutes all but one of them. In no. 178 White's aim is to play his b-rook to the h-file to threaten mate on h1.

178

OPTION COMBINATION

W.von Holzhausen
Deutsche Schachzeitung 1928
Mate in three

Tries 1 ♖b8?/♖b6?/♖b5?/♖b4?/♖d8?/
♖d6?/♖d4?/♖d3? a1♕!
Key 1 ♖d5! (>2 ♖h7 ... 3 ♖h1)

There seem to be several ways to do this: moves of the b-rook itself to b8, b6, b5 and b4, plus moves of the d-rook to d8, d6, d5, d4 and d3, all appear to achieve what is required. However, Black has the single defence 1...a1♕!, followed by 2...♕a8, guarding the mating square. Only one of White's many possible first moves will deal with this, namely 1 ♖d5!, closing the line a8-h1 in anticipation.

No. 179, in which White has a choice between only two plausible moves, nonetheless has more interesting strategic play. White would like to move his knight to d6 in order to deprive the black king of his two flights and thus to mate with the queen on d1. Clearly it is useless to play 1 ♘xd6? at once, as this is stalemate. In order to provide a reply to 1...♔b5 (2 ♕xd7+), the white king must move, and not of course to a dark square, where it would attract checks from the bishop. So the option is: g6 or e4? 1 ♔g6? allows 2 ♘d6 after random bishop moves, but Black continues the stalemating theme by playing 1...♗xf4!, after which 2 ♘d6? is no longer useful. Therefore only 1 ♔e4! will work, and the sole reason why it will work, and why 1 ♔g6? will not, is the prevention of stalemate after 1...♗xf4. The king has no other role to play, a fact that is underlined by the presence of the ♙e3, which in any case suffices to guard d4 after 1...♔b5 2 ♕xd7+ ♔c5 3 ♕c6. The pawn's presence is required by the principle of purity of aim, for without it the white king would have to move to e4 for two reasons. Incidentally, this problem shows

179

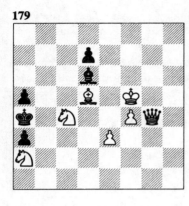

**OPTION COMBINATION
(+ UMNOV I)**

E.Zepler
1st prize, Olympic Tourney 1936
Mate in three
Try 1 ♘xd6? stalemate!
Try 1 ♔g6?
　　...　♗~　　2 ♘d6
　　　　♗xf4! (2 ♘d6? stalemate!)
Key 1 ♔e4!　　zugzwang
　　...　♗xf4 2 ♘d6　♗xd6 3 ♕xd7
　　　　♔b3　2 ♕e2　♔a4 3 ♘b6
　　　　♔b5　2 ♕xd7+　♔a6 3 ♕b7
　　　　...　　　　　♔c5 3 ♕c6

an effect which subsequently became known as **Umnov I** (a white piece oc-cupies a square just vacated by a black piece: 1...♗~ 2 ♘d6).

Like many areas of chess problem theory, logical problems have given rise to a great deal of debate, much of it centred on the principle of purity of aim. Speckmann's views do not meet with universal approval. In a book entitled *Hans+Peter+Rehm=Schach* (Editions feenschach-phénix, 1994) the distin-guished German authority Hans-Peter Rehm, writing in collaboration with Stephan Eisert, gives a slightly different view in an article reprinted from the German problem magazine *Die Schwalbe* (1977). Newcomers to the logical problem are advised to concentrate on the essential elements before embark-ing on a study of the intricate details!

Madrasi

This form of **fairy chess** was invented by the Indian composer A.J.Karwatkar. Like pieces (except kings) of opposite colour are paralysed when they at-tack one another, and are thus deprived of all powers until the attack ceases.

In no. 180 the white rook and black rook on the c-file are mutually para-lysed, and the key 1 ♘b4 is not check, because the white knight and the black knight are now paralysed. White's threat is a capture of the black knight, so that mate is given from b4. There seem to be three pieces available to make this capture, the ♗a2, the ♖d1 and the queen. However, d5 is guarded by the B♖d8 and B♗g8, which means that capture by the wrong piece will give the black king a flight-square: 2 ♗xd5? paralyses the white bishop, leaving b3 unguarded, and d2 is without a guard after 2 ♖dxd5?, the rook being now

180

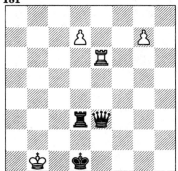

MADRASI

N.A.Macleod
Springaren 1984
Mate in two: Madrasi

Key 1 ♘b4 (>2 ♕xd5)
   ...   ♕e6   2 ♗xd5
       ♕d6   2 ♖dxd5
       ♕c6   2 ♖cxd5

paralysed. Therefore 2 ♕xd5 is the correct threat. Black defends by guarding d5 with his queen, for now 2 ♕xd5?, paralysing the queen, would allow Black a flight at d1. 1...♕e6, interfering with the ♗g8, allows 2 ♗xd5 (the bishop is not now paralysed), while 1...♕d6, an interference with the ♖d8, leads to 2 ♖dxd5 (no flight at d2 now). A third interference occurs on c6: 1...♕c6 'unparalyses' the ♖c5 and so permits 2 ♖cxd5. In this very clear example of interference between like-moving pieces, the Scottish grandmaster Norman Macleod (1927-1991) revealed his absolute mastery of an exciting fairy form.

181

MADRASI: HELPMATE

M.Rittirsch and A.Schöneberg
1st prize, *Die Schwalbe* 1987
Helpmate in two: Madrasi
(a) Diagram; (b) ♖e6→e5

(a) 1 ♕h3 g8♖ 2 ♖g3 d8♖
(b) 1 ♖a3 g8♕ 2 ♕b3 d8♕

No. 181 is an attractive **helpmate** miniature with promotions determined by the need for Madrasi paralysis. The diagram position is solved by 1 ♕h3 g8♖ 2 ♖g3 d8♖. The promotion on g8 is required to paralyse the black rook, and the mating promotion on d8 must not be to a queen, because Black would have the paralysing move 3 ♕h4 available. The second position has the ♖e6 on e5, and now the black **clearance** moves go in the opposite direction: 1 ♖a3 g8♕ 2 ♕b3 d8♕. This time the promotion on g8 paralyses the queen, while the mating promotion on d8 cannot now be to a rook (3 ♖a8!).

Composers sometimes extend the Madrasi rule to the two kings, which may then stand on adjacent squares. Solvers will see 'Madrasi RI' (= Rex inclusive) beneath the diagram when this additional rule applies.

Mari

The Mari theme is an important passive **dual avoidance** mechanism. Black opens a white line, thereby allowing White an apparent choice between two mates. But one of these mates would re-close the line which Black has just opened, and thus only the other one can be played.

MARI

182

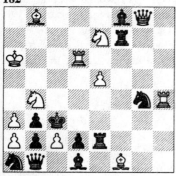

L.Lačný
1st hon. mention, Czech Chess Club
Tourney 1948
Mate in two

Key	1 ♗a7	(>2 ♖c6)
...♖e4	2 ♘ed5	(2 ♖d3? 2 ♗d4?)
♖xe5	2 ♗d4	(2 ♖d3? 2 ♘ed5?)
♖f6	2 ♗d4	(2 ♘ed5? 2 ♖d3?)
♖f4	2 ♖d3	(2 ♘ed5? 2 ♗d4?)
♘e3	2 ♖d3	(2 ♗d4? 2 ♘ed5?)
♘xe5	2 ♘ed5	(2 ♗d4? 2 ♖d3?)

No. 182 is a complicated rendering of the theme, combining it with other dual-avoidance effects. The key, 1 ♗a7, threatens 2 ♖c6. Black has a flight, c4, and White's three thematic mates, 2 ♘ed5, 2 ♗d4 and 2 ♖d3, cannot be played until Black has obligingly opened a white line of guard to that flight-square. This occurs when one of three units moves, the ♖e2, the ♖f7 and the ♘g4. 1...♖e4 allows only 2 ♘ed5; the move 2 ♖d3? would re-close the opened line f1-c4, while 2 ♗d4? is prevented by direct guard. 1...♖f6 allows only 2 ♗d4, since 2 ♘ed5? would shut the line g8-c4, and 2 ♖d3? is prevented by the pin of the white rook. After 1...♘e3, only 2 ♖d3 can be played, since 2 ♗d4? would close h4-c4, while d5 is guarded by the black knight.

It would be possible to end the discussion of this problem at this point, since we have now seen how the Mari theme works. But part of the point of this rendering lies in three further defences, which lead to the same three mates but which eliminate the other two mates in the reverse order. 1...♖xe5 prevents 2 ♖d3? (Mari) and 2 ♘ed5? (direct guard). 1...♖f4 rules out 2 ♘ed5? (Mari) and 2 ♗d4? (direct guard). Finally, after 1...♘xe5, 2 ♗d4? (Mari) and 2 ♖d3? (direct guard) are not playable.

MARI: RECIPROCAL CHANGE

183

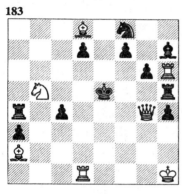

M.Kovačević
1st prize, *Kotelec* 1988
Mate in two

Set	1...	c3	2 ♖d5	
		g5	2 ♗f6	
		d5	2 ♖e1	
Try	1 ♘c7? (>2 ♖d5)		♖a5!	
Try	1 ♖d6? (>2 ♗f6)		♘e6!	
Key	1 ♕f3! (>2 ♖e1)			
	...	c3	2 ♗f6	(2 ♖d5?)
		g5	2 ♖d5	(2 ♗f6?)
		♔e6	2 ♕f6	

The Mari theme is not found in the set play of no. 183: 1...c3 2 ♖d5; 1...g5 2 ♗f6. Each black defence opens a white line of guard to a square on which the piece that guards that square in the diagram position can give mate. There are two tries that threaten those mates: 1 ♘c7? (>2 ♖d5) ♖a5!; and 1 ♖d6? (>2 ♗f6) ♘e6!. By placing a second guard on the mating squares but also giving a flight e6, the key 1 ♕f3! (>2 ♖e1) brings about a curious **reciprocal change**. Now the Mari theme comes into operation: 1...c3 2 ♗f6 (not 2 ♖d5?, because the line a2-e6 must not be closed again; and 1...g5 2 ♖d5 (not 2 ♗f6?, since the line h6-e6 has to be left open). A tireless worker on behalf of chess problems, Marjan Kovačević is one of the most original and inventive of two-move composers.

Mate transference

The majority of changed-play problems feature changed mates: Black's defences remain the same, but White's mates are different. An almost equally important, if less fruitful, changed-play concept is that of mate transference, in which the mates remain the same but the defences are changed; in other words, the mates are transferred from one group of defences to another. Transference of moves is the idea underlying a number of themes of recent development, and further discussion of the principle will be found under several other headings, particularly **reversal themes**, **Rukhlis** and **threat-correction**. The two examples quoted here illustrate mate transference in its simplest form.

MATE TRANSFERENCE

184

G.Popov
Thèmes 64 1961
Mate in two

Set	1...	♖b7	2 e4
		♗a4	2 c4
		♘d7	2 ♕xd7
		♘e6	2 ♕f3
		♘b7	2 ♕g8
Key	1 ♘xc6		(>2 ♘e7)
	...	♖xc6	2 e4
		♗xc6	2 c4
		♘bxc6	2 ♕d7
		♔xc6	2 ♕f3
		♘dxc6	2 ♕g8

185

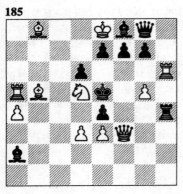

MATE TRANSFERENCE (THREE PHASES)

I.Grossman and A.Hirschenson
2nd prize, *Probleemblad* 1966
Mate in two

Set	1...	♔xd5	2 ♗d7
		♗xd5	2 d4
Try	1 ♘f4?		(>2 ♕xe4/♗c4)
	...	♔f5	2 ♗d7
		f5	2 d4
		♗d5!	
Key	1 ♘f6!		(>2 ♗c4)
	...	♔e6	2 ♗d7
		♗e6	2 d4

The key of no. 184 transfers five mates altogether, by means of a flight-giving sacrifice. The mates which follow the defences 1...♖b7, 1...♗a4, 1...♘d7 and 1...♘b7 in the set position follow the captures on c6 by these same four pieces after the key, 1 ♘xc6 (>2 ♘e7). The fifth transference is of the mate 2 ♕f3, which follows 1...♘e6 before the key and 1...♔xc6 after it.

Change of mate in three phases is very common (see **Zagoruiko**). Yet good examples of three-phase mate transference are comparatively rare. The thematic mates of no. 185 are 2 ♗d7 and 2 d4. These follow 1...♔xd5 and 1...♗xd5 in the set play, 1...♔f5 and 1...f5 after the try 1 ♘f4? (refuted by 1...♗d5!), and 1...♔e6 and 1...♗e6 following the key 1 ♘f6! (>2 ♗c4).

Maximummer

A maximummer is a kind of **fairy chess** problem in which Black must always play his geometrically longest move. If he has two moves of equal length, he may choose between them. If he is in check, he must play the longest move to get him out of check. The distances between the squares are measured from the square-centres, which means that a1 to b3 is longer than a1 to a3, and a1 to f6 is longer than a1 to a8 (this can be verified with a ruler – or by considering that $5^2+5^2 > 7^2$). Most maximummers are **selfmates**, like no. 186.

186

MAXIMUMMER

P.Raican
2nd prize, *feenschach* 1991
Selfmate in six: Maximummer

1 c8♖ ♕d8 2 ♖c3+ ♕d3 3 g8♖ b5
4 ♖e8 ♔g2/♔g4 5 ♖a8 ♕h7 6 ♖a3 ♕b1

It will be obvious that White has a much greater control over Black's moves than in most other kinds of selfmate. In this example, two promotions to rook are needed to set up the mating position. Notice that Black must be prevented from playing 4...♔e4, which would eliminate 5...♕h7 and allow the queen to escape up the d-file.

Meredith

A problem with at least eight and not more than twelve units is known as a Meredith, after an American composer of the 19th century who made a number of small-scale problems.

Merry-go-round → Round trip

Miniature

A problem with seven pieces or fewer is termed a miniature.

Minimal

A minimal is a problem in which the force of the mating (or self-mating) side consists purely of the king and one other unit.

Model mates

A model mate is a mating position in which no square in the black king's field is guarded more than once by White, and no square is guarded by White and simultaneously blocked by Black, and in which all the white men on the board, with the permitted exception of the king and pawns, play some part in the mate by guarding squares. The interest in a model-mate problem centres generally on the beauty of the actual mating positions. Consequently the two-mover offers little scope to the model-mate enthusiast, and few satisfactory examples are to be found. In the three- and more-move field, however, the possibilities are much greater, and it is difficult to give more than the sketchiest idea of what has been achieved.

Four distinct models are found in no. 187. The key 1 ♝h7 introduces a threat which itself ends in a model if Black plays a capture on d5: 2 ♞b5 ♚xd5 3 ♞fd4. In this position the mating piece, the white queen, holds e5 and c5; d4 and d6 are guarded by the ♞b5; the ♞d4 holds c6 and e6, and finally the ♝h7 controls e4. If Black plays 1...♖xa3, White has the quiet (i.e. non-checking) continuation 2 ♛xd2, and after 2...♚e5 3 ♛d4 gives us the second model mate. The third model occurs after 1...c3: 2 ♞g7+ ♚d4 3 ♞e6; and the fourth in the variation 1...♚xd5 2 ♞d4+ ♚xd4 3 ♞b5.

Echo-models are featured in no. 188. The key is 1 ♝f5. If 1...♚f3, then 2 ♚g1 ♚e2 3 ♝c2 ♚f3 4 ♝d1 – model mate. The reader should study carefully the relative positions of the white rook and bishops before considering the second variation. The reason is that after 1...♚f1 2 ♝g4 ♚f2 3 ♝d2 ♚g3

187

MODEL MATES

Y.G.Vladimirov
1st prize, Kubbel Tourney 1991
Mate in three

Key 1 ♗h7 (>2 ♘b5 ♚xd5 3 ♘fd4)
... ♖xa3 2 ♕xd2 ♚e5 3 ♕d4
c3 2 ♘g7+ ♚d4 3 ♘e6
♚xd5 2 ♘d4+ ♚xd4 3 ♘b5

188

MODEL MATES (ECHOES)

O.Wurzburg
1st prize, Cheney Miniature Tourney
1937
Mate in four
Key 1 ♗f5 (>2 ♗g4 ♚~ 3 ♗e3 ♚~ 4
♖a1)
... ♚f3 2 ♚g1 ♚e2 3 ♗c2 ♚f3 4 ♗d1
...   ♚e1 4 ♖e4
♚f1 2 ♗g4 ♚f2 3 ♗d2 ♚g3 4 ♗e1
...   ♚f1 4 ♖f4

4 ♗e1, the position of the three pieces in question is *echoed*; they stand in the same relationship to the black king in the two variations. (Echoed lines in which the king ends up on squares of different colours, as here, are known as *chameleon echoes*.) This elegant problem has two more model mates. If in the first variation Black plays 3 ♚e1, White mates with 4 ♖e4. This mate is echoed by the one that follows 3...♚f1 in the second variation, namely 4 ♖f4. It is probably true to say that elegance is the key-note of model-mate compositions; economy of means and beauty of effect contribute to this elegance.

Not all model-mate problems contain play of this character, however, for many composers have combined models with themes of considerable strategic complexity. In no. 189 we find **critical** and anti-critical play, self-blocks and other interesting strategy besides the echo-models.

The key, 1 ♕c6, threatens 2 ♘f6+ ♚f4 (if 2...♚e3, 3 ♕c5+) 3 ♕e4+ ♖bxe4/♖exe4 4 ♘d5. 1...♕a1 defeats the threat by means of an anti-critical defence, over the critical square f6, bringing the black queen into a position

189

ECHO-MODELS

O.Wurzburg and J.Buchwald
1st place, 1st International Team Match
1962-4
Mate in four

Key 1 ♛c6   (>2 ♞f6+ ♚f4 3 ♛e4+)
    ...   ♛a1   2 ♞c3+ ♚f4 3 ♛e4+
           ♛d4   2 ♞g5+ ♚e5 3 ♛e6+
           ♛e5   2 ♞xd2+ ♚d4 3 ♛c4+

to interpose on d4 after 2 ♞f6+ ♚e3 3 ♛c5+?. But the defence turns out to be a critical error, crossing a second critical square c3: 1...♛a1 2 ♞c3+ ♚f4 3 ♛e4+ ♖bxe4/♖exe4 4 ♞d5. Two further defences by the black queen introduce play involving the opening of the ♗+♞ battery in the south-east corner of the board. 1...♛d4 allows 2 ♞g5+ ♚e5 3 ♛e6+ ♖xe6 4 ♞f7 – model! And 1...♛e5 gives 2 ♞xd2+ ♚d4 3 ♛c4+ ♖xc4 4 ♞b3 – another model, and an echo of the previous one.

The fourth example shows models of a very popular type. In the course of the solution a black unit becomes pinned, and a *pin-model* results. In such a mate one of the white units is used to pin the black unit in question, and can thus be regarded as participating in the mate.

190

PIN-MODELS

G.Kozyura
1st prize ex aequo, Lobusov 40 Tourney
1992
Mate in three

Key 1 ♖b5   (>2 ♛f6+ ♚xh5 3 g4)
    ...   ♞xg3 2 ♛f4+ ♚h5 3 ♗xf7
           fxe6 2 ♛xh7+ ♚g5 3 ♛g6

There are three pin-models in no. 190. The good key 1 ♖b5, which gives up an apparently useful battery, prepares for a pin of the ♞e5 after black king moves to h5 and g5. The threat is 2 ♛f6+ ♚xh5 3 g4 – pin-model. 1...♞xg3 allows 2 ♕f4+ ♚h5 3 ♗xf7 – a second pin-model. The third pin-model is seen after 1...fxe6: 2 ♕xh7+ ♚g5 3 ♕g6. Even the solver who is not keen on model-mates will appreciate the play of this delightful work.

Munich

The Munich is a three- and more-move theme involving the following strategy. A black defence has a set mate. On his first move Black deprives himself of this defence, so that White is able to abandon the set mate on his second move. No. 191 is a clear illustration.

191

MUNICH

H.Garn
1st prize, German Ring Tourney 1948
Mate in three

Try	1 ♗g6?	♗b5!	(2 ♘g6??)
Try	1 ♗f5?	♕a6!	(2 ♘f5??)
Key	1 ♗c2!	zugzwang	
	... ♘c6	2 ♗g6	
	♘a6	2 ♗f5	
	c5	2 ♗d1	

The set replies to 1...♗b5 and 1...♕a6 are respectively 2 ♘g6 and 2 ♘f5. White has two tries which emphasise the character of the theme: 1 ♗g6?, refuted by 1...♗b5! (2 ♘g6? being no longer possible); and 1 ♗f5?, which fails to 1...♕a6!, since 2 ♘f5? is now ruled out. The key, 1 ♗c2!, puts Black in zugzwang and forces him to abandon his set defences by making them impossible. 1...♘c6 eliminates a pin of the white queen by the ♗e8, so that 2 ♗g6 can now be played. Likewise, after 1...♘a6, the black queen can no longer occupy a6, so that 2 ♗f5 is playable.

No. 192 is a more complex example. The set defences are 1...♘b5, 1...♘e6 and 1...f2, which lead respectively to the set mates 2 ♘c5, 2 ♖e5 and 2 ♕xe3. The tries 1 ♗c5?, 1 ♗e5? and 1 ♗xe3? occupy the squares needed for these mates, and so fail to the respective set defences. The key 1 ♖g5! completes the block. Black's principal defences now prevent the set defences from being played and thus allow, as second-move continuations, the three white bishop-moves shown as tries: 1...♖b5 2 ♗c5 (3 ♘c5 is not needed as a mate any more, because 2...♘b5 has been ruled out); 1...♖e6 2 ♗e5 (no need

192

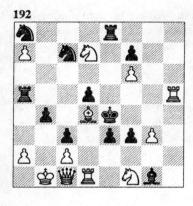

MUNICH

L.I.Loshinsky
1st prize, *Schach* 1956
Mate in three
Try 1 ♗c5?   ♘b5!
Try 1 ♗e5?   ♘e6!
Try 1 ♗xe3?   f2!
Try 1 ♖d3?   b3!
Key 1 ♖g5!   zugzwang
    ...   ♖b5   2 ♗c5
               ♖e6   2 ♗e5
               ♗f2   2 ♗xe3

to retain 3 ♖e5); and 1...♗f2 2 ♗xe3 (2...f2 cannot be played). Any other black first move either unguards a square to allow White to mate immediately, or else exposes a black unit to capture so that mate on the third move is inevitable.

Mutate

Mutate is the term given to a complete-block problem in which White, with no waiting-move at his disposal, is forced to abandon one or more of his set mates and introduce new replies to Black's defences, while at the same time keeping Black in zugzwang. No. 193 is a simple setting, illustrating a **focal** idea.

193

MUTATE: FOCAL PLAY

E.Zepler
Die Schwalbe 1928
Mate in two
Set 1...   ♖~4   2 ♕e6
               ♖~e   2 ♕d3
               c4   2 ♕c6
Key 1 ♘f7 zugzwang
    ...   ♖~4   2 ♘e7
               ♖~e   2 ♘xf4
               c4   2 ♕d6

In the set position White could mate with either 2 ♕e6 or 2 ♕d3 according to whether the black rook moved away along the rank or along the file. The key 1 ♘f7 changes the focal mates to 2 ♘e7 and 2 ♘xf4, and also introduces a new mate to follow 1...c4.

MUTATE: MULTIPLE CHANGES

R.T.Lewis
Version, *The Problemist* 1984
Mate in two

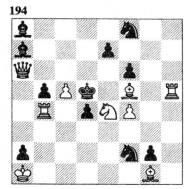

194

Set	1...	♘8~	2 ♕e6
		♘xe4	2 ♗e6
		d3	2 ♗e6
		e6	2 ♕d6
		♗b8	2 ♕xa8
		♗b6	2 ♕xa8
		♗xc5	2 ♕xa8
		♗c6	2 ♕xa2
Key	1 ♕xb5		zugzwang
	...	♘8~	2 ♕d7
		♘xe4	2 ♖xd4
		d3	2 ♘c3
		e6	2 ♘xf6
		♗b8	2 c6
		♗b6	2 cxb6
		♗xc5	2 ♕xc5
		♗c6	2 ♕c4
		♗b7	2 ♕xb7

Not all mutates are lightweight problems, as no. 194 proves. It may seem surprising to the solver that every black move is set with a mate in the diagram position. White has at least one good try which just fails to hold the position: 1 ♔xa2?, which will not work because of white self-obstruction (1...♗c6! 2 ♕xa2?). The key removes the queen from the a-file and the sixth rank, on both of which she can mate in the set play, and sets up a ♕+♙ battery, which opens twice in the post-key play. Importantly the queen also now guards c5 so that the ♘e4 is free to mate on c3 and f6. The composer, Tony Lewis, is well-known for his mutate two-movers, in which he largely specialises. No doubt he regrets the passive rôle of the ♖h5 after the key in this example, which shows five set mates changed to eight.

Neutral piece

Many composers of **fairy chess** problems have experimented with the effects that can be achieved with a neutral piece, which can be moved or captured by either side. No. 195 is a **helpmate** in two, with three solutions varying according to whether the ♗b2 is (a) white, as in the diagram, or (b) black, or (c) neutral.

195

NEUTRAL PIECE

P.B.van Dalfsen
Probleemblad 1968
Helpmate in two
(a) w.♗b2 (as diagram)
(b) b.♗b2
(c) Neutral ♗b2

(a) 1 ♗h7+ ♔f6 2 c2 ♔f7
(b) 1 c2 h6 2 ♗g7 hxg7
(c) 1 ♗a1 ♔f6 2 c2 ♔g6

Black moves first in each solution. Part (a) is solved by 1 ♗h7+ ♔f6 2 c2 ♔f7. With a black ♗b2 the solution is 1 c2 h6 2 ♗g7 hxg7. If the bishop is neutral, the play runs 1 ♗a1 ♔f6 2 c2 ♔g6. In (c) the bishop is used by Black to begin with, and then by White for the mate. That is why it must be moved into the corner first of all: if it remained on b2, Black would not be mated on the second move, since he would be able to play 3 ♗a3 or 3 ♗c1.

Nietvelt Defence

A Nietvelt defence occurs when Black defends by capturing on a battery-line so that the rear piece of the battery, in playing the threat, would crucially unpin the defending black unit. This is not actually as complex as it sounds! The defence is seen three times over in the set play of no. 196, and three times again after the key.

1 f8♘? threatens 2 ♕b7. Now a self-pin on d6 by the black queen defeats by threatening 2...♕c6!, and a pin-mate results: 2 ♘f4. Similarly 1...♖xd6 threatens 2...♖c6, but because of the self-pin White can play 2 ♗g8. 1...♘xd6 also defends (2 ♕b7? ♘xb7!), but allows 2 ♗e4 through line-opening (h7-e4) and self-pin. 2 ♗e4 also follows 1...♘xe7, but 1...♘d4! refutes the try. The flight-giving key 1 ♖e4! (>2 ♕b7) changes all three of the

196

NIETVELT DEFENCES

C.Ouellet (after K.Braithwaite)
Version, *The Problemist* 1989
Mate in two

Try	1 f8♘?	(>2 ♕b7)
	...	♕xd6	2 ♘f4
		♖xd6	2 ♗g8
		♘xd6	2 ♗e4
		♘d4!	
Key	1 ♖e4!	(>2 ♕b7)
	...	♕xd6	2 ♖e5
		♖xd6	2 ♘f6
		♘xd6	2 c4
		(♘xc5 | 2 ♘c3)
		(♔xe4 | 2 ♕xf5)

mates following the Nietvelt defences, and once again the mates exploit Black's self-pin: 1...♕xd6 2 ♖e5; 1...♖xd6 2 ♘f6; and 1...♘xd6 2 c4.

Nightrider

The Nightrider (♘)is a **fairy chess** piece invented by T.R.Dawson in 1925. It performs one or more knight-leaps in a straight line as a single move. Thus a nightrider on a1 has access on a clear board to b3, c5, d7, c2, e3 and g4. The nightrider is therefore a line-piece (known in fairy terminology as a *rider*) just like the queen, rook or bishop of the orthodox chess-set, and can consequently be used to achieve interference and pinning effects. A very popular fairy piece, the nightrider is seen in no. 197. To inflict the stipulated mate in five, the nightrider visits e7, g3, e4 and finally d2. Mate can be forced against a lone king with ♘+♘, but not, of course, with ♘+♘.

Some of the more complex effects which may be produced with a nightrider are to be found in no. 198. The key is 1 d8♘, which pins the ♗c6 and thereby threatens 2 ♕xb5. It is a convention in fairy problems that promotion to a fairy piece is permissible provided there is a piece of that type on the board already. So, since there are plenty of nightriders about, 1 d8♘ is a perfectly legal promotion, though perhaps a rather strong key. Black defends against the threat by moving the ♘b5, but five of the six moves of this piece produce interferences. 1...♘a7 interferes with the ♖a8, permitting the white ♘g3 to play to a6 to mate. 1...♘d6 leads to 2 ♘xc6, exploiting the interference with the black queen on the sixth rank, while 1...♘d4 allows 2 ♕c4,

197

NIGHTRIDER

T.R.Dawson
British Chess Magazine 1925
Mate in five
Nightrider c6

1 ♘e7 ♔a7 2 ♘g3 ♔a8 3 ♘e4 ♔a7 4
♘b5+ ♔a8 5 ♘d2

198

NIGHTRIDERS

P.Monréal and J.Oudot
2nd prize, *Thèmes 64* 1964
Mate in two
Nightriders b7, g3, h7, b5
Key 1 d8♘ (>2 ♕xb5)

...	
♘a7	2 ♘ga6
♘d6	2 ♘dxc6
♘d4	2 ♕c4
♘f3	2 ♘hxd5
♘h2	2 ♘gxh1
♖a5	2 ♘bd3

owing to the interference with the ♖g4. In the latter variation Black cannot reply 2...dxc4?, since the ♙d5 is pinned by the white ♘h7. 1...♘f3 enables this same ♘h7 to come into play as a mating-piece with 2 ♘xd5 (2...cxd5? cannot be played because the ♙c6 is still pinned by the ♘d8). The fifth interference by the black nightrider is 1...♘h2, which interrupts the black queen's line of guard down the h-file and so permits 2 ♘xh1. The capacity for producing spectacular interference-variations like this last is one of the many entertaining properties of the nightrider. (A further variation featuring one of the white nightriders is the self-block 1...♖a5 2 ♘d3.)

Novotny

The Novotny, one of the most popular themes for problems of all lengths, is a close relation of the **Grimshaw**. A white piece plays on to a square which is the cutting-point of the lines of (typically) a black rook and a black bishop, with the result that the capture of that piece leads to the same effects as straightforward interferences would produce. Merely stated in words, this theme may sound either complicated or dull. In fact it has given rise to a very large number of extremely fine problems, of which we can quote no more than a handful here.

NOVOTNY

199

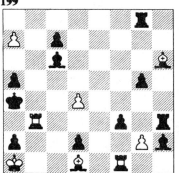

V.F.Rudenko
1st place, W.C.C.T. 1972-5
Mate in six

Key 1 g3 (>2 a8♕ ♗xa8 {2...♖xa8 3 ♖b8+ ♚a3 4 ♗f8}3 ♖b7+ ♚a3 4 ♖xf3) ... ♖xg3 2 ♖b7+ ♚a3 3 a8♕ ♖xa8 4 ♖b3+ ♚a4 5 ♖b8+ ♚a3 6 ♗f8 ... ♗xg3 2 ♖b8+ ♚a3 3 a8♕ ♗xa8 4 ♖b3+ ♚a4 5 ♖b7+ ♚a3 6 ♖xf3

We start our brief survey with an excellent six-mover, no. 199, in which the key is the Novotny move, but the interferences are not exploited until later in the solution. 1 g3 threatens 2 a8♕ (>3 ♕xc6); if 2...♗xa8, 3 ♖b7+ ♚a3 4 ♖xf3, and if 2...♖xa8, 3 ♖b8+ ♚a3 4 ♗f8. In each line the white rook shuts off the black unit capturing on a8 to allow the mate to occur. Black therefore defends by capturing on g3, so that an additional guard is placed on White's mating square (f3) or line (f8-a3). White replies by playing his threatened third move as second move, taking care to select the continuation that will ensure an eventual mate from the direction which Black has failed to control with his initial capture. 1...♖xg3 2 ♖b7+ ♚a3 3 a8♕ ♖xa8 4 ♖b3+ ♚a4 5 ♖b8+ ♚a3 6 ♗f8; and 1...♗xg3 2 ♖b8+ ♚a3 3 a8♕ ♗xa8 4 ♖b3+ ♚a4 5 ♖b7+ ♚a3 6 ♖xf3. In each line the white ♗+♖ battery must open twice with check, firstly to eliminate an unwanted black defence, and secondly to shut off the black piece that has captured on a8.

The very close affinity between the Grimshaw and Novotny themes may be clearly seen from no. 200. The solver with experience of the former theme will be quick to see two promising-looking Grimshaws with set mates, the interferences between black rook and black bishop on b4 and e6. White has two Novotny tries, 1 ♗b4? and 1 ♖b4?, both threatening the two mates set in

200

NOVOTNYS + GRIMSHAWS

W.Tura
1st prize, *Europe Echecs* 1962
Mate in two

Try 1 ♗b4?	(>2 ♕e1/♕xd4)
... ♖e6!	(2 ♖b5?)
Try 1 ♖b4?	(>2 ♕e1/♕xd4)
... ♗e6!	(2 ♗d6?)
Key 1 ♗e6!	(>2 ♖b5/♗d6)
... ♖b4	2 ♕e1
♗b4	2 ♕xd4

reply to the interferences on this square, 2 ♕xd4 and 2 ♕e1. However, these tries constitute a *white Grimshaw*, for the two white pieces get in each other's way. 1 ♗b4? is refuted by 1...♖e6!, because 2 ♖b5? cannot now be played. And 1 ♖b4? fails to 1...♗e6!, because 2 ♗d6? is now impossible. The key of this problem is a third Novotny, this time on e6: 1 ♗e6!. The threats are now the two moves 2 ♖b5 and 2 ♗d6, and Black's defences, the interferences on b4, lead to the mates threatened by the tries, 2 ♕xd4 and 2 ♕e1. The double threat, an extremely common feature of Novotny-key problems, is reduced to a single mate by the captures of the key-piece on its arrival square: 1...♖xe6 2 ♖b5 only; and 1...♗xe6 2 ♗d6 only.

One of the principal Novotny tasks which composers have set themselves is the achievement of a record number of different Novotnys in a single problem, on the same square or on different squares. Such problems are sometimes not of the greatest strategic interest, but may well be fiendishly difficult to solve. No. 201, an elegant pawnless setting (an *aristocrat*), shows great artistic restraint as well as some interesting play.

There are three set mates, but these are not the main points of the work, which lies in the choice of Novotny and the manner in which the wrong choices fail. 1 ♗e5? threatens 2 ♘g7 or 2 ♖e7 (as usual the threats are forced separately by the two captures on the Novotny square), but is refuted by 1...♘xh7!. 1 ♘d4? (>2 ♘f6/♖d8) fails to 1...♖e7!. 1 ♖d4? (>2 ♘f6/♘d6) provides no mate in reply to 1...♖e6! (but 1...♘e4? does not refute, since it is answered by 2 ♖e7). The key is 1 ♗d4! (>2 ♘g7/♖d8), and if 1...♘e6, then 2 ♖e7. The way in which the white pieces exchange roles, now making tries, now giving mates, is most entertaining.

Interestingly enough, no. 202 took first prize ahead of no. 201 in the same tourney. There are eight different threats in its four Novotnys, two on each of two squares. What adds considerably to the effect of this fine problem is the

201

NOVOTNYS: TRY-PLAY

M.Lipton
2nd prize, BCPS Ring Tourney 1966
Mate in two

Try	1 &e5?	(>2 ♘g7/♖e7)
...	♘xh7!	
Try	1 ♘d4?	(>2 ♘f6/♖d8)
...	♖e7!	
Try	1 ♖d4?	(>2 ♘f6/♘d6)
...	♘e4	2 ♖e7
	♖e6!	
Key	1 &d4!	(>2 ♘g7/♖d8)
...	♘e6	2 ♖e7

NOVOTNYS: TRY-PLAY

202

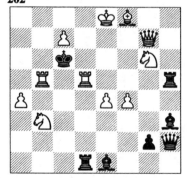

C.Goldschmeding
1st prize, BCPS Ring Tourney 1966
Mate in two

Try	1 ♖f5?	(>2 c8♕/♘e5)
...	♖d7	2 ♕xd7
	♖d8+	2 cxd8♘
	♕xf4!	
Try	1 f5?	(>2 ♕d7/♖dc5)
...	♕e5+	2 ♘xe5
	♖dxd5	2 exd5
	♕d6!	
Try	1 ♖d2?	(>2 ♘a5/♘d4)
...	♖xb5!	
Key	1 ♘d2!	(>2 ♕c3/♖d6)
...	♖e5+	2 ♘xe5
	&d7+	2 ♕xd7
	♖hxd5	2 exd5

large amount of by-play which the composer brilliantly worked in alongside the Novotnys and the play they introduce. The pattern of changed and transferred mates is quite bewildering. 1 ♖f5? threatens 2 c8♕ and 2 ♘e5 (separated, of course, by the captures on f5). Three defences defeat both threats: 1...♖d7, answered by 2 ♕xd7; 1...♖d8+, to which the reply is 2 cxd8♘; and 1...♕xf4!, which has no reply and therefore refutes this try. 1 f5? carries the threats 2 ♕d7 and 2 ♖dc5. Once again there are three defences defeating both threats: 1...♕e5+ (2 ♘xe5), 1...♖dxd5 (2 exd5), and 1...♕d6! (no reply). White therefore turns his attention away from the unproductive Novotny attempts on f5 and tries Novotnys on d2 instead. 1 ♖d2? (>2 ♘a5/♘d4) fails to 1...♖xb5!. So White is left with 1 ♘d2! (>2 ♕c3/♖d6). Again there are three total defences, but this time all have replies: 1...♖e5+ 2 ♘xe5; 1...♗d7+ 2 ♕xd7; and 1...♖hxd5 2 exd5. All this complex play is achieved with extraordinary economy and clarity. The brilliant Dutch expert Cor Goldschmeding made several examples of this theme, but surely none finer than this.

NOVOTNYS

203

R.C.O.Matthews
British Chess Magazine 1957
Mate in three

Key 1 b4	(>2 ♗xb1 ... 3 ♖a3)		
... ♗b6	2 ♖d5	♗xd5 3 ♘b5	
...		♖xd5 3 ♘e4	
♗c5	2 ♖b7, etc.		
♖bxb5	2 ♕d5, etc.		
♗b7	2 ♖c5	♗xc5 3 ♘b5	
...		♖xc5 3 ♗xd4	
♗d5	2 ♖bb6, etc.		
♖hxb5	2 ♖b6, etc.		

Interest in the Novotny in three-movers among British composers is largely due to several excellent examples produced by R.C.O.Matthews, a composer of remarkable inventiveness and constructional ability. One of his most famous problems is no. 203, with its brilliant combination of interference and Novotny play. In the three-mover the Novotny occurs more usually on White's second move than on his first, and that is the case here. The key, 1 b4, threatens 2 ♗xb1 followed by 3 ♖a3. Black has six thematic defences, each leading to a Novotny. 1...♗b6 allows 2 ♖d5, with the threats 3 ♘b5 and 3 ♘e4 (separated by the captures 2...♗xd5 and 2...♖xd5). This continuation is made possible because the black bishop initially interferes with the ♖b8. 1...♗c5 is an interference with the ♖h5 and permits the continuation 2 ♖b7, with the same threats as before. 1...♖bxb5 is an unguard of b5, allowing 2 ♕d5 (same threats). 1...♗b7 is a second interference with the ♖b8, and White can now play 2 ♖c5, this time threatening 3 ♘b5 and 3 ♗xd4. The same third-move threats are found after 1...♗d5 2 ♖bb6 (exploiting the interference with the ♖h6), and 1...♖hxb5 2 ♖b6 (a second unguard of b5). As with the two-mover by Tura, the affinity between the Grimshaw and Novotny themes stands out clearly.

204

NOVOTNYS + PICKANINNY

N.Littlewood
1st prize, B.C.P.S. Ring Tourney 1966
Mate in three

Key 1 ♖e6 (>2 ♘h7)

...	fxe6	2 c6
	fxg6	2 ♗c7
	f6	2 ♖d6
	f5	2 ♖c6

No. 204 combines Novotnys with a **Pickaninny**, the name given to maximum activity (four moves altogether) of a single black pawn. The key is somewhat perfunctory and threatens immediate mate: 1 ♖e6 (>2 ♘h7). Now each move of the ♙f7 leads to a Novotny continuation, with the usual double threat separated by the captures of the white unit: 1...fxe6 2 c6; 1...fxg6 2 ♗c7; 1...f6 2 ♖d6; and 1...f5 2 ♖c6. It is a slight blemish that this last continuation carries a third threat, 3 ♖xf5, which can be played, as an alternative to 3 ♖xg3, after 2...♖xc6.

Three variants of the Novotny theme deserve brief mention here. One is the *Finnish Novotny*. In the initial position a black pawn stands on the intersection-square of the lines of a black rook and black bishop. White has a try threatening two mates, both defeated simultaneously by the move of the black pawn to open the rook's and bishop's lines. The key is a capture of this pawn, and the play thereafter is exactly as in a normal double-threat Novotny. The second variant has been named the *English Novotny* by its inventor, Michael Lipton. A white piece plays on to the intersection-square of the lines of a pinned black queen and another black line-piece.

An extension of this idea is seen in no. 205, a *cyclic Novotny*, in which three black lines are cut simultaneously, in both try and key, with three threats, separated in cyclic fashion according to the captures. 1 ♘ec4? threatens 2 ♘dxf7, 2 b6 and 2 ♕c5, and these mates appear singly after the captures 1...♕xc4, 1...♖xc4 and 1...♗xc4. The try fails, however, to 1...♖xe8!. The key is 1 ♘dc4!, with three threats once again, but two of them different

205

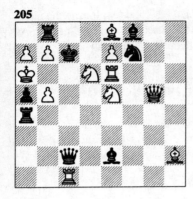

CYCLIC NOVOTNY

M.Lipton
2nd prize, *British Chess Magazine* 1967
Mate in two
Try 1 ♘ec4?

...	♕xc4	2 ♘dxf7
	♖xc4	2 b6
	♗xc4	2 ♕c5
	♖xe8!	

Key 1 ♘dc4!

...	♕xc4	2 ♘exf7
	♖xc4	2 b6
	♗xc4	2 ♖c6
	♗xe7	2 ♕xe7

from before: 2 ♘exf7, 2 b6 and 2 ♖c6. They are separated by the same three captures as after the try. The richness of this ingenious work is enhanced by the set play (1...♗xb5+ 2 ♘xb5; 1...♕c6+ 2 ♖xc6; 1...♖a8 2 bxa8♘; 1...♖c8 2 bxc8♕; and 1...♖xe8 2 ♘xe8 – this last defence being the one which defeats the try), and by the use made of the white queen after the key: 1...♗xe7 2 ♕xe7.

Obstruction

Obstruction occurs when a piece moves to a square so that another piece is prevented from occupying that square. In the two-mover this is restricted to obstruction of the black king, i.e. **self-block**. In three-movers and longer problems, however, the possibilities are much greater.

No. 206 shows obstruction in combination with **Nietvelt defences**: the black ♗a1 and ♘d1 get in each other's way as they pin themselves on c3. The key 1 ♔c7 threatens 2 ♕b6 followed by 3 ♘h4. The self-pins by the bishop and knight defeat the threat because, after 2 ♕b6?, checks on the white king would be possible as a result of the unpin. But 1...♗xc3 allows 2 c5 (>3 ♕d5), because the bishop, by occupying c3, has prevented the knight from self-pinning on that square. The parallel variation, in which the knight obstructs the bishop, is 1...♘xc3 2 ♕a3 (>3 ♕f8). The bishop cannot now self-pin on c3 to defeat the third-move threat. The white second-move continuations are also first-move tries, refuted by the self-pins 1 ♕a3? ♗xc3! and 1 c5? ♘xc3!.

206

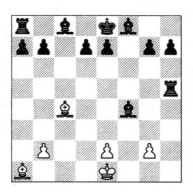

OBSTRUCTION (NIETVELT DEFENCES)

J.Hartong
3rd prize, *Parallèle 50* 1949
Mate in three

Try 1 ♕a3?   ♝xc3!
Try 1 c5?   ♞xc3!
Key 1 ♔c7!   (>2 ♕b6 ... 3 ♞h4)
    ...   ♝xc3 2 c5   (>3 ♕d5)
            ♞xc3 2 ♕a3   (>3 ♕f8)

Obtrusive force

The diagram accompanying this paragraph is not a problem. The pieces have been arranged on the board to illustrate what is meant by (1) *obtrusive force*, (2) *promoted force*, and (3) *illegal position*.

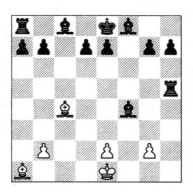

The w♝c4 is obtrusive: there is only one other white bishop on the board, yet it is evident, from the fact that the white e-pawn and g-pawn are still on their starting squares, that this ♝c4 can only have arisen through the promotion of a white pawn. (It is also evident from the position, though irrelevant to the present discussion, that this promotion could only have taken place on e8 or g8, which means that Black is unable to castle, since the pawn must have passed over f7, giving check, if the black king were then on e8, before promoting.) The b♜h5 is also obtrusive: the original h-rook must have been captured on h8 or g8, since it could never have escaped from that corner, just as the a-rook can only have moved to b8. We should not normally refer to either the ♗c4 or the ♖h5 as 'promoted', though they clearly are promoted pawns, because the number of white bishops and black rooks on the board does not exceed two in each case. But the black ♗f4 is *promoted*, because it is a third black bishop. The white ♗a1, on the other hand, makes for an *illegal position*: it could never have reached a1, promoted or not, with the white b-pawn still on its starting square. By convention, promoted force is not normally admitted in orthodox (i.e. direct-mate, helpmate and selfmate) problems, but obtrusive force, though not tolerated by some purists, is usually accepted if it cannot be avoided. But illegal positions are definitely out!

Opposition

Opposition, a kind of **correspondence**, can take various forms. Many a **duel** between pieces of opposite colour may exemplify opposition, when the duel produces moves that bear an optical similarity, as in no. 207.

OPPOSITION

207

J.M.Rice (after J.Szöghy)
The Problemist – Supplement 1996
Mate in two

Try	1 ♕c7?	(>2 ♕g7)	♗d7!
Try	1 ♕d6?	(>2 ♕f6)	♗e6!
Try	1 ♕f4?	(>2 ♕f6)	♗f5!
Try	1 ♕g3?	(>2 ♕g7)	♗g4!
Try	1 ♕h2?	(>2 ♕h8)	♗h3!
Key	1 ♘c3!	(>2 ♘b5)	
...	♗d7 2 ♕h8		
	♚xc3 2 ♕e5		
	bxc3 2 ♕f4		

Tries by the white queen, moving in a south-easterly direction and threatening mate on the diagonal d4-h8, are answered by equivalent bishop-moves. Following the key, defensive moves by the black bishop allow the queen to mate on that diagonal after all.

In no. 208 Black's three replies to White's threat of 2 ♖d8 determine White's checking continuations: 1...♕f8 is answered by 2 ♕a3+, so that after 2...♖a4 the sacrifice 3 ♕f3+ will either divert the black queen from her guard of the rook's mating square, or else allow White to mate by capturing the

208

OPPOSITION

A.Johandl
1st prize, *Deutsche Schachblätter*
1969-70
Mate in four

Key 1 ♖d7   (>2 ♖d8)
     ...   ♕f8 2 ♕a3+ ♖a4 3 ♕f3+
           ♕g8 2 ♕a2+ ♖a4 3 ♕g2+
           ♕h8 2 ♕a1+ ♖a4 3 ♕h1+

queen. 1...♕g8 and 1...♕h8 are consequently followed by 2 ♕a2+ and 2 ♕a1+ respectively, so that equivalent sacrifices can be made on g2 and h1.

Organ-pipes

Organ-pipes is the name given by F.Janet to the formation b♗, b♖, b♖, b♗ (as on the eighth rank in no. 209) in which each bishop interferes with each rook and vice versa. This arrangement normally produces four interference-variations, each mate being allowed by two of the interferences. Such is the case in the original organ-pipes problem, composed by Sam Loyd in 1859.

ORGAN-PIPES

209

J.Hartong
1st prize, *Problem* 1951
Mate in two
Key 1 exf6 zugzwang
     ...   ♗d7/♗d6 2 ♕d5
            ♗e7/♗e6 2 ♖e5
            ♖d7   2 ♗f5
            ♖d6   2 ♘bc5
            ♖e7   2 ♘dc5
            ♖e6   2 ♕xh7
            (♗xg4   2 ♕xg4)
            (♘~   2 ♘f2)

In Hartong's example, however, the organ-pipes produce a total of six variations, thanks to some ingenious **dual-avoidance** play. The key 1 exf6 waits for Black to commit himself. The defences 1...♗d7 and 1...♗d6 both lead to 2 ♕d5 (exploiting the interference by the bishops with the ♖d8). Similarly 1...♗e7 and 1...♗e6 are both followed by 2 ♖e5, since the line of guard of the ♖e8 has been cut. But 1...♖d7 and 1...♖e6 lead to two different mates, the former to 2 ♗f5 and the latter to 2 ♕xh7. 2 ♗f5? will not work after 1...♖e6 because the black rook has cut the line g8-d5, with the result that the white bishop cannot close h5-d5 without giving the black king a flight on d5. 1...♖d6 and 1...♖e7 also lead to distinct mates: 1...♖d6 2 ♘bc5 (not 2 ♘dc5? since this knight must remain at d3 to hold f4 now that the line b8-f4 is closed); and 1...♖e7 2 ♘dc5, the other knight being pinned.

210

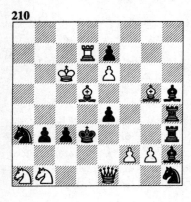

ORGAN-PIPES: NOVOTNY TRIES

C.Mansfield
1st prize, *Die Schwalbe* 1956
Mate in two
Try 1 g4? (>2 ♕d1/♕xe4) ♘xf2!
Try 1 g3? (>2 ♕e3/♗xb3) ♘c2!
Try 1 f4? (>2 ♕xe4/♗xb3) e3!
Key 1 f3! (>2 ♕d1/♕e3)

...	
♗f4	2 ♕xe4
♖f4	2 ♗xb3
♔d4	2 ♕xc3

No. 210 caused a sensation when it first appeared. Comins Mansfield had long been associated with the development of the traditional two-mover. In his teens and twenties he had been a prominent contributor to the Good Companion Folders, with beautifully constructed examples of the basic themes and elegant elaborations and combinations of them. For this problem he took just such a theme (double Grimshaw) and turned it into a first-class modern two-mover with **Novotny** tries and key. Significantly, Mansfield sent the work to *Die Schwalbe*, where the two-move editor was Hermann Albrecht, a great connoisseur and devotee of the art whose enthusiasm did much to stimulate the development of the two-mover in the post-war years, not only in Germany but throughout the chess problem world.

In Mansfield's problem the three tries, 1 g4?, 1 g3? and 1 f4?, each carry the usual Novotny double threat, the two mates occurring in turn after the captures on the Novotny square by rook and bishop. The key 1 f3! has the same effect, but the composer ingeniously arranged that the two black units not shut off by the key should produce a Grimshaw interference on f4 to defeat both threats and allow the other two mates threatened by the tries to reappear. The present writer still remembers the thrill experienced when Comins Mansfield showed this fine piece of work at a meeting of the British Chess Problem Society.

Overload

A black unit is overloaded if it is made to guard more squares than it can cope with.

OVERLOAD

211

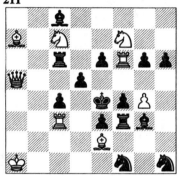

R.C.O.Matthews
1st prize, *British Chess Magazine*
1986-7
Mate in three
Key 1 ♘xd5 (>2 ♖xe6+ ♗xe6 3 ♘f6
　　　　　　　　...　　　　♖xe6 3 ♖xc4)
... ♗a6 2 ♖xc4+ ♗xc4 3 ♘c3
　　　　　　　...　　　　♖xc4 3 ♖xe6
♘d2 2 ♖xf4+ ♗xf4 3 ♘f6
　　　　　　　...　　　　♖xf4 3 ♖xe3
♗h4 2 ♖xe3+ ♘xe3 3 ♘c3
　　　　　　　...　　　　♖xe3 3 ♖xf4
exd5 2 ♕xd5+ ♔xd5 3 ♗xf3
♖c5 2 ♕xc5 exd5 3 ♕d4

The key of no. 211, 1 ♘xd5, threatens 2 ♖xe6+. The threatened move is a vacation of f6, allowing 3 ♘f6 if Black plays 2...♗xe6. But if Black plays 2...♖xe6, White can mate with 3 ♖xc4, because the black rook, having been overloaded, cannot maintain its guard on e6 and c4 at the same time. The first variation works in much the same way: 1...♗a6 2 ♖xc4+ (vacating c3, so that if 2...♗xc4, 3 ♘c3). If Black now plays 2...♖xc4, 3 ♖xe6 is playable. Two further defences allow White to exploit the overload of the ♖f3. Once again the second-move continuations are square-vacations allowing mate by a knight on the vacated square after one of Black's second-move captures. 1...♘d2 permits 2 ♖xf4+ ♖xf4 (if 2...♗xf4, 3 ♘f6) 3 ♖xe3; and 1...♗h4 leads to 2 ♖xe3+ ♖xe3 (2...♘xe3 3 ♘c3) 3 ♖xf4. In his book *Mostly Three-Movers*, the composer remarks of this problem: 'The by-play 1...exd5 2 ♕xd5+ makes a virtue of necessity. The white queen is the only piece available to guard d5, but it plays no part in the thematic variations, so it is good to find something else for it to do.' The point is well made; new composers could learn much from a study of Robin Matthews' compositions.

Paradox

PARADOXICAL KEY

212

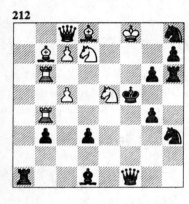

D.Shire
The Problemist 1995
Mate in two

Set	1...	♘f4	2 ♗e4
		♘g5	2 ♖f6
Try	1 ♖e4?		(>2 ♘b8)
	...	g5	2 ♘f6
		♘f4!	(2 ♗e4?)
Try	1 ♗f6?		(>2 ♘b8)
	...	♘g5!	(2 ♖f6?)
Key	1 ♘c6!		(>2 ♘b8/♘de5)
	...	♘f4	2 ♘d4
		♘g5	2 ♘e7
		♔e6+	2 ♘f6

In tackling no. 212, the solver soon sees that there are mates set for the self-blocking moves by the ♘h3: 1...♘f4 2 ♗e4, and 1...♘g5 2 ♖f6, both attractive white-interference mates. It may also be noticed that the further self-block 1...g5 would likewise allow a white-interference mate by 2 ♘f6 if only e5 were guarded by a second white unit. This leads naturally to two tries. 1 ♖e4?, with the threat of 2 ♘b8 (the only square available to this knight because all other possible destinations except f6 are plugged by white units), looks promising (1...g5 2 ♘f6 now works), but the white rook has occupied the square needed for the mate after 1...♘f4! (2 ♗e4?), so that this defence refutes the try. The same thing happens after the equally plausible-looking try 1 ♗f6?: 1...♘g5! refutes because 2 ♖f6? cannot be played. It is a nice touch that white interference works to White's advantage in the set mates, but to his disadvantage in the try-play. The square e5 can also be guarded by the knight standing there if it moves away. But most of its possible arrival squares are guarded by black units, and capture of the knight would clearly refute the threatened 2 ♘b8 and 2 ♘de5 as well as any other threats that might arise, e.g. 1 ♘f7? (>2 ♘b8/♘de5/♘xh6) 1...♘xf7!. So what can the solution be? The key is the astonishing move 1 ♘c6!, astonishing because it seems to shut out the two pieces that give the set mates on e4 and f6, so that it looks as if they will take no further part in the proceedings. Yet it works because it introduces new white-interference mates after the defences by the ♘h3, mates which, after all, give the ♗b7 and ♖c6 a rôle to play in guarding squares: 1...♘f4 2 ♘d4, and 1...♘g5 2 ♘e7. For the solver the paradox of the key is enhanced by the realisation that a flight is also granted, and that 1...♔e6 gives check. The reply to this defence is 2 ♘f6, a move transferred from the virtual play. In this mate the white king and w♘c5 also guard squares – so they are not just plugs! The double threat introduced by the key (2 ♘b8 and 2 ♘de5) is of no consequence, since each threat is separately forced (e.g. by 1...♖a8 and 1...♕e1). This is a fine piece of work by a highly talented composer, a specialist in two-movers and helpmates.

Ever since chess problems began, composers and solvers have been fascinated by the unpredictable and the bizarre. The well-known German problemist and theoretician J.Kohtz wrote in *Deutsches Wochenschach* in 1907: 'Ein Zug, der schlecht aussieht und tatsächlich sehr gut ist, ist ein echter Problemzug' (a move that looks bad but is actually very good is a genuine problem-move). Throughout this book you will find problems whose piquancy is enhanced by some element of paradox, whether in the key itself or in the pattern of the moves or in some other aspect of the play. Several themes depend on paradox for their effect: the *Dombrovskis* (→ **Reversal themes**) is one such, where the very defences that refute tries by defeating the threats they introduce actually allow those threats as mates after the key; another is **Umnov I**, in which White, on his second move, occupies the square just vacated by a black piece. Kipping's celebrated miniature no. 35 is a fine example of a paradoxical key: why on earth should White allow Black to promote to queen with check?! An equally bizarre key is seen in no. 213.

Here White might try 1 ♖e7?, to improve the possibility of mating on e2, but the white rook and white queen are the wrong way round (>2 ♕xe2+? ♗xe2 3 ♖xe2+ ♔d1!). So White tries a **doubling** manoeuvre (a **Turton** of the type known as *Loyd-Turton*): 1 ♕e8? (>2 ♖e7 ... 3 ♖xe2+ ♗xe2 4 ♕xe2), but this is not quick enough, as Black has time to get his queen into action to disrupt White's plan. The solver will see that the white king is at present well protected by the ♖d7, and that if the b♖h2 moves, the ♘f4 can mate on g2. What solves this problem is the amazing move 1 ♔a8!, with the threat of 2 ♖h7 ... 3 ♖xh2 ... 4 ♘g2. Black must, of course, check: 1...♖h8+. Now comes the second surprise, for the continuation is 2 ♕e8!, an apparently suicidal way to parry the check. If Black now plays 2...♖h2 (to guard g2), White carries on with 3 ♖e7, and there is nothing Black can do to stop 4 ♖xe2+ ♗xe2 5 ♕xe2. But Black also has 2...♖xe8+, to which White replies with

213

PARADOXICAL PLAY

S.Schneider
1st place, Switzerland v Austria 1977
Mate in five

Try 1 ♖e7? (>2 ♕xe2+ ♗xe2 3 ♖xe2+?
♔d1!) ♕~!
Try 1 ♕e8? (>2 ♖e7 ... 3 ♖xe2+ ♗xe2 4
♕xe2) ♕~!

Key 1 ♔a8! (>2 ♖h7 ... 3 ♖xh2 ... 4
♘g2)
   ... ♖h8+ 2 ♕e8 ♖xe8+ 3 ♔a7
       ... ♖h2 3 ♖e7, etc.

3 ♔a7!. The point is that the black rook cannot now get back to guard g2, so that even 3...♖a8+ is of no avail: 4 ♔xa8 ... 5 ♘g2. We can see why the white king cannot play to b8 or c8 on the first move, as 1...♖h8+ vacates the square h2 for the bishop to occupy with a pin of the ♘f4 if the white king should find himself on c7 or b8: 1 ♔b8? ♖h8+ 2 ♕e8 ♗h2!; or 1 ♔c8? ♖h8+ 2 ♕e8 ♖xe8+ 3 ♔b7 ♖b8+ 4 ♔xb8 ♗h2!. What makes this problem memorable is that the element of paradox arises not just in the key but in the subsequent play as well.

The **helpmate** is a fertile field for those in search of paradox. One of the most popular of helpmate ideas is the capture of white force, which is paradoxical in the sense that one would imagine that White would need whatever pieces he had in order to bring about the mate. The complex play of no. 214 well illustrates this kind of paradox.

In order to effect a mate with the ♗+♖ battery on the long diagonal, Black and White must between them organise a guard for the square g1, which is not too easy. In fact the only way it can be done is by means of the capture by Black of the two strong white pieces on the second rank, the first on its diagram square and the second on e1. The solution to position (a) runs: 1 ♕xd2 ♖e1 2 fxe1♗ ♖c4; and to position (b): 1 ♕xe2 ♕e1 2 fxe1♖ ♖c2. This outstanding helpmate relies for its paradoxical effect not just on the capture of strong white pieces, but also on the differentiated promotions (Black would be better off not promoting at all!), and on the twinning mechanism: removal of the ♖b4 ensures that the capture by Black switches from the queen to the rook, so that the occupation of e1 switches from the rook to the queen.

214

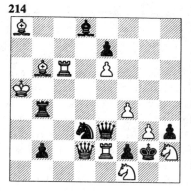

HELPMATE: CAPTURE OF WHITE FORCE

N.A.Macleod
1st prize, *feenschach* 1986
Helpmate in two
(a) Diagram
(b) Remove ♖b4

(a) 1 ♕xd2 ♖e1 2 fxe1♗ ♖c4
(b) 1 ♕xe2 ♕e1 2 fxe1♖ ♖c2

Paralysis

Paralysis, also known as *incarceration*, occurs when a black piece is prevented from playing away from a particular square. (This is, of course, the reverse of **obstruction**, where a piece is prevented from reaching a particular square.) No. 215 is a fine four-mover with echoed effects.

PARALYSIS

215

L.Zagoruiko
1st place ex aequo, 1st International
Team Match 1962-3
Mate in four

Key 1 ♔g6 (>2 ♘f6+ ♔f4 {2...♖e3 3 ♖xd3+ ♔f4 4 ♕xf5} 3 ♕xf5+ ♔e3 4 ♖xd3)
...♖f4 2 ♗c8 (>3 ♕xf5+ ♖xf5 4 ♗xf5)
... ♖gf3 3 ♕a7 (>4 ♘f6)
...♖e3 2 ♕b5 (>3 ♕xd3+ ♖xd3 4 ♗xd3)
... ♖ff3 3 ♔g5 (>4 ♘f6)

The threat introduced by the key 1 ♔g6 is 2 ♘f6+ followed by 2...♔f4 3 ♕xf5+ ♔e3 4 ♖xd3; or if 2...♔e3, then 3 ♖xd3+ ♔f4 4 ♕xf5. Black defends by moving his rooks, in an effort to gain flights for himself on his third move. But the rooks must retain their respective guards over f5 and d3, and so are limited as to their choice of defence. 1...♖f4 is followed by 2 ♗c8 (>3 ♕xf5+

♖xf5 4 ♗xf5). All Black can do is to double his rooks on the f-file so as to add a second guard to f5: 2...♖gf3. But this move has the effect of stopping the ♖f4 moving away from that square; it has been incarcerated, and White can therefore continue 3 ♕a7 (>4 ♘f6) – and the ♖f4 is powerless to gain a flight for the king. This variation is echoed by the play following the defence 1...♖e3: 2 ♕b5 (>3 ♕xd3+ ♖xd3 4 ♗xd3). Again Black must double his rooks, this time on the third rank: 2...♖ff3. Now the ♖e3 is paralysed, and White can play 3 ♔g5, for the rooks cannot now prevent 4 ♘f6. What is echoed in this beautiful problem is not only the paralysis of each black rook in turn, but also the **doubling** manoeuvres, which are performed by both Black and White. The black rooks give each other all the support they can, while White's queen and bishop collaborate in similar fashion. Fine use is also made of the white king.

Pericritical play

In a normal **critical** move a piece moves over a *critical square*, with the result that an interference takes place on that square. In a pericritical move, however, a piece moves round a critical square. No. 216 features pericritical tries by the white queen.

PERICRITICAL TRIES

216

M.Schneider
1st prize, *Main-Post* 1964

Mate in two

Try	1 ♕g7?		(>2 ♘e7)
	...	♖e5	2 ♕xe5
		e5!	
Try	1 ♕g4?		(>2 ♘e7)
	...	♗e4	2 ♕xe6
		♖e4!	
Try	1 ♕f2?		(>2 ♘e7)
	...	♕e3	2 ♗xc4
		♖e3!	
Try	1 ♕d2?		(>2 ♘e7)
	...	♕d3	2 ♕xa5
		♗d3!	
Key	1 ♕b2!		(>2 ♘e7)
	...	♕c3	2 ♕b5
		c3	2 ♕xb3

White wishes to threaten 2 ♘e7, and for this purpose the queen must set up a guard on d4. She has five possible ways of doing this, but four of her moves fail because a black piece is able to interpose between the queen and the square d4. 1 ♕g7? will not work because of 1...e5! (1...♖e5? leads to 2 ♕xe5). 1 ♕g4? provides a mate for 1...♗e4 (2 ♕xe6), but fails to 1...♖e4!. 1 ♕f2? is adequate to deal with 1...♕e3 (2 ♗xc4), but 1...♖e3! refutes. 1 ♕d2? introduces 2 ♕xa5 to follow 1...♕d3, but there is no reply to 1...♗d3!. Therefore only 1 ♕b2! will work. 1...♕c3 is answered by 2 ♕b5, while the reply to 1...c3 is 2 ♕xb3.

Pericritical play in three-move form is seen in no. 82, under **Doubling**, and in more-move form in no. 245 (→ **Roman**).

Pickaninny

A black pawn standing on its starting square (other than a7 or h7) has a maximum of four moves available to it. When all four moves of a single black pawn occur at some stage in the course of a problem's solution, the term Pickaninny is applied. There are two pickaninnies in no. 217.

PICKANINNY

217

N.G.G.van Dijk
American Chess Bulletin 1958
Mate in two

Key 1 b3		zugzwang
...	bxa6	2 ♖xa5
	b6	2 ♘c7
	b5	2 ♖c5
	bxc6	2 ♖d4
	exd6	2 ♕xe4
	e6	2 ♗xe4
	e5	2 ♕d2
	exf6	2 ♘xf6

The key, 1 b3, puts Black in zugzwang, and there follows a wealth of interference and self-block play, centring on the moves by the b7- and e7-pawns. Only one of the eight variations involves a mating capture of the pawn in question, which testifies to the composer's constructional skill.

Similar skill is evinced by Christopher Reeves in no. 218, in which the four mates following the moves of the ♗d7 are changed from set to post-key

218

PICKANINNY: CHANGED PLAY

A.C.Reeves
Die Schwalbe 1965
Mate in two

Set	1...	dxc6+	2 ♗xc6
		d6	2 ♘d5
		d5	2 ♕b4
		dxe6	2 ♗c8
Key	1 ♕xe5		(>2 exd7)
	...	dxc6+	2 ♘xc6
		d6	2 ♕f6
		d5	2 ♕c7
		dxe6	2 ♕xe6

play. The only (small) weakness of this problem is that the ♖a7 and the ♗b7 play no part in half of the solution. But their existence is justified by the fact that without them there would be no changed Pickaninny. (For a further comment on the justification for inactive force, see **Economy**.)

219

PICKANINNY + ALBINO

G.H.Drese
2nd prize, *Tijdschrift v.d. K.N.S.B.* 1935
Mate in three

Key	1 ♗d3 zugzwang	
	...	exf6	2 f4
		exd6	2 f3
		e6	2 fxe3
		e5	2 fxg3

No. 219 combines the Pickaninny with the **Albino** (maximum activity of a white pawn). After the key 1 ♗d3, which completes the block, the four moves of the ♙e7 are answered by the four moves of the ♙f2: 1...exf6 2 f4; 1...exd6 2 f3; 1...e6 2 fxe3; 1...e5 2 fxg3. In the first two variations the white pawn must replace the guard which the black pawn has just removed, so that zugzwang is maintained, while in the last two mate must be threatened with the bishop on c4 or e4.

No. 14 (→ **Albino**) shows four tries by a white pawn refuted by the four moves of a black pawn.

Pin

Pinning and unpinning is one of the problemist's favourite devices. The possible combinations of pin- and unpin-mechanisms are far too numerous to mention, and in any case copious examples will be found throughout the book. Suffice it to say that some of the most beautiful problems ever composed have featured pin-mates, or else mates brought about by means of unpinning defences. It would be difficult to find a more elegant illustration of pin-mates than no. 220.

220

PIN-MATES

L.I.Loshinsky
1st prize, *Abastumansky Shakhmaty Bureau* 1933
Mate in two
Key 1 ♔a5 (>2 ♘e2)

...	♛xf2 2 ♘f5
	♛xe5+ 2 ♘b5
	♖xd4 2 ♘d3
	♛xd4 2 ♖xd4
	(♛e4 2 ♘e2)

In the initial position the ♘d4 is pinned by the black queen, which itself is **half-pinned**, like the ♖d2, by the white queen. The key 1 ♔a5 unpins the ♘d4 to threaten a double checkmate by 2 ♘e2. Black now has four self-pinning defences, three of them leading to *double pin-mates* (a double pin-mate occurs when two black units are essentially pinned in the mating position): 1...♛xf2 2 ♘f5; 1...♛xe5+ 2 ♘b5; 1...♖xd4 2 ♘d3; and 1...♛xd4 2 ♖xd4.

Pin-mates are extremely common in three- and more-movers, where they may well be combined with **model-mates** to form *pin-models*, as in no. 190.

Plachutta

The Plachutta is a three- and more-move interference theme in which a white piece sacrifices itself on the intersection square of the lines of two like-moving black pieces (e.g. rook and rook, or queen and bishop). As each black piece captures the white unit, it becomes **overloaded**, being forced to take over the duties of the other black piece as well as its own. This effect can be clearly seen in the threat-line of the four-mover, no. 221.

PLACHUTTA

221

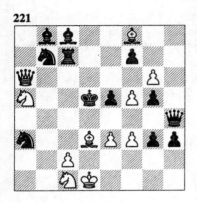

M.R.Vukcevich
1st prize, *Chess Life* 1988
Mate in four

Key 1 ♘a2	(>2 c4+	♕xc4 3 ♘c3+	
	...	♖xc4 3 ♘b4+)	
...	♕a4 2 ♕c4+	♕xc4 3 ♘c3+	
	...	♖xc4 3 ♗e4+	
	♖xc2 2 ♗c4+	♕xc4 3 ♕c6+	
	...	♖xc4 3 ♘b4+	
	♘xc2 2 ♕b5+		
	♕c4 2 ♘c3+		
	♗d7 2 ♕xb7+		
	e4 2 ♘b4+		

1 ♘a2 threatens the Plachutta-style sacrifice 2 c4+. If 2...♕xc4, White continues 3 ♘c3+, and after 3...♕xc3, 4 ♗e4 is mate. Similarly, after 2...♖xc4, 3 ♘b4+ is played, followed by 4 ♕c6 to follow 3...♖xb4. Black defends on his first move by playing an *anti-critical* move (→ **Critical Play**) with one of his thematic pieces, so that White's threatened Plachutta interference is thwarted. Now, however, White plays a different piece to the intersection square: if 1...♕a4, 2 ♕c4+, which Black can only answer with a capture leading to overload of the capturing unit: 2...♕xc4 3 ♘c3+ ♕xc3 4 ♗e4#; or 2...♖xc4 3 ♗e4+ ♖xe4 4 ♘c3. Analogous play is introduced by 1...♖xc2: 2 ♗c4+ ♕xc4 3 ♕c6+ ♕xc6 4 ♘b4; or 2...♖xc4 3 ♘b4+ ♖xb4 4 ♕c6. White must choose his second move with care: if the wrong piece checks on c4, White will lose one of his eventual mating units. Interference between like-moving pieces is very common in problems of more than two moves. When such an interference is not introduced by a white sacrifice, the effect is termed **Wurzburg-Plachutta** if the variations are paired, or **Holzhausen** when only a single interference takes place. (Compare the two-move terminology: **Grimshaw** – mutual interference between unlike-moving pieces; **Novotny** – the same with white sacrifice.)

Promoted force → Obtrusive force

Promotion

The rules governing pawn-promotion in problems are exactly the same as in the game. In a two-mover the useful choice is between queen and knight, since the queen combines the powers of rook and bishop. Consequently it is felt that a white second-move choice between queen and rook or between queen and bishop is not a **dual**, and that a black promotion to rook or bishop immediately before the mate does not cause a dual either.

222

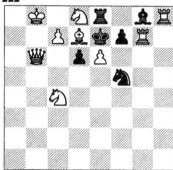

SIX PROMOTIONS BY ONE WHITE PAWN

S.Leites
1st prize, *Shakhmaty v SSSR* 1946
Mate in two
Key 1 exf7 zugzwang

...	d5	2 fxe8♕
	♔f6	2 fxe8♘
	♗h7	2 f8♕
	♔xd7	2 f8♘
	♔f8	2 fxg8♕
	♖f8	2 fxg8♘

No. 222 shows the maximum task of six distinct promotions of a single white pawn, choosing between queen and knight on three different squares. 1 exf7 puts Black in zugzwang and gives the king a third flight, d7, to add to those he already has, f6 and f8. The six mates occur after the king-moves to these flights (1...♔f6 2 fxe8♘; 1...♔xd7 2 f8♘; and 1...♔f8 2 fxg8♕), after a self-block by the black rook (1...♖f8 2 fxg8♘), and after two line-opening defences (1...d5 2 fxe8♕; and 1...♗h7 2 f8♕).

Promotion by a black pawn is featured in the three phases of no. 223. The try 1 ♕b5? threatens 2 ♕d3, and Black defends with 1...b1♕ (allowing 2 ♕e2) and 1...b1♘ (2 ♗d1). This try fails to 1...♘c4!, and so 1 ♕f4? is tried instead. Now the mates after the promotions are respectively 2 ♕d2 and 2 ♕c1, but 1...♘b3! refutes. The key is 1 ♕g3!, which introduces the mates 2 ♕c3 and 2 ♖a2 to follow 1...b1♕ and 1...b1♘. In this fine **Zagoruiko**, the two Argentinian experts achieved a great deal of play with very small means.

Promotion effects in three- and more-movers are considerably more varied. In no. 224 a single white pawn promotes on the same square to four different pieces in reply to the four moves of the b♗e7. The key brings the white pawn in question into position for promotion: 1 gxf7. 1...e6 leads to 2 f8♕.

223

PROMOTION: ZAGORUIKO

A.Ellerman and H.L.Musante
3rd prize, *Die Schwalbe* 1955
Mate in two

Try 1 ♕b5?		(>2 ♕d3)
...	b1♕	2 ♕e2
	b1♘	2 ♗d1
	♘c4!	
Try 1 ♕f4?		(>2 ♕e4)
...	b1♕	2 ♕d2
	b1♘	2 ♕c1
	♘b3!	
Key 1 ♕g3!		(>2 ♕d3)
...	b1♕	2 ♕c3
	b1♘	2 ♖a2

224

**ALLUMWANDLUNG +
PICKANINNY**

M.Niemeijer
1st prize, *Tijdschrift v.d. Nederlandse
Schaakbond* 1928
Mate in three

Key 1 gxf7 zugzwang		
...	e6	2 f8♕
	exd6	2 f8♖
	exf6	2 f8♗
	e5	2 f8♘+

But after 1...exd6 this continuation would fail because of stalemate! So *underpromotion* is necessary: 2 f8♖. Underpromotion is again required after 1...exf6, for the same reason: 2 f8♗. Finally, after 1...e5, Black must not be permitted to play 2...exd4, thereby gaining himself a flight c6, so a check is needed: 2 f8♘+. The four promotions in a single problem have no jargon name in English, and it is therefore quite common to refer to the task by its German name, *Allumwandlung* (literally 'total promotion'). (Other examples of the maximum task of four defences by a single black pawn will be found under **Pickaninny**.)

Allumwandlung as white tries is found in the very ingenious miniature no. 225. It is highly likely that the solver will look first at the ♙c7 as a possible

225

ALLUMWANDLUNG: TRIES

F.Abdurahmanović
1st prize, Yugoslav Republic Tourney
1957
Mate in two
Try 1 c8♕? stalemate!
Try 1 c8♖? ♔e6!
Try 1 c8♗? ♔c6!
Try 1 c8♘? ♔c4!
Key 1 ♘e4!   zugzwang
...   ♔e6   2 ♕f7
              ♔c6   2 ♕d6
              ♔c4   2 ♕f7
              ♔xe4   2 ♕f3

key-unit, and the question of a choice of promotions will naturally occur. 1 c8♕? fails because it produces stalemate. So underpromotion must be tried. 1 c8♖? leaves Black a single move, 1...♔e6!, but this is sufficient to refute. 1 c8♗? allows two moves, 1...♔c4 (after which 2 ♗e6 is mate) and 1...♔c6! – no mate. 1 c8♘? provides mates to follow 1...♔c6 and 1...♔e6, but fails to 1...♔c4!. The key, therefore, has nothing to do with this pawn, but is the surprising sacrifice 1 ♘e4!. The black king now has four flights (*star-flights*), each answered by a mate by the white queen.

Proof games

SHORTEST PROOF GAME

226

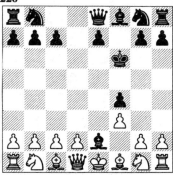

M.Caillaud and J.Rotenberg
Europe Echecs 1991
a) Position after Black's 7th move
b) Position after White's 8th move
How did each game go?

a) 1 ♘f3 f5 2 ♘e5 f4 3 ♘xd7 ♔f7 4 ♘e5+ ♔f6 5 ♘f3 ♗g4 6 ♘g1 ♗xe2 7 f3 ♕e8

b) 1 e4 f5 2 e5 ♔f7 3 e6+ ♔f6 4 exd7 ♕e8 5 d8♕ f4 6 ♕d3 ♗g4 7 ♕e2 ♗xe2 8 f3

Many solvers are attracted by the task of working out, from a diagrammed position, what moves must have been made in the putative game leading to it. In no. 226, if White and Black have each played seven moves, there is a unique sequence involving a capture on d7 by the W♘g1 and its return to that square followed by 7 f3, while Black's sequence is partially determined by the need to fit in with White's. Amazingly, the solution is different if White has played one move more, because there is no way of slotting an additional move into the first sequence. Now it is possible to prove that White has promoted his e-pawn on d8 to a queen, which has then been captured on e2!

Readers who would like to see more of this kind of problem are referred to an excellent little book by two authorities on the subject, Gerd Wilts and Andrei Frolkin, entitled *Shortest Proof Games*. Written in English and published in Germany in 1991, this book contains 170 positions, with some really astonishing works, including one that runs for no fewer than 58 moves!

Pseudo-two-mover

A pseudo-two-mover is a three- or more-mover in which White would have an immediate mate if it were Black's turn to play in the diagram position, but has no waiting move and so must delay giving mate until the third move or later. No. 227 is a simple four-move example.

227

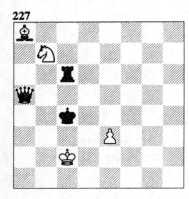

PSEUDO-TWO-MOVER

W.Massmann
1st prize, *Die Schwalbe* Theme Tourney 1942
Mate in four
Set 1... ♖~c   2 ♘d6
            ♖~6   2 ♕c5
Key 1 ♘d8 ♖d6 2 ♗c6 ♖xc6 3 ♘b7 ♖b6/c7 4 ♕c5/♘d6
            ... ♖d2+ 3 ♕xd2
♔c5 4 ♕d4

If White could find a waiting move, he could mate in two, as the black rook must unguard c5 or d6. But, there being no such move, White deliberately sacrifices a piece which is unnecessary to his plans, merely in order to gain a tempo. After the key 1 ♘d8, the black rook must move. A random departure from c6 allows immediate mate by 2 ♗d5, and the correction 1...♖c5 leads to 2 ♕a4. But after the further correction 1...♖d6, White has no immediate mate, and so plays 2 ♗c6, which carries the threat 3 ♕b5. If the rook captures the bishop, White continues 3 ♘b7, reverting to the initial position but with Black to play. Wherever the rook goes, White now mates with either 4 ♕c5 or 4 ♘d6, the two mates set in the diagram position.

Radical change

228

RADICAL CHANGE

M.Lipton
1st commendation, *Probleemblad* 1965
Mate in two

Set	1...	♕xh6	2 ♖h7
		♕h8	2 ♖g7
		♕f7	2 ♖xf7
		♕c6	2 ♖e6
Key	1 ♖xe5		(>2 ♗xf6)
	...	♘d4	2 ♖h5
		d4	2 ♖xe4

The set play of no. 228 contains four mates by the masked ♗+♖ battery: 1...♕xh6 2 ♖h7; 1...♕h8 2 ♖g7; 1...♕f7 2 ♖xf7; and 1...♕c6 2 ♖e6. The key 1 ♖xe5 renders all these defences and mates impossible by destroying the masked battery and pinning the white rook and black queen. The threat of 2 ♗xf6 is now defeated by two moves which unpin the B♘e4 to guard f6, but these moves also unpin the newly-pinned white rook, which consequently is able to give mate: 1...♘d4 2 ♖h5; and 1...d4 2 ♖xe4. This is radical change: changed defences and mates with a complete change of theme, here battery mates in the set play changed to unpin of White after the key.

Reciprocal play

Several of the simplest problem themes are reciprocal in character: the **Grimshaw**, the **Plachutta**, **half-pin**, **half-battery** and many others. What these themes have in common is a relationship between two elements. In the Grimshaw, a black rook interferes with a black bishop in one variation, and in a second variation the bishop interferes with the rook. In the half-pin one piece moves off the half-pin line in one variation, leaving the other totally pinned, while in the second variation the other piece returns the compliment.

One of the reciprocal themes most frequently encountered is partial **dual avoidance**: the mate avoided in one variation is the one that can be played in the other, and vice versa.

This discussion of reciprocal play will not be concerned with the themes mentioned already, for these are dealt with under the appropriate headings. In fact the term 'reciprocal play' is used to denote two reciprocal strategies in particular: *reciprocal correction* and *reciprocal change*.

229

RECIPROCAL CORRECTION

H.Knuppert
Tidskrift för Schack 1946
Mate in two

Key 1 ♕e7   zugzwang

...	♗d~	2 ♕c5	(A)
	♗c4	2 ♗b2	(B)
	♗c~	2 ♗b2	(B)
	♗e5	2 ♕c5	(A)
	♔c3/c4	2 ♕b4	

No. 229 is a simple illustration of the former. The key 1 ♕e7 grants Black a second flight c3 and puts him in zugzwang. If the ♗d5 moves at random, White can play 2 ♕c5 (mate A). The correction 1...♗c4 prevents this mate by cutting the line c5-c3 (and therefore stops the queen from guarding c3 after 2 ♕c5?), but blocks the flight c4, allowing 2 ♗b2 (mate B). Random moves by the ♗c7 open the line of guard of the w♖c8 to Black's two flights: 2 ♗b2 (B) can thus be played. The correction 1...♗e5 cuts the white queen's guard of e3 to prevent 2 ♗b2?, but, by blocking e5, permits 2 ♕c5 (A) once again. The reciprocal effect is clear: the random move of each black piece is followed by the same mate as the correction move of the other.

The same thing happens in no. 230, except that the mates are both changed from set to post-key play. In the diagram position 1...♖~ allows 2 ♘g6 (A) by opening the line d5-f3, while the correction 1...♖xe5 (self-block) enables White to mate by 2 ♕g5 (B). The random move of the ♘d4 opens the line a1-e5, so that 2 ♕g5 (B) is again playable, while the correction 1...♘f3, by blocking f3, allows 2 ♘g6 (A) to recur. The key eliminates both these mates: 1 ♕d6, completing the block position. Now 1...♖~ gives 2 ♘d3 (C), and the correction 1...♖xe5 leads to 2 ♕h6 (D). These two mates D and C reappear respectively after the random and correction moves of the ♘d4. The relationship AB:BA is replaced by CD:DC.

230

RECIPROCAL CORRECTION: CHANGES

V.F.Rudenko and V.I.Chepizhny
1st prize, *Tijdschrift v.d. K.N.S.B.* 1958
Mate in two

Set	1...	♖~	2 ♘g6	(A)
		♖xe5	2 ♕g5	(B)
		♘d~	2 ♕g5	(B)
		♘f3	2 ♘g6	(A)
Key	1 ♕d6		zugzwang	
	...	♖~	2 ♘d3	(C)
		♖xe5	2 ♕h6	(D)
		♘d~	2 ♕h6	(D)
		♘f3	2 ♘d3	(C)

Reciprocal change consists of the following. In the set (or virtual) play black move X is followed by mate A, and black move Y by mate B. The key reverses this pattern, so that B follows X and A follows Y. No. 231 is a simple virtual-play example, in which the black defences involved are king-flights.

RECIPROCAL CHANGE: FLIGHTS

231

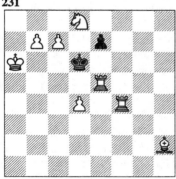

V.I.Chepizhny
1st place, 4th USSR Team
Championship 1963
Mate in two

Try	1 ♖f8?			
	...	♔xc7	2 ♖xe7	(A)
		♔d7	2 ♖d5	(B)
		e6!		
Key	1 ♖f7!		zugzwang	
	...	♔xc7	2 ♖d5	(B)
		♔d7	2 ♖exe7	(A)
		e6	2 c8♘	

The try 1 ♖f8? introduces 2 ♖xe7 (A) to follow 1...♔xc7 (X), while 1...♔d7 (Y) leads to 2 ♖d5 (B). 1...e6! refutes. The key 1 ♖f7! brings in the reversal of mates: 1...♔xc7 (X) 2 ♖d5 (B); 1...♔d7 (Y) 2 ♖exe7 (A). (1...e6 allows 2 c8♘.)

232

**RECIPROCAL CHANGE:
GRIMSHAW TO SELF-PINS**

C.P.Sydenham
1st prize, *I Due Alfieri* 1981
Mate in two

Set	1...	♗e4	2 ♘b5	(A)
		♖e4	2 ♘b6	(B)
Key	1 e4	(>2 ♘b5/♘b6)		
	...	♗xe4	2 ♘b6	(B)
		♖xe4	2 ♘b5	(A)
		♔d4	2 ♘c7	
		♖xb2	2 ♘b4	

Reciprocal change has been incorporated into almost every known two-move theme; there must be thousands of examples. No. 232 shows a curious effect in which the mates following Grimshaw interferences in the set play are reversed by a key which turns the interferences into self-pins. The set play is 1...♗e4 2 ♘b5; and 1...♖e4 2 ♘b6. The key, 1 e4, is a Novotny that threatens both these mates. However, the separation of the mates does not work as one might expect. After 1...♗xe4, 2 ♘b5? is not playable because of the opening of the black queen's line from h3 to c3. The other self-pin, 1...♖xe4, allows 2 ♘b5, and not 2 ♘b6? because of the vacation of f4, now held only by the ♘d5. A highly paradoxical idea.

The attractive, open setting of no. 233 conceals an intricate mechanism by means of which the composer has achieved a doubling of the theme of reciprocal change. After three tries and the key there are different mates for each of the black defences 1...♘xa4 and 1...♘d7. It is worth examining the effect of these defences. In the diagram position each one would gain two flights for the black king, on b3 and b5 after the capture of the bishop, and on d3 and d5 after the shut-off of the rook. The first try, 1 ♖e3? (>2 ♖c3), provides a second guard for b3 and d3, so that, in mating, White has only to take care of the other flights: 1...♘xa4 2 ♕f1, and 1...♘d7 2 ♕xe6. 1...♖h8! refutes, however. The second try, 1 ♖e5? (>2 ♖xc5), reverses the mates: 1...♘xa4 2 ♕xe6, and 1...♘d7 2 ♕f1. This reversal comes about because now b5 and d5 are doubly guarded, but not b3 and d3. 1 ♕f2! refutes the second try. The third try and the key show a *sequence reversal* (see **Reversal themes**) as compared with the first two tries. 1 ♕f1? (>2 ♖e4) introduces the following play: 1...♘xa4 2 ♖e3; and 1...♘d7 2 ♖e5. But this fails to 1...♘d3!. The key

233

DOUBLE RECIPROCAL CHANGE

P.Einat
3rd prize, Israel Ring Tourney 1975
Mate in two

Try	1 ♖e3?	(>2 ♖c3)		
	...	♘xa4	2 ♕f1	(A)
		♘d7	2 ♕xe6	(B)
		♕h8!		
Try	1 ♖e5?	(>2 ♖xc5)		
	...	♘xa4	2 ♕xe6	(B)
		♘d7	2 ♕f1	(A)
		♕f2!		
Try	1 ♕f1?	(>2 ♖e4)		
	...	♘xa4	2 ♖e3	(C)
		♘d7	2 ♖e5	(D)
		♘d3!		
Key	1 ♖xe6!	(>2 ♖e4)		
	...	♘xa4	2 ♖e5	(D)
		♘d7	2 ♖e3	(C)

is 1 ♖xe6! (>2 ♖e4), and now the mates after the third try reappear in reverse: 1...♘xa4 2 ♖e5; and 1...♘d7 2 ♖e3. It is surprising that this outstanding problem gained no more than a third prize.

234

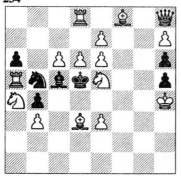

RECIPROCAL CHANGE

A.Kopnin and A.Kuznetsov
1st prize, Chigorin Memorial Tourney 1959
Mate in three

Set	1...	♗xd6	2 e8♗	♔xe6	3 ♗f7
		♘xd6	2 e8♘	♔xe6	3 ♘c7
Key	1 ♘f3	(>2 ♕e5+)			
	...	♗xd6	2 e8♘	♔xe6	3 ♕g8
		♘xd6	2 e8♗	♔xe6	3 ♕e5

No. 234 is a splendid three-move setting of reciprocal change, with black half-pin and self-pinning, and white underpromotions. In the set play 1...♗xd6 leads to 2 e8♗ (not 2 e8♕ – stalemate!), so that White can play

3 ♗f7 after 2...♔xe6. 1...♘xd6, on the other hand, allows 2 e8♘, with 3 ♘c7 to come after 2...♔xe6. The key, 1 ♘f3, threatens 2 ♕e5+. Now 1...♗xd6 leads to 2 e8♘, to allow 3 ♕g8 after 2...♔xe6 (f7 being no longer guarded). 1...♘xd6, however, enables White to play 2 e8♗ (2...♔xe6 3 ♕e5). The reversal of White's second moves is caused by the removal of the key-knight's guard of f7 and the substitution of an additional guard on e5, a deceptively simple mechanism.

Reflex-mate

The reflex-mate is fundamentally a **selfmate** with the added stipulation that either side must give mate on the move if this becomes possible. When this applies to Black only, the problem is termed a *semi-reflex-mate*. The traditional style of reflex-mate usually had a try or tries by White which failed because Black's reply forced White to give mate. But nowadays many reflex-mates feature complex play, like that found in no. 235, by a German expert who is among the greatest of all problem composers.

235

REFLEX-MATE

H.-P. Rehm
1st prize, *Die Schwalbe* 1963
Reflex-mate in two
Key 1 ♕f5 (>2 ♖g8 ♕e7)

...	♘d~+	2 ♕e6 ♗xe6
	♘b4+	2 ♔e7 ♘c6
	♘e7+	2 ♔xf8 ♘g6
	♘f6+	2 ♔g7 ♘xe8
	♘c3+	2 ♔f6 ♘e4
	♘f~	2 ♔e6 ♘c7/♘f4
	♕e7+	2 ♔g8 ♘f6

The key, 1 ♕f5, threatens 2 ♖g8, after which Black must mate by 2...♕e7. To try to avoid giving mate on his second move, Black gives check on his first. A random move of the ♘d5 allows 2 ♕e6, forcing 2...♗xe6. This same knight has four **corrections**, leading to **plus-flights** of the white king: 1...♘b4+ 2 ♔e7 ♘c6; 1...♘e7+ 2 ♔xf8 ♘g6; 1...♘f6+ 2 ♔g7 ♘xe8; and 1...♘c3+ 2 ♔f6 ♘e4. Two further defences by Black lead to other white king-flights: 1...♘f~ 2 ♔e6 ♘c7/♘f4; and 1...♕e7+ 2 ♔g8 ♘f6. Problems of this calibre show what kind of possibilities are inherent in the reflex-mate for the composer tiring of direct-mates!

Retrograde analysis

Before the solution to a problem can be discovered, the solver may have to decide whether or not castling is legal, or whether an *en passant* capture key is possible. Problems where such considerations come into play must be solved by retrograde analysis. Two examples will be quoted here, though no. 151 (→ **Key**) also illustrates the idea, as does no. 223 (→ **Proof games**).

RETROGRADE ANALYSIS (TWIN)

236

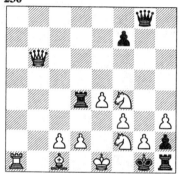

B.P.Barnes
2nd prize, *Problem* Theme Tourney 1964
Mate in two
a) Diagram
b) Add b♟g7

a) Try	1 ♔e2?	♛xg2! (2 ♘e2?)
Key	1 ♗a3!	(>2 ♔e2)
...		♖b4 2 0-0-0
		♖xd2 2 ♔xd2
b) Try	1 ♗a3?	♖b4! (2 0-0-0?)
Key	1 ♔e2!	(>2 ♗~)
...		♖b4 2 ♗b2
		♖xd2+ 2 ♗xd2
		♛a8 2 ♗a3

No. 236 is a **twin** problem: there are two positions, differing from one another in only one respect. The question in the diagram position is whether it can be proved that it is illegal for White to castle after the ♗c1 has moved. (Castling is always deemed to be legal unless it can be proved otherwise.) Can the black king and black rook have reached g1 and h1 respectively with the white king remaining on e1? The black king can certainly have got there, via g3 and h2. And if the ♖h1 is a promoted pawn, then that too could well have reached its present position without going via f1. So castling will be legal, and White can therefore play 1 ♗a3 (>2 ♔e2). If 1...♖b4, 2 0-0-0; and if 1...♖xd2, 2 ♔xd2. The try 1 ♔e2? is refuted by 1...♛xg2!, since the white king has occupied the square on which the ♘f4 could otherwise mate. Position (b) is the same as (a), but with the addition of a black pawn on g7. This clearly rules out the defence 1...♛xg2, so the solver should now wonder why both 1 ♔e2 and 1 ♗a3 cannot be played. Further retrograde analysis is required to determine the correct key. White has twelve units on the board, which means that only four have been captured. If the ♖h1 is a promoted pawn, can the black pawn-formation be legal? At least two captures must have been made by the ♙h2, since it has passed the white h-pawn. That leaves only two for the promoted ♙h1, but this must have come from the e-file, and in order to get to h1 it would have had to make three captures. Therefore the ♖h1 is an original rook (or a pawn promoted, e.g., on e1), and so the white king must have moved in the imaginary game leading to the present position. White castling is thus illegal, and so 1 ♗a3? fails to 1...♖b4!. Q.E.D.

237

PARTIAL ANALYSIS

L.Ceriani
Europe Echecs 1960
Mate in two

Solution in text

No. 237 is an example of *partial analysis*. The solver must first of all decide whether White can play 1 0-0, and whether Black can play 1...0-0-0. The crucial piece is the W♖a6. If it started life on h1, obviously White cannot castle. If it is White's original a-rook, it must have moved from a1 to a6 via e1 (thereby invalidating 1 0-0), since the move ♙(a2)xb3 cannot have been played until after ♘(b3)a1, and B♗(a2)a1♘ would require one black pawn-capture too many. If on the other hand this rook is a promoted pawn, then castling by Black is ruled out, because the pawn must have passed over d7 or f7 before promoting, forcing the black king to move if indeed he was standing on e8 at the time. Whichever is the case, therefore, either castling by White or castling by Black is impossible. If White is in a position to play 1 0-0, then this works as a solution because Black cannot defeat the threat of 2 ♖f8 by means of 1...0-0-0. But if 1...0-0-0 can be played, 1 0-0? is not legal. Instead, White is entitled to play 1 cxb6 e.p.+, because Black's last move must have been ...b7-b5 if the king and rook have not moved. (Note that ...b6-b5 cannot have been Black's last move because White would not then have had a possible previous move. As it is, with ...b7-b5 as Black's last move, White's previous move can only have been ♖(c6)xa6+.)

Reversal themes

REVERSAL: TRY/KEY + THREAT

238

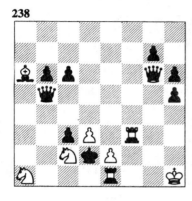

N.A.Macleod
3rd prize, *Mat* 1980
Mate in two

Try	1 ♕g2?	(>2 e4)
	... ♕c5	2 e3
	♕g5!	
Try	1 e4?	(>2 ♕g2)
	... ♕g5	2 ♖f2
	♕c5!	
Try	1 ♖f2?	(>2 e3)
	... ♕d5+	2 e4
	♕f5!	
Key	1 e3!	(>2 ♖f2)
	... ♕d5	2 ♕g2
	♕xd3	2 ♕xd3

In no. 238, if White tries 1 ♕g2?, he will threaten 2 e4. However, 1...♕g5! refutes. It is possible to play the threatened move as a try: 1 e4?. Now the threat is 2 ♕g2, the move which constitutes the first try. The refutation this time is 1...♕c5!. What we see here is a reversal of White's first and second moves. The position contains a second reversal, for there is another try, 1 ♖f2?, with the threat of 2 e3 (refuted by 1...♕f5!). Finally the key, 1 e3! (the move threatened by the third try) brings in 2 ♖f2 as its threat. This is a *sequence reversal* involving White's first moves and threats. Incidentally, the skilful composer of this fine example arranged that in each phase a further black defence introduces, as the mate, a thematic move from one of the other phases.

It might be helpful to summarise the pattern of this problem with the aid of letters to represent the white moves:

Try 1 **A**? (>2 **B**). Try 1 **B**? (>2 **A**). Try 1 **C**? (>2 **D**). Key 1 **D**! (>2 **C**).

The sequence reversal in no. 239 is of a slightly different character, for it involves White's first moves and the mates following a specific black defence. 1 ♘c3? (>2 ♘f7) allows 2 ♕e1 after 1...♘e6, but fails to 1...d3!. 1 ♕e1? (>2 ♘xc5) then brings in 2 ♘c3 to meet the defence 1...♘e6, but is refuted by 1...♘d3!. As in the previous problem, there is a second pair of reversed white moves: 1 ♕e3? (>2 ♘xc5), with 2 ♘f6 after 1...♘e6 (refuted by

239

REVERSAL: TRY/KEY + MATE

Z.Tanić
1st prize, *Die Schwalbe* 1983
Mate in two

Try 1 ♘c3?		(>2 ♘f7)
...	♘e6	2 ♛e1
	d3!	
Try 1 ♛e1?		(>2 ♘xc5)
...	♘e6	2 ♘c3
	♘d3!	
Try 1 ♛e3?		(>2 ♘xc5)
...	♘e6	2 ♘f6
	b2!	
Key 1 ♘f6!		(>2 ♘f7)
...	♘e6	2 ♛e3
	♖h7	2 ♛xg5

1...b2!), and the key 1 ♘f6! (>2 ♘f7), allowing 2 ♛e3 as the mate to follow
1...♘e6. The appeal of this problem lies in the differentiated queen-moves to
the e-file. In the following summary of the pattern, upper-case characters
represent white moves, and lower-case black moves:

   Try 1 **A**? 1...**a** 2 **B**. Try 1 **B**? 1...**a** 2 **A**. Try 1 **C**? 1...**a** 2 **D**. Key 1 **D** 1...**a** 2
C.

   The reader may perhaps be wondering whether a reversal of White's threat
and the mate following a specific defence in two phases can produce interesting play. This kind of reversal actually has its own name, the **le Grand**, and
its importance is such that it deserves an entry in this book all to itself.

   There are four other reversal themes, each named after a composer who
made an early example: *Dombrovskis, Hannelius, Vladimirov* and *Banny*. To
these may be added *Salazar* (mentioned under **Switchback**). The term 'reversal' is not a particularly accurate description of what happens in these
themes, but it is often used to denote them and seems to have gained general
acceptance. As in the examples of sequence reversal shown above, the
themes have to do with the relationship between white moves that appear and
reappear at different points in the solution of a multi-phase problem.

   Dombrovskis: A white try threatens move **A**, but is refuted by black defence **a**. After the key, which carries a different threat, defence **a** leads to
move **A**. A second try threatens move **B** and is refuted by defence **b**. In the
post-key play defence **b** is followed by move **B**.

240

DOMBROVSKIS

A.Dombrovskis
1st prize, *Probleemblad* 1958
Mate in two

Try 1 ♗c1?		(>2 ♘f4)
...	♗d2!	
Try 1 ♘g3?		(>2 ♖d4)
...	♕e2!	
Key 1 ♘e3!		(>2 ♕c2)
...	♗d2	2 ♘f4
	♕e2	2 ♖d4
	♔e2	2 ♕d1

No. 240 was the first consciously composed example of this paradoxical idea and is still one of the clearest. 1 ♗c1? threatens 2 ♘f4 [A], but fails to 1...♗d2! [a]. 1 ♘g3? threatens 2 ♖d4 [B], but 1...♕e2! [b] refutes. By crucially closing two white lines and, in anticipation, two black lines as well, and granting two flights, the key 1 ♘e3!, with the threat of 2 ♕c2, introduces the reversal pattern: 1...♗d2 [a] 2 ♘f4 [A]; and 1...♕e2 [b] 2 ♖d4 [B].

As readers will realise, it is possible to extend the idea to include three or more tries each threatening a mate that is playable after the key in answer to the very defence that refutes the try. In practice, however, constructional difficulties supervene beyond three Dombrovskis tries, although some **fairy chess** forms offer greater possibilities.

The pattern of the two-phase Dombrovskis is this:
Try? (>2 A) 1...a!. Try? (>B) 1...b!. Key (>threat) 1...a 2 A; 1...b 2 B.

Hannelius: White's first try threatens move A, refuted by defence a. The second try threatens move B, failing to defence b. After the key, defences a and b lead to moves B and A respectively. This is, therefore, an inversion of the Dombrovskis effect. A further try may introduce move C as the threat, refuted by defence c. In this cyclic form of the theme, defences a, b and c lead to moves B, C and A in the post-key play. Some ingenious composers have extended such a cycle to as many as six points. The theme is named after the Finnish expert Jan Hannelius, for many years President of the FIDE Permanent Commission for Chess Compositions (PCCC).

No. 241 is a clear illustration with two thematic tries: 1 ♘g3?, threatening 2 ♖e4 [A], failing to 1...♗xe6! [a], and 1 ♘f4?, with the threat of 2 ♘c6 [B], refuted by 1...♗e8! [b]. The key 1 ♘xf6! (>2 ♘d7) grants Black a flight, to which the thematic bishop-moves open a guard-line: 1...♗xe6 [a] 2 ♘c6 [B],

241

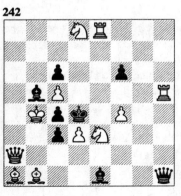

HANNELIUS

U.Degener
1st prize, Rizzetti Memorial Tourney
1985
Mate in two

Try	1 ♘g3?	(>2 ♖e4)
	...	♗xe6!
Try	1 ♘f4?	(>2 ♘c6)
	...	♗e8!
Key	1 ♘xf6!	(>2 ♘d7)
	...	♗xe6	2 ♘c6
		♗e8	2 ♖e4
		♔xf6	2 ♕xh8
		♕xf6	2 ♕b8
		exf6	2 ♕d6
		♗xf6	2 ♗f4
		♘c3+	2 ♗xc3

and 1...♗e8 [b] 2 ♖e4 [A]. Unlike the Dombrovskis, this pattern has nothing paradoxical about it, and if the problem contained no other play the result would be a dull piece of work. However, this example has five further variations, four of them involving captures on f6. The basic pattern is:

Try? (>2 A) 1...**a**!. Try (>2 B) 1...**b**!. Key (>threat) 1...**a** 2 **B**; 1...**b** 2 **A**.

DOMBROVSKIS + HANNELIUS

242

L.Szwedowksi
1st prize, *Szachy* 1988-9
Mate in two

Try	1 dxc4?	(>2 ♘f5)
	...	♕d5!
Try	1 ♕e2?	(>2 ♘c2)
	...	cxd3!
Try	1 ♖h3?	(>2 ♘e6)
	...	♕d5	2 ♘c2
		cxd3	2 ♘f5
		♕f3!
Key	1 ♕f2!	(>2 ♘e6)
	...	♕d5	2 ♘f5
		cxd3	2 ♘c2

The composer of no. 242 has ingeniously combined the Dombrovskis and Hannelius themes by incorporating a third try-play phase and **reciprocal change** between this phase and the post-key play. 1 dxc4?, threatening 2 ♘f5 [A], is refuted by 1...♕d5! [a]. 1 ♕e2?, with a threat of 2 ♘c2 [B], fails to 1...cxd3! [b]. The third try is 1 ♖h3?, this time threatening 2 ♘e6, which is not part of the pattern. Now defences **a** and **b** (1...♕d5 and 1...cxd3) are answered by mates **B** and **A** (2 ♘c2 and 2 ♘f5) respectively – the Hannelius theme. However, 1...♕f3! refutes (not, of course, 1...♕xh3, because 2 ♖e4 is always available). The key 1 ♕f2!, with the same threat of 2 ♘e6, reverses the two mates found after the third try: 1...♕d5 2 ♘f5 (a-A), and 1...cxd3 2 ♘c2 (b-B) – Dombrovskis. All this is brought about by an intricate pattern of line-effects, with double-checkmate in the post-key phase.

Try? (>2 A) 1...**a**!. Try? (>2 B) 1...**b**!. Try? (>threat) 1...**a** 2 **B**; 1...**b** 2 **A**. Key! (>threat) 1...**a** 2 **A**; 1...**b** 2 **B**.

Vladimirov: White's try (move A) is refuted by defence **a**. In the post-key play, defence **a** leads to **A** as a second move. A second try (move B) fails to defence **b**. Then defence **b** is followed by **B** after the key.

The theme is named after the outstanding Russian composer Yakob Vladimirov.

VLADIMIROV

243

M. Velimirović
1st prize, *diagrammes* 1978
Mate in two

Try 1 ♖de5?   (>2 d5)
...   ♕f7!
Try 1 ♗e5?   (>2 ♖d6)
...   ♖xa8!
Key 1 ♖e6! (>2 ♗e7)
...   ♕f7   2 ♖de5
        ♖xa8   2 ♗e5
        ♖d8   2 cxd8♘
        ♕xf5   2 ♖xf5

This idea is quite hard to construct unless capture of the try-piece(s) is used. No. 243 avoids this unconvincing arrangement. 1 ♖de5? [A] threatens 2 d5 but fails to 1...♕f7! [a]. 1 ♗e5? [B] carries the threat of 2 ♖d6, but is refuted by 1...♖xa8! [b]. After the key 1 ♖e6! (>2 ♗e7), defences **a** and **b** (1...♕f7 and 1...♖xa8) allow White to mate by **A** and **B** respectively (2 ♖de5 and 2 ♗e5).

Try 1 **A**? (>threat) 1...**a**! Try 1 **B**? (>threat) 1...**b**! Key! (>threat) 1...**a** 2 **A**; 1...**b** 2 **B**.

Banny: White's two tries **A** and **B** fail respectively to defences **a** and **b**. After the key, defence **a** allows move **B** as the mate, while defence **b** leads to move **A** as the mate. This theme, therefore, has the same relationship to the Vladimirov as the Hannelius has to the Dombrovskis. The Russian composer Dmitri Banny provides the name for this theme.

BANNY

244

V.Chepizhny
1st prize, *Revista Romana de Sah* 1984
Mate in two

Try 1 ♗c7?	(>2 ♘d6)	
...	♖xc4	2 ♖b8
	♘xc4!	
Try 1 c7?	(>2 ♖d4)	
...	♘xc4	2 ♖d6
	♖xc4!	
Key 1 ♖b7!	(>2 ♘d6)	
...	♘xc4	2 c7
	♖xc4	2 ♗c7
	♔xc4	2 ♕d3

Like the above example of the Vladimirov, no. 244 makes use of a **half-battery** to achieve the required effect. 1 ♗c7? [A] (>2 ♘d6) fails to the reply 1...♘xc4! [a]. 1 c7? [B] (>2 ♖d4) is refuted by 1...♖xc4! [b]. Notice, incidentally, that each of the defences **a** and **b** has an answer in the phase in which it is not a refutation. The key 1 ♖b7!, by placing another guard on b6, threatens 2 ♘d6. Now 1...♘xc4 [a] leads to **B** (2 c7), while 1...♖xc4 is answered by **A** (2 ♗c7). Splendid unity is achieved in this problem by virtue of the fact that White's two thematic moves involve the square c7, while Black's thematic moves are both captures on c4.

Try 1 **A**? (>threat) 1...**a**!. Try 1 **B**? (>threat) 1...**b**!. Key! (>threat) 1...**a** 2 **B**; 1...**b** 2 **A**.

The possibilities for these reversal themes in three-movers and longer problems are considerable. Indeed, there are many problems from the past, composed long before the themes became popular in the two-mover, which show similar effects in the variation play (e.g. white moves 2 and 3) without there being any try-play at all. But because in the three-mover there is an additional move to play with, it is possible to combine two or even more of the reversal themes without any sense of strain, as no. 245 amply demonstrates. It is by one of the foremost three-move composers of the late 20th century, an expert whose problems display their ideas with the utmost clarity and restraint.

245

DOMBROVSKIS + VLADIMIROV

M.Keller
1st prize, *diagrammes* 1991
Mate in three
Try 1 ♖f8?   (>2 ♗d5)
   ... hxg6! (2 ♗d5+? ♚xf4!)
Try 1 ♘d5?   (>2 ♖xd4)
   ... ♗xe2! (2 ♖xd4+? ♚f3!)
Key 1 ♔g3! (>2 ♘h4 ... 3 ♗d5)
   ... hxg6 2 ♗d5+ ♚xf5 3 ♖f8
        ♗xe2 2 ♖xd4+ ♚e3 3 ♘d5

There are two tries: 1 ♖f8? [A1] and 1 ♘d5? [B1], threatening respectively 2 ♗d5 [A2] and 2 ♖xd4 [B2]. However, **A1** fails to 1...hxg6 [a] because Black now has a flight on f4. And **B1** is refuted by 1...♗xe2! [b], securing a flight on f3. The key 1 ♔g3!, providing additional guards on these potential flights, threatens 2 ♘h4 ... 3 ♗d5 (notice that 2 ♖f8? and 2 ♘d5? are not threatened because of the impending check 2...h4+). Now 1...hxg6 [a] allows 2 ♗d5+ [A2] ♚xf5 3 ♖f8 [A1], while 1...♗xe2 [b] enables White to continue with 2 ♖xd4+ [B2] ♚e3 3 ♘d5 [B1]. So we have here the Dombrovskis theme on move 2, and the Vladimirov theme on move 3.

The same composer provides a convincing illustration of how to combine the Hannelius and Banny themes in no. 246. 1 ♖d2? [A1] threatens 2 ♗d4 [A2], but 1...fxe5! [a] refutes. It is no use White then trying 2 ♗g2? [B1] (>3 ♘e4) because of 2...♗xd2!, securing a potential flight on d5. The second try is this same move 1 ♗g2? [B1], with the same threat (2 ♘e4 [B2]), but it fails to 1...f5! [b], because 2 ♖d2? [A1] (>3 ♗d4) is answered by 2...♖xg2!, which again secures Black a potential flight on d5. The key and threat shift

246

HANNELIUS + BANNY

M.Keller
Die Schwalbe 1992
Mate in three
Try 1 ♖d2?   (>2 ♗d4)
        ...   fxe5! (2 ♗g2? ♗xd2!)
Try 1 ♗g2?   (>2 ♘e4)
        ...   f5!   (2 ♖d2? ♖xg2!)
Key 1 ♔b7!   (>2 ♔a6 ... 3 ♖c6)
        ...   fxe5 2 ♗g2   (>3 ♘e4)
                      ...   exd4 3 ♗xd4
              f5   2 ♖d2   (>3 ♗d4)
                      ...   fxe4 3 ♘xe4

attention briefly to the top of the board: 1 ♔b7! (>2 ♔a6 ... 3 ♖c6). Moves by the ♘f6 defend by threatening 2...♖h6. 1...fxe5 [a] leads to 2 ♗g2 [B1], with its threat of 3...♘e4 [B2], and if Black continues 2...exd4, then 3 ♗xd4 [A2] will mate. The other pawn-move, 1...f5 [b], allows 2 ♖d2 [A1] (>3 ♗d4 [A2]). If 1...fxe4, 3 ♘xe4 [B2] reappears. The Banny theme is seen in the recurrence of the two tries as continuations after the defences that refuted them, but in reverse order. The Hannelius theme brings the two try-play threats back as third-move threats, again reversed with respect to the original refutations. The fact that the two thematic defences are carried out by the same black unit makes for great unity, and it is an added bonus, though not part of the scheme, that moves **A2** and **B2** come in again after further moves by the defending black pawn. This magnificent problem makes an apt conclusion to this brief survey of reversal themes. Many other combinations and syntheses have been attempted in recent years, with varying degrees of success, and there is no doubt plenty of life left in them yet, more especially, perhaps, in the three- and more-move fields.

Roman

The Roman is a three- and more-move theme, an elaboration of simple decoy tactics. What happens is this. If White were to make a certain threat straightaway, a black unit would have an adequate defence. This black unit is therefore first decoyed away from the square from which it can play its adequate defence, and to a square from which it can play a new defence. But this new defence will carry a weakness not present in the original defence. No. 247 is a simple illustration.

247

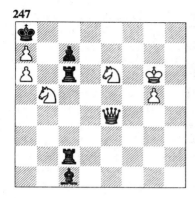

ROMAN

J.Møller
Skakbladet 1911
Mate in three

Try 1 ♕d5? ♗xg5!
Key 1 ♕h1! (>2 ♕h8)
... ♗b2 2 ♕d5 (>3 ♕d8)
... ♗f6 3 ♘exc7

The try 1 ♕d5? (>2 ♕d8) is refuted by 1...♗xg5!. If White is to play 2 ♕d5 as his second move, the black bishop must first be induced to abandon this defence. The key 1 ♕h1! serves White's purpose. Black's best defence is 1...♗b2, which now allows the continuation 2 ♕d5. 2...♗xg5 is no longer possible; it has been replaced by the defence 2...♗f6, countering the threat of 3 ♕d8. But 2...♗f6 is an interference-unpin of the ♘e6 and allows White to mate by 3 ♘exc7. Romans are usually classified according to the weakness of the substitute defence (e.g. interference-Roman, self-block-Roman, etc.). This one is an unpin-Roman. No. 176 (p.163) is a self-block Roman.

DECOY + ROMAN

248

H.-P. Rehm
1st prize, Leipzig Olympiad 1960
Mate in seven

Try	1 ♔g8?	♖g2+
	2 ♘g4+	♖xg4+
	3 ♔f8	♖e3!
Key	1 ♔e8!	♗a4+
	2 b5	♗xb5+
	3 ♔f8	♗d3
	4 ♔g8	♖g2+
	5 ♘g4+	♖xg4+
	6 ♔f8	♖e4
	7 ♖xf5	

No. 248 shows a Roman in combination with **pericritical** moves of two black pieces. The try 1 ♔g8? (>2 f8♕) fails to 1...♖g2+, for if 2 ♘g4+?

♖xg4+ 3 ♔f8 then Black continues with 3...♖e3!, and the rook from a3 has taken over the guard of e7, which the ♖e2 holds in the diagram position. White must therefore prevent this defence by the ♖a3, so that Black's only continuation after the moves given above will be to play the other rook from g4 to e4 – an interference permitting mate on f5. White does this by means of a three-move decoy of the ♗c2, so that this piece ends up on d3: 1 ♔e8! ♗a4+ 2 b5 ♗xb5+ 3 ♔f8 ♗d3 – the bishop must return to this diagonal in order to retain its guard of f5. Now any defence by the ♖a3 on the e-file has been ruled out, and so White can pursue the line shown as the try-play: 4 ♔g8 ♖g2+ 5 ♘g4+ ♖xg4+ 6 ♔f8 ♖e4 – necessary to restore the guard on e7 – and then White mates with 7 ♖xf5, exploiting the interference with the bishop. The beauty of this remarkable problem lies not merely in the strategy, but also in the echo effects of the pericritical moves of the black bishop and the ♖e2: both are made to move round three sides of a rectangle so that they finish up exactly where White wants them.

German composers have very strong views with regard to the Roman and related themes (e.g. **Dresden, Hamburg**). They regard the thematic try or tries as essential. Furthermore, Black's first move must allow the continuation only through the defence-substitution and not additionally because of some further weakness. A more detailed discussion of these points will be found under **Logical problems**.

Readers to whom the distinctions between the Roman, Dresden and Hamburg themes are not quite clear may find the following summary helpful:

Roman: move by piece **A** substitutes defence by **A** for defence by **A**;
Hamburg: move by piece **B** substitutes defence by **A** for defence by **A**;
Dresden: move by any piece substitutes defence by **B** for defence by **A**.

Rössel → Knight-tour

Round trip

One of the optical effects beloved of more-move composers is the round trip (a rough translation of the German *Rundlauf*). In the course of the solution a unit leaves its diagram square and eventually returns to it by a roundabout route. This effect, sometimes termed *merry-go-round*, differs from the **switchback**, where a piece returns to its starting square by the same route.

In no. 249, 1 f5+? would lead to mate on White's second move were it not for the black g-pawn (1...♔xe5 2 f4+? gxf3 e.p.!). The task of the ♗c2 is to eliminate this pawn, which it does by threatening mate from different directions, capturing on g4 on the way: 1 ♗a4! ♔f5 2 ♗d7+ ♔e4 3 ♗e8 ♔f5

249

ROUND-TRIP

S.Schneider
1st prize, *Deutsche Schachzeitung* 1956
Mate in ten
Try 1 f5+? ♚xe5! (2 f4+? gxf3 e.p.!)
Key 1 ♗a4! (>2 ♗d7)

	...	♚f5
	2 ♗d7+	♚e4
	3 ♗e8	♚f5
	4 ♗g6+	♚e6
	5 ♗h5	♚f5
	6 ♗xg4+	♚e4
	7 ♗d1	

(7 ♗h5? ♚f5 8 ♗g6+ ♚e6 9 f5+ ♚xe5
10 f4+? ♚e4!)

	7 ...	♚f5
	8 ♗c2+	♚e6
	9 f5+	♚xe5
	10 f4	

4 ♗g6+ ♚e6 5 ♗h5 ♚f5 6 ♗xg4+ ♚e4 7 ♗d1 ♚f5 8 ♗c2+ (now the bishop is back home and the black pawn has gone) 8...♚e6 9 f5+ ♚xe5 10 f4. While the bishop is busy performing its round trip, the black king executes two switchbacks, to e4 and back via f5. Writing of this splendid problem, the distinguished German composer and critic Herbert Grasemann said: 'Show this to over-the-board players, so that they too can see how beautiful chess can be!'

Royal battery

A royal battery consists of line-piece + king aimed at the opposing king or at a square in the king's field. The royal battery in no. 250 is diagonal, with the ♗b2 as the rear-piece. In the two-mover a direct royal battery can open at most six times; in this example there are six set mates, moves of the king from d4. After 1 ♚c3? (>2 ♚xb3) the king again visits six squares, four of them different from those visited in the set play. The key 1 ♚e5! (>2 ♚e6) leads once again to six openings of the battery, with four completely new variations: 1...g5 2 ♚f5; 1...♞g5 2 ♚f4; and 1...♗d6+ 2 ♚xd6. Many other composers have experimented with this matrix, with varying degrees of success.

250

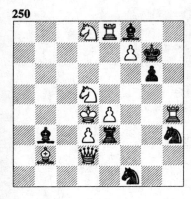

ROYAL BATTERY

B.W.Dennis
The Problemist 1968
Mate in two

Set 1...	♖xe4+	2 ♔xe4
	♖xd3+	2 ♔xd3
	♘f~	2 ♔xe3
	♗xd5	2 ♔xd5
	♗a4	2 ♔c4
	♗c5+	2 ♔xc5
Try 1 ♔c3?		(>2 ♔xb3)
...	♖xd3+	2 ♔xd3
	♘xd2	2 ♔xd2
	♗xd5	2 ♔c2
	♗a4	2 ♔c4
	♗b4+	2 ♔xb4
	g5!	
Key 1 ♔e5!		(>2 ♔e6)
...	g5	2 ♔f5
	♘g5	2 ♔f4
	♖xe4+	2 ♔xe4
	♗xd5	2 ♔xd5
	♗d6+	2 ♔xd6
	(♖f3	2 ♕h6)

Rukhlis

The Rukhlis is a pattern of moves combining mate-change and mate-transference. At least two set or virtual-play mates are transferred to different defences after the key, while the original defences gain new mates. No. 251 is an outstanding example. Four self-blocks are set: 1...♘e5 2 ♘e2; 1...♕e5 2 ♕xd1; 1...♗xd5 2 ♗c5; and 1...♖xd5 2 ♖a4. The apparently very simple key 1 ♗e4 (>2 ♖d3) transfers the third and fourth of these mates so that they now follow the first two defences, while the mates which followed the first two defences in the set play recur after two new defences, once again self-blocks: 1...♘e5 2 ♗c5; 1...♕e5 2 ♖a4; 1...♗xe4 2 ♘e2; and 1...♖xe4 2 ♕xd1. The open setting, combined with the richness of the self-blocks and the pattern of changed and transferred mates, makes this a memorable problem.

The Rukhlis differs from straightforward mate-transference in that the set defences must have new mates after the key. When the defences which

251

RUKHLIS

L.I.Loshinsky
1st prize, Chigorin Memorial Tourney
1950
Mate in two

Set 1...	♘e5	2 ♘e2
	♛e5	2 ♕xd1
	♗xd5	2 ♗c5
	♜xd5	2 ♖a4
Key 1 ♗e4 (>2 ♖d3)		
...	♘e5	2 ♗c5
	♛e5	2 ♖a4
	♗xe4	2 ♘e2
	♜xe4	2 ♕xd1

acquire the transferred mates in the post-key play also have set mates, the Rukhlis is described as *ideal*. Stated in simple terms, this is what happens in an ideal Rukhlis: the mates following four black defences are changed, two of them being transferred (without reciprocal effect). The scheme may be found in no. 252 – and just look at the date of this problem!

IDEAL RUKHLIS

252

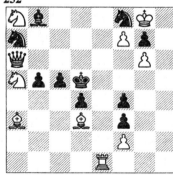

A.Moseley
2nd prize, Good Companions, April
1914
Mate in two

Set 1...	♗d6	2 ♘b6
	♗e5	2 ♗e4
	♘c6	2 ♕xc6
	b4	2 ♗c4
Key 1 ♘c4 zugzwang		
...	♗d6	2 ♕xd6
	♗e5	2 ♖xe5
	♘c6	2 ♘ab6
	b4	2 ♗e4

It is unlikely that Moseley realised, in 1914, that his work would be the precursor of a number of masterpieces many decades later. The set play runs:

1...♗d6 2 ♘b6; 1...♗e5 2 ♗e4 (both self-blocks with white interference); 1...♘c6 2 ♕xc6; and 1...b4 2 ♗c4. The key 1 ♘c4 (zugzwang) changes two mates and transfers two mates: 1...♗d6 2 ♕xd6; 1...♗e5 2 ♖xe5; 1...♘c6 2 ♘ab6; and 1...b4 2 ♗e4. There is also a third transferred mate, for the new defence 1...bxc4 brings back 2 ♗xc4, which previously followed 1...b4. But it would be asking too much to expect 2 ♕c6 to reappear as well. The white ♗a3, which completes the pre-key block (set 1...c4 2 ♘b6), is idle after the key and irrelevant to the thematic play. Most composers nowadays would remove it.

IDEAL RUKHLIS

253

O.Stocchi
Sah 1950
Mate in two

Set 1...	c3	2 ♘xe3	(2 ♘b4?)
	e2	2 ♘b4	(2 ♘e3?)
	♘c6	2 ♖d6	(2 ♖f5?)
	♘f5	2 ♖xf5	(2 ♖d6?)
Key 1 ♘e6		(>2 ♕d1)	
...	c3	2 ♖d4	
	e2	2 ♕d4	
	♘c6	2 ♘xe3	(2 ♘b4?)
	♘f5	2 ♘b4	(2 ♘xe3?)
	♔d6	2 ♘c7	

No. 253 is by the brilliant Italian composer Ottavio Stocchi, one of the half-dozen greatest two-move specialists of all time. The four set mates all show **dual avoidance**: 1...c3 2 ♘xe3 (not 2 ♘b4?, since White must not close the line which Black has just opened – the **Mari** theme); 1...e2 2 ♘b4 (not 2 ♘e3? for the same reason); 1...♘c6 2 ♖d6 (not 2 ♖f5, prevented by direct guard); and 1...♘f5 2 ♖xf5 (2 ♖d6?). The dual avoidance by direct guard is maintained in the post-key play, but the mating-squares guarded are different. After 1...♘e6 (>2 ♕d1), 1...c3 allows 2 ♖d4 and 1...e2 leads to 2 ♕d4. The mates by the ♘c2 are transferred: 1...♘c6 2 ♘xe3 (not 2 ♘b4?); and 1...♘f5 2 ♘b4 (not 2 ♘xe3?). All this is brought about by the fact that the key rules out the mates given in the set play by the ♖f6, grants Black a new flight on d6, guards d4 again to free the ♘c2, and makes possible, by **square-vacation**, the mates by the w♖a4 and ♕d4. Observe the additional defence 1...♔d6, leading to 2 ♘c7.

254

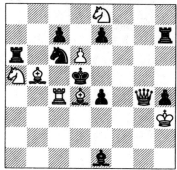

EXTENDED RUKHLIS

V.F.Rudenko
1st prize, *Praca* 1959
Mate in two

Set	1...	cxd6	2 ♘c7
		exd6	2 ♘f6
Try	1 ♗c5?		(>2 ♕xe4)
	...	♘e5	2 ♘c7
		e5	2 ♘f6
		♘d4!	
Key	1 ♗b6!		(>2 ♕xe4)
	...	♘e5	2 ♖d4
		e5	2 ♗xc6
		♘d4	2 ♖c5

The change and transference effects of the Rukhlis may be spread over three, rather than two, phases of the problem's solution. One of the ways in which this can be done is illustrated by no. 254. The set play has 1...cxd6 2 ♘c7, and 1...exd6 2 ♘f6. These mates are transferred by the try 1 ♗c5? (>2 ♕xe4) so that they follow self-blocks on the new flight e5: 1...♘e5 2 ♘c7; 1...e5 2 ♘f6. But this try is refuted by 1...♘d4!. The key changes the mates which follow the defences of the virtual play: 1 ♗b6! (>2 ♕xe4) ♘e5 2 ♖d4; and 1...e5 2 ♗xc6. (1...♘d4 2 ♖c5.) Numerous problems exist with changed and transferred effects spread over three phases; this example shows set/virtual transference + virtual/actual change, but other combinations are, of course, possible. Such patterns can conveniently be termed *extended Rukhlis*.

Rundlauf → Round-trip

Schiffmann Defence

The flight-giving key of no. 255, 1 ♗f1, sets up a ♗+♙ battery which opens in the threat, 2 e4. This move closes the line g4-c4, which means that a black unit other than a bishop can defeat the threat by capturing with self-pin on d4. Such a capture is a defence because the black unit, being unpinned by 2 e4, could interpose on the line f1-c4. In each of the four thematic variations White exploits the black self-pin: 1...♕xd4 2 ♘b6; 1...♘xd4 2 ♕b5; 1...♖xd4 2 ♕e6; and 1...exd4 2 e3. The Schiffmann defence, in which a black unit self-pins on a line where it would be released by interference unpin in

255

SCHIFFMANN DEFENCES

M.McDowell (after P.Mussuri)
Version, *Schiffs with Everything* 1982
Mate in two

Key 1 ♗f1 (>2 e4)
... ♛xd4 2 ♘b6
♞xd4 2 ♕b5
♜xd4 2 ♕e6
exd4 2 e3

the threat, is closely related to the **Nietvelt defence** (in which the unpin would be effected by removal of the pinning piece). The basic matrix of no. 252 was first shown by P.Mussuri in 1929. This new setting, saving five units and eliminating a cook, was produced by Michael McDowell, a gifted young problemist from Northern Ireland, for a monograph by Robert McWilliam on Schiffmann defences, *Schiffs with Everything*, published in 1982, when Michael was still a teenager.

Self-block

Self-block is the term used to describe a move by a black unit which restricts the mobility of the black king. In the two-mover the self-block must occur on a square adjacent to the king, since White must be able to exploit the weakness straight away. In three-movers and longer problems, however, the self-block may well occur on a square outside the king's initial field, but within the eventual scope of his mobility.

The maximum number of self-blocks attained in a single two-mover is eight. This record was set by A.J.Fink and J.F.Stimson in 1920, and it seems unlikely that it will ever be surpassed. No. 256 shows only six self-blocks, but they all occur on flight-squares.

The key, 1 ♜d8, threatens 2 ♗f5. 1...♜d4 allows 2 ♘bc5, 1...♛d4 leads to 2 ♕e2, and 1...♞d4 gives 2 ♜xe3. The blocks on the other flight are: 1...♜e4 2 ♗b5; 2 ♕e4 2 ♜d1; and 1...e4 2 ♘b2.

Dr Werner Speckmann, with his amazing capacity for reducing practically everything to miniature form, attains two changed self-blocks with only seven units in no. 257. The try 1 ♔g3? (>2 ♜e3) introduces the play 1...♗d5 2 ♕e3, and 1...e5 2 ♕c4, but fails to 1...♞c2!. The key is 1 ♕d6! (>2 ♜f5), and the mates after the same two defences are now 2 ♕f4 and 2 ♕d3. The

256

SIX SELF-BLOCKS ON FLIGHTS

T.Siapera
1st prize, *Sah* 1949
Mate in two
Key 1 ♖d8 (>2 ♗f5)

...	♖d4	2 ♘bc5
	♕d4	2 ♕e2
	♘d4	2 ♖xe3
	♖e4	2 ♗b5
	♕e4	2 ♖d1
	e4	2 ♘b2

CHANGED SELF-BLOCKS

257

W.Speckmann
Schach-Echo 1961
Mate in two
(a) Diagram
(b) ♘a1→h8

(a)	Try	1 ♔g3?	(>2 ♖e3)
	...	♗d5	2 ♕e3
		e5	2 ♕c4
		♘c2!	
	Key	1 ♕d6!	(>2 ♖f4)
	...	♗d5	2 ♕f4
		e5	2 ♕d3
(b)	Try	1 ♕d6? ♘g6!	
	Key	1 ♔g3!	

♘a1 serves merely to defeat the try, and if it is moved to h8 the try and key are reversed. The task of two changed self-blocks in miniature form was first achieved by H.Weenink in 1917, but without the twinning device.

Curious as it may seem, the task of four changed self-blocks is a difficult one to achieve. No. 258, one of the first examples to appear, shows this task in splendid style, with a setting which, incidentally, incorporates a **Rukhlis**. The square e6 is a flight in the diagram position; set self-blocks on this flight lead to mates separated by **dual avoidance**: 1...♖xe6 2 ♖xd4 (not 2 c4? because the pawn is pinned); and 1...♘xe6 2 c4 (not 2 ♖xd4?, eliminated by direct guard). Captures on e5 also have set mates, again with dual avoidance:

258

CHANGED SELF-BLOCKS (RUKHLIS)

M.Parthasarathy
1st prize, *British Chess Magazine* 1969
Mate in two

Set 1...   ♖xe6   2 ♖xd4
           ♘xe6   2 c4
           ♕xe5   2 ♕b3
           ♘xe5   2 ♘f4

Key 1 ♕g4 (>2 ♖c5)
      ...   ♖xe6   2 ♕xd4
            ♘xe6   2 ♕e4
            ♕xe5   2 c4
            ♘xe5   2 ♖xd4

1...♕xe5 2 ♕b3 (not 2 ♘f4?); and 1...♘xe5 2 ♘f4 (not 2 ♕b3?). The key 1 ♕g4 threatens 2 ♖c5 and changes all four replies to the captures by switching the flights. The mates on c4 and d4 now follow the captures on e5: 1...♕xe5 2 c4 (2 ♖xd4?); and 1...♘xe5 2 ♖xd4 (2 c4?). There are new mates after the captures on e6, which show **correction** rather than dual avoidance: 1...♖xe6 2 ♕xd4; and 1...♘xe6 2 ♕e4 (2 ♕xd4? is ruled out by the knight's arrival on e6, but e4 is unguarded at the same time). The ideal Rukhlis pattern is seen in the transference of two set mates to different post-key defences, with new mates for the original defences and set mates for the new defences (cf. no. 249). This remarkable problem was first published in the *British Chess Magazine*. The author of this book, who was *BCM* Problem Editor at the time, can still recall the excitement it aroused.

259

ANTICIPATORY SELF-BLOCKS

L.I.Loshinsky and V.I.Schiff
2nd prize, *Shakhmaty* 1961
Mate in three

Key 1 ♔f8   (>2 ♗f6+ ♔xd6 3 ♗d4)
      ...   ♖c6   2 ♖xg5+ ♔xd6 3 ♖d5
            ♖c5   2 ♕e2+ ♔d4 3 ♗f6
            ♖c4   2 ♕xg5+ ♔d4 3 ♕e3
            ♖c3   2 ♕f5+ ♔d4 3 ♕xd5

The self-blocks in the three-mover no. 259 are of an *anticipatory* nature. After the key, 1 ♔f8, the ♖c7 must move in order to create a flight in the black king's field to defeat the threat of 2 ♗f6+ ♔xd6 3 ♗d4. But each rook-move is a self-block of a square in the king's extended field. 1...♖c6 allows 2 ♖xg5+ ♔xd6 3 ♖xd5. 1...♖c5 leads to 2 ♕e2+ ♔d4 3 ♗f6. 1...♖c4 permits 2 ♕xg5+ ♔d4 3 ♕e3. And after 1...♖c3 White can play 2 ♕f5+ ♔d4 3 ♕xd5. In each variation White is able to exploit the fact that the black king's potential mobility has been restricted by the rook. Theoreticians may like to note that this problem is a good illustration of the combination of a theme with its **antiform**, the antiform of self-block being unblock, which is the motivation of the defences.

260

SELF-BLOCK

A.Johandl
1st prize, *Die Schwalbe* 1964
Mate in seven
Key 1 ♘f8 (>2 ♘fd7)

...		♔xf6
2	♘h7+	♔e5
3	exd3	a1♕
4	♘d7+	♔d5
5	♘hf6+	♕xf6
6	♘b5+	♔e5
7	d4	

No. 260, by a talented Viennese composer, is a witty seven-mover in which White would like to be able to mate on d4 (e.g. 1 exd3? > 2 d4). But Black has what seems at first sight to be an adequate defence: 1...a1♕!. White's plan must therefore be to allow this promotion to queen but then to force the queen to move out of harm's way. The play runs: 1 ♘f8 (>2 ♘fd7) ♔xf6 2 ♘h7+ ♔e5 3 exd3 (>4 d4) a1♕ 4 ♘d7+ ♔d5 5 ♘hf6+! ♕xf6 6 ♘b5+ ♔e5 7 d4. First the ♟f6 must go. This is so that the knight can check on that square and be captured by the black queen, which finds itself blocking the square in the final mating position, where the black king interferes with the queen on the **critical** square e5.

Selfmate

The stipulation for diagram no. 261 reads *Selfmate in two*. This means that the solver must discover how White, moving first, forces Black to inflict

261

SELFMATE

R.Prytz
Chemnitzer Tageblatt 1925
Selfmate in two

Key 1 &d2 (>2 ♕g2+ &xg2)
... ♖b7   2 ♕b1+   ♖xb1
    ♖c6   2 ♕c4+   ♖xc4
    ♖d5   2 ♕d3+   ♖xd3
    ♘d5   2 ♕xf4+ ♘xf4
    f3   2 ♕e2+   fxe2

mate on his second move. White
hopes to play 2 ♕g2+, forcing 2....&xg2. So e1 must be guarded by a move of
the bishop standing on that square. 1 &d2 is the key, and no other bishop
move will work, because Black must be prevented from defending with
1...♖b2 (1 &c3? ♖b2! 2 ♕g2+? ♖xg2!). Black is striving to avoid giving
mate, so he plays a unit on to the long diagonal to frustrate the threat. However, in doing so he unpins the white queen and simultaneously sets up a
masked battery, a situation which White can exploit by means of a queen-
check, forcing the battery to open, giving mate. In each case the queen must
check on a square controlled by the unpinning unit, so that Black is com-
pelled to capture. (This arrangement, quite common in selfmates, has ac-
quired the name *Dentist theme*.) 1...♖b7 allows 2 ♕b1+, forcing 2...♖xb1.

262

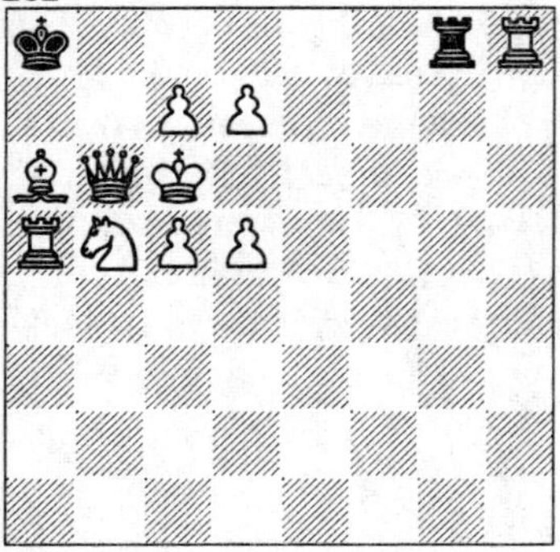

SELFMATE

E.Holladay
1st prize, *British Chess Magazine* 1965
Selfmate in ten

Key 1 ♘a7   ♖f8
    2 ♖g8   ♖e8
    3 ♖f8   ♖d8
    4 ♖e8   ♖c8
    5 ♖d8   ♖b8
    6 ♖c8   ♖xc8
    7 ♕b8+   ♖xb8
    8 &b7+   ♖xb7
    9 ♘b5+   ♖a7
    10 ♖a6   ♖xa6

1...♖c6 and 1...♖d5 lead to checks on c4 and d3 respectively, while 1...♘d5 permits 2 ♕xf4+ ♘xf4. Finally even a pawn gets in on the act: 1...f3 2 ♕e2+ fxe2.

No. 262 is a selfmate of a very different type. It takes White no fewer than ten moves to force Black into a position where he cannot avoid giving mate. The way the white rook follows the black rook along the eighth rank, restricting its mobility with each move, is elegant and ingenious.

Readers who would like to know more about selfmates are referred to an excellent book by an authority on the subject, Friedrich Chlubna, entitled *Das Matt des weißen Königs* (Vienna, 1995). The book is in German, but even if you are not much of a linguist, the problems speak for themselves.

Series-movers

Series-movers are **fairy chess** problems in which one side remains stationary all or nearly all of the time. There are many possible types, the following being the most common:

Series-mate: White plays a given number of consecutive moves ending in mate.

Series-helpmate: Black plays a given number of consecutive moves to reach a position in which White can mate in one.

Series-selfmate: White plays a given number of consecutive moves to reach a position in which Black is forced to give mate.

Series-reflex-mate: White plays a given number of consecutive moves to reach a position in which Black can (and therefore must) give mate. Throughout the sequence White must avoid positions in which he could himself give mate in one.

In all the above forms no check may be given until the last move of the se-

263

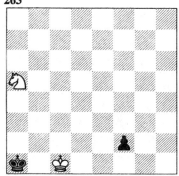

SERIES-HELPMATE

T.R.Dawson
Fairy Chess Review 1947
Series-helpmate in seventeen

1 ♔a2 2 ♔a3 3 ♔b4 4 ♔c3 5 ♔d3 6 ♔e2 7 ♔e1 8 f1♖ 9 ♖f2 10 ♔e2 11 ♔d3 12 ♔c3 13 ♔b4 14 ♔a3 15 ♔a2 16 ♔a1 17 ♖a2 ♘b3

quence. Each of the types listed has its equivalent ending in stalemate.

No. 263, by the King of chessboard unorthodoxy, T.R.Dawson, is a simple illustration of the series-helpmate. While White remains motionless, Black plays 17 consecutive moves to reach a position where White is able to give immediate mate. This example, with a **switchback** of the black king, shows a typical series-helpmate manoeuvre in which the white king has to be shielded from check while Black makes the necessary arrangement of his own pieces.

Square-vacation

As the name implies, square-vacation consists of the removal of a piece from a square so that another piece, nearly always of the same colour, may occupy that square. Square-vacation by Black is a defensive tactic: in the two-mover a black unit standing next to the black king may move in order to obtain a flight, thereby defeating White's threat. Such strategy, often known as *unblock*, is the **antiform** of **self-block**, and is illustrated, in conjunction with

264

SQUARE-VACATION

L.N.Gugel
2nd prize, *64* 1935
Mate in two

Key 1 ♘7f5	(>2 ♘g3)
...	♘e~ 2 ♖e7
	♘d7 2 ♖b6
	♘c6 2 ♘d6
	♗~ 2 ♖b4
	♗b6 2 ♖e7

black correction and battery play, in no. 264.

The key, 1 ♘7f5, threatens 2 ♘g3, which closes the line h2-e5. Black can therefore defend by removing his knight from e5, since 2 ♘g3? would then allow 2...♔e5!. A random departure from e5 allows the double-checkmate 2 ♖e7. The corrections 1...♘d7 and 1...♘c6 both close white and black lines and lead respectively to 2 ♖b6 and 2 ♘d6. Square-vacation can also be effected by the black bishop (1...♗ moves 2 ♘g3? ♔d4!): 1...♗~ 2 ♖b4; 1...♗b6 2 ♖e7. This last move, 2 ♖e7, is the same as that found after 1...♘~, but because it is brought about by completely different black strategy, it may be regarded as a distinct variation.

265

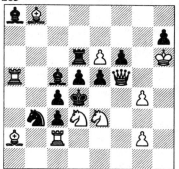

SQUARE-VACATION

S.Seider
2nd prize, Israel Ring Tourney 1964
Mate in three

Key 1 ♘f2 (>2 ♕xf6 ... 3 ♘f5)
     ...   ♖xe6   2 ♕f4+ exf4 3 ♘f5
            ♗b6   2 ♕e4+ dxe4 3 ♘f5
            ♘xa5 2 ♕d3+ cxd3 3 ♘f5
            ♔xe3 2 ♕f3+ ♔d4 3 ♕xc3

Square-vacation by White is used as a means of attack. In no. 265 the white queen four times vacates f5 to allow the ♘e3 to mate on that square. The first such vacation is found in the threat: 1 ♘f2, threatening 2 ♕xf6 followed by 3 ♘f5. Each of Black's three thematic defences opens a white line, allowing White to sacrifice his queen: 1...♖xe6 2 ♕f4+ exf4 3 ♘f5 (the ♗b8 now holds e5); 1...♗b6 2 ♕e4+ dxe4 3 ♘f5 (d5 held by the ♖a5); and 1...♘xa5 2 ♕d3+ cxd3 3 ♘f5 (c4 held by the ♗a2).

Stocchi

266

STOCCHI

P.Bekkelund
1st prize, *Sjakk-Nytt* 1947
Mate in two

Key 1 ♘e4 (>2 ♖b8)
     ...   axb4 2 ♖c5
            ♖xb4 2 ♘c3
            ♗xb4 2 ♗c4
            ♘xb4 2 ♘d6

The Stocchi is a self-block theme in which at least three self-blocks on a single square lead to mates differentiated by means of **dual avoidance**. No. 266 is one of the neatest and clearest examples of the theme. 1 ♘e4 threatens 2 ♖b8, and the blocks, four of them in all, occur on the flight-square b4. If a

dummy black unit with no powers at all, except the ability to self-block, were
to arrive on b4, four mates would be possible: 2 ♖c5, 2 ♘c3, 2 ♗c4 and 2
♘d6. These mates are forced individually by the captures 1...axb4, 1...♖xb4,
1...♗xb4 and 1...♘xb4 respectively. The first two of these defences are unblocks as well as being self-blocks.

STOCCHI

267

M.Kwiatkowski
1st prize, *Szachy* 1988
Mate in three

Key 1 ♖c6   (>2 ♖d6+ ♔e5 3 ♖xd3)
    ...   ♖d4 2 ♗e6+ ♘xe6 3 ♘f6
         ♘d4 2 ♘f6+ ♖xf6 3 e4
         ♕d4 2 e4+ ♘xe4 3 ♗e6
         ♔d4 2 ♘xf5+ ♔~ 3 ♘f6
         ♘e4 2 ♗e6+ ♔d4 3 ♘xf5
         ♘f7 2 ♘f6+ ♔d4 3 ♘xf5
         bxc6 2 ♕xc6+ ♔d4 3 ♘xf5

Stocchi blocks are not uncommonly found in the three-mover. In no.
267 the key 1 ♖c6 threatens 2 ♖d6+ ♔e5 3 ♖xd3. Blocking d4 clearly defeats this. 1...♖d4 allows 2 ♗e6+ ♘xe6 3 ♘f6, exploiting the **half-pin** of the
black units on f5 and g5. 1...♘d4 again exploits the half-pin: 2 ♘f6+ ♖xf6 3
e4. The third Stocchi-block on d4, 1...♕d4, does not lead to an exploitation
of the half-pin, but it does allow White to complete a cycle of continuations and mates (A-B, B-C, C-A): 2 e4+ ♘xe4 3 ♗e6. As with the two-
move example of the theme quoted above, an arrival on d4 by a dummy black
unit with only self-blocking power would allow all three white continuations.

Strategy, Change of

The set play of no. 268 consists of interferences on d5 (1...♘bd5 2 ♖c6; and
1...♘cd5 2 ♗xa6), and self-blocks with dual avoidance on c3 (1...♖xc3 2
♕e4; and 1...♗xc3 2 ♕e2). The key 1 ♘d5 introduces the threat 2 ♕b4. The
same defences now lead to the same mates, but for quite different reasons:
1...♘bxd5 and 1...♘cxd5 are now self-blocks, while 1...♖c3 and 1...♗c3
have become interferences. What changes is the strategy of the variations.

268

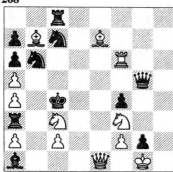

CHANGED STRATEGY

K.Hannemann
1st place, Denmark v Norway 1946
Mate in two

Set 1...   ♘bd5   2 ♖c6
            ♘cd5   2 ♗xa6
            ♖xc3   2 ♕e4
            ♗xc3   2 ♕e2
Key 1 ♘d5 (>2 ♕b4)
   ...   ♘bxd5   2 ♖c6
            ♘cxd5   2 ♗xa6
            ♖c3   2 ♕e4
            ♗c3   2 ♕e2

Switchback

A switchback occurs when a piece returns by the same route to a square which it has occupied already at some previous point in the problem's solution. In the two-mover only white pieces can perform switchbacks: White's key piece returns to its starting square on its second move. No. 269 shows a switchback in each of two phases, combined with other closely related play.

SWITCHBACKS

269

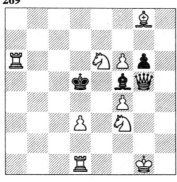

F.Salazar
2nd prize, *Die Schwalbe* 1968
Mate in two

Try 1 ♘e5?
   ...   ♗xe6   2 ♘f3
            ♗xd3   2 ♕g2
            ♗h3   2 ♘g4
            ♗e4!
Key 1 ♕g2!   (>2 ♕a2)
   ...   ♗xe6   2 ♕g5
            ♗xd3   2 ♘e5

The try 1 ♘e5? just waits for Black to commit himself. If the unpinned black bishop pins itself on e6, unmasking the ♕+♘ battery, White replies 2

♘f3 – switchback. The self-pin 1...♗xd3 leads to 2 ♕g2, a second pin-mate. 1...♗h3 and 1...♗g4 allow 2 ♘(x)g4, but there is no reply to 1...♗e4!. White must therefore play 1 ♕g2!, a move we have already seen as the second-move reply to 1...♗xd3 in the virtual play. The key carries the threat 2 ♕a2, which Black defends against by means of the self-pins of the bishop on e6 and d3. 1...♗xe6 permits the switchback mate 2 ♕g5, while 1...♗xd3 allows 2 ♘e5, the same move as White's try. The pattern of white moves in this well-constructed setting has led to the problem's being quoted as the pioneer of a **reversal theme** where White's first move and the mate following a defence are interchanged (try 1 A? 1...a 2 B; key 1 B! 1...a 2 A.) But Salazar's delightful problem, with its reciprocally interchanged batteries, goes much further than that, and it hardly does justice to the composer to link his name with a more basic idea that is (often unintentionally) a feature of many problems.

Task

In a sense, every problem is a task, since it is the composer's aim to produce the best setting of his idea with the fewest possible units. But the term is usually applied only when the composer has striven for a maximum effect. In his book *Chess Problems: Tasks and Records* (Faber & Faber, 1995), Sir Jeremy Morse rightly uses the term *record* to describe a problem showing a theoretical maximum, e.g. 6 mates by a **Royal battery** in the post-key play of a two-mover, or the maximum so far achieved, e.g. four changed mates after self-blocks in the post-key play of a two-mover. All records are *tasks*, but not all tasks are necessarily records.

It often happens that, in achieving a maximum task, a composer builds on work previously done by others. Such is the case with no. 270. Earlier problems by Vojko Bartolović and Michael Lipton, composed independently, were subsequently improved by Gustav Jönsson, who published his version in *Die Schwalbe* in 1962. It showed a seven-phase **Zagoruiko**: six tries and the key introduced a different pair of mates in reply to two black defences. In 1986, Miloš Tomašević, using much the same matrix, pushed this record up to *nine* phases (no. 270). The first six tries, 1 b3?, 1 ♕a3?, 1 h8♕?, 1 ♘b3?, 1 ♘de4? and 1 a8♘?, all differently refuted, create a block position in which moves by the two black knights produce different mates. The remaining two tries, 1 ♕a6? and 1 e8♕?, carry threats which demand specific moves by the knights. Finally the key, 1 e8♘!, reverts to the block position. As often happens with extreme tasks, the composer has justifiably ignored one of the desirable elements in the principle of **economy**.

270

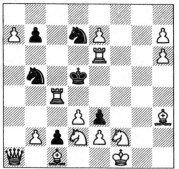

TASK: MULTI-PHASE ZAGORUIKO

M.Tomašević
(after Bartolović, Lipton and Jönsson)
Neue Zürcher Zeitung 1986
Mate in two

Try 1 e8♕?	(>2 ♗g2)	♘d~	2 ♖c5
...	♘d4 2 ♕xd7	♘d6!	
	♘e5 2 ♕xb7	Try 1 ♘de4?	
	♘c5 2 ♕h5	...	♘b~ 2 ♘c3
	♘d6!		♘d~ 2 ♘f6
Try 1 b3?			exf2!
...	♘b~ 2 ♕d4	Try 1 a8♘?	
	♘d~ 2 ♕e5	...	♘b~ 2 ♘c7
	♘c3!		♘d~ 2 ♘b6
Try 1 ♕a3?			b6!
...	♘b~ 2 ♕d6	Try 1 ♕a6?	(>2 ♕xb7/♗g2)
	♘d~ 2 ♕c5	...	♘d4 2 ♕d6
	♘xa3!		♘e5 2 ♕xb5
Try 1 h8♕?			♘c5!
...	♘b~ 2 ♕d4	Key 1 e8♘!	zugzwang
	♘d~ 2 ♕e5	...	♘b~ 2 ♘c7
	♘f6!		♘d~ 2 ♘f6
Try 1 ♘b3?		b6	2 a8♕
...	♘b~ 2 ♖d4	e~	2 e4

Ever since the early days of the chess problem, composers have been attracted by the notion of a task. In Tasks and Echoes (1915), A.C.White used the word 'accumulation' to refer to the build-up of effects found in task problems. He wrote: "Each country, each period, each composer has turned more or less consciously to some form of accumulation, and however far apart the results arrived at may be, their kinship in aim remains the vital, underlying principle in composition and the most helpful guide in any attempt towards a general classification of problems."

Themes A-H → Line-themes

Third-pin

On a **half-pin** line two pieces are arranged so that if one moves off the line, the other becomes totally pinned. Three pieces are needed to form a third-pin line, and therefore at least three moves are required for the solution if the third-pin is to be utilised, for two pieces have to move away before the third remains pinned.

271

THIRD-PIN

M.Niemeijer
Good Companions 1924
Mate in three

Key 1 ♗f5   (>2 ♔xg1 ... 3 ♘h2)
     ...   ♘xe5 2 ♘xe5+ ♕xe5 3 ♖d3
            ♕xe5 2 ♖d3+ exd3 3 ♘xe5
            e3   2 ♘f6 ♘xe5 3 ♘xd4

The key of no. 271, 1 ♗f5, threatens 2 ♔xg1 followed by 3 ♘h2. Black has a first-move defence by each of his third-pinned units: 1...♘xe5, which allows 2 ♘xe5+ ♕xe5 3 ♖d3 – the pawn is now left pinned; 1...♕xe5, leading to 2 ♖d3+ exd3 3 ♘xe5, with the knight now pinned; and finally 1...e3, permitting 2 ♘f6 (>3 ♗g4) ♘xe5 3 ♘xd4 – the queen is the only piece left on the pin-line. Partly because of the difficulties of construction, the third-pin has enjoyed far less popularity than the half-pin. Indeed, really good examples are hard to find, whereas the half-pin theme has inspired many a masterpiece.

Threat-correction

This is a white first-move tactic related to **white correction**. It can best be explained by reference to an example, no. 272. If the rook on the d-file plays southwards (over the square d6), White's threat can be 2 ♘d6. So try 1 ♖xd2?. This fails, however, to the pinning defence 1...♖a7!. Now the white rook has no way of preventing this defence or of providing a mate in reply

272

THREAT CORRECTION

M.Lipton
3rd prize, *Die Schwalbe* 1962
Mate in two

Try 1 ♖xd2?		(>2 ♘d6)
...	♗e5	2 ♖xe5
	♖a7!	
Try 1 ♖d3?		(>2 ♖e3)
...	cxd3	2 ♘d6
	♔xd3	2 ♘c5
	♗d4	2 ♖xd4
	♗e5!	
Try 1 ♖xg5?		(>2 ♘c5)
...	♗d4	2 ♖xd4
	♖a5!	
Key 1 ♖f5!		(>2 ♗c2)
...	gxf5	2 ♘c5
	♔xf5	2 ♘d6

to it. So instead of correcting the general error of removing itself from the seventh rank, it corrects the actual threat, by playing to d3 instead of d2. The new threat is 2 ♖e3; 2 ♘d6? is impossible as a threat now, because the black king has a flight d3. But 2 ♘d6 can be played after the self-blocking defence 1...cxd3. 1...♔xd3 leads to 2 ♘c5, while 1...♗d4 allows 2 ♖xd4, but this white first move is also only a try, since there is no reply to 1...♗e5!. (After 1 ♖xd2?, 1...♗e5 is followed by 2 ♖xd5, but the flight d3 makes this reply impossible after 1 ♖d3?) The solver's attention must now turn to the other white rook, which can threaten 2 ♘c5 by moving eastwards as far as g5. 1...♗d4 is met by 2 ♖xd4, but there is no reply to 1...♖a5!. Therefore the threat must be corrected once again: 1 ♖f5! (>2 ♗c2). The original threat returns after the self-block 1...gxf5, while 2 ♘d6 reappears when Black plays 1...♔xf5. The theme is therefore threat-correction twice over, by each white rook.

The close affinity between White Correction and Threat Correction may be seen from no. 273. A random move by the ♘e4 threatens both 2 ♕f4 and 2 ♘f5, but is refuted by 1...♖f8!. The correction try 1 ♘f6!?, closing the line f8-f4 in anticipation of the rook's defence, fails to 1...♗xg6!, because White has deprived himself of the reply 2 ♕xh8. No other tries by the ♘e4 can preserve the original threats and at the same time deal with 1...♖f8!. So a new threat must be substituted, in the hope that Black will have no adequate defence. 1 ♘xc5!? is tried, threatening 2 ♘b3. Black can capture the knight,

273

WHITE CORRECTION + THREAT CORRECTION

V.F.Rudenko
1st prize, Odessa Tourney 1986
Mate in two

Try 1 ♘4~?		(>2 ♕f4/♘f5)
...	♖f8!	
Try 1 ♘f6?		(>2 ♕f4/♘f5)
...	♗g6!	(2 ♕xh8?)
Try 1 ♘xc5?		(>2 ♘b3)
...	♖xc5	2 ♕f4
	♘xc5	2 ♘f5
	♔xc5	2 ♕e5
	♖b4!	
Key 1 ♘xc3!		(>2 ♘e2)
...	♖xc3	2 ♕f4
	♘xc3	2 ♘f5
	♔xc3	2 ♕d2
	♗xg4	2 ♕xh8

but in so doing allows White's original threats to reappear in turn: 1...♖xc5 2 ♕f4; and 1...♘xc5 2 ♘f5 (notice that these two variations display **dual avoidance**). 1...♔xc5 leads to 2 ♕e5, but Black still has a defence, 1...♖b4!. So a second threat-correction must be played, and this is the key: 1 ♘xc3!! (>2 ♘e2). Once more the captures of the knight lead to the original threats, again with dual avoidance: 1...♖xc3 2 ♕f4; and 1...♘xc3 2 ♘f5. This perfectly conceived problem is rounded off by two further variations: 1...♔xc3 2 ♕d2; and 1...♗xg4 2 ♕xh8 – this last line re-introducing a mate seen earlier in the solution. Incidentally, the mate-transference effects in both these examples of threat correction, by means of which the original threat which has to be corrected reappears in the post-key play in one of the variations, is regarded by many purists as a *sine qua non* of the theme. There are two such threats in Rudenko's example, both recurring in each of the threat-correction phases.

Total change

Total change occurs when the defences and mates of a two-mover are all changed between set and/or virtual and post-key play, but the theme remains the same throughout the various phases. No. 274 is an entertaining three-phase example featuring *en passant* captures by Black.

THREE-PHASE TOTAL CHANGE

274

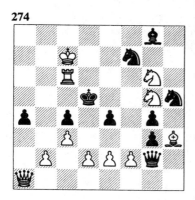

M.Myllyniemi
Version, *Problem* 1968
Mate in two

Try	1 b4?	(>2 ♖c5)	
	...	axb3 e.p.	2 ♕a5
		cxb3 e.p.	2 c4
		♕xf2!	
Try	1 f4?	(>2 ♘e7)	
	...	exf3 e.p.	2 e4
		gxf3 e.p.	2 ♗e6
		♘xf4!	
Key	1 d4!	(>2 ♖c5/♘e7)	
	...	cxd3 e.p.	2 ♕a2
		exd3 e.p.	2 ♗xg2

One try is 1 b4? (>2 ♖c5) axb3 e.p. 2 ♕a5; 1...cxb3 e.p. 2 c4; but it is defeated by 1...♕xf2!. So try 1 f4? (>2 ♘e7) exf3 e.p. 2 e4; 1...gxf3 e.p. 2 ♗e6; but 1...♘xf4! refutes. So only 1 d4!, with its double threat of 2 ♖c5 and 2 ♘e7, will work, and the defences and mates are now 1...cxd3 e.p. 2 ♕a2; and 1...exd3 e.p. 2 ♗xg2. The actual strategy of the problem is not very profound, but there is unity in the fact that all the mates are made possible by **line-opening** or **square-vacation**.

Tourneys

Competitions for chess problems are known as *tourneys*. There are five main types:

1. *Formal tourneys*. These are usually held to commemorate some special event (for example, a jubilee) or as a memorial to a recently deceased composer. There may be a set theme. Entries are sent to a nominated *controller*, whose functions are outlined below. The name of the judge is made known when the tourney is first announced, and he receives the competing problems on anonymous diagrams, so that he is unaware of the identity of the composers. When the award is published, only those entries honoured by the judge

are published, other entries being then at the composers' disposal, for publication elsewhere if they wish.

2. *Informal tourneys.* Problems published in many chess magazines and in magazines devoted exclusively to problems compete in these. The problems are seen and solved by the magazine's readers, and all those of the same type (e.g. mates in two) published within a specified period, usually a year, are arranged in order of merit by the judge, whose name should be made known before the beginning of the period in question.

3. *Team matches.* These are of two kinds:
i) Matches between two or more countries, usually formal, with an independent controller and neutral judge. (It is actually unusual to refer to such matches as tourneys.)
ii) The World Chess Compositions Tournament, a fully international event held every few years. Countries compete in a variety of sections, with different types of problem, which are judged as in a formal tourney. Points are awarded for the best entries in each section, and the competing countries are then ranked in order of their scores.

4. *Theme tourneys.* A magazine may announce a tourney on a set theme, frequently in conjunction with an article containing examples of the theme. Such tourneys are often, though not necessarily, formal.

5. *Quick composing tourneys.* Since the mid-1970s, gatherings of problemists have become common, several being held each year, in various parts of the world. At these gatherings composing tourneys are often run, with sometimes a few days' composing time allowed, sometimes only a few hours'.

The task of the controller of a formal or theme tourney is to receive the entries, to test them for soundness (this can now be done by computer for all types except endgame studies and the longer more-movers, and a few complex or lengthy fairy forms), to print anonymous diagrams and to send these to the judge. On receipt of the judge's award, he must prepare the text and diagrams (with composers' names) for publication. A period of a few months is normally allowed between the publication of the award and the finalisation of the tourney, to enable claims of **anticipation** to be lodged. The controller will have to get in touch with the judge in the event of such claims, and will finally draw up the definitive award once the judge has reached his decision regarding possible anticipations.

The judge of a composing tourney should be a problemist with an established reputation and an up-to-date knowledge of developments in the relevant genre. He will probably wish to check the entries for anticipation by consulting the holder of a collection of published problems, though relatively few comprehensive collections exist. As a general rule, he will award a number of *prizes*, and then single out a further selection of entries for *honourable mention* and for *commendation*. The judge of a team match will normally be asked simply to place the entries in order of merit.

It is not the purpose of this book to lay down the principles by which judges should assess problems, but it is perhaps worth quoting the views of the late Hermann Albrecht, a distinguished collector, editor and critic, and a recognised authority on two-move problems, even though he composed almost none himself. He thought a prize-winning problem ought to display formal perfection, though the combination of such perfection with great originality is rare. Originality + convincing form = prize; originality with formal weaknesses = honourable mention; attractiveness without particular originality = commendation. Not all judges will necessarily agree with Albrecht's views, but there can be no denying that those called upon to assess the works of others should base their assessment on some principles of this kind. In the end, personal preference will inevitably play a part. The British three-move expert R.C.O.Matthews poses the dilemma like this: 'If I am faced with two problems in a tourney, one of them original but having constructional defects and the other perfectly constructed but less original, I might ask myself: "Which of these problems would I be pleased to have composed?" '

Experienced judges may be holders of the FIDE title 'International Judge for Chess Compositions'. Such judges may be called upon to assess the entries for the *FIDE Album*, an anthology of the best problems of a three-year period. There is no order of merit involved here; instead, judges award points from 0 (not suitable for the Album) to 4 (must go in). Three judges work on each section, and as a general rule any entry receiving a total of at least 8 points qualifies for inclusion. The judging is very time-consuming, particularly in the more popular sections (e.g. two-movers and helpmates), where there might be well over 2000 entries. However, there are compensations: some of the entries are outstanding problems which it is a pleasure to study in depth, and in any case the exercise is a good way of keeping up to date with recent developments, as any self-respecting judge should wish to do. How does one become an International Judge? Applicants for the title must have already judged a number of appropriate tourneys (currently six), and must have the backing of their country's problem society. Applications are then considered by a sub-committee of the FIDE Problem Commission.

Tries

In the two-mover a try, which is normally defined as a white move which nearly solves the problem but is refuted by a single black defence, may have one of several functions:

1) A two-mover of the traditional style (where the interest is centred on the play which follows the key) may have a try which adds to the difficulty (and thus to the pleasure) of solving the problem, but which in no way affects the rest of the play. A good composer would never add extra force to create such a try; it should be inherent in the problem's position, and a composer will regard it as a matter of luck if a try of this sort happens to exist. A complete block problem, solved by a waiting move, may very well have a number of tries, each one failing because a set mate is thereby abandoned.

2) A try may serve to emphasise the set play of a problem. A try of this type is likely to be misleading to the solver, who is often reluctant to sacrifice whatever set play the position may contain.

3) New play may be introduced by a try, and this new play will contrast with the set play (if any) and with the post-key play. The solver's enjoyment of a problem should not be impaired if he happens to discover the key first and the try afterwards, though ideally the try should be the more obvious move. For this reason a composer will generally attempt to obtain the most obscure refutation for his try, to mislead the solver as much as possible. However, a problem with a try refuted by the most evident of defences should not be dismissed as worthless if the play this try introduces is of some genuine value in itself. The obvious refutation may have been forced on the composer by the nature of the setting.

4) A series of tries may be of interest in themselves through their relationship to one another. Tries of this type may conveniently be classified according to whether they are related through a *common aim* or through a *common error*. Tries showing **white correction**, such as in no. 275, are illustrative of the former type.

It is not hard to see that the ♘d6 must move to threaten 2 ♕e5, but the solver can easily go wrong in trying to determine where the knight should play to. The 'random' try 1 ♘f7? fails to the 'random' defence 1...♘4~! (this is a case where a genuine try is refuted by more than one black move, for that is part of the composer's thematic idea). The common aim is to provide for moves of this black knight. There are six 'correction' tries, which fail to single black refutations, some of them being corrections by the ♘f4, and finally the key, 1 ♘db7!, which of course provides for everything.

TRIES WITH COMMON AIM:
WHITE CORRECTION (WS-TOUR)

N.A.Macleod
1st prize, *Mat* 1988
Mate in two

Try 1 ♘f7?	(>2 ♕e5)	
	...	♘4~!
Try 1 ♘c8?	(>2 ♕e5)	
	...	♘4~	2 ♘e7
		♘4g6!
Try 1 ♘e8?	(>2 ♕e5)	
	...	♘4~	2 ♘f6
		♘h5!
Try 1 ♘f5?	(>2 ♕e5)	
	...	♘4g6	2 ♘e3
		♘g2	2 ♘e7
		cxd4!
Try 1 ♘e4?	(>2 ♕e5)	
	...	♘h5	2 ♘xc3
		♘e2	2 ♘f6
		♔xd4!
Try 1 ♘dc4?	(>2 ♕e5)	
	...	♘4~	2 ♘e3
		♘g2!
Try 1 ♘b5?	(>2 ♕e5/♖g5)	
	...	♘4~	2 ♘xc3
		♘e2!
Key 1 ♘db7!	(>2 ♕e5)	
	...	♘4~	2 ♕xc6
		♘d7	2 ♕d6
		♘8g6	2 ♕xd8
		♔xd4	2 ♖d1
		cxd4	2 ♖g5

Tries related by common error are found in no. 276. In playing to each of the squares d6, e5, e3 and d2, the W♘c4 prevents a necessary white mate from taking place: 1 ♘xd6? ♘c6! (2 ♕xd6? cannot be played); 1 ♘e5? ♘d5! (2 ♖e4?); 1 ♘e3? ♘d3! (2 e3?); 1 ♘d2? ♘c2! (2 ♖d1?). The only square the knight can safely occupy without obstructing one of his own men

276

TRIES WITH COMMON ERROR

C.Goldschmeding
2nd prize, *Probleemblad* 1964
(Version by J.M.Rice)
Mate in two

Try	1 ♘xd6?	(>2 ♕c4/♗e5)
...	♘c6!	(2 ♕xd6?)
Try	1 ♘e5?	(>2 ♕c4/e3)
...	♘d5!	(2 ♖e4?)
Try	1 ♘e3?	(>2 ♕c4)
...	♘d3!	(2 e3?)
Try	1 ♘d2?	(>2 ♕c4)
...	♘c2!	(2 ♖d1?)
Key	1 ♘a5!	(>2 ♕c4)
...	♘c6	2 ♕xd6
	♘d5	2 ♖e4
	♘d3	2 e3
	♘c2	2 ♖d1
	♗c6	2 ♕xa7
	♗c5	2 ♕g7
	♕xa5	2 ♘b3
	d5	2 ♗e5

is a5. The ingenious way the black knight follows the white knight round provides a fine example of **correspondence**.

Other problems showing tries related either by common aim or by common error will be found throughout the book. Three- and more-movers may also have tries introducing new play, or common-aim or common-error tries, and examples of these may be found elsewhere. For a comment on tries in defence-substitution themes (e.g. **Roman**), see **Logical problems**.

Turton

The Turton is a **doubling** manoeuvre. What happens is that the key of a three-mover (or continuation of a more-mover) is a clearance move away from the main action of the problem over a critical square, played so that a second white piece can move on to the same line (on the critical square) and subsequently down that line in the opposite direction. In the 'normal' form of the Turton, the less powerful of the two pieces involved makes way for the more powerful (e.g. rook for queen). No. 277 illustrates the so-called *Loyd-Turton*: the more powerful piece makes way for the less powerful.

277

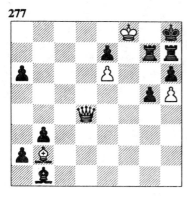

TURTON

A.P.Grin
1st prize ex aequo, Birnov Memorial
Tourney 1991
Mate in five

Try 1 ♕xg7+? ♖xg7 2 ♗xg7+ ♔h7!
Key 1 ♗c1! (>2 ♕a1 ... 3 ♗b2 ... 4
♗xg7+)

   ... b2 2 ♗xg5 a1♕ 3 ♗xh6
(>4 ♗xg7+)

       ...   hxg5 3 h6
(>4 hxg7+)

The reason why this must happen is underlined by the try 1 ♕xg7+? ♖xg7! (2 ♗xg7+? ♔h7!). It often happens in over-the-board play that a white bishop and white queen are the wrong way round, the queen being needed on a square nearer to the black king. Here the situation is reversed, for the bishop must be sacrificed before the queen can mate. The key is therefore 1 ♗c1!, which threatens the Loyd-Turton move 2 ♕a1, followed by 3 ♗b2 and then the bishop captures on g7 with the queen mating on move 5. If Black defends with 1...b2, the white bishop gets to g7 via a different route: 2 ♗xg5 a1♕ 3 ♗xh6 (>4 ♗xg7+), and if 2...hxg5, 3 h6. The alternative route via e7 will not work: 1 ♗a3? b2 2 ♗xe7 a1♕ 3 ♗f6? ♕a3+!.

In addition to the Loyd-Turton shown here, there is a further form of Turton doubling known as the *Brunner-Turton*. This involves two identical pieces (i.e. two rooks in orthodox chess) as the thematic pieces. It is illustrated in one variation of no. 82, under **Doubling**: 1 ♖e8 c1♕/♖ 2 ♖ce5. When the first thematic piece moves forward towards the main action so that the second piece can come in behind it, the manoeuvre is termed **Zepler-doubling**.

Twin

This is the term used to denote a problem with more than one setting, each differing from the others in only a very small respect, and with play which is in some way different in the various settings. Composers have come to accept twinning as a useful and fruitful method of achieving changed and other effects. Here are some of the ways in which twins may be created (in each case it is implied that there are two settings altogether):

(1) one unit of either colour may be moved to a different square;

(2) one unit may be removed from or added to the diagram position;

(3) one unit may be replaced by another of either colour on the same square (or, less commonly and less acceptably, on a different square);

(4) the board may be given a quarter- or half-turn, to alter the moves of the pawns, castling possibilities etc.;

(5) the position may be moved *en bloc* to a different part of the board;

(6) the post-key position of a block problem may itself be a sound problem.

The diagram may present a *zeroposition* (not to be solved), from which all settings may be derived as in (1) to (3) above.

In each case the twinning mechanism should be a single action only (e.g. shift of one piece, not two). Some problemists are prepared, in exceptional cases, to accept double-action twinning.

TWIN: PLUS- AND STAR-FLIGHTS

278

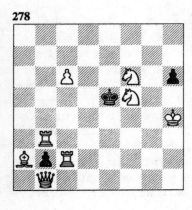

J.J.Gill (after G.Latzel)
The Problemist 1967
Mate in two
a) Diagram
b) ♘f5→e7

a) 1 ♘h5   zugzwang
   ...   ♚xf5   2 ♖e2
             ♚e4   2 ♖c5
             ♚d5   2 ♖e3
             ♚e6   2 ♖b5
b) 1 ♖e3+
   ...   ♚xf6   2 ♛xb2
             ♚f4   2 ♘fd5
             ♚d4   2 ♘f5
             ♚d6   2 ♘e8

The possibilities of twins have been most fully explored by the composers of **helpmates**, but some idea may be gained, from the four examples quoted here, of what can be done in twin-form in the two-mover. In no. 278 the shift of a single unit changes the *plus-flights* found after the key of the diagram position (1 ♘h5) to *star-flights*, introduced by the checking key 1 ♖e3+. No. 279 again shows the shift of a single unit, but this time there are six different settings, all with different keys and play.

TWIN: FLIGHTS

279

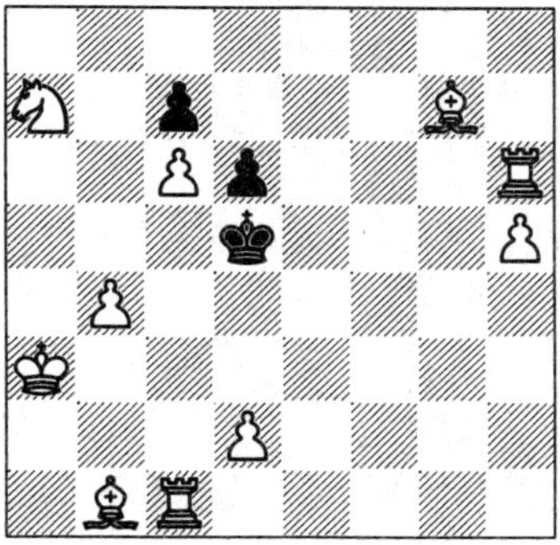

C.Mansfield
1st prize, BCPS Twin Tourney 1965
Mate in two
a) Diagram
b) w♔→d7
c) w♔→e2
d) w♔→f8
e) w♔→g3
f) w♔→g5

a) 1 ♗c2 ♔c4 2 ♗e4
b) 1 ♖f6 ♔e5 2 ♖f5
c) 1 ♗c3 ♔c4 2 ♗a2
d) 1 ♗g6 ♔e6 2 ♗e4
e) 1 ♖c2 ♔e4 2 ♖c5
f) 1 ♔f6 ♔d4 2 ♔e6

In the initial position in each case Black has no move, and it is a matter of deciding which white piece can be shut off to allow Black a king flight.

No. 280 illustrates how a quarter-turn of the board anticlockwise can transform the try of setting (a) into the key of setting (b) and vice versa. 1 ♔e2? fails in the diagram position because the △e4 can move to e3. But when the board is given a quarter-turn to the left, the pawn becomes immobile. However, 1 ♘f3? now fails, because castling is no longer possible!

Finally we have a **mutate** twin, no. 281, where the second setting cannot be solved until the key of the first setting has been found. The set mate of position (a) is of great importance: 1...♔xf3 2 0-0. The key 1 ♖h2 changes the reply to 1...♔xf3 to 2 ♖f2, a pin-mate. The solver must now decide why the solution to position (b) is not a simple return to the status quo, since the problem is a complete block. The answer lies in that set mate: the try 1 ♖h1? in (b) is refuted by 1...♔xf3!, because castling is illegal. The key is 1 ♖d2!, with further changed play after 1...gxf3 (changed from 2 ♖h4 to 2 ♖xd4), and 1...e2 (previously 2 ♗d2, now 2 ♖xd4).

280

TWIN: HALF-BATTERY

B.P.Barnes
The Tablet 1961
Mate in two
a) Diagram
b) Give board a quarter-turn anti-clock-wise

a) Try 1 ♔e2?   (>2 ♘~)
    ...   e3!
    Key 1 ♘c3!   (>2 ♔e2)
    ...   ♖a4   2 0-0-0
            ♖xd2   2 ♔xd2
            e3   2 ♘e2
b) Try 1 ♘f3?   (>2 ♔g5)
    ...   ♖e1!
    Key 1 ♔g5!   (>2 ♘~)
    ...   ♖xg4+ 2 ♘xg4

281

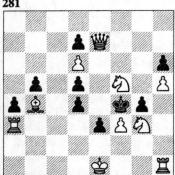

TWIN: MUTATE

J.A.Schiffmann
1st prize, *Aachener Anzeiger* 1928
Mate in two
a) Diagram
b) After key of (a)

a) Set 1 ... ♔xf3 2 0-0
    Key 1 ♖h2   zugzwang
    ...   ♔xf3   2 ♖f2
            d3   2 ♕xe3
            e2   2 ♗d2
            gxf3   2 ♖h4
b) Set 1 ... gxf3   2 ♖h4
            e2   2 ♗d2
    Key 1 ♖d2   zugzwang
    ...   gxf3   2 ♖xd4
            e2   2 ♖xd4
            exd2+ 2 ♗xd2
            d3   2 ♕xd3
            ♔xf3   2 ♖f2

Umnov

In 1975 the distinguished Russian problemist Evgeny Umnov published in the German chess magazine *Schach-Echo* an article in which he drew attention to a pair of related effects, at first sight paradoxical, which have to do with the relationship between certain white and black moves. Interest in these effects had hitherto been mainly confined to Soviet composers, but they have since developed a more general appeal. As with other effects such as **reciprocal play**, they are shown to best advantage when combined with clear strategic ideas.

Umnov I: A white unit moves to a square just vacated by a black piece, which could return to effect a capture.

UMNOV I

282

A.Kopnin
1st prize, All-Russian Tourney 1979
Mate in three
Key 1 ♖cc5   (>2 ♘xe5 ... 3 ♕xg6)
  ...   ♖cd3 2 ♗c3   (>3 ♖xe5)
             ...   ♖xd5 3 ♗xd5
                        ♖xc3 3 ♘d2
                        ♘f3 3 ♕xg6
  ♖ed3 2 ♗e3   (>3 ♖xe5)
  ♘cd3 2 ♗c1   (>3 ♘d2)
      ...   ♖xc4 3 ♖xc4
                    ♘f3 3 ♕xg6
  ♘ed3 2 ♗e1   (>3 ♘d2)
  ♘g2 2 ♖xe5+

No. 282 contains four Umnov I variations, in combination with **square-vacation** (the **anti-form** of square-occupation) and a white bishop-star. The key 1 ♖cc5 threatens 2 ♘xe5 followed by 3 ♕xg6. Black defends four times on d3: 1...♖cd3 is answered by 2 ♗c3 (>3 ♖xe5), the bishop vacating d2 for 3 ♘d2 after 2...♖xc3. Similarly 1...♖ed3 leads to 2 ♗e3. 3 ♘d2 is threatened after 1...♘cd3 2 ♗c1, and after 1...♘ed3 2 ♗e1. The composer has skilfully maintained the solver's interest by incorporating other second-move defences and third-move mates. One senses that at some point in the construction of this problem he must have considered the possibility of making 1

▤d3-d5 the key, to fit in with the pattern of square-vacation and square-occupation. Getting the position sound would undoubtedly have been a difficulty. Another three-mover illustrating Umnov I is Rehm's no. 26, under **Battery play**.

Note that the paradoxical nature of the effect rules out square-vacation by a black pawn, which cannot return to capture the white unit.

Umnov II: Black defends by playing a piece on to the square where a white piece will arrive in the threat.

283

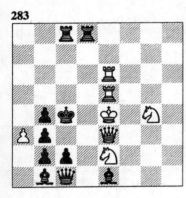

UMNOV II (+ PLACHUTTA & HOLZHAUSEN)

A.Kuzovkov
3rd prize, *Probleemblad* 1985
Mate in four
Key 1 ▤b6 (>2 ♛d2 ♛xd2 {2...♗xd2 3 ♞e3+ ♗xe3 4 ▤xb4}3 ▤xb4+ ♛xb4 4 ♞e3)
   ...♛d2 2 ♛c3+ ♛xc3 3 ▤xb4+ ♛xb4 4 ♞e3
   ...♗d2 2 ♛c5+ ▤xc5 3 ♞e3+ ♗xe3 4 ▤xb4

No. 283 shows the effect with great clarity. The key 1 ▤b6 threatens a **Plachutta** on d2: 2 ♛d2, with a dual continuation separated by Black's captures of the white queen: 2...♛xd2 3 ▤xb4+ ♛xb4 4 ♞e3; and 2...♗xd2 3 ♞e3+ ♗xe3 4 ▤xb4. There are good reasons why the threat will not work once the black queen or black bishop has occupied d2: 1...♛d2 2 ♛xd2? c1♛+!; and 1...♗d2 2 ♛xd2? ♛h1+!. But this square-occupation by Black sets up a **Holzhausen** interference, so that White can exploit an **overload** of the defending unit with a queen-sacrifice: 1...♛d2 2 ♛c3+ ♛xc3 3 ▤xb4+ ♛xb4 4 ♞e3; and 1...♗d2 2 ♛c5+ ▤xc5 3 ♞e3+ ♗xe3 4 ▤xb4.

Unpin

A black defence may effect an unpin of a white piece in one of two ways: (1) by *interference*, when another black unit plays on to the pin-line; or (2) by *withdrawal*, when the pinning piece itself moves off the pin-line. Both types are seen in no. 284.

284

UNPIN OF WHITE BY BLACK

C.Mansfield
1st prize, *South African Chessplayer* 1960
Mate in two

Key 1 ♕xf3		(>2 ♗xd5)
...	e4	2 ♕e3
	♘e4	2 ♕xa3
	♗xe6	2 ♕f8
	♘b5	2 ♕xd5
	♗e4	2 ♗xe4
	♗xf3+	2 ♗xf3
	♘b6	2 ♗e7

The key is thematic in that it pins the white queen, which is to be unpinned in three of the variations: 1 ♕xf3 (>2 ♗xd5). The unpins by interference are 1...e4, allowing 2 ♕e3, and 1...♘e4, which is followed by 2 ♕xa3. 1...♗xe6

285

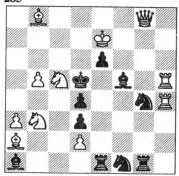

INTERFERENCE UNPINS

N.Easter
1st prize, *Bristol Times and Mirror* 1926
Mate in two

Key 1 ♘xe6		(>2 ♘bc5)
...	♘fe3	2 ♘ec5
	♘ge3	2 ♘g7
	♘e5	2 ♘c7
	♔e4	2 ♘g5
	♔c4	2 ♘bxd4
	♘xd2	2 ♘xd2

is the withdrawal unpin, leading to 2 ♕f8.

Four interference unpins of a white knight (the maximum so far achieved) are found in no. 285, a problem of extraordinary beauty. Again there is a thematic key, which also grants the black king a second flight: 1 ♘xe6 (>2 ♘bc5). The defence 1...♘fe3 leads to the **switchback** 2 ♘ec5 (the knight returns to its starting square). After 1...♘ge3 White no longer needs to put a guard on e4 when mating, because the black knight has opened the white rook's line of guard from h4. But another line has also been opened, that of the b♖g1, and White must see that this is closed if the ♕+♘ battery is to function effectively. The mate is 2 ♘g7 – not 2 ♘g5?, which would unpin the ♗f5, enabling it to interpose on e6. 1...♘e5, as well as being an interference unpin, is a self-block permitting the white interference mate 2 ♘c7. (2 ♘g7? will not work now because of 2...♗e6 or 2...♘f7.) The fourth interference unpin is effected by the black king himself: 1...♚e4 2 ♘g5. This move must be played (rather than 2 ♘bc5?) because of the need to put a guard on f3. Two variations leading to opening of the other battery round off a memorable problem: 1...♚c4 2 ♘bxd4; and 1...♘xd2 2 ♘xd2.

WITHDRAWAL UNPINS

286

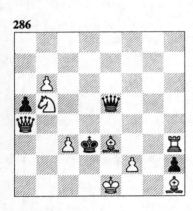

C.J.Morse
The Observer 1962
Mate in two
Key 1 c4   zugzwang

...	♕a1+	2 ♗c1
	♕c3+	2 ♗d2
	♕xb5	2 ♗c5
	♕d4	2 ♗xd4
	♕f6	2 ♗f4
	♕g7	2 ♗g5
	♕h8	2 ♗h6
	♕g3	2 ♕b3
	♕xe3+	2 ♖xe3

Sir Jeremy Morse has made systematic researches into two-move and other **tasks** and records. One of his own compositions, no. 286, illustrates a maximum task, equalling the record for withdrawal unpins of a white bishop. The key 1 c4 introduces a fine set of variations in which the bishop is thematically unpinned seven times.

The theme of white self-pin with subsequent unpin by Black in at least two phases lends itself to expression in various ways. A single white piece may pin itself on two different squares. Or two white pieces may stand in a **half-pin** situation in the diagram position; one moves away in the try, leaving the other pinned, while the key is made by the second, with subsequent unpins of the first. A third possibility is seen in no. 287, where two different white pieces pin themselves in try and key on the same square.

Try 1 ♖xf3? (>2 ♖xe3). The white rook is unpinned five times by the queen, with two variations in which the rook has to pin the queen herself to prevent her from interposing on the battery-line. The key, 1 ♘xf3! (>2 ♘b4),

287

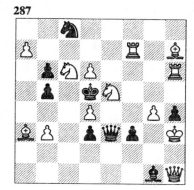

WHITE SELF-PIN + UNPIN

H.L.Musante
1st prize, *American Chess Bulletin* 1961
Mate in two

Try	1 ♖xf3?	(>2 ♖xe3)
...	♛xh6	2 ♖f6
	♛xe5	2 ♖f5
	♛d2	2 ♖f2
	♛f4	2 ♖xf4
	♛xd4	2 ♖xd3
	♛e4	2 ♗g8
	♛e2!	
Key	1 ♘xf3!	(>2 ♘b4)
...	♛xh6	2 ♘g5
	♛e6	2 ♘fe5
	♛xd4	2 ♘fxd4
	♛d2	2 ♘xd2
	♛e1	2 ♘xe1
	♚xc6	2 a8♛

pins the knight instead of the rook, and there follow five unpins once again, with two shut-offs and three captures of the queen – slightly less interesting strategy than in the virtual play, but clearly the composer could do nothing about the virtual play defence 1...♛e2! and had to accept it as the refutation of the try. The try-rook looks rather out of play on f7, but does at least have a small part to play in the post-key play, in guarding d7 after 1...♚xc6 2 a8♛. The key-knight performs the same function after the try.

All sorts of other unpinning effects are possible, of course. The key may thematically unpin a black unit, whose moves will then form the problem's principal variations. Alternatively Black may defend against a threat by un-pinning one of his own men. No. 285 shows, in the variation 1...♘ge3 2 ♘g7, how White must avoid unpinning a black unit when mating. Unpin of White by White is found in no. 288.

The key – yet again thematic – is the self-pin 1 ♖xe5, threatening 2 ♚f7 followed by 3 ♖f5 or 3 ♖e4. 1...♖c1 allows the white unpin 2 ♚f8, and if Black checks with 2...♛b4+, then 3 ♖c5 shuts off both the queen and the rook simultaneously. 1...♖d1 allows 2 ♚g8, and if 2...♛a2 or 2...♛b3+, then 3 ♖d5 – again a double shut-off. 1...♖e1 leads to 2 ♚xg6, and 1...♖a3 to 2 ♚h6.

288

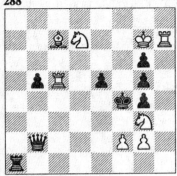

UNPIN OF WHITE BY WHITE

R.Burger and R.C.O.Matthews
1st prize, *British Chess Magazine* 1962
Mate in three

Key 1 ♖xe5		(>2 ♔f7)
...	♖c1	2 ♔f8
	♖d1	2 ♔g8
	♖e1	2 ♔xg6
	♖a3	2 ♔h6

Unprovided check

A check available to Black without a set white reply in the diagram position is said to be *unprovided*. Many solvers regard unprovided checks as intolerable, and will quite cheerfully dismiss a problem as worthless simply because of such a weakness. An unprovided check is only a weakness, however, inasmuch as it restricts the choice of key and therefore facilitates the solving process. But the play of the problem may well contain many a compensating factor.

289

UNPROVIDED CHECK

C.G.Watney
Good Companions 1920
Mate in two

Key 1 ♗f4 zugzwang		
...	h1♕+	2 ♘h2
	h1♘	2 ♘e3
	f1♕	2 ♘gf2
	f1♘	2 ♕d5
	♔h1	2 ♕d5
	♔f1	2 ♘e3

No. 289 may be cited as a case in point. 1...h1♕+ has no set reply. This automatically suggests 1 ♗f4 as the key, so that 1...h1♕+ may be met by 2 ♘h2. But it is not until the solver has found this key that he is likely to enjoy the full play of this delightful problem, with its four self-block promotions and two king-flights. As all this is achieved with only ten men altogether, perhaps the unprovided check may reasonably be excused?

This is not to condone all unprovided checks, or *unprovided flights* (b-moves with no set mate), or strong unprovided black moves, such as a capture of the white queen with a resulting gain of flight-squares. Where possible the composer will avoid non-provision of strong black defences – and this is often the difference between the good composer and the poor composer, for the latter will be more easily satisfied with a work containing strong unprovided black defences. But the solver should be wary of dismissing a problem as valueless (or a composer as poor!) merely because of the presence of such defences.

Valve

This term is used to denote a black move which simultaneously opens one line of a black rook, bishop or queen, but closes another. When the move opens the line of one piece but closes the line of another piece, the term *bivalve* is used.

290

VALVE AND BI-VALVE

L.I.Loshinsky and E.Umnov
1st prize, *Western Morning News* 1930
Mate in two

Key 1 ♘h6 (>2 ♕xe7)

...	♗h1	2 ♘xg4
	♗d1	2 ♖d5
	♗e2	2 ♘e4
	♗e4	2 ♘e2

The key of no. 290, 1 ♘h6, threatens 2 ♕xe7, against which Black can defend with any move of his bishop, opening a line to pin the white queen. This bishop *focuses* the squares g4 and d5, so that the mate 2 ♘xg4 can be played after a random bishop-move to north-west or south-east, while 2 ♖d5 follows a random move to the south-west. 1...♗e2 and 1...♗e4, however, prevent both mates by unpinning the black knight to guard the two mating squares. The first of these unpinning defences is a valve: the bishop opens the black queen's line northwards but closes her line westwards, so that 2 ♘e4 can be played. 1...♗e4, on the other hand, is a bi-valve: the queen's line is opened and that of the ♖g4 is closed. White therefore mates with 2 ♘e2.

291

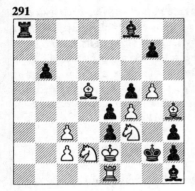

VALVES (HALF-BATTERY)

R.C.O.Matthews
The Problemist 1950
Mate in three
Key 1 ♘xe4   (>2 ♗f2 ... 3 ♘h4)

...	♗e7	2 ♘d4
	♗d6	2 ♘c5
	♗c5	2 ♘d6
	♗b4	2 ♘e5
	♗a3	2 ♖f1
	fxe4	2 ♗xe4

No. 291, with its key 1 ♘xe4 (>2 ♗f2, followed by 3 ♘h4), shows a five-fold valve. In this case the black line that is closed is a potential, rather than an actual, line, as a study of the variations will reveal. Any move by the ♗f8 will defeat the threat by allowing Black to play 2...♖h8. This is the line-opening, effected by departure of the bishop from f8. If 1...♗e7, White can continue 2 ♘d4, threatening mate by the ♗+♘ battery. No defence by 2...♖e8 is now possible, because the bishop has closed the line e8-e4. Similarly after 1...♗b4 White can play 2 ♘e5, since 2...♖a4 is ruled out as a defence (closure of a4-e4). 1...♗d6 allows 2 ♘c5, with a threat of mate from the other knight, now the remaining piece on the battery-line. 2...♖d8? cannot now be played as a defence, because of the closure of d8-d5. The parallel variation is 1...♗c5 2 ♘d6 – and 2...♖a5 is no defence (closure of a5-d5). Finally there is a fifth valve, 1...♗a3, which permits 2 ♖f1 (>3 ♘e1), and Black is unable to defend with 2...♖a1?. This problem, composed as long ago as 1950, is a fine illustration of the **half-battery** theme, which came into prominence in the two-mover several years later.

Vladimirov → Reversal themes

Wurzburg-Plachutta

The Wurzburg-Plachutta consists of a pair of **Holzhausen** interferences, i.e. interferences in a three-mover or longer problem between like-moving pieces (e.g. ♖+♖ or ♗+♕) standing on different lines. (See **Anti-Bristol** for interferences between like-moving pieces standing on the same line.)

292

WURZBURG-PLACHUTTA

J.Hartong
1st prize, *Tijdschrift v.d. Nederlandse Schaakbond* 1943
Mate in three

Key 1 ♗d2 (>2 ♕xc5+ ♖xc5 3 ♗xd3
       ... ♘xc5 3 ♘b2)
  ... ♖ad6 2 ♕xd7 ♖xd7 3 ♘b6
     ♖dd6 2 ♕f6 ♖xf6 3 ♗xd3

The key of no. 292, 1 ♗d2, threatens 2 ♕xc5+; if 2...♖xc5, 3 ♗xd3; and if 2...♘xc5, 3 ♘b2. The thematic interferences occur on d6: 1...♖ad6 2 ♕xd7 ♖xd7 3 ♘b6; and 1...♖dd6 2 ♕f6 ♖xf6 3 ♗xd3. Each rook becomes **overloaded** in turn; in playing to d6, each is expected to do duty for the other in the matter of guarding squares

WURZBURG-PLACHUTTA

293

V.Chepizhny
1st prize ex aequo, 40th Anniversary Tourney, *Shakhmaty v SSSR* 1966
Mate in three

Set 1...   ♗c3   2 ♖b4+
               ♕c3   2 ♖d4+
Try 1 ♔b6?   (>2 ♕c8)
    ...   ♗c3   2 ♖b4+
               ♕c3   2 ♘e5+
               ♘xc2!
Key 1 ♔d6!   (>2 ♕c8)
    ...   ♗c3   2 ♘a5+
               ♕c3   2 ♖d4+
               ♘xc2 2 ♘a5+

on which White can check or mate.

The very ingenious no. 293 shows the Wurzburg-Plachutta with changed play. The set replies to 1...♝c3 and 1...♛c3 (respectively 2 ♜b4+ and 2 ♜d4+) are emphasised by the try 1 ♛c8?. A second try 1 ♚b6? (>2 ♛c8) retains one of the set continuations but changes the other: 1...♝c3 2 ♜b4+; 1...♛c3 2 ♞e5+. But this try fails to 1...♞xc2!. The key 1 ♚d6! re-introduces the set continuation after 1...♛c3 (2 ♜d4+) but changes the reply to 1...♝c3: 2 ♞a5+. The position of the white king is crucial in the scheme of changed play, for White must avoid allowing checks.

Zagoruiko

This is a framework rather than a theme. In its simplest form a Zagoruiko has the following play: two black defences are followed by different mates (in the two-mover) or continuations (in the three- and more-mover) in three distinct phases of the solution. The scheme may well be extended so that there are more than two defences with changed mates, or more than three phases altogether.

294

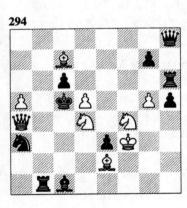

ZAGORUIKO: BLACK INTERFERENCE

O.Stocchi
Schach-Magazin 1949
Mate in two

Set	1...	g6	2 ♞de6
		♝b2	2 ♞b3
Try	1 ♞f5?		(>2 ♛d4)
	...	g6	2 ♝d6
		♝b2	2 ♝b6
		♜b4!	
Key	1 ♞c2!		(>2 ♛d4)
	...	g6	2 ♛xc6
		♝b2	2 ♛b4

No. 294 is a typical interference-Zagoruiko in three phases. The set play is 1...g6 2 ♞de6; and 1...♝b2 2 ♞b3. White tries 1 ♞f5? to threaten 2 ♛d4. The same black defences are now followed by 2 ♝d6 and 2 ♝b6 respectively. The try is refuted by 1...♜b4!. The key 1 ♞c2! (same threat) brings in a third pair of mates after the interferences: 1...g6 2 ♛xc6; and 1...♝b2 2 ♛b4.

295

ZAGORUIKO

L.Szwedowski
1st prize, *Il Due Mosse* 1960
Mate in two

Try	1 ♘d6?	(>2 ♕d4)
...	♘e6	2 ♕xf5
	♘e2	2 ♕f3
	fxg4	2 ♕e4
	c5!	
Try	1 ♘xf6?	(>2 ♕d4)
...	♘e6	2 ♘h5
	♘e2	2 ♖f2
	fxg4	2 ♖xg4
	♘f3!	
Key	1 ♘g5!	(>2 ♕d4)
...	♘e6	2 ♘xe6
	♘e2	2 ♘h3
	fxg4	2 ♖e4

The basic Zagoruiko scheme is extended in no. 295 to include three changes in each phase. Whereas in the previous example the phases were set, virtual and post-key play, Szwedowski's problem has two virtual and one post-key phase. Try 1 ♘d6? (the threat throughout is 2 ♕d4). 1...♘e6 leads to 2 ♕xf5, 1...♘e2 to 2 ♕f3, and 1...fxg4 to 2 ♕e4. But 1...c5! refutes. So try 1 ♘xf6?, and the same three defences now yield the mates 2 ♘h5, 2 ♖f2 and 2 ♖xg4. But now 1...♘f3! refutes. The key is 1 ♘g5!, with the play 1...♘e6 2 ♘xe6; 1...♘e2 2 ♘h3; and 1...fxg4 2 ♖e4. Despite the extra change in each phase, the problem may well be regarded as inferior to Stocchi's, since the errors committed by Black allowing the white mates are much less interesting, consisting mainly of simple unguards and lacking the unity of the interference errors of no. 294.

No such criticism can be levelled against no. 296, which also features an extension of the basic scheme. This time two defences lead to changed mates in four phases, the set play, the first virtual phase introduced by the try 1 ♘e6?, the second virtual phase (try 1 ♘xf5?) and finally the phase following the key, 1 ♘c6!. In this problem the error of Black's two thematic defences, 1...♖xd5 and 1...♘xd5, remains the same throughout, namely self-block on a flight-square. Valentin Rudenko, the composer of this very elegant work, is an outstanding problemist who will surely find a place in problem history as one of the most brilliant and versatile composers of all time.

296

ZAGORUIKO: SELF-BLOCKS

V.F.Rudenko
1st prize, Dutch Ring Tourney 1962
Mate in two

Set	1...	♖xd5	2 ♕c2
		♘xd5	2 ♗xf5
Try	1 ♘e6?	(>2 ♖d4)	
	...	♖xd5	2 ♘eg5
		♘xd5	2 ♘xc5
		f4!	
Try	1 ♘xf5?	(>2 ♖d4)	
	...	♖xd5	2 ♕xe3
		♘xd5	2 ♘d6
		♘d7!	
Key	1 ♘c6!	(>2 ♖d4)	
	...	♖xd5	2 ♘fg5
		♘xd5	2 ♘d2
		♔xd5	2 ♕d3
		♖c4	2 ♖e5

ZAGORUIKO (PIONEER)

297

F.Berhausen
1st prize, *Essener Anzeiger* 1927
Mate in two
a) Diagram
b) After key of (a)

a)	Set	1...	d2	2 ♖xd2
			♘g2	2 ♘xf3
	Key	1 ♖2xf3	zugzwang	
		...	d2	2 ♘e2
			♘g2	2 ♖xd3
b)	Key	1 ♘e3	zugzwang	
		...	d2	2 ♘c2
			♘g2	2 ♘xf5

As a constructional work of art, no. 297 is undoubtedly much inferior to the examples of the Zagoruiko so far studied. Its principal interest lies in the date of its composition, for it is one of the pioneers of the idea. (It also exemplifies a curious form of twinning, comparable with that of Schiff-mann's mutate no. 281, under **Twin**.) In the diagram position the defences 1...d2 and 1...♘g2 have the set mates 2 ♖xd2 and 2 ♘xf3. The key 1 ♖2xf3 changes these replies to 2 ♘e2 and 2 ♖xd3. Position (b), a second block position after the key of (a), is solved by 1 ♘e3, and there is now a third pair of replies to the thematic defences: 1...d2 2 ♘c2; and 1...♘g2 2 ♘xf5. Position (b) cannot be solved by a return to position (a), since the key of (a) is a capture and a self-pin which cannot be 'unplayed'.

ZAGORUIKO

298

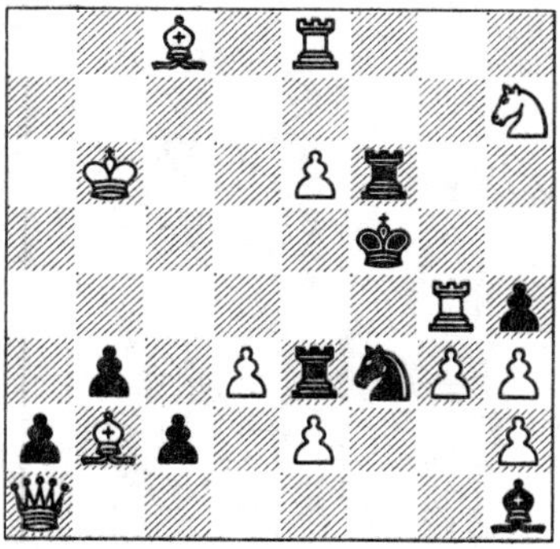

B.Zappas
Probleemblad 1983
Mate in three

Set 1...	♖exe6+	2 ♔a5
	♖fxe6+	2 ♔a7
Try 1 ♕c1?		(>2 ♕xe3)
...	♖exe6+	2 ♔c5
	♖fxe6+	2 ♔c7
	a1♕!	
Key 1 ♕f1!		(>2 ♖g5)
...	♖exe6+	2 ♔b5
	♖fxe6+	2 ♔b7

A simple mechanism brings about the changes in the three phases of no. 298. The set checks by black rooks self-pinning on e6 are answered in the set play by king moves to the a-file, the king selecting the square on which he cannot be checked again. The king cannot move to the b-file, where he would be checked by moves of the ♘f3, nor to the c-file, because of 2...c1♕+!. The try 1 ♕c1? (>2 ♕xe3) eliminates these continuations by enabling the black a-pawn to promote (2 ♔a5/♔a7? a1♕+!). But the c-pawn cannot now promote, so the king, in answer to the self-pinning checks, plays to c5 and c7. But 1...a1♕! refutes the try. The key 1 ♕f1!, with the short threat 2 ♖f5, pins the ♘f3, so that 1...♖exe6+ can be answered by 2 ♔b5, and 1...♖fxe6+ by 2 ♔b7. The black rook-moves weaken Black's position in each phase, which means that the white king-moves merely wait until 3 e4 or 3 ♖f8 can be played, depending on which rook has given the check. Byron Zappas, the composer of this attractive Zagoruiko, is a very versatile Greek with an outstanding constructional talent. The best of his work combines great originality with rich strategic play.

The *reduced Zagoruiko* fits the basic Zagoruiko requirements, but the total number of white mating moves is reduced, by means of **mate transference** or **reciprocal change**, from the normal minimum of six to four, or even (in examples of **cyclic change**) to three. No. 299 is a reduced Zagoruiko with four mating moves, those of the set play reappearing after the key but reciprocally changed.

REDUCED ZAGORUIKO

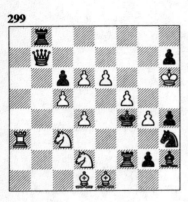

299

S.Shedey
1st prize ex aequo, *Sahs* 1963
Mate in two

Set	1...	♔e3	2 ♘e2
		♔g3	2 ♘d5
Try	1 ♕xc6?	(>2 ♘d5)
	...	♔e3	2 ♕e4
		♔g3	2 ♕f3
		♖b3!
Key	1 ♕g7!	(>2 ♕e5)
	...	♔e3	2 ♘d5
		♔g3	2 ♘e2

The set play is as follows: 1...♔e3 2 ♘e2; 1...♔g3 2 ♘d5. The try is 1 ♕xc6? (>2 ♘d5), with the mates 1...♔e3 2 ♕e4; 1...♔g3 2 ♕f3. It is refuted by 1...♖b3!. The key is 1 ♕g7!, and by means of a subtle alteration of the guards on squares in the black king's extended field the original mating moves are re-introduced, but reversed: 1...♔e3 2 ♘d5; and 1...♔g3 2 ♘e2. The reduction of mating moves in a Zagoruiko to three only is discussed under **Cyclic play**.

Zepler-doubling

Zepler-doubling is related to the **Turton**, but differs from it in that a white line-piece moves towards the black king so that a second line-piece can move on to the same line behind it. The manoeuvre is seen in no. 300.

The key, 1 ♖e4, prepares for the threatened continuation 2 ♖dd4, followed by 3 ♖f4. The variations are: 1...♔xe4 2 ♖d4+ ♔f5 3 ♗b1; and 1...♗c6 2 ♗e6+ ♔xe4 3 ♖d4. The point of the key is emphasised by the try 1 ♖dd4?, with the threat of immediate mate by 2 ♖f4. The rooks are now in the wrong order, for Black refutes the try with 1...♖xd8! (if 2 ♖b4?, then 2...♗~!). It is

300

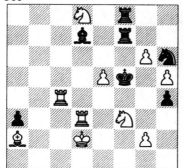

ZEPLER-DOUBLING

B.Sommer
1st prize, *Die Schwalbe* 1955/II
Mate in three

Try 1 ♖dd4? ♖xd8! (2 ♖b4? ♗~!)
Key 1 ♖e4! (>2 ♖dd4 ... 3 ♖f4)
... ♚xe4 2 ♖d4+ ♚f5 3 ♗b1
♗c6 2 ♗e6+ ♚xe4 3 ♖d4

essential that White should open the line a2-e6 before he makes his threat, rather than leaving it until later.

Section III

Problems for solving

The best composers are not usually the best solvers. Most composers don't take the solving business seriously, and only look in detail at some of the problems they see in print, to keep in touch with what other composers are doing. The serious solvers are those who send in regular sets of solutions to a magazine's originals and whose names appear in the solving ladder. Or they may take part in national solving competitions or even be members of a country's solving team, competing in the annual World Chess Solving Championships. Some people solve a chess problem by trial and error. A leading solver in *The Problemist*, the bi-monthly magazine of the British Chess Problem Society, once reported that his method was to examine and, if necessary, write down every single white move on the board, so that he would be sure of finding not only the key but also every cook the position might contain (this was in the days before home computers and fast solving programs helped to eliminate cooks before publication). Well, he had a solving trophy to show for his labours, but one can't help feeling he must have been bored to tears.

It is possible to find the key to a large number of problems by applying a few basic principles. Look for a way of arranging a reply to a strong, unprovided black defence, such as the capture of a unit guarding potential black king-flights; bring an out-of-play unit (i.e. one that is out of range of the black king) to a more promising-looking square; decide whether the problem will be a block, with Black in zugzwang after the key, or whether the key must introduce a threat. All this will certainly help. But by far the most satisfying method of solving chess problems, the method used by practically all top-class solvers, is that of 'theme-spotting'. The layout of the principal black and white units on the board may well suggest the theme of the problem to the experienced solver, and a realisation of what the problem is likely to be all about should lead to the key in due course, even if, on the way, there are a few pitfalls in the shape of tries.

The discovery of the key and the variation play will be sufficient for those taking part in solving championships to gain whatever points are on offer. But a full appreciation of a chess problem as a work of art demands more than this. If you find what you take to be the key after only a few seconds' search, don't stop there. Consider every variation, in itself and in its relationship to other variations. You might be dealing with an example of reciprocal or cyclic play, where the pattern of defences or mates or both is all-important. Or you might even have been deceived by a try. Ideally, a try should be defeated by as obscure a refutation as possible. But sometimes a composer is forced to accept an obvious refutation simply because the move is inherent in the position. A try which introduces new play different from that found after the key should not be dismissed merely because it is obviously refuted. That try may well be an integral part of the composer's idea – half the problem, even. The solution to a direct-mate problem is not just White's first move, but that and the variations it introduces, together with set play and any tries the position may contain and the play which they, in turn, introduce. The composer hopes you will see his try or tries first and not discover his key until later, but this may not always be the case.

The problems in this section range from the straightforward to the very difficult. They have been chosen in some cases as examples of themes dealt with in Section II, in others simply as typical illustrations of the art of chess composition. Note that they are in alphabetical order of composers. In some of the solutions that follow after all the diagrams for solving, black defences are given in sequence, separated by an oblique line (/), followed by the respective white mates or continuations in the same sequence, similarly separated.

F.Abdurahmanović
1st place, 1st WCCT 1971-3

301

H.Ahues
1st prize, *Deutsche Schachblätter*
1983-4

302

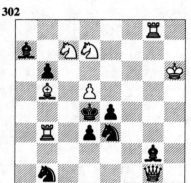

Helpmate in two
2 solutions

Mate in two

G.F.Anderson and V.L.Eaton
1st prize, *British Chess Magazine* 1953

303

G.F.Anderson
2nd prize, BCF Tourney 1946-7

304

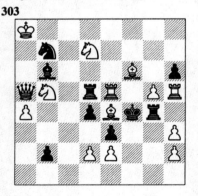

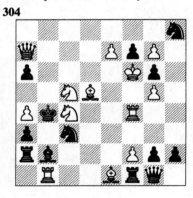

Mate in three

Selfmate in two

V.M.Archakov and A.G.Kopnin
1st prize, *Schach* 1980

305

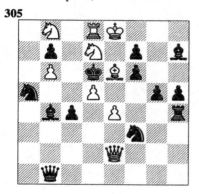

Mate in six

U.Avner
1st place, 2nd WCCT 1980-3

306

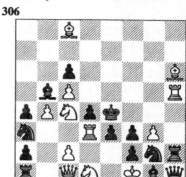

Selfmate in three

D.Banny
1st prize, Birnov Memorial Tourney
1986

307

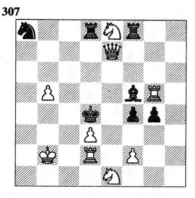

Mate in two

D.Banny
3rd prize, *Shakhmaty* 1984

308

Mate in two

B.P.Barnes
2nd hon. mention, Mansfield
Memorial Tourney 1986-7

309

Mate in two

M.Basisty
1st prize, Bogatyr Sports Club 1988

310

Mate in two

R.Bédoni
1st prize, Blikeng 80 Jubilee Tourney
1993-4

311

Mate in two

E.Bogdanov
2nd prize, *Shakhmaty/Sahs* 1985-6

312

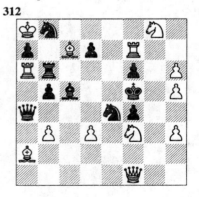

Mate in three

E.Bogdanov
4th prize, *Shakhmaty* 1986

313

J.-P.Boyer
2nd prize, *Europe Echecs* 1983

314

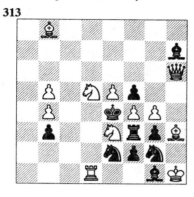

Mate in three

Mate in two

J.-P.Boyer
1st prize, *Europe Echecs* 1978

315

J.-P.Boyer
1st place, France v Israel 1985

316

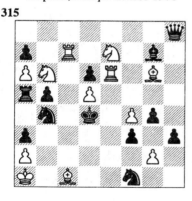

Mate in four

Mate in two: Circe

K.H.Braithwaite
1st prize, *The Problemist* 1982/II

317

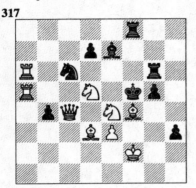

Mate in two

S.Brehmer and D.Kutzborski
1st prize, *Die Schwalbe* 1990

318

Mate in three

S.Brehmer
1st prize, *Schach* 1951

319

Mate in four

S.G.Burmistrov
1st prize, *diagrammes* 1987

320

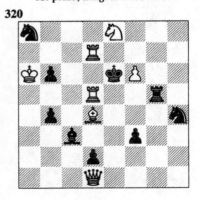

Mate in two

M.Caillaud and J.-M.Loustau
1st place, 3rd WCCT 1986-8

321

M.Caillaud
Probleemblad 1982

322

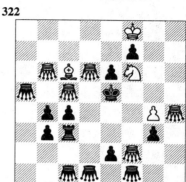

Mate in three

Mate in two: Grasshoppers

M.Caillaud and C.Poisson
1st prize, Andernach 1993

323

Y.Cheylan
3rd prize, *Die Schwalbe* 1983

324

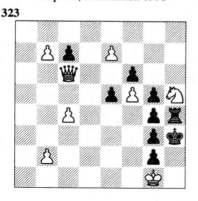
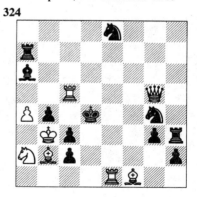

Mate in six: Andernach Chess

Mate in two: Madrasi

Y.Cheylan
1st prize, Anderson Memorial Tourney
1986-7

325

S.Clausen
1st prize, *Die Schwalbe* 1939

326

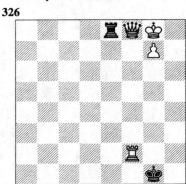

Reflex-mate in two

Mate in three

N.G.G.van Dijk
3rd hon. mention, *Hlas l'udu* 1986

327

G.Doukhan
1st prize, *Die Schwalbe* 1983/II

328

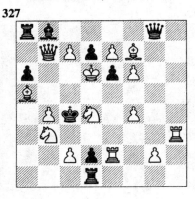
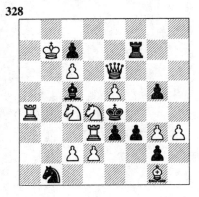

Mate in two

Mate in two

G.Doukhan
2nd prize, A.C.White Centenary
Tourney 1980-1

329

N.Easter
1st prize, *Bristol Times and Mirror*
1926

330

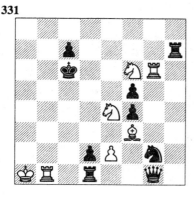

Mate in two

Mate in two

C.J.Feather
Die Schwalbe 1974

331

R.Fedorovich and I.Soroka
1st prize, *Probleemblad* 1983

332

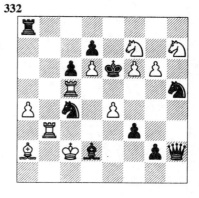

Helpmate in two
(a) Diagram; (b) ♘g2→h4
2 solutions in each part

Mate in two

E.Fomichev and Y.Gordian
1st prize, Rudenko Jubilee Tourney
1988

333

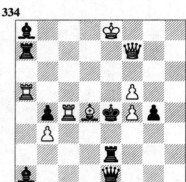

Mate in four

T.Garai
1st prize, *Deutsche Schachblätter*
1987-8

334

Helpmate in two
2 solutions

H.Gockel
1st prize, *Schach* 1993

335

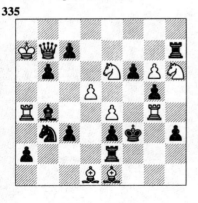

Mate in three

C.Goldschmeding
1st place, International Team Tourney
1969

336

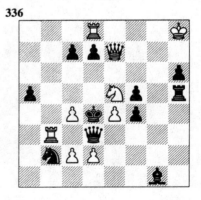

Mate in two

C.Goldschmeding
2nd hon. mention, *Die Schwalbe* 1959

337

A.R.Gooderson
4th prize, BCPS Olympic Tourney
1948

338

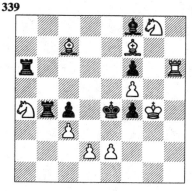

Mate in two

Mate in two

C.Goumondy
1st prize, *Thema Danicum* 1976-8

339

A.Gschwend
Schach-Echo 1974

340

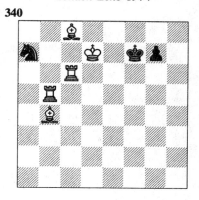

Mate in four

Helpmate in two
2 solutions

P.Gvozdjak
2nd prize, *The Problemist* 1989/II

341

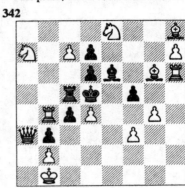

Mate in two

P.Gvozdjak
1st prize, *The Problemist* 1987/II

342

Mate in two

R.C.Handloser and B.Stucker
2nd prize, Olympic Tourney 1982-4

343

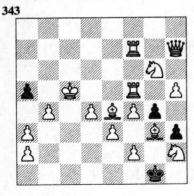

Mate in four

M.Havel
Šachové umění 1950

344

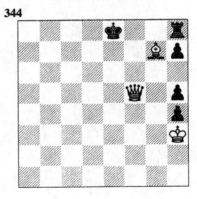

Mate in four

U.Heinonen
Probleemblad 1987

345

Helpmate in three: Chinese pieces
4 solutions

K.Junker
1st prize, *Deutsche Schachzeitung*
1956

346

Mate in five

M.Keller
1st prize, *Deutsche Schachzeitung*
1983-4

347

Mate in three

M.Keller
1st prize, *Schweizerische
Schachzeitung* 1985

348

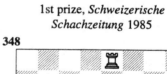

Mate in three

M.Keller
1st prize, *Schach-Aktiv* 1991

349

M.Kirtley
1st prize, *The Problemist* 1986

350

Mate in three

Selfmate in eight

I.Kiss
1st prize, *Molodezh Moldovei* 1981

351

H.Klug and M.Zucker
2nd prize, *Schach* 1967

352

Mate in two

Mate in five

V.Kopaev
Shakhmaty v SSSR 1986

353

Mate in two

M.Kovačević
1st prize, *The Problemist* 1991/II

354

Mate in two

J.Kricheli
1st prize, Olympic Tourney 1982-4

355

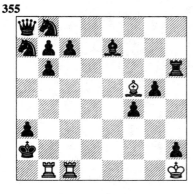

Mate in seven

J.Kricheli
1st prize, *Ideal Mate Review* 1983

356

Helpmate in four
(a) Diagram; (b) give board half turn

D.Kutzborski
1st prize, *Europe Echecs* 1973

357

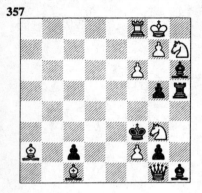

Mate in three

M.Kuznetsov and M.Marandiuk
1st prize, *Mat* 1980

358

Mate in six

B.Lindgren
1st prize, *Tidskrift för Schack* 1979

359

Helpmate in three
3 solutions

B.Lindgren
Mat 1984

360

Series-helpmate in eight
2 solutions

T.Linß
1st prize, *Thema Danicum* 1989

361

Mate in four

M.Lipton
Commended, *The Problemist* 1991

362

Mate in three

R.List
1st prize, *The Problemist* 1980

363

Helpmate in three
(a) Diagram; (b) Remove ♙d3

A.Lobusov
1st prize, *Shakhmaty v SSSR* 1976

364

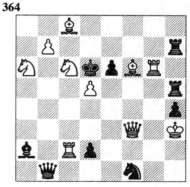

Mate in two

A.Lobusov
1st prize, *Shakhmaty v SSSR* 1982

365

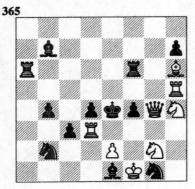

Mate in three

A.Lobusov
1st prize, *Neue Zürcher Zeitung* 1982-3

366

Mate in three

A.Lobusov and A.Spirin
Special prize, Zepler Memorial
Tourney 1985

367

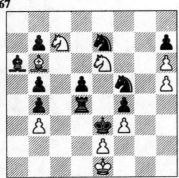

Mate in six

A.Lobusov and M.Marandiuk
2nd prize, *Probleemblad* 1987

368

Mate in seven

L.Loshinsky
1st prize, *Sahs* 1962

369

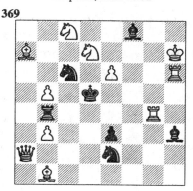

Mate in two

J.-M.Loustau and J.Rotenberg
2nd prize, *Phénix* 1988

370

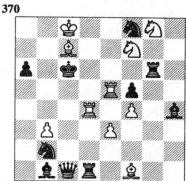

Mate in three

J.-M.Loustau
3rd prize, *Ideal Mate Review* 1985

371

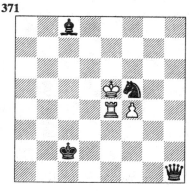

Selfmate in four: maximummer

V.Lukianov
3rd prize, *Chervony girnik* 1988

372

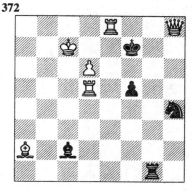

Mate in two

N.A.Macleod
1st prize, Israel Ring Tourney 1988

373

Mate in three

N.A.Macleod
1st prize, *diagrammes* 1990

374

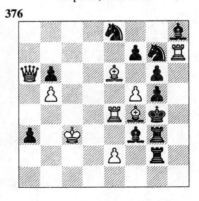

Mate in four

N.A.Macleod and C.P.Sydenham
1st prize, *Thèmes 64* 1982

375

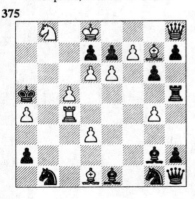

Mate in six

N.A.Macleod
1st prize, *Mat* 1981

376

Helpmate in two
2 solutions

T.Maeder
1st prize ex aequo, *The Problemist*
1988

377

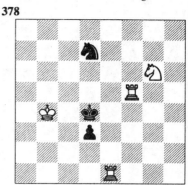

Mate in two

G.Maleika
Deutsche Schachzeitung 1985

378

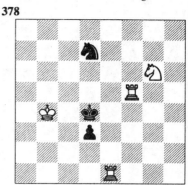

Mate in two

G.Maleika
1st prize, *U.S. Problem Bulletin* 1991

379

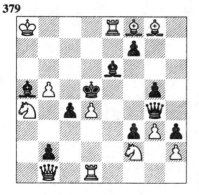

Mate in two

M.Manolescu and V.Nestorescu
Prize, *Revista romana de sah* 1984

380

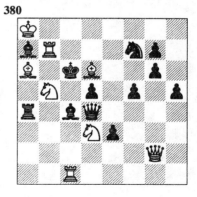

Mate in three

C.Mansfield
Version, *Chess Amateur* 1926

381

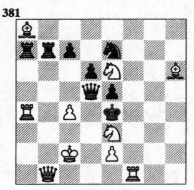

Mate in two

C.Mansfield
1st prize, *Chess Life and Review*
1970-1

382

Mate in two

C.Mansfield
4th prize, *The Problemist* 1970

383

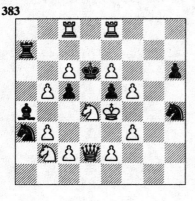

Mate in two

V.Marin
4th prize, Good Companions 1924
Version by J.M.Rice

384

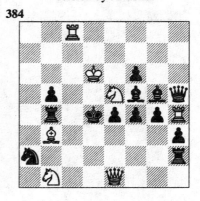

Mate in three

Z.Maslar
Mat Plus 1995

385

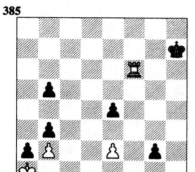

Helpmate in seven
2 solutions

R.C.O.Matthews
1st prize, *Problemisten* 1958

386

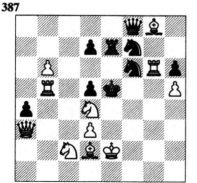

Mate in three

R.C.O.Matthews
1st place, 3rd WCCT 1984-8

387

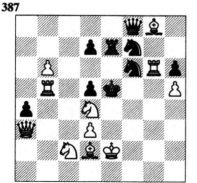

Mate in three

M.McDowell
1st prize, *Ideal Mate Review*
Nov.-Dec. 1984

388

Helpmate in three
2 solutions

V.Melnichenko
1st prize, Odessa 1988

389

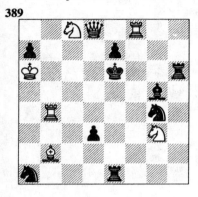

Mate in two

J.Meyers
2nd prize, *Chess Life* 1989

390

Mate in two

R.J.Millour
1st prize, Israel Ring Tourney 1989

391

Mate in three

M.Mladenović
1st place, 4th WCCT 1990-2

392

Helpmate in three
3 solutions

M.Mladenović
1st prize, *The Problemist* 1982

393

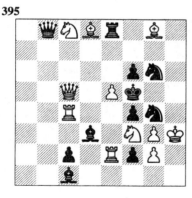

Reflex-mate in two

S.Mladenović
1st prize, *Sakkélet* 1988

394

Mate in two

J.Montgomerie
The Observer 1937

395

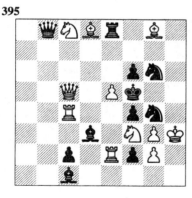

Mate in two

D.Müller
1st prize, Janos Kele Memorial
Tourney 1989

396

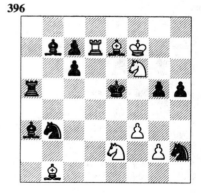

Mate in three

D.Müller and S.Brehmer
1st prize, *Schach* 1986

397

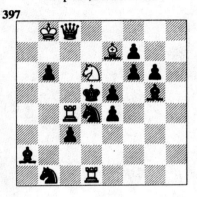

Mate in three

C.G.S.Narayanan
1st prize, *Northwest Chess* 1976

398

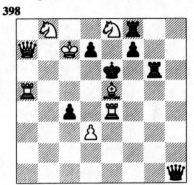

Mate in two

E.Navon
2nd prize, *The Problemist* 1990/I

399

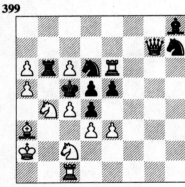

Mate in two

M.S.Nešić
4th prize, Fleck Jubilee Tourney 1983

400

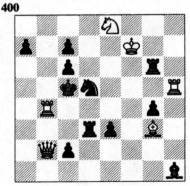

Mate in three

J.D.M.Nunn
2nd prize, *British Chess Magazine*
1984-5

401

Mate in three

J.Paavilainen
1st place, Baltic Sea Tourney 1991-3

402

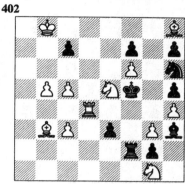

Mate in four

A.N.Pankratiev
1st prize, *Boletim da UBP* 1990-1

403

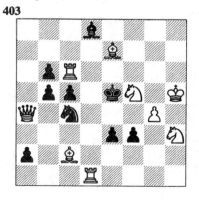

Mate in two

M.Parthasarathy
2nd prize ex aequo, *The Problemist*
1988/II

404

Mate in two

P.A.Petkov
2nd prize, *feenschach* 1985

405

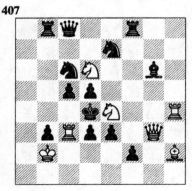

Helpmate in two
(a) Diagram; (b) ♙h4→h6

P.A.Petkov
4th prize, *feenschach* 1985

406

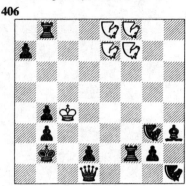

Helpmate in two: Nightriders
3 solutions

H.-P. Rehm
1st prize, *Springaren* 1978

407

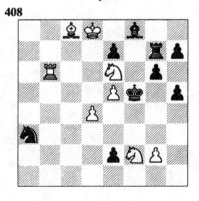

Mate in three

H.-P. Rehm
1st prize, Léon-Martin Memorial
Tourney 1971-2

408

Mate in five

H.-P. Rehm
1st prize, *Probleemblad* 1982

409

J.M.Rice
1st prize ex aequo, Mansfield
Memorial Tourney 1986-7

410

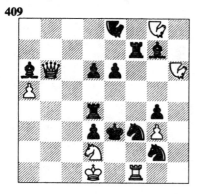

Mate in three: Nightriders

Mate in two

J.M.Rice
2nd place, GB v Hungary 1993-5

411

Y.Rossomakho
3rd place, Baltic Sea Tourney 1991-3

412

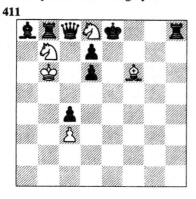

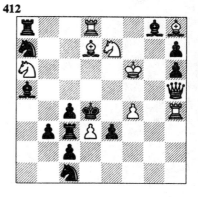

Series-helpmate in seven

Mate in two

Y.Rossomakho
3rd prize, *The Problemist* 1987

413

Mate in three

J.Rusinek
4th prize, *The Problemist* 1987

414

Mate in three

M.Schwalbach
5th prize, *feenschach* 1977

415

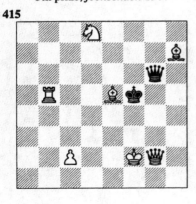

Selfmate in seven

M.Segers
Neue Leipziger Zeitung 1933

416

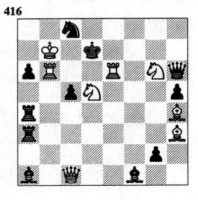

Mate in two

S.Seider
1st prize, *The Problemist* 1974

417

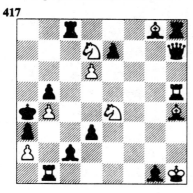

Mate in three

N.Shankar Ram
Die Schwalbe 1983

418

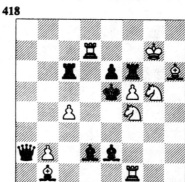

Mate in two

V.Shcherbina
1st prize, Popandopulo Memorial
Tourney 1990

419

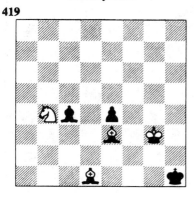

Mate in seven

D.J.Shire
Troll 1993
Version: *Problemist Supplement*

420

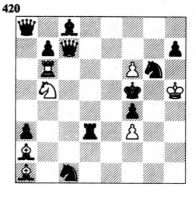

Mate in two

D.A.Smedley
2nd prize, *The Problemist* 1977
(Version by A.C.Reeves)

421

D.A.Smedley
2nd place, 1st WCCT 1973-5

422

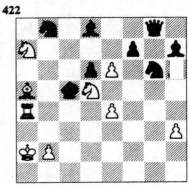

Mate in two

Mate in seven

W.Speckmann
1st prize, *Die Schwalbe* 1955

423

A.Stepochkin
1st prize, *Thema Danicum* 1991

424

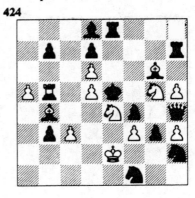

Mate in six

Mate in three

O.Stocchi
L'Italia Scacchistica 1953

425

C.P.Swindley
1st prize, *The Problemist* 1981/II

426

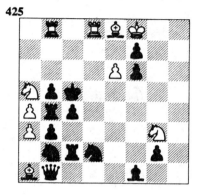

Mate in two

Mate in two

C.P.Sydenham
1st prize ex aequo, *Die Schwalbe*
1983/I

427

C.P.Sydenham
The Problemist 1976

428

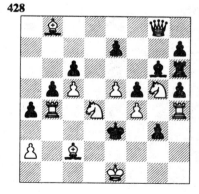

Mate in two

Mate in two

C.P.Sydenham
1st prize, *Probleemblad* 1993

429

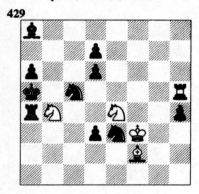

Helpmate in two: Duplex

T.Taverner
Chess Problems made easy 1924

430

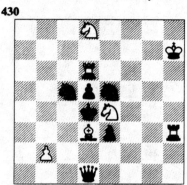

Mate in two

Touw Hian Bwee
1st prize, Visserman Memorial
Tourney 1980

431

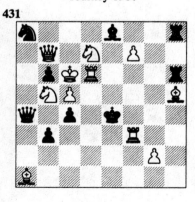

Mate in two

M.Tribowksi
1st place, Berlin v Munich 1988

432

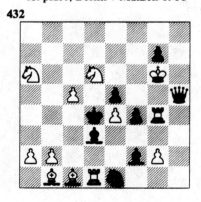

Mate in three

P.S.Valois
2nd prize, *Gazeta Czestochowska* 1972

433

J.Valuska
5th prize, Olympic Tourney 1982

434

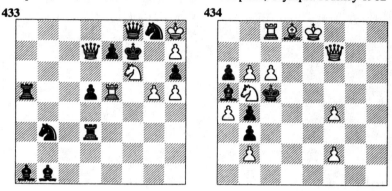

Selfmate in two

Mate in two

M.Velimirović
1st prize, *Mat* 1976

435

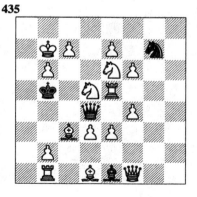

Mate in two

M.Velimirović
1st prize, *Die Schwalbe* 1986

436

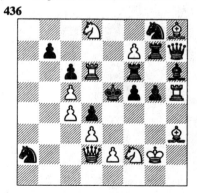

Mate in three

Y.G.Vladimirov and V.Kopaev
1st place, 2nd WCCT 1981-3

437

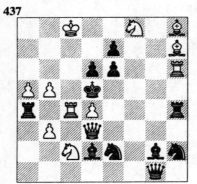

Mate in three

Y.G.Vladimirov
1st prize, 'October 70'
Commemoration Tourney 1987

438

Mate in three

Y.G.Vladimirov and L.Loshinsky
1st place, 1st WCCT 1973-5

439

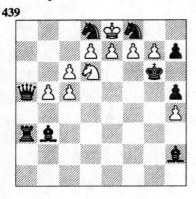

Reflex-mate in two

M.R.Vukcevich
1st prize, *U.S. Problem Bulletin* 1993

440

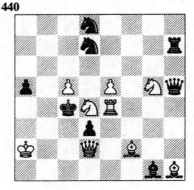

Mate in three

K.Wenda and F.Chlubna
1st prize, *Deutsche Schachblätter* 1972

441

Mate in four

L.Zagoruiko
1st prize, Vani C.C. 1987

442

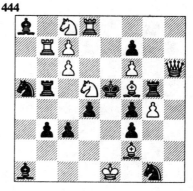

Mate in three

G.Zakhodiakin
1st prize, *Rochade* Miniature Tourney
1980

443

Mate in three

B.Zappas
1st prize, *The Problemist* 1988/II

444

Mate in two

B.Zappas
1st prize, *The Problemist* 1983/II

445

Mate in two

B.Zappas
1st prize, *The Problemist* 1986/I

446

Mate in two

B.Zappas
1st prize, *The Problemist* 1985

447

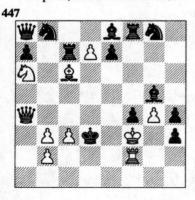

Selfmate in two

V.Zinoviev
2nd prize, *64* 1986

448

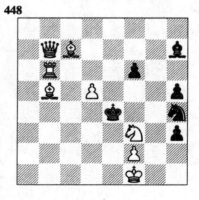

Mate in three

T.Zirkwitz
1st prize, *Deutsche Schachblätter* 1991

T.Zirkwitz
Prize, *Schach-Echo* 1985-6

449

450

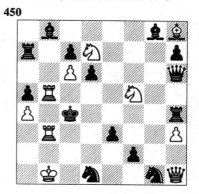

Mate in three

Mate in four

Solutions

301 1 Nf7 Be4 2 Kf4 Qh6, and 1 Nb5 Re4+ 2 Kd3 Rd8. Two perfectly matched solutions with pin-mates and diagonal/orthogonal correspondence.

302 1 Rg5? (>2 Ne6) Bh3! (2 Qg7?). 1 Rg4? (>2 Rxd3) Bf1! (2 Qg7?). 1 Rg3? (>2 Qxe3) Bf3! (2 Qg7?). 1 Ra8! (-) Bg~/Ba~/N~/Nc3/d2 2 Qg7/Ra4/Qa1/Rb4/Qxe3. Anti-Bristol tries, each failing to a different bishop-move. The key is a fine surprise.

303 1 Bb1 (-) Nxa5 2 Nd6 (>3 Re4) Rxe5/Rxd6 3 Bxe5/Rf5. 1...Nc5 2 Nc3 (>3 Nd5) dxc3 3 dxe3. 1...Nd6 2 Nf8 (>3 Ne6/Ng6). 1...Nd8 2 gxh6 (>3 Re4/Rhf5) Rg5 3 Bxg5. 1...Ba7,Bc5 2 Nc7 (>3 Ne6/Nxd5). 1...Bxa5 2 Nxd4 (>3 Ne6/Re4/dxe3). 1...Bc7 2 Rxd5 (>3 Rf5/Rxd4). 1...Bc5 2 Nxc5 (>3 Ne6/Nd3/Rf5). 1...Rxb5 2 Rf5+. 1...d3 2 Qb4+. 1...hxg5 2 Rhxg5. The white knights and Bg5 are pinned on bent lines: Black would have checks available if they moved. The main variations are unpins of these pieces. This is one of a number of joint compositions by these two very talented composers produced during the 1950s, when Gerald Anderson was working in Washington.

304 1 Nb7 (>2 Nd2+ Ne4) Kxa4/Kb3/Rxf2/Qxf2 2 Nd6+/Ne3+/Ne5+/Nb6+ Ne4/Nxd5/Rxf4/Qxf4,Qd4. Complex battery-play. Various effects force the WNc4 to choose its arrival square with care.

305 1 Qe3 (>2 e5+ Nxe5 3 Nxe5) Bxe4 2 Nf8+ Ke5 3 Ng6+ fxg6 4 Nd7+ Kd6 5 Nf8+ Ke5 6 Nxg6. 1...Rxe4 2 Nxf6+ Ke5 3 Ng4+ hxg4 4 Nd7+ Kd6 5 Nf6+ Ke5 6 Ng4. 1...Qxe4 2 Nc5+ Ke5 3 Nd3+ cxd3 4 Nd7+ Kd6 5 Nc5+ Ke5 6 Nd3. The black defences are anticipatory self-pins. The white knight forces a capture on a potential mating square so that its colleague can take over its rôle and mate there on move 6. The change of front piece on a battery line has been named the *Popandopulo* mechanism.

306 1 Bg7 (>2 Nc3+ dxc3 3 Rxe3 Nxe3) Rxh5 2 Nd6+ Kd5 3 Nxe3+ Nxd3. 1...Rxc1 2 Bf5+ Kd5 3 Ncxe3+ Nxe3. 1...Nxc2 2 Rxd4+ Nxd4 3 Qxe3+ Nxe3. 1...Nb1 2 Nxf2+ exf2 3 Nd2+ Nxd2. (1...Ng~ 2 Nd2+ exd2 3 Nf2+ B/Rxf2.) Each of the main lines in this fine work ends in a double pin-mate. The Israeli composer Uri Avner is one of the most brilliant of to-day's composers, an expert in all fields, though he has a particular talent for selfmates.

307 Set 1...Bxd3/Rd5 2 Qb4/Nc2. 1 Re2? (>2 Qe5) Bxd3/Rd5/Rdxe8 2 Qc5/Qb4/Qd6. 1...Rfxe8!. 1 Rc2! (>2 Qc5) Bxd3/Rd5/Kd5/Rc8 2

♕e5/♖c4/♕e4/♕d6. The le Grand mechanism, enriched in the form of a Zagoruiko.

308 1 f4? (>2 ♖2g5) ♘d7/♘xe6 2 ♖e2/♖d2. 1...♘e4!. 1 ♖e2? (>2 ♕xc5) ♗xd4/♘d7 2 ♘f4/f4. 1...♘xe6!. 1 ♖d2! (>2 ♘f4) ♗xd4/♘xe6 2 ♕xc5/f4. A study in repeated white moves: f4, ♖e2 and ♖d2 all appear both as first move and as mating move.

309 1 ♘f7? (>2 ♕e5) ♘xf7/♘xg7 2 ♗xe6/♖f4. 1...♖c5!. 1 ♘c4! (>2 ♕e5) ♘f7/♘xg7/♕xd6+/♕f6/♕h8 2 ♗xc2/♖xb5/♘xd6/♕xf6/♖d5. The key is both a white and a black Novotny, eliminating mates on e6 and f4 and introducing new mates that exploit the Novotny. An original concept which was unlucky not to be placed higher in its tourney.

310 1 ♘c7? (>2 ♕d5) ♘c6/♘6b7 2 ♘e6/♘b5. 1...♖h5!. 1 ♘c3? (>2 ♕d5) ♘6b7/♖h5 2 ♘b5/♘e2. 1...♘c6!. 1 ♘f4? (>2 ♕d5) ♖h5/♘c6 2 ♘e2/♘e6. 1...♘6b7!. 1 ♘e7? (>2 ♕d5) ♘c6/♘6b7 2 ♘xc6/♘f5. 1...♖h5!. 1 ♘de3? (>2 ♕d5) ♘6b7/♖h5 2 ♘f5/♘c2. 1...♘c6!. 1 ♘b4! (>2 ♕d5) ♖h5/♘c6/♘6b7 2 ♘c2/♘xc6/♖c4. Cyclic refutation, taken several stages further than usual, with five tries plus key and multiple changes.

311 Set 1...♔c6/♔e6/♔xd4 2 a8♕/♕c4/♘ec3. 1 ♕g2 (>2 ♘g5) ♔c6/♔e6/♔xd4 2 ♘d6/♕g8/♘f2. The set pin-mates after the king-flights are abandoned and replaced by three new ones.

312 1 ♕e2 (>2 ♘d4+ ♗xd4 3 ♕g4) d6 2 ♖xf6+ [A] ♘xf6 3 ♘e7 [B]. 1...♖d6 2 ♘e7+ [B] ♔e6 3 bxa4 [C]. 1...♗d6 2 bxa4 [C] (>3 ♕/dxe4) ♘e~ 3 ♖xf6 [A]. A cyclic Grimshaw on d6, with the interferences exploited differently on White's second and third moves.

313 Set 1...♖xe3 2 ♘f6+ ♔f3 3 ♗xg2. 1...♖xf4 2 ♗xg2+ ♖f3 3 ♘f6. 1 ♕b6? (>2 ♘c3+ ♘xc3/♔xf4 3 ♕d4/♕h6) ♖xe3 2 ♗xg2+ ♖f3 3 ♕e3. 1...♖xf4 2 ♘f6+ ♔f3 3 ♗xg2. 1...♗g6!. 1 ♕c6! (>2 ♕c4+ ♘d4 3 ♕xd4/♖xd4/♕d3) ♖xe3 2 ♘c7+ ♔xf4 3 ♘e6. 1...♖xf4 2 ♘xg2 ♔f3 3 ♘dxf4. 1...♘xe3 2 ♘c3+ ♔f4 3 ♕h6. 1...♘d4 2 ♖xd4+ ♔xd4 3 ♕c4. The two principal defences have different replies in the three phases, with reciprocal change between the set play and the virtual play – hence, a reduced Zagoruiko, a comparative rarity in the three-move field.

314 1 ♕g1 (>2 ♕xd4) ♘f2!. 1 ♕f1? (>2 ♕c4/♕f7) ♘d6!. 1 ♕d1? (>2 ♕xd4/♕b3) ♘d2!. 1 ♕c1? (>2 ♕c4/♕c6) ♘c3!. 1 ♕h2? (>2 ♘b6) ♘g3!. 1 ♕h3? (>2 ♕e6/♕b3) ♘c5!. 1 ♕h5? (>2 ♕f7/♘b6) ♘g5!. 1 ♕h6? (>2 ♕e6/♕c6) ♘f6!. 1 ♕h8! (>2 ♘b6/♕g8/♕a8). Splendid duel between the white queen and the black knight, the latter making a wheel of refutations.

315 1 ♖e2 (>2 ♗e3+ ♘xe3 3 ♖d2+ ♘d3 4 ♖xd3) fxe2 2 ♘f5+ ♔~+ 3 ♘xg7+ ♔d4 4 ♘e7. 1...♘c6 2 ♘xc6+ ♔c5+ 3 ♘e5+ ♔d4 4 ♖e4. 1...♘xd5 2 ♖e4+ ♔d3+ 3 ♖e5+ ♔d4 4 ♖xd5. 1...♘c2+ 2 ♖cxc2 (>3 ♘c6) axb5,♕c8 3

♗e3+ ♘xe3 4 ♖d2. 1...♘d2 2 ♖xd2+ ♔e3+ 3 ♖b2+ ♔d4 4 ♖b4. A riot of checks by both sides.

316 1 ♗b8? (>2 ♖xe3) ♖xe1[♖a1]! (2 ♘xc3[♗c7]?) 1 ♗c8? (>2 ♕xf3) fxe5[♗e2]! (2 exd3[♗d7]?) 1 ♗e6! (>2 ♖a4) ♖b8/♖c8 2 ♖xe3/♕xf3; 1...♖xe1[♖a1]/fxe5[♗e2] 2 ♘xc3[♗c7]/exd3[♗d7]. The tries by the bishops occupying potentially fatal rebirth squares fail because the rebirth of a black pawn cuts a line of guard to a black king-flight. In the post-key play the black rook occupies the same squares and so allows the threatened captures (the captured pieces now disappear).

317 1 ♗h2 (>2 ♘c5) ♔g4+/♔e6+/♖e6/g4/♘e5/♘d4 2 ♘ef6/♘f4/♘d6/ ♘xe7/♘g3/♘ef6. Complex play by the direct and indirect batteries.

318 1 ♘c4 (>2 ♖e5+ ♖xe5/♗xe5 3 ♕d4/♕d5) d5 2 ♘ce5 (>3 ♖c6) ♖c4/♗c4 3 ♕d5/♕d4. 1...♖xc4 2 ♕d5+ ♖xd5 3 ♖xd5. 1...♗xc4 2 ♕d4+ ♗xd4 3 ♗xd4. 1...♘c3 2 ♕e3+ ♔xc4 3 ♘d2. 1...♖a1 2 ♗d4+ ♗xd4 3 ♕xd4. The key is a simultaneous Novotny and anti-Novotny, and the continuation after 1...d5 reverses the situation. With a white rook and white bishop ambushed behind the thematic black units on the f-file, White can safely play his queen to d5 or d4 on his second move after the Novotny-captures on c4. A brilliant piece of work by two outstanding composers.

319 1 ♔d7 (>2 ♖g8+ ♔f7 3 ♖g7) ♗a4+ 2 ♘c6 ♗xc6+ 3 ♔c7 (>4 ♕h5) ♗f3 4 ♖xf6. 1...♖d2+ 2 ♘d3 ♖xd3+ 3 ♔c8 (>4 ♖xf6) ♖f3 4 ♕h5. The two thematic black units are decoyed away in turn so that when they play to f3 to guard a potential mating-square a Grimshaw interference takes place.

320 1 ♕a4? (>2 ♕c6) ♖xd5/♘f5 2 ♘g7/♖e5. 1...b5!. 1 ♕b3? (>2 ♖e7) ♖xd5/♘f5 2 ♕xd5/♖5d6. 1...♖e5!. 1 ♕c2! (>2 ♖5d6) ♖xd5/♘f5/♗xd4 2 ♖e7/♕e4/♕c6. A Zagoruiko with paradoxical elements: 1...♖xd5 defeats 2 ♖e7 in the second try but allows it after the key, while 1...♘f5 allows 2 ♖5d6 in the same try but defeats it in the post-key play.

321 Set 1...♖xe5 2 f8♘+ ♔f6/♔xd6 3 e8♘/exd8♕. 1...♘xe5 2 e8♕+ ♔f6/♔xd6 3 f8♕/♘b5. 1 ♕h2 (>2 ♕h3+; 1...♖xh5 2 ♕h3+ ♖f5 3 f8♘)) ♖xe5 2 e8♕+ ♔f6/♔xd6 3 f8♕/♘b5. 1...♘xe5 2 f8♘+ ♔f6/♔xd6 3 e8♘/ exd8♕. 1...♔f5/♘c5+ 2 ♗xd3+/♘xc5+. Reciprocal change, plus additional promotion play.

322 Set 1...♖d3/♖e3/♖f3 2 ♘d7/♜ce7/♜he7 [A/B/C]. 1 ♜d2 (>2 ♗d5) ♖d3/♖e3/♖f3 2 ♜ce7/♜he7/♘d7 [B/C/A]. Cyclic shift (Lačný) brought about by an apparently simple switch of square-control.

323 1 ♕e4 c5 2 ♕e1 e4 3 b8♖ e3 4 ♖b3 e2 5 ♖xg3[=B♖] ♖~ 6 ♕g3. 1...c6 2 e8♗ c5 3 ♕e2 e4 4 ♗c6 e3 5 ♗xg2[=B♗] ♗~ 6 ♕g2. The queen must wait until a mating-square has been vacated, by a piece which cannot recapture without inflicting self-check. White's promotions are neatly differentiated by the black c-pawn's first move.

324 1 ♘xc3 (>2 ♘b5) c1♕/c1♖/c1♗/c1♘+ 2 ♘e4/♘d1/♖d1/♘a2. 1...♘d6/♘c7/g2 2 ♖d5/♖e4/♕d5. A fine illustration of the Madrasi rules of paralysis. After 1...c1♕ and 1...c1♖, the white knight must regain control of flights. 1...c1♗ eliminates a battery-mate but allows the ♖e1 to mate because the bishop is paralysed, and 1...c1♘+ requires the white knight to paralyse the black knight.

325 1 ♘a6? (>2 c7 ♕xb6) ♖d8+/0-0-0+/♔f8/♔d8 2 ♔c7/♔e7/♘c7/ ♘xc5 ♕xb6/♗g5/♖d8/♕xc5. 1...♘xb6!. 1 ♘d7! (>2 ♘xe5 ♗xe5) ♖d8/0-0-0/ ♗g5/♗b5 2 c7/e7/♘xc5/♔xd5 ♕xb6/♖f6/♕xc5/♕d4. In the virtual play the white king moves to c7 or e7 after the checks on d8; after the key, which prevents the checks, the same squares are occupied by white pawns, with pin-mates to follow.

326 1 ♖d2? ♖d8!. 1 ♖c2? ♖c8!. 1 ♖b2? ♖b8!. 1 ♖a2! (-) ♖xf8+ 2 gxf8♕ ♔h1 3 ♕f1. 1...♖e2 2 ♖xe2. 1...♖d8 2 ♕xd8 (3 ♕d1). 1...♖c8/♖b8/♖a8 2 ♕x♖. 1...♔h1 2 ♕xe8. Opposition tries and correspondence, all with six units.

327 1 ♖ee3? (>2 ♖c3) ♕g3!. 1 ♖e4? (>2 ♘d~) ♕xg2!. 1 ♖e5? (>2 ♖c5) ♕g5!. 1 ♖xe6! (>2 ♕d5) ♕g3/♕xg2/♕g5 2 ♖e3/♖e4/♖e5. 1...dxe6/♗xc7+ 2 ♕c6/♕xc7. Vladimirov: the try-moves reappear on White's second move in answer to the refutations. This is a rare example of the 'pure' form (i.e. without capture of the black unit) with three thematic variations.

328 1 ♘c~? (>2 ♖xe3) ♗b4!. 1 ♘xe3? (>2 ♕d5) ♖d7 2 ♕f5. 1...♘c3!. 1 ♘d~? (>2 ♘d6) ♗d4 2 ♖xd4. 1...f2!. 1 ♘xf3! (>2 ♘xg5) ♗e7/♖f5/♖xf3/ ♔xf3 2 ♖xe3/♕d5/♘d6/♕g4. Threat-correction by each of the two white knights, in a half-battery setting.

329 1 ♕d2? (>2 ♘e8) ♖xe7 2 ♗f3. 1...♖d3!. 1 ♗f3? (>2 ♘e8) ♖xe7 2 ♕d2. 1...♖e4!. 1 ♖d1? (>2 ♘e8) ♖xe7 2 ♗b3. 1...♕xb4!. 1 ♗b3! (>2 ♘e8) ♖xe7/♖xb3/♕xb3 2 ♖d1/e8♘/cxb7. A half-pin arrangement is skilfully used to show double sequence-reversal between White's first move and the mate after a defence.

330 1 ♕h7 (>2 ♕d3) ♘c5/♗c4/♗c2/♖xd1/♖xc3+ 2 ♘b5/♘e2/♘b1/ ♘xd1/♗xc3. A lovely example of unpin with two white interference mates, by a master from the past.

331 (a) 1 ♕c5 ♘d7+ 2 ♕d6 ♘ec5; and 1 ♖d7 ♘c5+ 2 ♖d5 ♘fd7. (b) 1 ♘xf3 ♖g3 2 ♘d4 ♖c3; and 1 ♘xg6 ♗h5 2 ♘e7 ♗e8. In part (a) interchange of functions between the two white batteries, with features of the Umnov I theme (White occupies a square just vacated by Black); in (b) the batteries are dismantled, the bishop being captured in one line, with the rook giving the mate, and the rook in the other, with the bishop mating (the *Zilahi* theme).

332 Set 1...♘a3+/♘e3+/♘b2/♘b6 2 ♖xa3/♖xe3/♖xb2/♖xb6. 1 ♖d3? (>2 ♗xc4) ♕xd6/♖xa4 2 ♖xd6/♘d8. 1...♘xf6!. 1 ♖e3? (>2 ♗xc4) ♕xd6/♘xf6 2 ♘fg5/♘hg5. 1...♖xa4!. 1 ♖xf3? (>2 ♗xc4) ♘xf6/♖xa4 2 ♖xf6/♘f8. 1...♕xd6!. 1 ♖b8! (>2 ♗xc4) ♕xd6/♘xf6/♖xa4/♕e5 2 ♘d8/♘f8/♖e8/♖xe5. An excellent example of cyclic refutation, enriched by set play (unconnected to the theme) and mate transference.

333 1 ♕c3 (>2 ♘e5+ ♔xd6 3 ♘f7+ ♔e6/♔d7 4 ♕c8/♕c6) g5 2 ♕a5+ ♔d4 3 ♘f5+ ♔xc4 4 ♗d5. 1...e5 2 ♘b6+ ♔xb6 3 ♘c8+ ♔b5 4 ♗c6. 1...♗xd6 2 ♘e3+ ♔b5 3 ♗c6+ ♔b6 4 ♘d5. 1...♖c1 2 ♘xe4+ ♔b5 3 ♕a5+ ♔xc4 4 ♕a4. 1...♗c7 2 ♘c~+ ♔xd6 3 ♕d4+ ♔e6 4 ♕d5. 1...e6 2 ♘b7+ ♔b5/♔d5/♔c6 3 ♘a3+/♘e3+,♘e5/♘b6+. 1...f5 2 ♕a5+ ♔d4 ♕e5. A fine blend of variations, many lines ending in model mates.

334 1 ♖xa5 ♗f6+ 2 ♔xf5+ ♗e5; and 1 ♖xf7 ♗c5+ 2 ♔d5+ ♗e7. Paradoxical play in both solutions: Black captures a strong white unit to allow the king to move, and when he does a cross-check ensues.

335 1 ♕c6 (>2 ♘xg5+ fxg5 3 ♕f6) ♖f7 2 e5 [A] (>3 d6 [B]) ♗d6 3 ♖g3 [C]. 1...♖xh6 2 d6 [B] (>3 ♖g3 [C]) ♗d6 3 e5 [A]. 2...♔xg4 3 ♗xe2. Cyclic change of function between the white e-pawn, d-pawn and ♖g4.

336 Set 1...♕xc4/♘xc4/♕xe4/fxe4 2 ♘f3/♘c6/c3/♖xd7. 1 ♘xd7 (>2 ♘b6) ♕xc4/♘xc4/♕xe4/fxe4/♔xc4 2 ♕e5/♖xd3/♕c5/♘e5/♘e5. Four changed self-blocks. The lack of a set mate for 1...♔xe4 is a slight blemish, but if there had been one, 1 ♖xd7+ would probably have cooked.

337 1 ♘e3 (>2 ♕c3) ♘f~/♘fe6/♘xd5/♘g~/♘ge6/♘e8 2 ♕c7/♕d6/♕xd5/♖c7/♖c6/b8♘. Each knight plays at random and twice corrects its general error. The arrivals on e6 are of particular interest, as 1...♘ge6 also corrects the error of allowing 2 ♕d6 (the white queen is pinned, but 2 ♖d6 will now mate because c7 is guarded by the ♖h7).

338 1 ♖e8 (>2 ♘g8) ♖f4/♗f4 2 ♕d6/♘e3. 1...♘gf4 2 ♗d4 (2 ♕d6/♘e3?) 1...♘df4 2 ♕b2 (2 ♕d6/♘e3/♗d4?) First there is a Grimshaw on f4. Then the g-knight corrects the error of occupying f4 by preventing both the mates allowed by the Grimshaw interferences. Finally the d-knight corrects the error of placing a knight on f4 by opening the line a5-e5, but of course allows a new mate, none of the other three being playable. Splendid use of white and black lines.

339 Set 1...♖d6 2 ♘c5+ ♔e5 3 ♘xf6. 1...♗d6 2 ♘xf6+ ♔e5 3 ♘c5. 1 ♖h3 (>2 d3+ cxd3 3 exd3) ♖d6 2 ♘xf6+ ♔e5/♖xf6 3 ♘d7+/d3+. 1...♗d6 2 ♘c5+ ♔e5/♗xc5 3 ♘d7+/d3+. Reciprocal change of continuation between set and post-key play. The two moves ♘xf6 and ♘c5 recur at various points in both phases.

340 1 ♘xc8 ♖b8 2 ♘a7 ♖f8; and 1 ♘xb5 ♗a6 2 ♘a7 ♗c4. The *Zilahi* theme (see no. 331) with switchback, in as elegant a setting as one could wish for.

341 1 ♘e5? [A] (>2 ♕c6) ♖c4 2 ♘dxc4 [B]. 1...♖xe5 2 ♖xe5 [C]. 1...♗b5!. 1 ♘c4! [B] (>2 ♘b6) ♖xc4 2 ♖xe5 [C]. 1...♖e5 2 ♘dxe5 [A]. This is the *Kiss* theme (named after Ivan Kiss): A, B and C are shifted between White's first move and the replies to two defences.

342 1 ♗f7? ♗xf7/♖b5/♖a5 2 ♖xd6/♖xb5/♕xa5. 1...f5/c3/♖c7 2 ♖h5/♘f6/♘xc7. 1...♖c6!. 1 ♖b5! (-) ♗f7/♗g8/♖xb5 2 ♗xf7/hxg8/♕xd6. 1...f5/c3 2 ♗e4/♕xb3. A novel study in changed play, by one of today's most original and daring composers. Don't look too critically at the ♖h6, which is idle after the key!

343 1 ♗a8 axb4 2 ♖a7 b3 3 ♕b7 (>4 ♕h1). 2...bxa3 3 ♖b7 ♔~ 4 ♖b1. 1...a4 2 ♖d5 ♔~ 3 ♘h4(+) ♔g1 4 ♕b1. Bristol clearances and line-vacations (by both sides).

344 1 ♗f6 (>2 ♕e6+ ♔f8 3 ♕e7+ ♔g8 4 ♕g7) ♔f7 2 ♗g5+ ♔g8 3 ♕e6+ ♔~ 4 ♗h6. 2...♔g7 3 ♗h6+ ♔xh6 4 ♕f6. 1...0-0 2 ♕d5+ ♖f7 3 ♕g2+ ♔f8 4 ♕a8. Model mates in the Bohemian style, with a lovely line to follow the castling defence.

345 1 ♘c5 e8♘ 2 ♘d4 ♔f7 3 ♚e5 ♘f6. 1 ♚e5 e8♚ 2 ♘d4 ♚h5 3 ♚c5 ♚f3. 1 ♘cd4 e8♚ 2 ♚c6 ♚a8 3 b5 ♚a5. 1 ♚b5 e8♚ 2 ♚c5 ♚xa4 3 ♚d4 ♚b5. Allumwandlung to Chinese pieces, the whole family of them.

346 1 ♔c2 (>2 ♖a1+) ♘e1+ 2 ♔d1 ♘c2 3 ♖e3 ♘xe3+ 4 ♔e2 ♘xg4 5 ♘f3. 1 ♖a1? ♘c1!. 1 ♖c3? ♘e1!. 1 ♖a2? ♘e5!. It seems amazing that two of White's pieces must be sacrificed before mate can be given.

347 1 ♘c4 (>2 ♘xe3+ ♖xe3 3 ♕xe6) ♖d5 2 ♗f3+ ♘xf3 3 ♖e4. 1...♗d5 2 ♖xg5+ ♗xg5 3 ♘e5. 1...♘f1 2 ♖d5 ♖xd5/♗xd5 3 ♗f3/♘e5. 1...♗b6 2 ♗d5 ♖xd5/♗xd5 3 ♖e4/♖xg5. 1...c1♕ 2 ♕e2+. In the first two variations the Grimshaw on d5 leads to checks with square-vacation. The second pair of variations allows Novotnys with the customary double threats.

348 1 ♗b6? (>2 ♕xd4) ♘f3!. 1 ♗c7? (>2 ♖xd6) ♘e4!. 1 gxf4! (>2 ♕xh1+ ♘f3,♘e4 3 ♕x♘) ♘f3 2 ♕xd4+ ♘xd4/♔xd4 3 ♘e3/♖xd6. 1...♘e4 2 ♖xd6+ ♘xd6/♔xd6 3 ♖e5/♕xd4. 1...♗f3 2 ♗b6 (>3 ♕xd4). 1...♗e4 2 ♗c7 (>3 ♖xd6) ♘xf6 3 ♘xf6. The Dombrovskis paradox: the defences against the threats of the try-play are followed in the post-key play by the very moves they defeat. And there is more, for a reciprocation arises between the first two variations when the black king captures on d4/d6 (3 ♖xd6 and 3 ♕xd4). In addition, the occupation of f3 and e4 by the black bishop allows the tries to be played as continuations, because the black knight is denied access to the appropriate square to defend.

349 1 ♖c4 (>2 ♕e2+ ♔f4 3 ♖xd4) ♖xh4 2 ♘xb4 (>3 ♘d3) ♕xb4/♗xc2 3 ♗d7/♗c8. 1...♗xc2 2 ♕g4 (>3 ♕xd4) ♕b6/♖xh4 3 ♗g8/♗c8. 1...♕b6 2 fxg6 (>3 ♕f5) ♖h5/♗xc2 3 ♗d7/♗g8. Three black pieces control the white ♖+♗ battery. When one moves away, White plays so as to draw each of the other two away in turn, so that the third can be shut off as the battery opens. The quiet (i.e. non-checking) second moves add to the attractiveness of the problem.

350 1 ♘b1+ ♔b3 2 ♕d1+ ♔c2 3 ♗c1 axb6 4 ♖a1 b5 5 ♖h1 bxc4 6 ♔e1 c3 7 ♘g1 f3 8 ♗f1 f2. In longer selfmates a checking key is not regarded as a blemish, especially when the problem is a task. If you have not spotted what task the composer has achieved here, take a good look at the final position! An amazing achievement.

351 1 ♗c3? (>2 ♕d1) ♔d3/♔b3 2 ♕b1/♕b2. 1...e2!. 1 ♘c3! (>2 ♕b1) ♔d3/♔b3 2 ♕d1/♕b1. Le Grand, in miniature.

352 1 ♘d5? (>2 ♕xf6+ ♘xf6 3 ♘e7) g4!. 1 ♗g4? (>2 ♕/♗f5) ♖xg4! (2 ♘d5? a1♕!) 1 ♗d1! (>2 ♗c2+ ♖d3 3 ♕e4) a1♘ 2 ♗g4 ♖xg4 3 ♘d5 ♖f4 4 ♕e8+ ♔f5 5 ♘e3. 1...g4 2 ♗c2+ ♖d3 3 ♕e4+ ♖f5 4 ♕e8+ ♔g5 5 ♘e6. The main-plan cannot work until the ♙g5 has been blocked and the ♙a2 induced to promote to knight to prevent promotion to queen (the Holst theme). Wonderful use is made of the small white force.

353 1 ♘e1? (>2 ♘xd5) ♖b5 2 ♗h3. 1...♕a5!. 1 ♘d2? (>2 ♘xd5) ♕a5 2 ♗h3. 1...♖b5!. 1 ♗h3? (>2 ♘xd5) ♖b5/♕a5/♖h5 2 ♘e1/♘d2/♖xg6. 1...g5!. 1 ♘g5! (>2 ♘xd5) ♖b5/♕a5/♖f2/♕xf1/gxf5/♗xe7 2 ♗b1/♗c2/♗a3/♗b4/ ♕xf5/♗e5. Good variety from the half-battery, with the Banny theme hidden in the try-play.

354 1 ♕g7? (>2 ♕xg5) ♕d4!. 1 ♕f6? (>2 ♕xg5) ♕c3!. 1 ♕h6? (>2 ♕xg5) ♖xh5!. 1 ♕e7! (>2 ♕xg5) ♕d4+/♕c3+/♖xh5+ 2 ♘g7/♘f6/♘h6. Self-obstruction tries by the white queen fail to pinning defences. After the key these defences lead to cross-checks.

355 1 ♖e1? (>2 ♖e2) f3 2 ♗c2 (>3 ♗b3). 1...♖c6!. 1 ♗e4? (>2 ♗d5) c6 2 ♖e1. 1...♖d6! (2 ♗c2? ♖d3 3 ♗xd3 b5 4 ♗c2 b6+!) 1 ♗c2! (>2 ♗b3) ♖h3 2 ♗g6 (>3 ♗f7) ♖h7 3 ♗e4 (>4 ♗d5) c6 4 ♗f5 (>5 ♗e6) ♖h6 5 ♖e1 (>6 ♖e2) f3 6 ♗c2 (>7 ♗b3). Two foreplans are needed to block the diagonal a8-h1 (3...c6) and to confine the black rook to the h-file. Even then White must take care; if for instance 4 ♖e1? instead of 4 ♗f5, Black defends with 4...♗f6!, but after 4 ♗f5 ♖h6 5 ♖e1, 5...♗f6 allows 6 ♗e6.

356 (a) 1 ♖d6 ♔f4 2 ♖a6 ♔f5 3 ♔c6 ♔e6 4 ♖b6 ♖c8. (b) 1 ♖f2 ♖h1 2 ♗d1 ♔e6 3 ♔f3 ♔f5 4 ♗e2 ♖h3. Tempo moves by different black pieces in the two solutions, with echoed mates. Josef Kricheli was one of the finest helpmate composers.

357 1 Rd8? Rh3! (2 Bd5+? Kg4 3 Rd4?) 1 Rc8? Bxg7! (2 Rc4? B~ 3 Bd5?) 1 Rb8? Rh4! (2 Rb3+? Kg4 3 Be6?) 1 Ra8! (-) Rh3 2 Bd5+ Kg4 3 Ra4. 1...Bxg7 2 Ra4 (>3 Bd5) Rh4 3 Nxg5. 1...Rh4 2 Ra3+ Kg4 3 Be6. 1...Rh2 2 Be6 (>3 Ra4) g4 3 Bd5. 1...g4 2 Ng5+ Rxg5/Bxg5 3 Ra3/Bd5. 1...Kg4 2 Be6+ Kf3/Kh4 3 Ra3/Qh2. The tries fail due to self-interference between rook and bishop. After the key the Novotny following 1...g4 is an attractive feature.

358 1 Rc4 (>2 Rxe4 ... 3 Nd~) Re1 2 Nf8+ Ke5 3 Rxe4+ Bxe4 4 Nd7+ Kf5 5 Nb6+ Ke5 6 Nc4. 1...Qxh4 2 Nb6+ Ke5 3 Rxe4+ Rxe4 4 Nd7+ Kf5 5 Nf8+ Ke5 6 Nxg6. A Siers battery, with the 'Rössel' (the Nd7) returning to the battery-line before moving away again and ultimately giving mate.

359 1 Ncb5 Ba8 2 Rb7 cxb7 3 Kc6 b8N. 1 Ne6 Bb8 2 Rd7 c7 3 Kd6 c8N. 1 Ke6 Bc8 2 Rdd7 cxd7 3 Nd5 d8N. Each solution starts with a white bishop-move to the eighth rank and ends with a promotion to knight, different squares being used each time. An attractive idea by an inventive and adventurous Grandmaster-composer.

360 1 g1N 2 Ne2 3 Kg2 4 Kg1 5 Nc1 6 a1Q 7 Qa8 8 Qh1 Bd4. 1 g1B 2 Be3 3 Bc1 4 a1R 5 Ra4 6 Bf4 Ke3 8 Re4 Rb3. Contrasting mating positions after analogous promotion play, including Allumwandlung. A fine achievement with only six men!

361 1 Bf2? (>2 Nc5) Ne3!. 1 Rf2? (>2 Nf6) Nf4!. 1 Rf7! (>2 Bxd5+ Kxd5 3 Nf6+ Kd6 4 Rd7) Ne3 2 Nc5+ Kd4 3 Na4+ Ke4 4 Nc3. 1...Nf4 2 Nf6+ Kf5 3 Nh7+ Ke4 4 Ng5. White's anti-critical tries fail to line-closing defences. After the key, which introduces a fine full-length threat, the same defences allow the mates threatened by the tries to work as continuations – the Dombrovskis effect.

362 Set 1...Bf3+ 2 Nxf3 h6 3 Qg1/Qh2. 1...Rh3 2 Nxh3 h6 3 Qg1. 1 Kh6 (-) Bf3 2 Nh3 (>3 Qg1). 1...Rh3 2 Nf3 (>3 Qg1/Qh2). In the set play the bishop must be captured because Black has another move available. The key eliminates this move, so now the bishop must not be captured. The result is reciprocal change!

363 (a) 1 Ke5 Be3 2 Bd5+ Kg6 3 Ke4 Bxd2. (b) 1 Kc5 Re3 2 Rd5 Kf6 3 Kd4 Rxf3. Interchange of squares (German: *Platzwechsel*) between the black king and black bishop in (a) and the black king and black rook in (b), with an attractive diagonal/orthogonal correspondence.

364 1 Bb2? (>2 Rxe6) Qe1/Bxd5/Rh7h6 2 Ba3/Qa3/b8Q. 1...Re7!. 1 Bg5? (>2 Rxe6) Bxd5/Rh7h6/Rh5h6 2 Qf4/Be7/Rf4. 1...Qe1!. 1 Bg7! (>2 Rxe6) Rh7h6/Rh5h6/Qe1/Bxd5 2 Bf8/Be5/b8Q/Qf8. A wealth of changed and transferred mates dependent on White's line-closing tries and key.

365 1 ♗g7 (>2 ♕f5+ [A] ♖xf5 3 ♖xd4 [B]) ♗c8 2 ♖xd4+ [B] ♔xd4 3 ♕xf4 [C]. 1...♗f2 2 ♕xf4+ [C] ♖xf4 ♗e5 [D]. 1...♖ad6 2 ♖e5+ [D] ♔xe5 3 ♕f5 [A]. 1...♖a5/♘xd3 2 ♕e6+/♕f3+. The diagonal g7-d4 is crucial in this example of cyclic play: in two lines of play the ♖f6 is drawn away so that the white bishop guards e5/d4, and in two others the rook is pinned by a move of the black king.

366 Set 1...bxc5/♗d5/♗xe5 2 ♘g4+/♗e4+/♘fe4+ [A/B/C]. 1 ♕e7? (>2 ♕xd6+) bxc5/♗d5/♗xe5 2 ♗e4+/♘fe4+/♘g4+ [B/C/A]. 1...cxd3!. 1 ♕c7! (>2 ♕xd6+) bxc5/♗d5/♗xe5 2 ♘fe4+/♘g4+/♗e4+ [C/A/B]. The complete cyclic shift (Lačný) over three phases, making a cyclic Zagoruiko. See no. 392 for the same task in reflex-mate form.

367 1 ♘e8 (>2 ♘f6 ... 3 ♘g4) ♘g8 2 ♘6c7 (>3 ♘xd5) ♘fe7 3 ♘g7 (>4 ♘xd5+/♘f5+) ♘xh6 (3...♘f6? 4 ♘ce6) 4 ♘ge6 (>5 ♗xd4) ♘hf5 5 h6 ♘e~/♘f~ 6 ♘xd5/♗xd4. White's plan is to gain a tempo by forcing Black to capture the ♙h6. In the course of the solution the white knights swap places – and so do the black knights!

368 1 ♕b5 (>2 ♖f6 ♕xd7 3 ♕xd7) ♖c6 2 ♘g4+ ♔e6 3 ♘e3+ ♔e5 4 ♘c4+ dxc4 5 ♗f4+ ♔f6 6 ♗e3+ ♔e5 7 ♗xd4. 1...♗c6 2 ♗f4+ ♔f6 3 ♗e3+ ♔e5 4 ♗xd4+ cxd4 5 ♘g4+ ♔e6 6 ♘e3+ ♔e5 7 ♘c4. (4...♔xd4 5 ♕c4+) 1...♘c6 2 ♖f7 ♘xf7 3 ♗f4+ ♔f6 4 ♘g4+ ♔e6 5 ♘e3+ ♔f6 6 ♘xd5. Elaborate checking manoeuvres by the white pieces force the half-pinned pawns on c5 and d5 to weaken their hold on eventual mating squares.

369 1 ♕c2? (>2 ♕xc6) ♘c~/♘cd4/♘e5/♘e7 2 ♕f5/♕e4/♘db6/♕c5. 1...♘c3!. 1 ♕a6! (>2 ♕xc6) ♘c~/♘cd4/♘e5/♘e7 2 ♖h5/♗e4/♘f6/♕d6. Changed mates after random moves of the ♘c6 and three corrections.

370 1 b4 (>2 b5+ axb5 3 ♗xb5) ♖d3 2 ♘g5 ♖xg5/♗xg5 3 ♘e7/♗g2. 1...♗d3 2 ♘f6 ♖xf6/♗xf6 3 ♘d8/♖d6. 1...♘d3 2 ♗g2+ ♖xg2 3 ♖d6. 1...♕c4 2 ♖xc4+ ♘xc4 3 ♖c5. The Grimshaw on d3 leads to Novotnys involving the other black rook and black bishop, on two different squares.

371 1 ♖d4 ♕a8 2 ♖d5 ♕a1+ 3 ♔e4 ♕h8 4 ♖e5 ♕h1. While the black queen visits all four corners, the white king and white rook swap places. Try 1 ♔d5? ♕a1! (2 ♖e8? ♕h8 3 ♔e4 ♕a1 4 ♖e5 ♕a8+!)

372 1 ♕h6? (>2 ♖f8) ♖g6/♖g7/♖g8/♔xe8 2 ♕f8/♕e6/♖e7/♖e5. 1...♘g6!. 1 ♖e6! (>2 ♖f6) ♖g6/♖g7/♖g8/♔xe6 2 ♖e7/♕e8/♕f6/♖e5. Three changed self-blocks and mate transference after the king-flight, in an elegant setting.

373 1 ♗f6 (>2 ♗d8 ... 3 ♗c7) d4 2 ♘de4+ ♖xe4/♗xe4 3 ♖d5/♗xe5. 1...f4 2 ♘ge4+ ♗xe4/♖xe4 3 ♗xe5/♖xd5. Black's two defences are anticipatory interferences leading to Novotnys.

374 1 ♗a4? c1♘! (2 ♘h3? ♔xe6!) 1 ♘h3? c1♕! (2 ♗a4? ♔xe6!) 1 ♔g8! (>2 h8♕ ... 3 ♕/♖xe5+) c1♕ 2 ♗a4 ♕c2 3 ♗xb3+ ♕xb3 4 ♖c5. 1...c1♘ 2

♘h3 ♘xd3 3 ♘xf4+ ♘xf4 4 ♖xe5. White's tries are premature: he must wait to play these moves until Black has decided which promotion unit to choose.

375 1 ♗a1? ♗a8!. 1 g5! (>2 ♔xe7) ♗d5 2 ♔xe7 ♗xc4 3 ♕d8+ ♔b4 4 ♕b6+ ♗b5 5 ♕xb5+. 1...♗d2 2 ♗a1 ♗a8 3 ♕b2 ♕b7 4 ♕xd2+ ♘c3 5 ♗xc3+. White anti-Bristol try answered by black anti-Bristol defence – a fine illustration of correspondence.

376 1 ♗xe4+ ♗e3 2 ♗xf5 ♕a4; and 1 ♘xe6+ f6 2 ♕xf4 ♕c8. Black starts by capturing an unwanted white unit, checking as he does so, and then White parries the check with a second (otherwise unnecessary) unit so that the queen can use the line that has been vacated after the thematic black piece has pinned itself.

377 1 ♖e3? (>2 ♕xf4/♘xf3) ♖f7! (2 ♖xe6?) 1 ♗e3? (>2 ♕xf4/♘xf3) ♗f7! (2 ♕g7?) 1 ♘g5? (2 ♖xe4) ♖e3! (2 ♕xf4?) 1 gxf3? (>2 ♖xe4) ♗e3! (2 ♘xf3?) 1 g5! (>2 ♕f6) ♖f7/♗f7/♖e3/♗e3 2 ♖xe6/♕g7/♕xf4/♘xf3. Excellent example of Novotny self-obstruction tries and double Grimshaw after the key, with two further tries adding to the already intricate pattern.

378 1 ♘e7 (>2 ♘c6/♖d5/♖f4 [A/B/C]) ♘g8 2 A/B/C. 1...♘c5 2 A/B. 1...♘b6 2 A/C. 1...♘b8 2 B/C. 1...♘f6 2 A. 1...d2 2 B. 1...♘e5 2 C. Combinative separation, in miniature.

379 1 ♗xf7 (-) ♗c3 2 ♖d8/♘b6/♘c3 [A/B/C]. 1...♕h5 2 ♕e4/♕f5/♗xe6 [D/E/F]. Other moves by the ♗a5 yield complete combinative separation of mates A, B and C, while other moves by the queen do the same for mates D, E and F. Two defences give new mates altogether: 1...♗xf7/c4 2 ♖e5/♕a2.

380 1 ♕g3 (>2 ♗c5) ♕c5 2 ♘d4+ ♕xd4 3 ♗b5. 1...♗c5 2 ♘a7+ ♗xa7 3 ♗b5. 1...♕e5/f4 2 ♕xe5/♕h3. A combination of Umnov I and Umnov II: Black defends by playing a piece to the threat-square (Umnov II), and White then occupies the square the black unit has just vacated (Umnov I).

381 1 ♘d1 (>2 ♘c3) ♕xd1+/♕d2+/♕a5/♕xe6/♖b2+/♖b3/♕d3+/♕d4 2 ♔xd1/♔xd2/♔c1/♔c3/♔xb2/♔xb3/exd3/♘g5. Six Royal-battery mates, all resulting from the black half-pin. The set 2 ♖xc4 after 1...♕xc4+ is replaced by the threat.

382 1 ♕c8 (>2 d8♕) ♔e7/♔d6/♔f6/♔f5/♕d8 2 d8♕/♘f7/♘xg4/♘d3/♘c4. An excellent key, giving four flights, leads to attractive battery-play.

383 1 c4? (>2 ♘c2) ♘b1! (2 ♘c4?) 1 b4? (>2 ♘b3) cxd4! (2 ♕b4?) 1 b6? (>2 ♘b6) ♖c7!. 1 c7? (>2 ♘c6) ♗xb5! (2 ♘xb5?) 1 e7? (>2 ♘e6) ♘xf5! (2 ♘xf5?) 1 f6? (>2 ♘f5) ♖e7!. 1 f4? (>2 ♘f3) exd4! (2 ♕f4?) 1 e3! (>2 ♘e2) exd4/♘b1/cxd4/♗xb3/♗xb5/♘xf5/♘xf3 2 ♕h2/♘c4/♕b4/♘xb3/♘xb5/♘xf5/♘xf3. A rich variant on the white knight-tour: seven tries and the key all vacate squares for the knight, most of the tries failing through white self-obstruction. There's no shortage of post-key play, which is rare with tasks of this kind.

384 1 ♖c3 (>2 ♕d1+ ♖d2 3 ♕xd2) g3 2 ♕e3+ [A] fxe3 3 ♖d3 [B]. 1...f3 2 ♖d3+ [B] exd3 3 ♘xf3 [C]. 1...e3 2 ♘f3+ [C] gxf3 3 ♕xe3 [A]. 2...♔e4 3 ♗d5. 1...♘c1 2 ♖c5 (>3 ♖d5/♕c3) ♘e2/e3 3 ♕d2/♕xb4. Cycle of white continuations and mates based on Black's third-pinned pawns. In Marin's original setting one of the thematic white moves was also the threat. The new version eliminates that weakness and introduces a little by-play, at the cost of some additional black force.

385 1 g1♘ ♖g6 2 ♘f3 exf3 3 e3 f4 4 e2 f5 5 e1♗ f6 6 ♗c3 f7 7 ♗h8 f8♘; and 1 e3 ♖f2 2 exf2 e4 3 f1♗ e5 4 g1♖ e6 5 ♖g7 e7 6 ♗c4 e8♕ 7 ♗g8 ♕h5. Excelsior – doubled! In the first solution a black unit is sacrificed to allow the e-pawns to pass each other, in the second it is the white rook that has to go.

386 1 ♗f1 (>2 ♖gd7 ... 3 ♖xd5; 2...♖d2/♖d1 3 ♕xb5/♘xa4) ♖b3 2 ♖g4 (>3 ♗d6/♗d4) ♖e3/♖e1 3 ♕xb5/♘xa4. 1...♖a3 2 f7 (>3 f8♕) ♖f2/♖f3 3 ♕xb5/♘xa4. 1...♖b4/♖xf1/♖e2 2 ♘xd5/♘xa4+/♗xe2. After the key, 2 ♖g4? (>3 ♗d6/♗d4) won't work because 2...♖e2! pins the ♗e5 and shuts off the ♗f1. Similarly 2 f7? (>3 f8♕) fails to 2...♖xf1!. But when the black rooks move to the third rank, they lose the benefit of occupying the diagonal f1-b5 as they move eastwards to defend, so that 3 ♕xb5 or 3 ♘xa4 will now mate. This variant of the Roman theme is known as the *Sackmann*.

387 Set 1...♘xh5 2 ♕d6+ ♘xd6 3 ♖xd5. 1...♘g5 2 ♖xd5+ ♘xd6 3 ♕d6. 1 ♔f1 (>2 ♘f3+ ♔~ 3 ♘cd4) ♘xh5 2 ♖xd5+ ♔xd5 3 ♕d6. 1...♘g5 2 ♕d6+ ♔xd6 3 ♖xd5. 1...d6 2 ♕c1 (>3 ♗f4) ♘xh5 3 ♕e1. A superb example of reciprocal change, brought about by the position of the white king (checks must be avoided). The by-play variation 1...d6 makes good additional use of the white queen.

388 1 ♖c4 ♗h2 2 ♗d4 ♔e6 3 ♘c3 ♗g1; and 1 ♘d4 ♗a2+ 2 ♔e4 ♔d6 3 ♘f3 ♗b1. An attractive chameleon echo with ideal mates.

389 1 ♘b6? (>2 ♕d7/♕d5) axb6 2 ♖xb6. 1...♘f6!. 1 ♖b7? (>2 ♕d7) ♘f6 2 ♖xe7. 1...♘e5!. 1 ♖b5? (>2 ♕d5) ♘f6/♘e3 2 ♕xe7/♖e5. 1...♘e5!. 1 ♖d4! (>2 ♕d5) ♘e3/♘f6/♖e5/♔e5+ 2 ♖e4/♕xe7/♕d7/♖d6. Threatening two mates turns out to be less effective than threatening only one! An elegant example of the *Barnes* theme: two mates are threatened by the first try, but only one of them by the second try and the other by the key.

390 1 ♘b3? (>2 ♖d4) ♘c6! (2 ♗d5?) 1 ♘c6? (>2 ♖d4/♗d5) ♘b3! (2 ♕xb7?) 1 ♘e6? (>2 ♖d4) ♘f5! (2 ♕xf5?) 1 ♘f5? (>2 ♖d4) ♘e6! (2 ♕h7?) 1 ♘c2! (>2 ♖d4) ♘c6/♘b3/♘f5/♘e6/♗e5/♖xe2 2 ♗d5/♕xb7/♕xf5/♕h7/ ♖xe3/♖xf4. The white knight duels with the two black knights, in an interesting example of correspondence (reciprocal occupation of squares).

391 1 ♖a~a? ♗a1! (2 a8♕? ♔g7!) 1 ♖b6? ♗b2! (2 b8♕?) 1 ♖c6? ♗c3! (2 c8♕?) 1 ♖d6? ♗d4! (2 d8♕?) 1 ♖a1! (–) ♗xa1 2 a8♕ (>3 ♕xf8/♕xa1) ♗g7 3 ♘g6. 1...♗b2/♗c3/♗d4 2 b8♕/c8♕/d8♕. 1...♗xh6 2 ♕xh6 ♘~ 3 ♘g6. Opposition-tries which fail through white self-interference: the newly promoted queen must have access to the square to which the black bishop plays.

392 1 ♕xf6 ♗e6 2 ♔e4 ♖g2 3 ♔f3 ♗d5. 1 ♘xf5 ♖g2 2 ♘d6 ♖g5 3 ♘c4 ♖d5. 1 exf2 ♔b3 2 ♔e3 ♔xc3 3 f3 ♗d5. A cyclic form of the *Zilahi* theme: a white unit that is captured in one solution gives the mate in another. In this beautifully unified setting, the three white pieces all mate on d5.

393 Set 1...♕xh1/♕f1/♕d1 2 c3/c5/g5 [A/B/C] ♕xe4/♘f7/♘f7. 1 ♖xd4? (>2 ♔e4 ♕xe3) ♕xh1/♕f1/♕d1 2 g5/c3/c5 [C/A/B] ♘f7/♕xe4/♘f7. 1...♘g5!. 1 ♖xf4! (2 ♔e4 ♕xe3) ♕xh1/♕f1/♕d1 2 c5/g5/c3 [B/C/A] ♘f7/♘f7/♕xe4. The cyclic Zagoruiko has never been achieved in a direct-mate two-mover, except in a Zeroposition, but here it is shown by a talented composer in reflex-mate form. The three-mover no. 366 achieves the same task.

394 Set 1...♗c3/♖d3/♕e3 2 ♕xd5/♕b4/♕xe3. 1 ♖c8? (>2 ♔g7) ♗c3/♖d3/♕e3 2 ♕xc3/♕xb6/♕xd5. 1...♖e1!. 1 ♘e5! (>2 ♘f3) ♗c3/♖d3/♕e3 2 ♕xb6/♕xd3/♕b4. The white queen is kept very busy in this well-constructed 3x3 Zagoruiko.

395 1 ♕d5 (>2 ♕xd3) ♕xe5/♖xe5/♘6xe5/♘4xe5/fxe5/♗d~ 2 ♘d6/♘e7/♗h7/g4/♘d4/♕e4. Five Nietvelt defences.

396 1 ♘g4+? hxg4 2 ♗f6. 1...♘xg4!. 1 ♖d5+? cxd5 2 ♘d7. 1...♖xd5!. 1 ♗d6+? cxd6 2 ♘e7. 1...♗xd6!. 1 g3! (>2 f4+ gxf4 3 gxf4) ♘xf3/♖a4/♗c1 2 ♘g4+/♖d5+/♗d6+. The 'cook-tries' underline the theme: cyclic square-vacation by the white pieces, playable only when black pieces move away to defend against the threat.

397 1 ♘b5? (>2 ♕c6) ♘d2 2 ♘xc3. 1...♗d2!. 1 ♘e8? (>2 ♕c6) ♗d2 2 ♘xf6. 1...♘d2!. 1 ♗f8! (>2 ♕b7+ ♔e6 3 ♕xf7) ♗d2 2 ♘e8 (>3 ♘xf6) ♗g5 3 ♕c6. 1...♘d2 2 ♘b5 (>3 ♘xc3) ♗b1 3 ♕c6. The *Swiss* theme: Black's defence changes the threat carried by a given white move from one that Black can defeat to one that he cannot defeat without causing a new error. Here it is combined with the Banny theme.

398 1 ♔b6 (>2 ♕xd7) ♕g1+/♕b1+/♔e7+/♔f5+ 2 ♗d4/♗b2/♗f6/♗d6. Four cross-checks are allowed by the key.

399 1 ♖xe5? (>2 ♖xd5) ♖xb4!. 1 ♕e7? (>2 ♕xd6) dxc4!. 1 ♕a7? (>2 ♕xb6) ♘xc4!. 1 ♘xd4! (>2 ♘b3) ♖xb4/dxc4/♘xc4 2 ♕a7/♖xe5/♕e7. The Banny theme in cyclic form.

400 Set 1...♖f6+/♖g7+ 2 ♘xf6/♘xg7. 1 ♗e1? (>2 ♕xc2+ ♖c3 3 ♕xc3) ♖f6+ 2 ♕xf6 (>3 ♕e7). 1...♖g7+ 2 ♕xg7 (>3 ♕f8). 1...♖g5!. 1 ♗e5! (>2

♗d4+ ♖xd4 3 ♕xd4) ♖f6+ 2 ♗xf6 (>3 ♗e7). 1...♖g7+ 2 ♗xg7 (>3 ♗f8). A three-move Zagoruiko in a simple but attractive setting.

401 Set 1...♔f4 2 ♕e3+ ♔g4 3 ♕g3. 1...d4 2 ♕c5+ ♔f4/♔e6 3 ♕f5/♗f5. 1 ♕c6 (-) ♔f4 2 ♕c3 ♔g4 3 ♕g3. 1...♔d4 2 ♗xh7 ♔e5 3 ♕f6. Good variety in this mutate miniature, in which the key brings in quiet continuations to replace the checks of the set play.

402 1 ♘c6 (>2 ♘e7+ ♔e5 3 ♗d5 (>4 ♖e4) ♗f5 4 ♘c6) e2 2 ♗c2+ ♔e6 3 ♔xc7 (>4 ♖d6) ♘f5 4 ♗b3. 1...♘g8 2 ♖d5+ ♔e4 3 ♗c4 (>4 ♖e5) ♖f5 4 ♖d4. (2...♔g6 3 ♖g5+ ♔h6 4 ♗g7) Self-blocks by Black on f5 on his third move (defending against different threats by the ♖d4) lead to switchback-mates. A novel concept, superbly shown.

403 1 ♘g7? (>2 ♖e6) ♘d6 2 ♕f4. 1...♘d2!. 1 ♘xe3? (>2 ♖d5) ♘d2 2 ♕f4. 1...♘d6!. 1 ♘f4! (>2 ♘g6) ♘d2/♘d6/♔xf4 2 ♖e6/♖d5/♗d6. The Dombrovskis paradox, with ingenious use of white lines.

404 1 ♘e~? (>2 ♕xe4) ♘f7!. 1 ♘xc5? (>2 ♖c2) dxc5/♔xc5 2 ♕xe4/♖xc6. 1...♖xe2!. 1 ♘b~? (>2 ♖c2) d4!. 1 ♘xd5! (>2 ♕xe4) cxd5/♔xd5 2 ♖c2/♘f4. Black has an adequate refutation to the random move by each knight, so threat correction is required. Here the effect is reciprocal: the threat introduced by the random move of the ♘e6 is the same as that carried by the correction of the ♘b4, and vice versa.

405 (a) 1 ♔g5 ♔b3 2 ♘c3 ♕c1. (b) 1 ♔g6 ♔b2 2 ♖e6 ♕g3. Black unpins Black and White unpins White, the white king's choice of square depending on where the black king has gone. Black's second move opens a white line and interferes with the black queen.

406 1 ♖f5 ♔d4+ 2 ♔c2 ♔e3. 1 ♗f5 ♔d5+ 2 ♔c3 ♔c6. 1 ♕f5 ♔d3+ 2 ♔c1 ♔e4. A cycle of black interferences on f5, followed by Royal-battery checks and mates.

407 1 ♕g5 (>2 ♖c4+ dxc4 3 ♕xc5) ♕f5 2 ♘xc5+ ♕g4 3 ♘xe6. 1...♗f5 2 ♘xf2+ ♔e4 3 ♖xd3. 1...♖f5 2 ♘d2+ ♖f4 3 ♘f3. 1...♘f5 2 ♘f6+ ♘xh4 3 ♕xd5. The white knight aims for a mating-square which a black piece must lose control of in parrying the check.

408 1 ♗b7? (>2 ♗e4) e1♕!. 1 ♗a6? (>2 ♗d3) e1♘ 2 ♗b7. 1...♘b5! (2 ♗xb5? e1♘ 3 ♗c6 ♔xe6!) 1 g3! (>2 ♘xg7+ ♔g5 3 ♘h3+ ♔h6 4 ♘f5) ♖f7 2 ♗a6 ♘b5 3 ♗xb5 e1♘ 4 ♗c6 ♔xe6 5 ♗e4. Finding that his first try fails to a queen-promotion, White tries to induce a knight-promotion, but Black has an escape-square on f7. The key and threat force Black to block this square, with the result that the try inducing the knight-promotion will now work as the continuation.

409 1 ♕b2 (>2 ♘c4+ ♗/♖xc4 3 ♕f2) ♖f6 2 ♕xd4+ [A] ♘xd4 3 ♘xg4 [B]. 1...♕f6 2 ♖xf3+ [C] gxf3 3 ♕xd4 [A]. 1...♗f6 2 ♘xg4+ [B] ♖xg4 3

♖xf3 [C]. The double interferences on f5 produce a white cycle which arises from the fact that the B♖d4, ♗g4 and ♘f3 form a cycle of guards.

410 Set 1...♗~/g3/fxg2 2 ♕xh7/♕h4/♕xg2. 1 ♘e1? d2! (2 ♕b1?) 1 ♘e3? e1! (2 ♕xe1?) 1 ♘f4? g3! (2 ♕h4?) 1 ♘h4! (-) ♗~/♗xg5/g3/d2/e1/ ♘~ 2 ♖xg4/♘xg5/♕xf3/♕b1/♕xe1/♘d6. Mutate with white-interference tries.

411 1 0-0 2 ♖xd8 3 ♔f7 4 ♖h8 5 ♕g8 6 ♖f8 7 ♔e8 ♘xd6. Only the h-rook can capture on d8 to let the other rook out so that the unpinned white knight can mate. After castling, the black king and black rook return to their original squares.

412 1 ♕f3 (>2 ♕e4) cxd3/♖xd3/♘xd3/♗xd3 2 f5/♔f5/♘f5/♗f5. Stocchi blocks on d3, with White occupying f5 in all the mates. One wonders why the composer used an expensive W♘a6 to guard c5 when a black pawn would have served well enough to block the square.

413 1 ♖f6 (>2 ♖c6+ ♔d5 3 ♕d7) ♕xd4 2 ♕f7+ ♔c5+/♕d5 3 b4/♖c6. 1...♖xd4 2 ♕c7+ ♔d5+ 3 c4. 1...♔xd4 2 ♖f5+ ♔c4/♔e3 3 ♕c3/♘f1. 1...♔d5 2 ♕d7+ ♔c4 3 ♖c6. Anticipatory self-pins on d4 lead to cross-checks with mates from the two white pawns, which look as if their only function is to guard squares.

414 1 ♗xd6? (>2 ♗xe5/♕c5) ♖gc3!. 1 ♘e7? (>2 ♕xd5/♘f5) ♖cf3!. 1 ♖g4! (>2 ♖xe4+ dxe4 3 ♕xe4) ♖be3 2 ♗xd6 ♘d3 3 ♕c3. 1...♖gd3 2 ♘e7 ♘e3 3 ♘f3. 1...♖xg4 2 ♗xb3. Anti-Bristol defences by the black rooks, which do their best to defeat White's double threats. The tries serve to underline the defensive play.

415 1 ♔g1 ♕xh7 2 ♗b2+ ♔f4 3 ♘e6+ ♔e3 4 ♖b3+ ♕d3 5 ♖c3 ♕xc3 6 ♗c1+ ♕d2 7 ♔f1 ♕xc1. The black queen captures one pinning piece only to find herself successively in two further pins. White's key is subtle: if 1 ♔f1?, there is no tempo-move at the end of the sequence.

416 1 ♕d1 (>2 ♘f6) ♖d4/♗d4/♖d3/♗d3/♕d2/♘d6+ 2 ♘e5/♖e3/♕xa4/ ♖e4/♘f8/♖xd6. A lovely example of Levman defences, with two Grimshaws on the d-file.

417 1 ♗e1 (>2 ♗b3+ ♗xb3 3 axb3) e6 2 ♘dc5+ ♗xc5/♖xc5 3 ♕xc2/ ♘b6. 1...d2 2 ♘ec5+ ♗xc5/♖xc5 3 ♘c3/♕a7. 1...♖hxg8 2 ♖c5 ♗xc5/♖xc5 3 ♘c3/♘b6. 1...♖c4 2 ♗xc4. Anticipatory line-openings by the black pawns allow Novotnys on c5 by the knights. The third Novotny, by the rook, is playable because Black has deprived himself of a potential check by 1...♖xh7.

418 1 ♕a3 (-) ♗c1/♗e1/♗d1/♗xf1/♖a6/♖c8/♖f8/♖h6 2 ♕c3/♕e3/ ♘d3/♘f3/♕c5/♕d6/♘g6/♘f7. Focal play by each of four black pieces.

419 1 ♗c2? ♗d5!; 1 ♗g4? ♗e6! (2 ♗h5? ♗f7!); 1 ♗a7? ♗f1! (2 ♘d3 ♗g2 3 ♘f2+ ♔g1 4 ♗e2 e3!). 1 ♘d3! (>2 ♘f2+ ♔g1 3 ♘xe4+ ♔f1 4 ♗f2) ♗xd3 2 ♗h5 ♗e3 3 ♗g6 ♗f3 4 ♗h7 (4 ♗f5? ♗g2!) ♗g2 5 ♗f5 ♗f3 6 ♗h3.

Black uses the threat of stalemate as a refutation. In the post-key play a duel arises between the white bishop and the black bishop.

420 1 f7? (>2 ♖f6) ♘e5/♗e6/♖d6/♖d4 2 ♕xe5/♗xe6/♘xd6/♘xd4. 1...♕a6!. 1 ♕c2? (>2 ♘d6 – not 2 ♘d4?) ♘e5/♘b3 2 ♘d4/♕xd3. 1...♕b8!. 1 ♗b1! (>2 ♘d4 – not 2 ♘d6?) ♗e6/♘b3/♕a4 2 ♘d6/♗xd3/♕xc8. David Shire has made a particular study of the *Sushkov* theme: a pseudo le Grand with dual avoidance in the threats, the avoided mate reappearing after a prominent defence. The first try shown, though adding appreciably to the interest of the problem, is not part of the theme.

421 1 ♘h5 (>2 g4) ♘b2 2 ♖xf7 [A] (2 d4? [D]). 1...♘e5 2 ♘g3 [B] (2 ♖xf7? [A]). 1...♘d6 2 ♕d7 [C] (2 ♘g3? [B] 2 ♖xf7? [A]). 1...♘b6 2 d4 [D] (2 ♕d7? [C]). 1...gxh5/♕f4 2 ♖g5/♖xf4. Four-point dual-avoidance cycle based on black interferences, by a talented and versatile composer.

422 1 b3? (>2 ♖c4) ♘e5!. 1 ♗c3? (>2 ♗d4) ♘c6!. 1 ♗d2? (>2 ♗e3) ♖xh3!. 1 ♗e1! (>2 ♗f2) ♗h4 2 ♗d2 (>3 ♗e3) ♗g5 3 b3 (>4 ♖c4) ♘e5 4 ♗c3 (>5 ♗d4) ♘c6 5 ♗d4+ ♘xd4 6 ♖c4+ ♘xc4 7 b4. 2...♗f2 3 ♗a5 (>4 ♗b6) ♘d7 4 b3 (>5 ♖c4) ♘e5 5 ♗c3 (>6 ♗d4) ♕b8 6 ♖a5+ ♕b5 7 ♖xb5. If White were to try 1 b4+?, he would find that Black had two king-moves available: 1...♔c4/♔d4. His task, therefore, will be to arrange for Black to block those squares with his own men.

423 1 ♔d7 (>2 ♔c7/♔c8) d5 2 ♔c6 d4+ 3 ♔b6 d3+ 4 ♔a6 ♗a7/♗f4 5 ♕e8+ ♗b8 6 ♕xe4. White must force Black to block an orthogonal flight with the ♗e3. The black pawn turns out to be useful to White, as it interferes with each bishop in turn, thus allowing the king to get through to a6. Elegant minimal setting.

424 1 ♘c5 (>2 ♘d3+ ♔f6+ 3 ♘e6) ♔f6+ 2 ♘ge6+ ♔e5 3 ♘d3. 1...♔xd6+ 2 ♘ce6+ ♔e5 3 ♕xf4. 1...♔xd5+ 2 ♘ce4+ ♔~ 3 ♖c5. 1...♘xf3 2 ♘xd7+ ♖xd7 3 ♘xf3. Cross-checks after king-moves, with all three flights granted by the key.

425 Set 1...♖xa4/bxa4/♘b~/♖c~/♘d~/♗~ ♖xb5/axb4/♗d4/♕f5/♘e4/ ♕g1. 1 ♘xc4 (>2 ♖bc8) ♖bxc4/bxc4/♘bxc4/♖cxc4/♘dxc4/♗xc4 2 ♖xb5/ axb4/♗d4/♕f5/♘e4/♕g1. A superb study in mate transference, with six self-blocks on the flight-square granted by the key. Two eminent Russian composers reproduced this setting piece-for-piece in a well-known prizewinner a decade later.

426 1 ♖e5? (>2 ♘xf4/♘c5) f2!. 1 ♗c5? (>2 ♘f2) ♗e5! (2 ♘c5?) 1 ♗xf4? (>2 ♘f2) ♗e5! (2 ♘xf4?) 1 ♗d2? (>2 ♘f2) ♘e3! (2 ♖d2?) 1 ♗d4? (>2 ♘f2) ♖e7! (2 ♕d4?) 1 ♗b6! (>2 ♘f2) ♗e5/♖e5/♘e3/♖e7/♗e6 2 ♘c5/♘xf4/♖d2/♕d4/♕xf1. A Novotny try on e5 fails because Black can close the line h2-e2. White's further tries carry a threat which opens a second guard-line to e2, but all are self-interferences which allow Black to close that new line, with Levman defences. A brilliantly conceived problem.

427 1 ♘d~? (>2 ♖xd3/♕g6) ♘d~!. 1 ♘de4? (>2 ♖xd3/♕g6) ♘e3 2 ♘xf2. 1...♘c7!. 1 ♘b5? (>2 ♖xd3/♕g6) ♘f6 2 ♕e6. 1...♘b6!. 1 ♘df5! (>2 ♖xd3/♕g6) ♘f6/♘b6 2 ♖g7/♘e3. A speciality of the composer: white correction answered by black correction.

428 1 ♕e6? (-) ♗~/a3 2 ♘xf5/♕b3. 1...g2!. 1 e6? (-) g2/♗~ 2 ♖h3/♘xf5. 1...a3!. 1 ♘de6? (-) a3/g2 2 ♖b3/♖h3. 1...♗~!. 1 ♘ge6! (-) a3/g2/♗~ 2 ♖b3/♖h3/♕xg3. White arrival correction in quaternary form: arrival on e6 by the queen fails to provide for 1...g2; 1 e6? corrects but eliminates 2 ♕b3 after 1...a3. Arrival by the d-knight on e6 corrects again by introducing 2 ♖b3, but the mate on f5 has been lost. Finally the g-knight corrects yet again by bringing in 2 ♕xg3 after the bishop-move.

429 Black plays: 1 ♘d5 ♘xc5 2 ♘xb4+ ♘b7. White plays: 1 ♘d5 ♘xe4 2 ♘xe3+ ♘g5. An appealing study in reciprocal line-effects.

430 Set 1...♘c~/♘e~ 2 ♘e6/♘c6. 1 ♘d2 (-) ♘c~/♘e~/♘cxd3/♘exd3/ ♔xd3/e2 2 ♘b3/♘f3/♘e6/♘c6/♖xd5/♕g1. Thomas Taverner was composing fine two-movers even before the Good Companions got to work. This Rukhlis appeared without source or date in Taverner's little book from 1924, *Chess Problems made easy*, but was very likely composed well before this date, and may even have pre-dated Moseley's well-known early Rukhlis of April 1914 (see no. 252).

431 1 cxb6? (>2 ♔c5) ♕a6/♗xf7/♖xh5/♖xd6+/♘xb6 2 ♘c3/♘c5/♖d4/ ♔xd6/♔xb6. 1...♕b4!. 1 ♖g6! (>2 ♔d6) ♕a6/♗xf7/♖xh5 2 ♘d6/♘f6/♖g4. 1...♕xb5+/♗xd7+/♖xg6+/♘c7 2 ♔xb5/♔xd7/♗xg6/♔xc7. A brilliant piece of work in which the mates given by three unpinned white units are changed from virtual to post-key play. The Royal battery works hard!

432 1 b3 (-) ♘c2 2 ♘c4 (>3 ♕xe5 [A]) ♔c3 3 ♗b2 [B]. 1...♗g1 2 ♕h3 (>3 ♗b2 [B]) ♔c3 3 ♘b5 [C]. 1...♗h4 2 ♕f5 (>3 ♘b5 [C]) ♔c3 3 ♕xe5 [A]. 1...♔c3 2 ♖xd3+ ♘xd3 3 ♘b5. The cyclic le Grand familiar from the two-move field (see no. 162) is here shown in third-move threats and mates.

433 1 ♖f5 (>2 hxg8♕+ ♕xg8) d4 2 ♘d5+ ♘f6. 1...♖c3,♖d4 2 ♘e4+ ♘f6. 1...♘d4 2 ♘xg8+ ♘xf5. 1...♘xf6+ 2 ♖xf6+ ♘xf6. Black defends by unpinning the white knight, which the key has pinned, but the unpins work to White's advantage. The variation starting 1...♘d4 is particularly attractive: no shut-off by the white knight is possible, but a self-pin will do instead.

434 Set 1...♗xb6 2 ♗e7. 1 ♗c7? (-) ♔xc6/♗xb6 2 ♗d8/♗d6. 1...axb5!. 1 ♘d6? (-) ♔xd6/♔d4 2 ♗e7/♕c4. 1...♗xb6!. 1 ♘c7! (-) ♔d6/♔xc6/♔xb6/ ♔d4 2 ♕d5/♘b5/♘e6/♕d5. 1...♗xb6 2 ♕d5. It is not enough to grant the black king one flight or even two: it has to be four! A fine paradoxical key guaranteed to appeal to solvers.

435 1 b4 (>2 ♘xd4) ♕xe5/♕e4/♕xf4/♕xe3/♕xd3/♕xc3 2 d4/dxe4/
♘dxf4/♘xe3/♕xd3/♘xc3. 1...♕c4/♕xb4/♕c5/♕xb6+/♕xd5+/♘xe6 2
dxc4/♘xb4/bxc5/♘xb6/♖xd5/e8♕. Eleven dual-free variations by the black
queen.

436 1 ♔g3? (>2 ♕e3+ dxe3 3 d4) g4 2 ♖e6+ [A] ♖xe6 3 ♘xg4 [B].
1...♖xd6 2 ♘g4+ [B] fxg4 3 ♕f4 [C]. 1...f4+ 2 ♕xf4+ [C] ♖xf4 3 ♖e6 [A].
1...♘c3!. 1 ♔f3! (>2 ♕e3+ dxe3 3 d4) g4+ 2 ♘xg4+ [B] ♖xg4 3 ♖e6 [A].
1...♖xd6 2 ♕f4+ [C] gxf4 3 ♘g4 [B] (2...♔f6 3 ♕xd6) 1...f4 2 ♖e6+ [A]
♖xe6 3 ♕xf4 [C]. Black's two half-pin lines give rise to a cycle of continuations and mates in each phase, and to a cyclic shift of continuations and
mates between the virtual and post-key play. Everything hinges on the position of the white king. An outstanding concept, brilliantly executed by a
composer of rare talent.

437 1 ♘d7? (>2 ♘b6) ♗xa5! (2 ♘e3+? ♕xe3!) 1 ♘xe6? (>2 ♘c7/♕f5)
♗h3! (2 ♗e4+? ♖xe4!) 1 ♘g6? (>2 ♘xe7) ♗g5! (2 ♘b4+? ♖xb4!) 1 ♖c6!
(>2 ♕c4+ ♖xc4 3 bxc4) ♕xd4 2 ♘d7 ♗xa5 3 ♘e3. 1...♖hxd4 2 ♘xe6 ♗h3
3 ♗e4. 1...♖axd4 2 ♘g6 ♗g5 3 ♘b4. The tries fail because each potential
mating-square is doubly guarded. Black's queen and two rooks carry out
Nietvelt defences in self-pinning on d4, and each self-pin allows one of the
tries to work as a continuation, with a pin-mate on move 3.

438 1 ♖c6 (>2 ♘xf6+ ♖3xf6/♖7xf6 3 ♖e5/♘c7) ♖e7 2 ♖d6+ ♔xe4 3
♕xf3. 1...♗e7 2 ♘c7+ ♔xe4 3 ♖e6. 1...♖d3 2 bxc4+ ♔xd4 3 ♗xf2. 1...♗d3
2 ♘c3+ ♔xd4 3 ♖xc4. 1...♘xe4 2 ♖e7 ♖xe7/♗xe7 3 ♘b4/♘c7. 1...♘xg4 2
♕d3 ♖xd3/♗xd3 3 bxc4/♘c3. An attractive blend of Grimshaws, Novotnys
and pin-mates.

439 1 ♘b7 (>2 gxf8♗ ♗xf7) 1...♔h6 2 gxf8♘ ♗xf7. 1...♘de6 2 gxf8♖
♘g7. 1...♘fe6 2 f8♖ ♘g7. 1...♘xd7 2 f8♗ ♘f6. 1...♗a4 2 exf8♖ ♖e3.
1...♔xg7 2 exd8♖ ♕e1. 1...♘xf7 2 exf8♖ ♕e1. 1...♕~ 2 ♔xd8 ♕/♖xa8.
1...♗xf7+ ♔xf8 2 ♘e6. A tour-de-force of white promotions.

440 1 ♕b2 (>2 ♕b3+ ♔xc5 3 ♕b5) ♘xc5 2 ♘c6+ ♔d5/♘xe4 3 ♖d4/
♕b3. 1...♘xe5 2 ♘de6+ ♔d5 3 ♖d4. 1...♕d1 2 ♘e2+ ♔d5 3 ♖h4. 1...♕f7 2
♘f5+ ♔d5 3 ♖h4. Another composer of rare talent combines self-blocks,
battery play and shut-offs in a skilfully constructed setting.

441 1 ♕e8? (>2 ♘b8+ ♗xb8 3 ♕b5) ♗b8! (2 ♘xb8+? ♕xb8!). 1 ♖e5!
(>2 ♘b8) ♗xe2 2 ♕e8 (>3 ♘b8+) ♗b8 3 ♕xe2+ ♕xe2 4 ♘xb8. The try
fails because Black has two line-pieces guarding b8, one behind the other. As
things stand, the white queen cannot get to e2 from e8 in order to draw the
black queen away, so Black must first be induced to annihilate the e-rook to
clear the line. Combination of Umnov II with clearance moves by both sides.
The composers are two of Austria's most talented problemists. From 1986 to
1994 Klaus Wenda was the distinguished President of the FIDE Permanent

Commission for Chess Compositions. Friedrich Chlubna has a number of excellent problem books to his credit (see references in the Bibliography).

442 1 ♖f8 (>2 ♕d6+ ♚xf6 3 ♕xe6) ♚xf6 2 ♖xe6+ ♚xf5 3 ♕xe4. 1...♚xf5 2 ♕xe4+ ♚xf6 3 ♖xe6. 1...♖xh4 2 ♖xe6+ fxe6 3 ♕d6. A well-concealed key and threat, with black self-pins by king-moves.

443 1 ♔d4? (>2 ♘c7) ♛d8!. 1 ♚c5? (>2 ♘c7) ♛g5!. 1 ♔b4? (>2 ♘c7) b1♛+!. 1 ♔c3! (>2 ♘c7) b1♘+ 2 ♔b4 ♛f8+ 3 ♘e7. The first two tries fail because Black can pin the knight again. The third try shows why the key works: Black must be forced to promote to knight so that promotion to queen is not available (the Holst theme).

444 1 ♘db6? (>2 ♖e8/♗xd4) ♘xc6 2 ♘c4. 1...♖xg4!. 1 ♘de7? (>2 ♗xd4/♖xb5) ♖b4 2 ♖d5. 1...♖xf5!. 1 ♘e3? (>2 ♖xb5/♖e8) fxe3 2 ♗g3. 1...♖g6!. 1 ♘xf4! (>2 ♘d3) ♖xg4/♖xf5/♖g6/♚xf4 2 ♖xb5/♖e8/♗xd4/♕h2. A move by the ♘d5 would appear to carry three threats, but in fact each try eliminates one, thus introducing only two, in cyclic fashion. Consequently the tries fail to different moves by the ♖g5. After the key, which carries a new threat, the original threats return after the rook-moves, à la Hannelius.

445 Set 1...♛c6/c5/♘e6/♖d4/♘c4/♘bd7 2 ♕f5/♕e4/♖f5/♖xd4/♕xc4/♕c4. 1 ♗d4 (>2 ♕b5) ♛c6/c5/♘e6/♖xd4/♘c4/♘bd7 2 ♕xc6/♖d6/♗xe6/♖f5/♕e4/♕a2. Six mates changed with two of the set mates transferred – an ideal Rukhlis with additional play.

446 1 ♘b4? (>2 ♗c6) ♖xf5!. 1 ♘f4? (>2 ♗c6) ♛d4!. 1 ♘e5? (>2 ♗c6) ♘e3!. 1 ♘e3? (>2 ♕c6) ♛e5!. 1 ♘d4? (>2 ♕c6) ♖f4+!. 1 ♘e7! (>2 ♕c6) ♖xf5/♛d4/♘e3/♛e5/♖f4+ 2 ♕xf5/♖xd4/♖xe3/♖xe5/♖xf4. Correction-tries by the white knights, which prevent the rooks from playing one necessary mate each time.

447 Set 1...♖xc6/♘xc6/♕xc6+ 2 ♕c4+/♕d4+/♕e4+ ♖xc4/♘xd4/♕xe4. 1 ♕xf4 (>2 ♗e4+ ♕xe4) ♗f7/♗f6/♘f6 2 ♕c4+/♕d4+/♕e4+ ♗xc4/♗xd4/♘xe4. 1...♖xc6/♘xc6/♖b7 2 ♘c5+/♘b4+/♗b5+ ♖xc5/♘xb4/♖xb5. Rukhlis in selfmate form: the three set continuations are transferred to new defences, and two of the original defences allow new continuations.

448 1 ♕a6 (>2 ♕a4+) ♗f5 2 ♖xf6+ ♚e4/♚g4 3 ♕e6/♖f4. 1...♚xf3 2 ♗e2+ ♚e4 3 ♕d3. 1...♘f5 2 ♖e6+ ♚xd5/♚xf3 3 ♕c6/♗e2. 1...♘xf3 2 ♗d3+ ♚xd5 3 ♕c4. 1...♚xd5 2 ♕b7+ ♚c5 3 ♗d6. Clearance moves by the white rook and white bishop, with a fine key and complete accuracy in all variations.

449 Set 1...♖g7 2 ♘e6+ ♗xe6 3 ♗c5. 1...♛xe2 2 ♘b3+ ♗xb3 3 ♗c5. 1 ♕a7 (>2 ♘cxd3+ ♚e4 3 ♘f2) ♖xd6 2 ♘e6+ ♚e4 3 ♘xg5. 1...♛a3 2 ♘b3+ ♚e4 3 ♘d2. 1...♖g7 2 ♘d7+ ♚e4 3 ♘f6. 1...♛xa2 2 ♘a4+ ♚e4 3 ♘c3. In the set play, White's second moves are simple square-vacations. The key gives a flight but sets up a battery, and the resulting Siers Rössel is used to produce an ingenious Rukhlis.

450 1 ♘xe3+? ♕xe3!. 1 ♘xd6+? ♕xd6!. 1 ♔a2! (>2 ♖c5+ dxc5 3 ♘e5) ♕f4 2 ♕e4+ ♕xe4 3 ♘xd6+ cxd6 4 ♘b6. 1...♕e6 2 ♕d5+ ♕xd5 3 ♘xe3+ ♘xe3 4 ♖c3. 1...♕f6/♕g7 2 ♗xf6/♗xg7. Holzhausen interferences combined with focal play.

Section IV

Composing

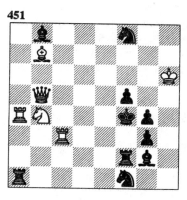

C.Mansfield
4th Prize, *The Problemist* 1953
Mate in two

Key 1 ♗e4 (> 2 ♕xf5)
..	♘e3 2 ♘d3
	♗e5 2 ♘d5
	♗xe4 2 ♕xb8
	fxe4 2 ♕g5
	♔xe4 2 ♘a2

No. 451 shows an attractive combination of two self-blocks leading to white interference mates, with the mating piece (the ♘b4) opening a white line of guard to the flight e4, and two self-blocks on the flight, plus a fifth variation after the black king-move, the whole mechanism being introduced by a thematic flight-giving key.

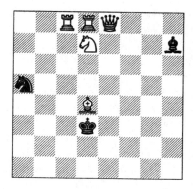

Let's try to imagine how the composer started this problem. The initial position may have been something like that shown on the left: the key is made, Black's flights are presumed to be guarded, except for d4. The threat is 2 ♕e3, and the thematic defences are 1...♘c4 and 1...♗e4. Not enough yet to make an interesting problem, even when the business of guarding Black's king-flights is attended to. At such a point in the construction of a problem the budding composer must take care; for it is all too easy to add fringe variations to a promising position like this one, in other words, variations which have no relation whatever to the theme of the problem. (However, it is often preferable to settle for a fringe variation, even with additional force, rather than to add force to eliminate a cook or serious dual, and then give that extra force nothing else to do.) Since here the two thematic lines are self-blocks, it would be logical and appropriate to arrange two further self-blocks, possibly on the flight-square. Furthermore, it would be sensible to give the white queen more work to do, since she might otherwise be uneconomically used. Best of all would be two captures of the ♗d4 leading to queen-mates. It is now a question of deciding on which squares it would be appropriate for the queen to give mate. The square e2 suggests itself immediately, and this can be managed if the whole position is given a quarter-turn anti-clockwise and a black pawn added on the new f5: 1...fxe4 2 ♕g5. Turning the board like this is a very useful procedure in the early stages of composing a problem, as new pawn-move possibilities arise. Where else could the queen mate? On the diagonal c7-f4? But there's a black bishop guarding that. Put the bishop on c7 so that the queen could capture it? No, because 1...♗xa5 would be a very strong defence, so strong as to be impossible to provide a mate for. The way to do it is to place the queen on b5, so that 2 ♕xb8 is the mate.

At this point the composer may well start thinking about the key his problem is to have. When there are flight-squares, it is a good thing if at least one of them can be granted by the key, since a flight-giving key offers Black some small advantage. In this case the ♗e4 could make the key, but where should it start from? The corner-squares a8 and h1 suggest themselves first. But if h1, then what piece is going to create the second self-block on e4, the one that will lead to 2 ♕xb8? This piece can only be the other black bishop, and this bishop cannot stand on b1, because of 1...♗d3!, a threat-defeating move for which it would be very difficult to arrange a reply. Nor can it be on a8, because of 1...♗d5!, another unwanted defence. So this black bishop must stand to the south-east of e4, which means that the white key-bishop will have to start to the north-west. The corner-square a8 seems all right. Thus we get the diagram at the top of the following page: the key will be 1 ♗e4; squares in the black king's field are presumed to be guarded.

Suddenly the composer realises he has a mate in one on his hands: 1 ♕xb8. Luckily this is easily dealt with: the key-bishop must stand on b7. So much for all the discussion about where it should start! There is another unwanted defence which must be prevented, namely 1...♘c3. It is a simple matter to shift this knight to f1, but then another defence arises, 1...♘g3. One way of dealing with this is to 'plug' g3 with a black pawn. Then a further black pawn can be added on g4 to continue the control of the black king's field. This second black pawn is more economical than a white pawn h3. (Some composers try to avoid white pawns altogether. One or two take this principle to absurd extremes, preferring a whole white piece where a pawn

would do just as well. There is no special merit in a problem without white pawns. I learnt my own lesson in this respect at the age of sixteen: I submitted to a well-known magazine, whose problem-editor favoured positions with no white pawns, a two-mover in which I had used a white bishop in order to achieve a pawnless setting, although a pawn would have been sufficient. It served me right: the setting was cooked, but it wouldn't have been if I had settled for a pawn to start with.)

Returning to the construction of the problem under discussion, we suddenly realise that we have done nothing to provide a mate for a defence which is inherent in the scheme and simply cannot be avoided, 1...♔xe4. By a piece of good luck, this move actually allows four mates in the position as we have constructed it so far: 2 ♘a6/♘c6/♘a2/♘c2. This is very satisfactory, because these can be reduced to a single mate by the addition of a black ♖a1, provided that the white ♖a3 is moved to b3 or c3 (it doesn't really matter which, though the composer probably chose c3 so as to avoid having too many pieces on one file – the question of the appearance of the problem must be considered). This new variation 1...♔xe4 2 ♘a2 blends harmoniously with the rest of the play, because the rook and knight battery, which remains masked in the mates by the knight, now becomes unmasked so that mate can be given by the rook when the knight moves away to shut off the black rook.

Now all that remains to be done is to arrange a guard for g5, and to make sure there are no cooks. The white king has not yet been put on the board, and since by convention he has to be there somewhere, he might as well do guard duty by standing on h6 (not h5, because g4 would be then both blocked and guarded, an undesirable situation). It is curious how often the white king can be used in this way: a glance through the problems in this book will show some of the methods by which economies of this sort can be achieved. What about cooks? 1 ♕e2 looks rather serious, with its threats of 2 ♘d3 and 2 ♘d5. Mansfield decided to prevent this cook by adding a black ♖f2, shifting the ♗h1 to g2 to stop 1...♖h2+. Another nasty-looking cook is 1 ♗c8, which has the same effect as the intended key. A black ♘f8 will prevent this. At this point the present-day composer owning a personal computer would do a quick check for soundness, but of course in 1953 there was no such aid available. In any case there is a danger that a composer might come to rely on his computer to show him where the cooks are; it is therefore much better to eliminate the cooks *before* the computer reveals them! The finished problem (no. 451) is not in the top class, since some of the strategy is on fairly simple lines (self-blocks on flights are among the most straight-forward of black errors), but good enough for publication back in 1953, and, as it turned out, good enough to win a prize. It is worth emphasising, however, that nowadays, more than forty years on, a problem-editor would very likely reject a work such as this, for all its elegance and solver-appeal, on the grounds that its thematic content is too well-known to justify publication. This is one of the difficulties that a budding composer faces: all the most appealing strategic effects attainable in the post-key play of a two-mover have been shown over and over again, and one soon comes to dread the word 'anticipation'!

The majority of chess problemists learn their art by studying the works of others, though bad habits can easily be picked up if inferior works are used as models. In this book I have tried to present well-constructed examples of the themes and strategy discussed, in the hope that readers who are not already expert composers may see and appreciate the standards that can be attained. Those wishing to extend their knowledge of problems would do well to join the British Chess Problem Society, founded in 1918 and still going strong. This would entitle them to receive the Society's two bi-monthly magazines, *The Problemist* and its *Supplement*, both containing in each issue large numbers of problems of various types, along with articles and commentaries on selected problems. Members can also attend meetings held monthly in London from September to May, and an annual gathering one weekend in March or April, usually held away from London.

Where does a composer find his inspiration? The answer to this question will obviously vary from one problemist to another. Many will pick up an idea from the study of other problems. This cannot be regarded as plagiarism provided the composer consciously seeks a novel presentation of the idea. Sometimes one problem successfully completed will lead to the composition of another, along similar lines and showing the same theme, but in a different setting, perhaps with different thematic pieces, or with a diagonal rather than an orthogonal matrix (in other words, with, e.g., a battery or half-battery set on a diagonal rather than on a rank or file). In his excellent book on composing, *Adventures in Composition*, Mansfield called this technique 'The Adventure of the Stepping Stones'.

Theme tourneys, though despised by some composers, sometimes inspire the production of a series of worthwhile problems. For quick composing (see **Tourneys**) 'key-stipulation' generally provides a suitable challenge; composers are asked for problems where the key displays a particular effect. An example was the two-move quick-composing tourney at the British Chess

Problem Society's weekend gathering at Paisley in 1996. The theme was announced on Friday evening by the judge, Colin Sydenham, and the dead-

452

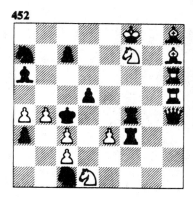

J.M.Rice
1st commendation, BCPS Paisley Weekend, March-April 1996
Mate in two

Try 1 ♖f6? (>2 ♘e5) ♖xe3! (2 ♘xe3?)
Try 1 ♗f6? (>2 ♘e5) ♘c6! (2 ♖xc6?)
Try 1 ♖f5? (>2 ♘e5) ♘d3! (2 ♗xd3?)
Key 1 ♗f5! (>2 ♘e5)
   ... d4   2 ♗e6 (2 ♖c5?)
      ♖xe3 2 ♘xe3
      ♘c6 2 ♖xc6
      ♘d3 2 ♗xd3

line for entries was 48 hours later. My entry was no. 452.

The required theme was: 'The key cuts both a black and a white line.' I was quite pleased to get my matrix to work satisfactorily in such a short time. The white organ-pipes (see p. 189) are appealing enough, but the setting has its weaknesses, such as the fact that the ♖h5 is idle after the key (though it is obviously essential to the idea), the rather under-used white queen, and the clumsy construction on the left side of the board. When you add to these defects the fact that the problem may well be anticipated, you appreciate why the judge gave it no more than a commendation. A further reason is the outstanding quality of the prize-winner in the tourney, a lovely example of reciprocal change (see p.207) by a grandmaster composer (no. 453).

It is remarkable that such a fine piece of work should have been produced in a quick-composing tourney, at a weekend gathering with other activities going on, such as lectures and a solving contest in which Michel Caillaud was actively involved. "The problem on its own made the weekend a success," wrote Editor Paul Valois in *The Problemist*.

No. 454 is in nothing like the same class, though it was lucky enough to win 1st prize in a quick-composing tourney at the FIDE meeting held in Belfort (France) in July 1994. The theme set for this tourney derived from a series of games played between Karpov and Kasparov in a variation of the Grünfeld Defence towards the end of the 1980s. The diagram on the next page shows a position after Black's 16th move.

453

M.Caillaud
Prize, BCPS Paisley Weekend, March-
April 1996
Mate in two

Try 1 ♘f~?   (>2 ♕f5)d4/♖f3!
Try 1 ♘d4?   (>2 ♕f5)
    ...   ♘xd4 2 f4
          ♘g3 2 ♕xe3
          ♖f3 2 ♘xf3
          ♘xe6 2 ♘dxe6
          ♗g3 2 ♘f3
          ♗xf2!
Key 1 ♘g3!   (>2 ♕f5)
    ...   ♘d4 2 ♕xe3
          ♘xg3 2 f4
          d4 2 ♘e4
          ♘xe6 2 ♘gxe6

In one of the world-championship
match-games at Seville in 1987, Karpov
(White) played 17 ♕e1, and the game
was drawn in 79 moves. The identical
position was reached by the same two
players at Amsterdam in 1988, when
Karpov played 17 ♕c2 (draw in 58
moves). Three months later, in the World
Cup tournament at Belfort, the same position arose yet again, and this time Karpov played 17 ♕a4! ('le coup de
Belfort'), securing a win in 38 moves –
this became known as the 'Belfort Variation'. The organisers of the FIDE
meeting in 1994 had the witty idea of holding a tourney for direct-mate problems of any length in which, with the white queen on d1, the moves ♕e1,
♕c2 and ♕a4 are all featured.

The two thematic tries and the key of No. 454 all set up batteries. After the
tries these batteries threaten to open immediately, but after the key the battery cannot function until the black knight has played to a7 or c7. The extra
try 1 ♕b3?, not required for the tourney, of course, is nonetheless a useful
addition to the problem from the artistic point of view; it brings in some new
play, and it provides some work for the black bishop and the pawn on g4,

454

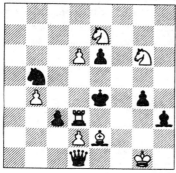

J.M.Rice
1st prize, Le Coup de Belfort, July 1994
Mate in two

Try	1 ♕e1?	(>2 ♗f1)
	... ♘d4	2 ♖e3
	cxd2!	
Try	1 ♕c2?	(>2 ♖d5)
	... cxd2	2 ♕c6
	♘d4	2 ♖e3
	♘a3!	
(Try	1 ♕b3?	(>2 ♕xe6)
	... e5	2 ♕d5
	♘c7	2 ♕c4
	♘d4	2 ♖e3
	g3!)	

Key	1 ♕a4!	(>2 ♕a8)
	... ♘a7,c7	2 b5
	♘xd6	2 ♕c6
	♘d4	2 ♖e3

both of them needed in any case to prevent cooks and duals on the right side of the board.

The requirement for the Belfort tourney can only loosely be described as a 'theme'. Equally broad in scope was the 'theme' set for the two-move tourney at another gathering in France (Messigny, June 1995): 'The key pins a black piece'; and it occurred to me that it might be interesting to start with the same basic arrangement as at Belfort (see diagram).

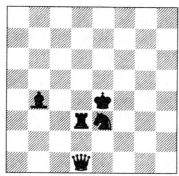

The idea would be to pin the knight and the rook with the tries, and the bishop with the key. 1 ♕e1? could threaten a bishop mate on the diagonal f5-h7, with a further bishop-mate on d5 after 1...♖d5, exploiting the pin of the knight. 1 ♕c2? might threaten a rook-mate on d4, and if the white rook stood on d7, 1...♗d6 could lead to a knight-mate on c3, to exploit the pin of the black rook. After 1 ♕a4! the threat could be 2

▨d7-e7, with 2 ♘c3 recurring after 1...▨xd7, etc. This looked promising, but for a variety of reasons I couldn't get it to work satisfactorily. It needed a turn of the board – and an abandonment of the 'Belfort' set-up! – to produce a tolerable setting, in which the pin of the bishop is a try and the pin of the rook the key.

J.M.Rice
1st place, Messigny, June 1995

455

Mate in two

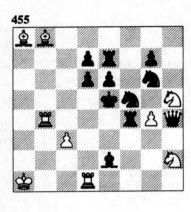

Try 1 ♕g5?   (>2 ♗xd6)
...   ▨d4 2 cxd4
      ♗xd1 2 ▨b5
      ♗d3!

Try 1 ♕e1?   (>2 ▨b5)
...   ▨d4 2 ♘f3
      ▨e4 2 ▨xe4
      ♘e3 2 ♗xd6
      ♘d4!

Key 1 ♕g3!   (>2 ▨e4)
...   ♗d3 2 ♘f3
      ♘xg3 2 ♗xd6
      ♘d4 2 cxd4

As originally submitted, the w♘h5 was on h3, and there was a b△f6 (try 1 ♕h5?). This, of course, was a relic of the Belfort matrix, and was inartistic as it gave the knight insufficient work to do. As it is, the other white knight is under-employed, but the matrix does not seem to allow it to do more than simply mate on f3. The b▨e7 is also an unfortunate necessity: that square must be plugged to prevent 1...♘f5-e7, and a pawn-plug would guard a crucial mating-square, d6. A further weakness is the absence of a role for the white king. The complex arrangement of changed and transferred mates in a *pseudo* **le Grand** pattern perhaps provides some compensation for the problem's defects.

It has been stated elsewhere in this book that the composer will normally keep the solver in mind as he builds his problem, by seeking well-hidden refutations for the tries and by making the key a less evident move, if the position allows for such desirable features. Problems composed specifically for solving contests may perhaps place the aim of baffling the solver above other artistic considerations. No. 456 is a case in point.

456

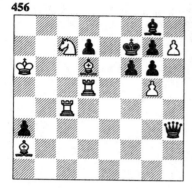

J.M.Rice
Chess Problems for Solving 1995
Mate in two

Try 1 ♖c3?   (>2 ♖f5)
...   ♕d3+ 2 ♖xd3
         ♕h2 2 ♖d2
         ♕h4 2 ♖d4
         fxg5 2 ♖f5
         ♕h1!
Try 1 ♖h4?   (>2 h8♘)
...   ♗xh7!
Try 1 ♖f5?   (>2 ♖c3)
...   gxf5!
Try 1 ♖g4?   (>2 ♖d3)
...   ♕h1!
Key 1 ♖d3!   (>2 ♖g4)
...   ♕xd3 2 h8♘
         ♕h2 2 ♖c2
         ♕h1 2 ♖e4
         fxg5 2 ♖f4

White half-batteries often present the solver with a tricky task, especially when combined, as here, with focal play involving the black queen, whose lines are cut in three different directions in the try-play. As an artistic creation the problem is negligible, particularly in view of the amount of work that has been done with half-batteries, but it certainly baffled the solvers! No. 457 was composed with much the same aim in view.

Here, too, White has a half-battery, and the tries look convincing. But all attempts to get the half-battery working are doomed to failure. So the key abandons it altogether, introducing a block position with an Albino (see p. 26) to follow the black rook's moves. Of 25 solvers in the Final of the British Solving Championship 1996, 11 were stumped by this one.

A composer searching for ways of widening his horizons may try to make a problem in a field where he has hitherto hardly ventured. In gathering material for this book, I found it difficult to lay hands on three-movers showing a complete third-pin, as in no. 271 (p. 240). The first one I composed turned out to be substantially anticipated (see no. 384), hardly to my surprise. The second (no. 458) took several weeks of work.

457

J.M.Rice
The Problemist 1996
Mate in two

Try 1 ♘dc4? (>2 ♘xd3/♘xd7)
  ... d6!
Try 1 ♘e4? (>2 ♘xd3/♘xd7/♖h4)
  ... ♖xd2!
Try 1 ♘xd7? (>2 ♘6~)
  ... ♘c4 2 ♘xc4
    ♖e3 2 ♘e4
    ♖xf3 2 ♖d4
    ♖xd5!
Key 1 ♕c1! zugzwang
  ... ♖c3 2 dxc3
    ♖e3 2 dxe3
    ♖xf3 2 ♖xf3
    ♖d4 2 d3
    ♖xd5 2 d4
    ♖xd2 2 ♕xd2
    ♘~ 2 ♘xd3

458

J.M.Rice
The Problemist 1996
Mate in three

Key 1 ♗g1 (>2 ♖c5+ dxc5 3 ♕xe5)
  ... ♗f6 2 ♕d4+ ♘xd4 3 ♗c4
    ♘e3 2 ♗c4+ ♘5xc4 3 ♘xf4
      ... ♘3xc4 3 ♕d4
    ♘d3 2 ♘xf4+ ♗xf4 3 ♕d4
      ... ♗xf4 3 ♗c4
    ♘xf3 2 ♗c4+ ♔e4 3 ♘hf2
    ♘c6 2 ♖xc6 (>3 ♗c4) ♗xf3 3 ♗xf3
    b2 2 ♕xa2+

The main constructional difficulty was presented by the variation 1...♘d3, where the dual continuation 2 ♗xd3 had to be eliminated. Eventually the b♗h1 proved to be the answer, and it was a source of considerable satisfaction that White's light-squared bishop could be placed on e2 (rather than f1) to give mate by 3 ♗xf3 after 1...♞c6 2 ♖xc6 ♗xf3. Another source of satis-faction was the key: the bishop must not stop on f2, where it would obstruct a necessary knight-mate. The two white knights are perhaps slightly under-employed, but at least each of them performs two valuable functions.

Many composers are content to work in the orthodox field, with direct-mate problems. Some, however, have found that fairy chess offers scope that would otherwise be denied to them. My love of the half-battery led me to compose no. 459 at the annual meeting of enthusiasts at Andernach in 1994. The set theme involved Andernach chess (see p. 29): White's key and/or threat captures a black unit, and Black defends by capturing a white unit.

459

J.M.Rice
3rd prize, Andernach 1994
Mate in two: Andernach chess

Try   1 ♞dxc4=b♞? (>2 ♞bxc4=b♞)
...   axb2=w♙   2 b4 (b3?)
...   ♞xd5=w♞!
Key   1 ♞bxc4=b♞! (>2 ♞dxc4=b♞)
...   exd2=w♙   2 d4 (d3?)
   ♞xd5=w♞   2 ♞f4
   ♚d3   2 ♞e4

In orthodox problems, a try or key should not generally involve the cap-ture of a black piece (capture of a black pawn is acceptable). In Andernach chess, however, this convention does not apply, for White appears to weaken his own forces by effecting a capture. Here the white knights must clear the second rank to threaten mate from the ♖a2, but their only arrival square is c4. Playing the captures on this square in the wrong order leaves White with no defence against 1...♞xd5=w♞!, which transforms the ♗d5 into a knight and so deprives White of a line of guard to f3. After Black has played his defen-sive capture on the battery-line, White has a pawn in place of a knight, and in each phase this new pawn must select its arrival square with care, to avoid self-interference (after the try) or unpin of Black (after the key). If you are wondering why three white knights are acceptable in this problem, or two white bishops on light squares, the answer lies in the rules of Andernach chess. The composer may use up to four knights of either colour (likewise four rooks and two queens), and two light-squared and two dark-squared bishops of either colour.

460

J.M.Rice
The Problemist – Supplement 1996
Series-helpmate in six: Andernach chess

1 ♘xg6=w♘ 2 ♚g7 3 ♗xg6=w♗
4 ♚f8 5 ♜xg6=w♜ 6 ♚e8 ♜g8

Andernach chess is one of many entertaining fairy forms. No. 460 is an illustration of the sort of effect that can be achieved. This is a series-helpmate (see p. 233): Black plays a sequence of moves to reach a position where White can mate in one. White's mating piece is on the board already, but to allow the black king access to e8, where he will be mated, Black has to transform the rook first into a knight, to permit 2 ♚g7, then into a bishop (for 4 ♚f8) and finally back into a rook. A problem of this kind is satisfying to compose provided it can be done with only the force required for the effects. According to reports received, this one has apparently given both amusement and satisfaction to solvers. In the end that is what makes it all worth while.

Bibliography

Lots of books have been written on chess problems, but relatively few are still in print and readily obtainable. The following list does not claim to be comprehensive, but offers some suggestions for a basic collection. Some of the otherwise unobtainable books occasionally turn up in second-hand shops, while others may be borrowed by members from the library of the British Chess Problem Society.

Those looking for anthologies should investigate the Albums published under the auspices of FIDE (the Fédération Internationale des Echecs). 15 of them have appeared so far, containing most (but unhappily not all) of the best problems and studies published between 1914 and 1988. Further Albums are being prepared. Other outstanding collections are: *The Good Companion Two-mover* (1922), by A.C.White and G.Hume, containing the best from the Good Companion folders; *A Century of Two-movers* (1941), with 100 of the most famous two-move problems selected by White, Mansfield, Gamage and Eaton; and *The Two-move Chess Problem in the Soviet Union* (1943), which contains some outstanding Russian work from the 1930s, the great era of dual avoidance and white line-themes. Colin Russ's *Miniature Chess Problems from Many Countries* (1981, rev. 1987) has 400 direct-mate miniatures of various lengths. Two paperbacks by Barry Barnes are worth looking out for: *Pick of the Best Chess Problems* (1976, rev. 1991), and *White to play and mate in two moves* (1991). Both contain Merediths (8-12 pieces only) by British composers. There are two superb anthologies of task problems, one in English: *Chess Problems: Tasks and Records* (1995), by Sir Jeremy Morse; and one in French: *Le Joueur d'Echecs au Pays des Merveilles* (1982), by André Chéron. *The Art of Israeli Chess Composition* (1983 – edited by Yoel Aloni and Uri Avner) contains some fine work by Israeli composers.

There are several excellent collections of the work of individual composers. The problems of Comins Mansfield feature in *A Genius of the Two-mover* (1936 – text by A.C.White), *The Modern Two-move Chess Problem* (1958 – Brian Harley) and *Comins Mansfield MBE: Chess Problems of a Grandmaster* (1976 – Barry Barnes). A further comprehensive collection is being prepared, as are collections of the work of N.A.Macleod, A.R.Gooderson, and G.W.Chandler (problems and writings). The complete output of R.C.O.Matthews is the subject of an outstanding book entitled *Mostly Three-movers* (1995). Three books with text in German contain some very fine work: *Hans+Peter+Rehm=Schach* (1994 – problems and text by Hans-Peter Rehm); *Michael Keller – ein Meister der Schachkomposition* (1994), by Friedrich Chlubna; and *Meine besten Schachprobleme* (1988), by Herbert Ahues.

Now for some books about problems, many of them being also anthologies. H.Weenink's *The Chess Problem* (1926 – a revised translation of the 1921 Dutch work *Het Schaakprobleem*) is a comprehensive survey of the early development of the chess problem. In his two books, *Mate in Two Moves* (1931, rev. 1941) and *Mate in Three Moves* (1943), Brian Harley aimed at a wide audience, explaining problems and their terminology simply and lucidly. Two Faber books appeared in the 1960s: *Chess Problems: Introduction to an Art* (1963 – Michael Lipton, R.C.O.Matthews and John Rice), and *The Two-move Chess Problem: Tradition and Development* (1966 – Rice, Lipton and Barnes). In the former stress is laid on the artistic side of the chess problem, while the latter contains essays on important two-move themes. Comins Mansfield's *Adventures in Composition* (1948) is unique, being all about the art of composing seen from the point of view of the expert. C.J.Feather's *Black to play* (1994) is the only critical survey of the helpmate. *Solving in style* (1985), by John Nunn, shows how the expert solver tackles even the toughest of problems. Study enthusiasts should look out for two books on the endgame study: John Roycroft's *Test Tube Chess* (1972), and *Endgame Magic*, by John Beasley and Timothy Whitworth (1996). A book to appeal to lovers of all aspects of chess is *Secrets of Spectacular Chess* (1995), by Jonathan Levitt and David Friedgood, which explores the links between the game, the study and the problem.

If your German is good, you will appreciate the instructive commentaries to be found in Herbert Grasemann's three collections, *Problemschach I & II* (1955 and 1959), and *Problemjuwelen* (1964). Equally illuminating are the commentaries in *Im Banne des Schachproblems* (1951, rev. 1971) and *Problemkunst im 20.Jahrhundert* (1956), both by A.Kraemer and E.Zepler. *Das Logische Schachproblem* (1965, rev. 1980), by Werner Speckmann, is a treatise on the theories of the New German School. Friedrich Chlubna's *Schach für Nußknacker* (1994) makes a good introduction to problems, while his *Das Matt des weißen Königs* (1995) is all about selfmates, the only recent book on this subject. Werner Sidler's *Problemschach* (1968), an alphabetical survey of problem terminology, has proved invaluable in the compilation of the present volume. In French there is *Problèmes d'Echecs en deux coups* (1983), by J.-P.Boyer, and also *Initiation au problème d'échecs* (1964 – Jean Bertin). For readers of Russian there are several excellent books to choose from, including three anthologies by E.Umnov, and collections of problems by V.F.Rudenko and L.I.Loshinsky.

Finally, a short list of magazines. Those devoted exclusively to problems include *The Problemist* (in English – the magazine of the British Chess Problem Society, published bi-monthly with a Supplement aimed more at beginners); *Die Schwalbe* (German), *Phénix* and *diagrammes* (both French), *Probleemblad* (Dutch), *Problemas* (Spanish), and the *U.S. Problem Bulletin* (English). *Mat Plus* (in English, though produced in Belgrade) has made a welcome appearance on the scene. Each of its issues is more like a book than a magazine. A few chess magazines have small problem sections, including the *British Chess Magazine* and *Chess Monthly*.

General Index

Certain problem themes and effects, such as Batteries, Black checks, Dual avoidance, Line-opening, etc. occur too frequently to warrant a comprehensive listing in this index. Readers are therefore referred only to problems where these themes or effects occur as the principal feature.

Zilahi theme pp. 311-2, 319; nos. 331, 340, 392

zugzwang p. 10
Zweckreinheit pp. 94, 163

Index of Names

Problem numbers in brackets indicate either that the named composer is responsible only for the version, or that substantial changes have been made in his original position.

Abdurahmanović, F. nos. 225, 301
Ahues, H. pp. 160, 339; nos. 48, 62, 173, 302
Albert, E. no. 130
Albrecht, H. pp. 190, 245
Aloni, Y. p. 339
Anderson, G.F. p. 308, nos. 64, 303, 304
Animitsa, K.S. no. 151
Aprò, L. no. 170
Archakov, V.M. no. 305
Avner, U. pp. 308, 339; no. 306
Babson, J.N. p. 33
Baev, G. no. 140
Bakcsi, G. no. 111
Banny, D. p. 218; nos. 307, 308
Barnes, B.P. pp. 104, 339; nos. 47, 72, 99, 236, 280, 309
Bartolović, V. p. 238; no. (270)
Barulin, M.M. p. 160; nos. 59, 171, 172
Basisty, M. no. 310
Beasley, J.D. p. 340
Bédoni, R. no. 311
Beers, W.A. no. 159
Bekkelund, P. no. 266
Berhausen, F. no. 297
Bernard, H.D'O. no. 13
Bertin, J. p. 340
Bettmann, H.W. p. 33
Bogdanov, E. nos. 312, 313
Bouma, G.J. no. 66
Boyer, J.-P. p. 48; nos. 314, 315, 316
Braithwaite, K. nos. (170), (196), 317
Brehmer, S. nos. 54, 68, 122, 318, 319,

397
Buchwald, J. nos. 87, 189
Burger, R.E. nos. 25, 288
Burgess, H.J. p. 136
Burmistrov, S.G. no. 320
Caillaud, M. p. 331; nos. 226, 321, 322, 323, 453
Casa, A. no. 46
Ceriani, L. no. 237
Chandler, G.W. p. 339
Chepizhny, V. nos. 24, 128, 230, 231, 244, 293
Chéron, A. p. 339
Cheylan, Y. nos. 324, 325
Chlubna, F. pp. 95, 232, 325, 339-40; no. 441
Clausen, S. no. 326
Davidenko, F. no. 89
Dawson, T.R. pp. 98, 112, 179, 234; nos. 106, 197, 263
Degener, U. no. 241
Dennis, B.W. no. 250
Dittrich, S. no. 175
Dombrovskis, A. p. 214; no. 240
Doukhan, G. nos. 328, 329
Drese, G.H. no. 219
Driver, J.E. p. 136
Easter, N. nos. 285, 330
Eaton, V.L. p. 308; no. 303
Ebend, T. no. 8
Einat, P. no. 233
Eisert, S. p. 166
Ellerman, A. nos. 145, 223
Ellinghoven, B. p. 29